# Reconstructing Keynesian Macroeconomics Volume 1

T0303923

*Reconstructing Keynesian Macroeconomics* lives up to its title. The authors present an up-to-date, technically sophisticated version of truly Keynesian macrodynamics along with a trenchant critique of mainstream modeling. The book represents the state of the art in an exciting area of macroeconomics.

This book represents the first of three volumes offering a complete reinterpretation and restructuring of Keynesian macroeconomics and a detailed investigation of the disequilibrium adjustment processes characterizing the financial, the goods and the labor markets and their interaction. It questions in a radical way the evolution of Keynesian macroeconomics after World War II and focuses on the limitations of the traditional Keynesian approach until it fell apart in the early 1970s, as well as the inadequacy of the new consensus in macroeconomics that emerged from the Monetarist critique of Keynesianism.

Professors Chiarella, Flaschel and Semmler investigate basic methodological issues, the pitfalls of the Rational Expectations School, important feedback channels in the tradition of Tobin's work, and theories of the wage–price spiral and the evidences for them. The book uses primarily partial approaches, the integration of which will be the subject of subsequent volumes. With its focus on Keynesian propagation mechanisms, the research in this book provides a unique alternative to the black-box shock-absorber approaches that dominate modern macroeconomics.

*Reconstructing Keynesian Macroeconomics* should be of interest to students and researchers who want to look at alternatives to the mainstream macrodynamics that emerged from the Monetarist critique of Keynesianism.

**Carl Chiarella** is currently Professor of Quantitative Finance in the Business Faculty at the University of Technology, Sydney, Australia.

**Peter Flaschel** is Professor Emeritus of Economics at Bielefeld University, Germany.

**Willi Semmler** is Professor of Economics at The New School for Social Research, USA.

# Routledge Frontiers of Political Economy

# Reconstructing Keynesian Macroeconomics Volume 1

## Partial perspectives

**Carl Chiarella, Peter Flaschel and Willi Semmler**

Routledge
Taylor & Francis Group

LONDON AND NEW YORK

First published 2012
by Routledge
2 Park Square, Milton Park, Abingdon, Oxfordshire OX14 4RN

Simultaneously published in the
by Routledge
711 Third Avenue, New York, NY 10017

First issued in paperback 2014

*Routledge is an imprint of the Taylor & Francis Group, an informa business*

*British Library Cataloguing in Publication Data*
A catalogue record for this book is available from the British Library

*Library of Congress Cataloging in Publication Data*
Chiarella, Carl.
  Reconstructing Keynesian macroeconomics: partial perspectives/by Carl Chiarella, Peter
  Flaschel, and Willi Semmler.
    p.;  cm.
  Includes bibliographical references and index.
  ISBN 978-0-415-66856-9 (hb)—ISBN 978-0-203-80576-3 (eb)    1. Keynesian economics.
  2. Macroeconomics. I. Flaschel, Peter, 1943– II. Semmler, Will. III. Title.
  HB99.7.c53 2011
  B39.5—dc22                                                              2011014501

ISBN 978-0-415-66856-9 (hbk)
ISBN 978-1-138-79995-0 (pbk)
ISBN 978-0-203-80576-3 (ebk)

Typeset in Times New Roman
by RefineCatch Limited, Bungay Suffolk

# Contents

# Figures

# Tables

# Notation

Steady state or trend values are indicated by a sub- or superscript "$o$" (sometimes also by an "*"). When no confusion arises, letters $F$, $G$, H may also define certain functional expressions in a specific context. A dot over a variable $x = x(t)$ denotes the time derivative, a caret its growth rate; $\dot{x} = dx/dt$, $\hat{x} = \dot{x}/x$. In the numerical simulations, flow variables are measured at annual rates.

As far as possible, the notation tries to follow the logic of using capital letters for level variables and lower case letters for variables in intensive form, or for constant (steady state) ratios. Greek letters are most often constant coefficients in behavioral equations (with, however, the notable exceptions being $\pi^c$, $\omega$). We use the abreviation "NAIRU" for the Non-Accelerating-Inflation Rate of Unemployment, but use this acronym also in the case of "Utilization" (of labor or capital) in the place of "Unemployment". And the acronym "RE (S)" stands for the "Rational Expectations (School)". Further acronyms are of a local nature only and will be explained in the sections where they are used. There will also be some chapter-specific (local) notation in some of the chapters.

| | |
|---|---|
| $B$ | outstanding government fixed-price bonds (priced at $p_b = 1$) |
| $C$ | real private consumption (demand is generally realized) |
| $E$ | number of equities |
| $F$ | neoclassical production function |
| $G$ | real government expenditure (demand is always realized) |
| $I$ | net investment in fixed capital |
| $I$ | desired real inventory investment |
| $J$ | Jacobian matrix in the mathematical analysis |
| $K$ | stock of fixed capital |
| $L^d$ | total working hours (labor demand is always realized) |
| $L^w$ | Employed workforce, i.e., number of employed people |
| $L$ or $N$ | labor supply, i.e., supply of total working hours per year |
| $M$ | stock of money supply |
| $N$ | inventories of finished goods |
| $N^d$ | desired stock of inventories |
| $S_f$ | real saving of firms |
| $S_g$ | real government saving |

| | |
|---|---|
| $S_p$ | real saving of private households |
| $S$ | total real saving |
| $T$ | total real tax collections |
| $T_w(t_w)$ | real taxes of workers (per unit of capital) |
| $T_c(t_c)$ | real taxes of asset holders (per unit of capital) |
| $W$ | real wealth of private households |
| $Y$ | real output |
| $Y^p$ | potential real output |
| $Y^f$ | full employment real output |
| $Y^d$ | real aggregate demand |
| $Y^e$ | expected real aggregate demand |
| $c$ | marginal propensity to consume |
| $e$ | employment rate |
| $U = 1 - e$ | unemployment rate |
| $f_x = f_1$, etc. | partial derivative |
| $r, i$ | nominal rate of interest on government bonds; |
| $k$ | capital intensity $K/L$ (or parameter in money demand) |
| $\sigma = 1/y$ | capital coefficient $K/Y$ |
| $l$ | labor intensity (in efficiency units) |
| $m$ | real balances relative to the capital stock; $m = M/pK$ |
| $n$ | inventory–capital ratio; $n = N/K$ |
| $p$ | price level |
| $p_e$ | price of equities |
| $q$ | return differential; $q = r - (i-\pi)$ or Tobin's $q$ |
| $r, \rho$ | rate of return on fixed capital: $r = (pY - wL - \delta pK)/pK$ |
| $s_c$ | propensity to save out of capital income, asset owners |
| $u, u^w, e^w$ | rate of capacity utilization $u = Y/Y^n = y/y^n$ |
| $v$ | wage share (in gross product); $v = wL/pY$ |
| $w$ | nominal wage rate per hour |
| $y$ | output–capital ratio; $y = Y/K$; |
| $y^d$ | ratio of aggregate demand to capital stock; $y^d = Y^d/K$ |
| $y^e$ | ratio of expected demand to capital stock; $y^e = Y^e/K$ |
| $z$ or $x$ | labor productivity, i.e., output per worker; $z = Y/L^d$ |
| $\alpha$ | symbol for policy parameters in Taylor rule |
| $\alpha_i$ | interest rate smoothing coefficient in the Taylor rule |
| $\alpha_p$ | coefficient on inflation gap in the Taylor rule |
| $\alpha_u$ | coefficient on output gap in the Taylor rule |
| $\beta_x$ | reaction coefficient in an equation determining $x$, $\dot{x}$ or $\hat{x}$ |
| $\beta_y$ | adjustment speed in adaptive sales expectations |
| $\beta_\pi$ | general adjustment speed in revisions of the inflation climate |
| $\beta_{xy}$ | reaction coefficient related to the determination of variable $x$, $\dot{x}$ or $\hat{x}$ with respect to changes in the variable $y$ |
| $\alpha_q$ | responsiveness of investment to changes in $q$ |
| $\alpha_u$ | responsiveness of investment to changes in $u$ |
| $\beta_n$ | stock adjustment speed |

| | |
|---|---|
| $\alpha_{n^d}$ | desired ratio of inventories over expected sales |
| $\beta_{pu}$ | reaction coefficient of $u$ in price Phillips curve |
| $\beta_{pv}$ | reaction coefficient of $(1+\mu)v-1$ in price Phillips curve |
| $\beta_{we}$ | reaction coefficient of $e$ in wage Phillips curve |
| $\beta_{wv}$ | reaction coefficient of $(v-v^o)/v^o$ in wage Phillips curve |
| $\gamma$ | government expenditures per unit of fixed capital; $\gamma = G/K$ (a constant) |
| $\tau$ | lump sum taxes per unit of fixed capital; $\tau = T/K$ (a constant) |
| $\delta$ | rate of depreciation of fixed capital (a constant) |
| $\eta_{m,i}$ | interest elasticity of money demand (a positive number) |
| $\kappa$ | coefficient in reduced-form wage-price equations $=\dfrac{1}{1-\kappa_p\kappa_w}$ |
| $\kappa_p$ | parameter weighting $\hat{w}$ vs. $\pi$ in price Phillips curve |
| $\kappa_w$ | parameter weighting $\hat{p}$ vs. $\pi$ in wage Phillips curve |
| $\kappa_{wp}$ | same as $\kappa_w$ |
| $\kappa_{wz}$ | parameter weighting $\hat{z}$ vs. $\hat{z}^o$ in wage Phillips curve |
| $\kappa_\pi$ | parameter weighting adaptive vs. regressive expectations |
| $\pi^c$ | general inflation climate; |
| $\theta$ | log of real wages |
| $\tau_c = T_c/K$ | tax parameter for $T^c$ (net of interest per capital); $T^c - iB/p$ |
| $\omega$ | real wage rate $w/p$ |

# Contributors

**Carl Chiarella** is a Professor of Quantitative Finance and also an Emeritus Professor at the University of Technology, Sydney. Carl has held visiting appointments at a number of Universities around the world including the University of Kyoto, Nanyang Technological University, Hitotsubashi University, Tokyo Metropolitan University, the University of Bielefeld and the University of Urbino. He is currently an Editor of the *Journal of Economic Dynamics and Control* and an Associate Editor of *Studies in Nonlinear Dynamics and Econometrics*, and the *European Journal of Finance and Computational Economics*.

**Peter Flaschel** is Professor Emeritus at Bielefeld University, Germany. He was on numerous occasions Visiting Professor at the University of Technology, Sydney, and was invited as Theodor Heuss Professor to the New School for Social Research, New York, in 2006. He received an Opus Magnum Grant from the Fritz Thyssen/Volkswagen Stiftungen in 2007/08.

**Willi Semmler** is a Professor of Economics at the New School for Social Research, New York. He was Visiting Scholar at Columbia University and Stanford University, has taught at the Universities of Bielefeld, Marseilles/Aix-en-Provence, Mexico City and the European Doctoral Program in Quantitative Economics. He worked as a consultant for the ILO, World Bank and the European Unions and has been appointed Fulbright Visiting Professor to the University of Economics and Business, Vienna, for Fall 2011.

# Introduction
## Keynesian macroeconomics

### The disarray in Keynesian macroeconomics

> So here's what I think economists have to do. First, they have to face up
> to the inconvenient reality that financial markets fall far short of per-
> fection, that they are subject to extraordinary delusions and the madness
> of crowds. Second, they have to admit – and this will be very hard for the
> people who giggled and whispered over Keynes – that Keynesian economics
> remains the best framework we have for making sense of recessions and
> depressions. Third, they'll have to do their best to incorporate the realities of
> finance into macroeconomics. Many economists will find these changes
> deeply disturbing.
>
> (Paul Krugman, *New York Times*, September 6, 2009)

As the Nobel laureate Paul Krugman states in the above quotation the financial
market meltdown of the years 2007–2009, and the subsequent world-wide great
recession, has posed a great challenge for macroeconomics. This concerns not
only the now dominant modern macroeconomic modeling framework, such as the
Dynamic Stochastic General Equilibrium (DSGE) Model, but also traditional
macroeconomics based on the Keynesian paradigm. This book takes the above
statement as point of departure by critically evaluating not only the DSGE models
but also the evolution of Keynesian macroeconomics after World War II.

Macroeconomics in the 1960s and 1970s was viewed as part of the old
Neoclassical synthesis of Patinkin and others, with the Classical version of this
synthesis on the one hand and the Keynesian variant of it on the other hand. From
this traditional consensus the Neoclassical Synthesis was however transformed
towards a new and extremely different one, the so-called New Neoclassical
Synthesis, with Real Business Cycle theory now representing the Classical variant
and New Keynesian theory now as the Keynesian variant.

This New Consensus in macroeconomics and its two basic variants could be
summarized under the general heading of DSGE model building. There is from a
general perspective much to be said for the first three letters in this acronym. Yet,
the fulfillment of them is heavily biased towards a stochastic explanation of the
business cycle, in particular in the Real Business Cycle (RBC) tradition. The DSGE

model variants also see the shocks as the main driving force for the business cycle, but they allow for other shocks than technology shocks, for example preference shocks, monetary and fiscal policy shocks. The equilibrium part of the DSGE acronym is generally constrained by the postulates that it has to be microfounded, to be operated under continual market clearing, and reflect forward looking behavior in its extreme case, namely as rational expectations versions.

Again there is nothing wrong with the demand for microfoundations and forward-looking behavior (attempts at this can already be found in Keynes), however there is a lot doubt, if this task is to be performed by means of market clearing representative agent models, where undifferentiated households make economy wide decisions and there is no heterogeneity such as workers, asset owners and others. Capitalist market economies are at the minimum characterized by a principal–agent relationship and thus modeled in a misleading way by such a single household type. This is a crucial misrepresentation of the complexity of market economies. Yet more extreme is the the rational expectations assumption, which assumes forward-looking behavior of a truly omnipotent type. This assumption as well as the proposition that decision making households can make smooth and continuous adjustments are essential, so that:

- the marginal conditions, describing the balance between current cost and future benefits, are instantaneously established,[1]
- actual market constraints such as income, liquidity and credit constraints are not operative and binding when decisions are made,
- there are no spillover and externality effects and no contagion effects,
- there are no macroeconomic feedback effects that significantly disturb the intertemporal arbitrage decisions,
- the impact of macroeconomy wide shocks can be sufficiently well studied by local linearizations and local impulse response functions, and
- there are no non-linear macroeconomic propagation effects.

In the purely forward-looking variant of the baseline DSGE model those assumptions for example imply that the economy would always be mean reverting and move back to its steady state position if unanticipated shocks are occurring over time. In higher dimensions there may be damped oscillations around the steady state position in the deterministic core of DSGE models, but persistent business fluctuations remain excluded by the very solution method of the rational expectations approach which generally only allows movements along the stable manifold of the full phase space representation.

The data generating process on the macro-level of an economy is from a modeling perspective by and large of a continuous type, though it is in fact discrete with very high, and in general non-synchronized, frequencies. This basic observation implies in our view that continuous time modeling (augmented by specific delays if necessary) is the more appropriate approach as compared to completely synchronized period modeling for the macro-level of whole economies. But in continuous time, the assumption of continual market clearing is very hard to accept implying that it is better then to describe macrodynamics in terms of adjustment processes towards a moving market equilibrium, which – even when convergent – may never be reached in situations of such moving temporary equilibria, in particular if stochastic elements are also added to the structural equations of the considered macrodynamic model under consideration.

The more appropriate model building philosophy in macrodynamics is therefore of a DSGD (disequilibrium) type where the "Dynamics" is given by the set of macroeconomic adjustment processes that drive the economy in its attempts to establish interacting real and financial market equilibria. The macro-economic adjustment processes can be stabilizing or destabilizing. The interaction of these adjustment processes on the labor markets, the goods markets and the markets for financial assets may then well be of a nature that allows for endogenously generated persistent business fluctuations – not possible under DSGE modeling – which of course could be further enhanced by stochastic processes that surround these dynamics. This in our view in sum provides the foundations for an alternative paradigm, the DSGD approach to (Keynesian) macroeconomic theory, where a system of feedback adjustment channels – well known from the history of macroeconomics – is driving the macroeconomy. We hereby can allow for a microstructure of principal–agent relationships which is characterized by heterogeneous expectations formation which can range from very naive to very sophisticated.

Microfoundations – whenever possible – are of course highly desirable, but they are of a subordinate nature as compared to the macrofoundations underlying the DSGD approach towards which this book is directed. This book as well as two planned companion volumes on integrated Keynesian macromodels, highlight coherent real and financial asset accumulation, stock-flow consistency as well as advanced stock-flow interactions. The DSGD scenario describes the foundations of the approach to macroeconomic model-building that is pursued in the three volumes of integrated Keynesian approaches to the real and the financial markets of the macroeconomy. This approach is pursued on the basis of the assumption – in line with the above statement of Krugman – that Keynes' theory of effective goods demand is in principle the correct approach to the modeling of the short- and medium-run relationship between the goods and the financial markets. In order to motivate this further we can go back to the roots, that is to Keynes' (1936) own views on the working of the trade cycle, from which we shall start our understanding of the processes of fluctuating growth that characterize the evolution of complex market economies.

## Keynes' Business Cycle Analysis

Since we claim to have shown in the preceding chapters what determines the volume of employment at any time, it follows, if we are right, that our theory must be capable of explaining the phenomena of the trade cycle.

(Keynes 1936, p.313)

Following this introductory remark of Keynes in his chapter *Notes on the Trade Cycle* we shall here briefly recapitulate his observations on the main sources and the pattern of the cyclical fluctuations which characterize the evolution of market economies, with owners of assets, workers and so on, in order to describe an important perspective for the application of the temporary (dis-)equilibrium analysis of the IS–LM type. We however only sketch here some basic medium-run implications of temporary equilibria of the kind envisaged by Keynes. We will therefore not provide a detailed and thorough presentation or even elaboration of Keynes' ideas on the causes that drive the business cycle.

Yet, since in particular most macroeconomics textbooks usually introduce IS–LM analysis without properly discussing its medium-run dynamic implications, which instead of being Keynesian in nature are often in fact of monetarist type. We hope that this brief overview may help to stimulate renewed interest in Keynes' particular approach to the analysis of the trade cycle – and the role that the future and expectations play in his arguments. Moreover, this brief section also provides the framework for this book as well as its companion volumes, a framework which we will try to follow from partial, integrated and financial models of a Keynesian variety.

There are three main elements of conventional approaches to IS–LM models – and their more elaborate forms – that can be used for an analysis of the phenomenon of the business cycle:

- the marginal propensity to consume ($c$),
- the marginal efficiency of (new) capital ($i$), and
- the state of liquidity preference ($l$).

The marginal propensity to consume out of disposable income is too well-known to need further explanation here. Elements which may explain shifts in this propensity (and thus shifts in the IS-curve) are, among others:

- changes in income distribution,
- changes in perceived wealth and perceived disposable income, and
- changes in the rate of time-discounting.

See Keynes (1936, Chs.8,9) for a discussion of the last three points. Moreover, the marginal propensity to consume can be depressed if expectations about the future become pessimistic, due to rising unemployment, tighter labor market policies and also expectations of a crisis in the financial sector of the economy. Keynes knew pretty well that the decision makers are constrained by the regimes of the business cycle. Shifts in the marginal propensity to consume are regime dependent. They decrease or increase the Keynesian multiplier and thus have expansionary or contractionary effects on the level of activity of the economy.[2]

The role of the future is also important for the marginal efficiency of capital (cf. Keynes 1936, Ch.11). It is defined in reference to certain time series $Q_1,...,Q_n$ of prospective returns or yields of investment projects. Without going into the details of its definition,[3] it can be seen that such an approach makes investment heavily dependent on expectations of future cash flows over a considerable amount of time that are complex in nature, hard to control and may be more of an animal spirit type than of a proper discounting of the future.

> The social object of skilled investment should be to defeat the dark forces of
> time and ignorance which envelop our future.
>
> (Keynes 1936, p.155)

It follows that investment demand can be very volatile and consequently may be of central importance for an explanation of the trade cycle. Multiplier effects (including changes in the multiplier as discussed before) may add to this volatility and its consequences. Nevertheless, in Keynes' view, they mainly transmit fluctuations in investment to ones in income and employment, but do not by themselves explain the business cycle (though they may explain certain phases of it).

Changes in liquidity preference (cf. Keynes 1936, Ch.15), refer to the stock of accumulated savings and are – as investment demand – highly dependent on the "state of confidence". This, of course, is particularly true for the speculative motive for holding cash balances, which through sudden changes in expectations may give rise to "discontinuous" changes in the rate of interest.

> Speculators may do no harm as bubbles on a steady stream of entreprise. But
> the position is serious when entreprise becomes the bubble on a whirl-pool of
> speculation. When the capital development of a country becomes a by-product
> of the activities of a casino, the job is likely to be ill-done.
>
> (Keynes 1936, p.159)

This quotation suggests that investment may drive the cycle via a time varying multiplier effect, but that investment may itself be dependent on forces that have little to do with the social function of financial markets to channel private savings, the additions to the financial assets of the household sector, into private investment and the proper evolution of the capital stock of a country.

We may provisionally summarize the above by means of the three fundamental parameters $c$, $i$ and $l$ and the three central behavioral relationships which underlie Keynes' (1936) General Theory and also the conventional IS–LM model namely consumption (C), investment (I) and real money demand ($M^d/p$) that satisfy

$$C(\underset{+ \; - \; +}{Y, r, c}), \quad I(\underset{- \; +}{r, i}), \quad \frac{M^d}{p}(\underset{+ \; - \; +}{Y, r, l}). \tag{0.1}$$

These parameters express the fact that the behavioral relationships may be subject to slow build ups, but also to sudden changes which are not explained by the IS–LM model (which on the basis of these parameters explains the temporary position of income $Y$ and the rate of interest $r$). These parameters are here added from the outside in an *ad hoc* fashion – due to the fact that an endogenous treatment in particular of the marginal efficiency of investment, is at the very least a quite demanding task.

> By a cyclical movement we mean that as the system progresses in, e.g. the upward direction, the forces propelling it upwards at first gather force and have a cumulative effect on one another but gradually lose their strength until at a certain point they tend to be replaced by forces operating in the opposite direction; which in turn gather force for a time and accentuate one another, until they too, having reached their maximum development, wane and give place to their opposite. We do not, however, merely mean by a cyclical movement that upward and downward tendencies, once started, do not persist for ever in the same direction but are ultimately reversed. We mean also that there is some recognizable degree of regularity in the time-sequence and duration of the upward and downward movements.
>
> (Keynes 1936, pp.313–314)

We would characterize this sketch of a description of the phases of the business cycle and their further development by the expression "Keynes Paradigm", in order to distinguish it from the so-called "Frisch Paradigm". The latter offers an explanation of persistent business cycles on the basis of at most damped oscillations which are turned into persistent ones through the addition of sufficiently pronounced stochastic processes. This latter approach – underlying the current macromodels – does not interpret the business cycle as being composed of accelerating forces into a boom situation as well into the establishment of a bust, which are subject to turning points through the systematic establishment of counteracting forces. Such forces – when agents realize these thwarting tendencies – can turn the boom more or less suddenly into a bust and which – if sufficient cost-reductions have occurred in the real as well as in the financial markets in the bust – can lead to renewed optimism of investors and from there back into an upswing of the economy. Such accelerating forces, setting in motion synchronized behavior and cumulative effects are simply not a topic in the DSGE or New Keynesian approach to macrodynamics which therefore do not appear as Keynesian in their core structure.

Keynes, by contrast, starts his discussion of fluctuations in investment, income and employment in the late stage of a boom period. In this stage of the boom, it may have become apparent to investors – due to the past effects of capital accumulation on the abundance of physical capital and the costs of production – that their views on the marginal efficiency of capital needs to be significant revised downwards($i \downarrow$). Such a revision of cash flow expectations – when it becomes sufficiently generalized – may lead to a significant change in $i$ and thus a fall in effective demand (via the multiplier process), which in turn may aggravate the pessimism that has started to become established so that the marginal efficiency of capital goes down even further($i \downarrow\downarrow$). The cumulative upward trends of the boom may thereby become reversed and turned into cumulative downward trends in income and employment and so generating recessions.

It appears intuitively plausible that this decline (or even collapse) in the marginal efficiency of capital ($i$) will give rise to an increase (or upward jump) in the liquidity preference parameter $l$, that is to a (sudden) increase in the demand for money. IS–LM analysis implies that this will lead to a (sharp) increase in the rate of interest $r$ and consequently to a further decrease in investment and income. The existing negative expectations are thereby confirmed and further strengthened. It follows that the parameters $i$ and $l$ may interact in such a way that this results in a collapse in economic activity. Of course, milder forms – such as the recessions of the 1960s or the 1990s are also conceivable in the above framework.

The upper turning point for economic activity is thus explained by the interaction of the three basic parameters of the IS–LM model which bring to an end a boom that is gradually losing force – since the gradual change in $i$ and $l$ has endogenous consequences (on $I$, $Y$, and $r$) that confirm the opinions which are responsible for this change in behavior. Finally, one effect of the boom may also have been that the marginal propensity to consume has risen (due for instance to an increase of the share of wages in national income). Yet, the parameter $c$ may also contribute to the decline in economic activity due to its own decline and a rise of savings in downturns.

Let us assume for the following discussion of the lower turning point in economic activity, that there has been a long period of economic prosperity, so that the movements described above have all worked with sufficient force and therefore induce a depression of considerable strength. Economic activity now being low means that the rapid accumulation of "capital" in the past has created a significant amount of idle capital-goods. It is obvious that this excess capacity in production must disappear before there can be any recovery in the parameter that characterizes the marginal efficiency of capital. A considerable amount of time will elapse therefore during which now unprofitable investments of the past are eliminated in physical or in value form.

Such a process of capital depreciation will not in general accelerate, since there is a floor to the level of gross investment (above zero) that helps to maintain a low level of economic activity. Once the capital stock has been reduced so far as to be in line again with the prevailing level of activity, a return to a more optimistic view on investment profitability becomes possible and may come about. The forces that operated downwards in the development of the depression may now allow a spreading optimism to gather force. Rising investment and thus rising income and economic activity confirm the positive change in the parameter $i$, eventually leading to its further increase. An improving state of confidence may then also give rise to a decline in $l$, the liquidity preference parameter and thus to a decline in the rate of interest, giving further force to the spreading investment optimism. The resulting cumulative upward effects may, of course, in some cases be weak and thus only lead to a minor recovery, but may in other cases be strong enough to generate once again a boom of significant duration and strength.

This brief sketch of the cumulative upward or downward forces at work and the gradual appearance of counteracting elements which bring an end to such upward or downward tendencies must suffice here as an outline of the potential of basic

IS–LM analysis (or more advanced Keynesian model building) to explain observed regularities in business fluctuations. The central role of the parameter $i$ (in comparison to the other two parameters)[4] in the explanation of such fluctuations should be obvious from the statements made above. What is also obvious is that there are macroeconomic feedback mechanisms at work generating externality effects and synchronized behavior with huge macroeconomic impacts that are rarely captured in the unconstrained[5] behavior of the optimizing agents in DSGE models.

Indeed, no such an analysis is possible when current modern macromodels are used (because of their reliance on Say's Law in the main). Business fluctuations in the market clearing approach are then, for example, explained by introducing local markets and misperceptions of information into such a setup, see Barro (1994, Ch.19), Sargent (1987, Ch.18),or by introducing misperceived technology shocks in the so-called "real" business cycle model, see Blanchard and Fisher (1989, Ch.7).

Keynes' (1936) approach to explaining the trade cycle has not received much attention in the discussion on growth and instability that developed after the appearance of the "General Theory". This may in particular be due to the strong psychological influences that appear in his explanation of the cycle as, for example in the following statement (p.317):

> ... it is not so easy to revive the marginal efficiency of capital, determined, as it is, by the uncontrollable and disobedient psychology of the business world.

Instead of the above speculative type of interaction of largely psychologically determined magnitudes (the parameters $i$, $c$, $l$), Keynesian dynamic economic analysis has unfortunately turned to the analysis of interactions of a more mechanical type in the sequel: the multiplier and accelerator – approaches and the like, later on replaced by models of inflation and stagflation when the monetarist critique of Keynesianism was impacting its evolution. Keynes' (1936) original approach to macrodynamics was therefore not taken seriously, neither by Neoclassical theory nor really the Keynesian approaches within the old Neoclassical synthesis that was developed by Patinkin and others from Hicksian IS–LM analysis. Those insights are also neglected by the New Keynesian reformulation of the building blocks of macrodynamic analysis. This topical issue will be considered in detail in the now following section.

## Keynes or Frisch Paradigm? Some further thoughts

We now discuss in more detail the methodological foundations of mainstream macroeconomics, and Keynesian alternatives. These foundations, in particular for models of DSGE type, often act in our view like an intellectual straight jacket for the further evolution of Keynesian macroeconomics. They enforce a research program for macroeconomics which in the words of Keynes (1936, p.3) maybe characterized as follows:

I have called this book the General Theory of Employment, Interest and Money, placing the emphasis on the prefix general. ... I shall argue that the postulates of the classical theory are applicable to a special case only and not to the general case, the situation which it assumes being a limiting point of the possible positions of equilibrium. Moreover, the characteristics of the special case assumed by the classical theory happen not to be those of the economic society in which we actually live, with the result that its teaching is misleading and disastrous if we attempt to apply it to the facts of experience.

We would add to this quotation from today's perspective that DSGE model building is in fact even no longer really a special, limiting case – as was the classical variant of the old Neoclassical synthesis with its assumption of market clearing prices. It represents in its present form a structurally unstable prototype model of the Wicksellian variety, with no neighboring Keynesian demand rationed situations and with little common ground with more traditional types of Keynesian theories. The following considerations will attempt to shed some light on the reasons behind such a statement.

Today's mainstream macroeconomics generally insists on the following three methodological principles in order to judge whether a macrodynamic model makes sense or not:

- Micro-foundations based on smoothly operating and unconstrained optimizing behavior of agents (however it could be disaggregated with respect to age structure in so-called Overlapping Generations (OLG) models).
- Market clearing on all markets (which in general results in the use of algebraic equations in place of dynamic adjustment equations).
- Extremely informed forward-looking agents and rational expectations (which ensure that the economy is always on its stable submanifold with all the marginal conditions fulfilled).

We will collect in this section some arguments which we believe show that such a methodological approach to the study of macrodynamic systems is much too narrow and one-sided to allow for a fruitful analysis of actual behavioral possibilities for economic agents, the stock-flow interactions that they imply, and the complex dynamics that such behavior may generate when cumulative processes and macroeconomic feedback mechanisms become effective in non-market clearing situations.

Indeed, as the *assumption* of the extremely well informed forward-looking agents and rational expectations by now have become an undeniable "truth" for many macroeconomists, the stability of the economy (and the well behaved impulse-response functions generated after anticipated and unanticipated shocks) implied by its mathematically very demanding structure has become a "goes without saying" matter in the current macroeconomics literature. Hand in hand with this development, the study of accelerating processes or divergent paths of the economy has by and large become superfluous or a pathological situation for the majority of the profession. However, as for example the recent financial crisis, and in fact common sense would suggest, not all agents *have the capability* to be fully "rational" or are sufficiently knowledgeable with respect to the future economic evolution, so that the modeling and study of *"non-rational"* and that means behaviorally founded macroeconomic dynamics is just as, if not more, important as the study of dynamics generated under the assumption of an omnipotent forward-looking and perfectly rational economic agents in a situation where markets clear at each moment in time.

By contrast, a topic that must be and is common to *all* thorough economic theorizing is the assumption of a complete set of budget restrictions which, when all debt financing is properly specified, must be fulfilled at all moments in time.[6] The type of behavior that takes place within given budget equations (or *restrictions* if credit rationing takes place) is however open to discussion, since there is no unique way to rationalize the behavior of economic agents taking place within these constraints (who may in particular use different optimization routines when solving problems of differing complexity). Furthermore, coordination between the plans of agents acting on a specific market may be very different, not only depending on the specific form of the market, but also on the restrictions economic agents experience – or have experienced – when operating on it. In the following subsections we will consider each of the above items in isolation before we come to a general evaluation of the importance of these topics in their interaction.

### Omnipotent forward-looking agents as microfoundation?

In our view the basic objection to the omnipotent forward-looking agent is given by the simple observation that for complex market economies it is the interaction of multiple agents (or at least at the minimum the interaction of two representative agents – workers and the owners of assets) that is relevant for economic outcomes. A very relevant aspect of the market interaction of the agents in market economies are therefore distributional issues.

Thus, the conflict over income and asset distribution (and over new techniques of production) is a very fundamental conflict in an economy where there is an uneven distribution of capital assets. It may even be claimed, as for example Richard Goodwin testifies with his work, that this is a core element in the explanation of the dynamics of capitalism, shaping distribution driven Keynesian goods market dynamics (based on the wage-led/profit-led distinction) as well as Schumpeterian innovation waves in the economic and the social structure of accumulation in significant ways. The nature of this distributive conflict is exemplified in detail with respect to the short- and long-phase cycles it implies for the case of the US economy in Chapter 16. It cannot be analyzed by means of so-called Overlapping Generations (OLG) models, since distribution of income and capital assets is not a matter of age. Instead, if the distinction between worker households and pure asset holders is made, we would get four types of economic agents, since social affiliations tend to be stable over time and are thus quite the opposite of the case considered in the single agent OLG framework.

There are of course more than just the two considered social classes, but our argument is not directed towards finding the most appropriate representation for a given economy, but to establish what should be assumed at a minimum level for an investigation of the dynamics of capitalist market economies. On the basis of such a minimum framework, one should then consider a situation which is more general than the case of classical saving habits where only savings out of profits are allowed for. In modern economies both asset owners and workers save so that personal income distribution will be different from functional income distribution[7] and there will be wealth accumulation also on the side of workers, though of a more basic type as compared to pure asset holders, the long-run effects of which have to be investigated.

Of course, there is the evolution of workers with different skill groups, the evolution of unions, public sector and fiscal policy, pension funds and more. Furthermore workers' preferences may also change in the course of wealth accumulation. Yet, these are issues that should be kept apart from the baseline version of the model that attempts to investigate the dynamics of wages, profits and wealth in a society where interests differ about the evolution of those groups, sectors and magnitudes.

There is however a second argument which questions the validity of the positions put forth by those who insist on the omnipotent forward-looking agent framework. Households in this approach are often modeled in a Walrasian manner, as not only price takers, but also as seeing no restrictions on the choice of jobs and the supply of labor they are offering as the result of their isolated single agent optimizing procedure. With respect to the Walrasian framework we know however from theorems proved by Sonnenschein, Mantel and Debreu[8] that nearly everything can be microfounded, once enough heterogeneity is assumed between economic agents. What therefore is the value of a microfoundation of consumption and labor supply schedules, which necessarily result in very special demand and supply behavior? The answer is that nothing can be proved in this way as being superior to well-specified macroeconomic supply and demand relationship that are formulated within well-specified budget restrictions. As mentioned above, this is not to say that forward-looking behavior should be irrelevant for macroeconomics. Already in Keynes the future plays an important role in decision making concerning the marginal efficiency of capital and the liquidity preference. Yet, in dynamic optimization models it is frequently overdone by assuming unrestricted optimizing behavior – usually with too much micro, and not enough macro, foundation.

Our basic methodological requirement is to exclude situations where economic behavior is introduced by assuming supply and demand relationships that are inconsistent with the stock-flow interactions generated by the budget restrictions of the various agents. This implies that these latter restrictions should always be carefully specified, but that the matter of what agents actually optimize within these constraints, for example given by the regimes of business cycles, should at the least be a matter of discussion, if not even be a matter of empirical investigation that cannot be subjected to theoretical analysis alone. All this also holds outside the counterfactual general equilibrium analysis of Walrasian production economies. It should be used to demand rigor on the side of stock-flow specifications of the considered economy, but – in the interests of research diversity – not be used to just refuse coherent models of this type simply because they are not based on the omnipotent agent assumption or related modeling devices.

We conclude that the starting point of the macroeconomic study of advanced market economies with uneven distribution of capital assets should be based on a principal–agent relationship which can explain differentiated wealth and income positions and the resulting saving propensities. Thus a long-phased demand driven distributive cycle can be generated from this situation as we have observed it in the form of prosperity phases and subsequent stagnant developments since World War II.

### Continual Walrasian market clearing?

Viewed from the perspective of the Non-Walrasian macroeconomics of the 1970s it is fairly perplexing to see that most currently fashionable New Keynesian models aimed at helping to understand observed business fluctuations are again being built on Walrasian household theory in particular. Consuming households may be price-takers on many markets for consumption goods, but the assumption that they choose their optimal consumption plans on the basis of their notional labor supply and resulting wage income plans is fairly far from what households actually do – or, given the constraints, can do – when optimizing the use of their resources.

One need not be convinced by the microeconomic dual decision hypothesis in the Non-Walrasian reformulation of household decision making, but may simply assume on the macroeconomic level as point of departure that households consider as their wage income what they receive from their current actual employment position (or – if unemployed – from their unemployment insurance). A great fraction of the households are thus constrained in consumption decisions by job opportunities, labor income and credit constraints, which in some of the New Keynesian literature have become known as "rule of thumb" consumers.[9] Compared to the Walrasian notional wage income concept, according to which the participants in the labor market assume that they can always realize the optimal consumption/labor supply decision they derive from given wages, prices and intertemporal choice given by the Euler equation, in complete isolation from all other economic information and macroeconomic feedback effects affecting next period's economic outcome, the hypothesis that we have sketched above is to be preferred. The great macroeconomists in the past knew this and it in fact was already part of the pre-Keynesian Neoclassical analysis of Pigou and others when they studied the causes of unemployment in the macroeconomy.

Whatever the microeconomic underpinnings of the macroeconomic analysis of (mass, non-frictional) unemployment may be, they cannot be of an omnipotent forward-looking agent type, but have to be derived from a different set of assumptions about the constrained behavior of households in the presence of the conditions of the labor market and in particular unemployment. Be that as it may, there is still another methodologically oriented argument that deeply questions the assumption of a universal market clearing, of Walrasian or any other type.

A basic empirical fact of macroeconomics is that the actual data generating process on the macroeconomic level concerning annualized data, like the inflation rate over a yearly period, is by and large a daily one, since the annual inflation rate is updated by the actual economic processes at least every day. This suggests that empirically oriented discrete time macromodels mirroring the actual data generating process should be iterated with a short period length and will then in general provide the same answer as their continuous time analogs.

Concerning expectations, the (slower) data collection process may however be of importance and may give rise to certain (smaller) delays in the revision of expectations, which however is overcome by the formulation of extrapolating expectation mechanisms and other ways by which agents smooth their expectation formation process. We do not expect here that this implies a major difference between period and continuous time analysis if appropriately modeled, a situation which may however radically change if proper delays – as for example gestation lags in investment – are introduced. Yet even this situation may only lead to continuous time systems involving time delays and not to the conventional period models with a uniform period and the corresponding totally synchronized actions over all the markets in the economy, as is also standard for example in some of the New Keynesian approaches to macrodynamics.[10]

Sims (1998, p.318) states in this regard:

> The next several sections examine the behavior of a variety of models that differ mainly in how they model real and nominal stickiness ... They are formulated in continuous time to avoid the need to use the uninterpretable "one period" delays that plague the discrete time models in this literature.

We completely agree with such a statement. We conclude from it that the use of temporary or intertemporal general equilibrium approaches with market clearing on all markets in an economic model that is operated in a continuous time framework is very unlikely to represent a reasonable approach at least for the real markets of the economy. Instead, there are gradual adjustment processes towards moving equilibrium positions at work that respond for example to disappointed sales expectations and unintended inventory changes experienced by firms in the manufacturing sector. We thus claim here that continuous time disequilibrium dynamics is much more relevant for the study of actual market economies than macrodynamic period models with their artificial synchronization of all economic activities (their virtual bunching at, for example, four points during the year). This is directly obvious for macrodynamic models of dimension one when situations of convergence in continuous time can lead to chaotic dynamics in period versions of the model when the period length becomes sufficiently large. The same also applies to statements of Erceg et al. (2000, p.302) when uniformly synchronized period lengths of two years are considered with respect to their economic implications.

Of course, there exist processes that are synchronized with certain calendar dates, like monthly wage payments or the data collection snapshots of the economy mentioned above, which are often taken at given points in time. The question however is whether these synchronized activities are so important that they challenge the use of continuous time models with their compelling implication of using non-market clearing formulations at least for the real markets of the economy rather than the assumption of perpetual equilibrium at all moments in time. Moreover the use of such non-market clearing adjustment processes is indeed the basis for the consideration of the various Keynesian macroeconomic feedback channels, like the impact of nominal changes on the real side, the Fisher debt deflation effect, the Pigou real balance effect, the Tobin price expectation effect (where an expected price fall will trigger instabilities) and the Keynes-effect in the context of a dynamic multiplier model: they all have been a characteristic in the traditional Keynesian approaches to macrodynamics but have mostly been forgotten in modern market clearing macroeconomics.

We conclude that period models that give different answers as compared to their corresponding continuous time analogs should be viewed with suspicion if it is claimed that they are applicable to the explanation of the observed behavior of actual economies. Such model types may be very misleading, in particular if we attempt to use them for macroeconomic policy advice.

### *Hyper-perfect expectations?*

We consider the rational expectations methodology here only with respect to continuous time deterministic models. The existence of uniquely determined rational expectations solutions for the forward-looking variables (called determinacy) is based on eigen-value calculations and the local search for a stable submanifold, as in Woodford's (2003) appendices, such that a one-to-one correspondence between the forward-looking variables and the number of unstable roots can be established. This guarantees determinacy in the reaction of the non-predetermined variables by means of the so-called jump-variable technique, which by assumption then allows the economy, after some change, to be put on a unique path back onto the stable submanifold of the full phase space of the dynamics. This is postulated to occur after unanticipated shocks. Rational expectations are therefore much more than just model-consistent expectations, since they select – by jumps of the forward-looking variables – from the set of all future paths with model-consistent expectations the single path that converges to the steady state of the economy as time goes to infinity. This type of an omniscient forward-looking agent is assumed to characterize the representative household's behavior as well as the decision making for firms and the results of their interactions.

Our basic objections to such a solution of the local stabilization of an in general (saddlepoint) unstable economy through a schematic application of a mathematical algorithm and the instantaneous adjustment to the marginal conditions are the following:[11]

- What are the microfoundations for this choice of behavior for the whole economy in models where the area of economic outcomes, that is the stable manifold, depends on the interaction between independent households' and firms' demand, supply and pricing decisions? Who is coordinating macroeconomically the behavior toward the establishment of the marginal conditions and the endogenous parameters of the partial decision problems of households and firms over the considered time horizon?
- How do agents master the complex rational expectations calculations that are needed to guarantee such a macroeconomic performance, in particular given that there are agents who will have to make choices in the future, and how do we know what they will decide and how they will get the appropriate information (in particular if information is costly)?[12]
- In a non-linear context: why do agents have rational expectations in loglinear approximations around the steady state, but apply their global rational expectations calculation (since they must know all unbounded trajectories) routines to the loglinear approximation instead of checking what the non-linear stable submanifold looks like?
- Increasing the dimension of an economic model simply by adding for example some stock-flow interaction may lead to totally different jumps than in the initially given situation, for example when the capacity effects of investment are added to the model, see Chiarella et al. (2009, Ch.7). The behavior of the economy is therefore structurally unstable, not only with respect to local approximations of the model, but also with respect to the number of state variables, even if they do not involve additional behavior from the side of the economic agents. The structural instability of rational expectations was first pointed out by George and Oxley (1985).
- Assuming for example a PPP-UIP model with rational expectations may lead to policy advice that would recommend increases in money supply in order to fight inflation. Clearly such perfection in a neoclassical framework implies strong policy conundrums, see Chiarella et al. (2009, Ch.11).
- There is no rigorous determinacy discussion for theoretical models of staggered wage and price setting and even more in applied DSGE models where this problem is thus only implicitly dealt with (usually in an *ad hoc* numerical manner).
- Purely forward looking models of New Keynesian type often perform poorly in empirical applications and need to be modified in an *ad hoc* fashion in order to improve their empirical applicability.
- Rational expectations approaches linearize about some steady states and then undertake VAR type impulse-response studies to show that the shocks (technology, preference or monetary and fiscal policy shocks) generate the expected responses that correspond to empirically observed patterns; often this done in one-regime models, and responses are not regime dependent.[13]

- Rational expectations approaches are very limited with respect to even slight generalizations in the framework of the model under consideration, for example with respect to an adequate treatment of the investment decisions of firms.

Taken together we would claim therefore that the rational expectations methodology may be a rigorous strategy for solving the performance of a macrodynamic model economy numerically, but it is far from producing realistic baseline cases in the sense of how the agents behave under disequilibrium constraints. Moreover, this solution strategy is structurally unstable (at least in the case of anticipated events). In addition, from the economic perspective it requires an extremely complex type of household behavior, and it is subject to bizarre reactions of the economy (in times of severe contractive shocks, see Chiarella et al. 2009, Chs.2,3 for example) or doubtful policy conclusions (in perfectly open economies, see Chiarella et al. 2009, Ch.11 and its consideration of *laissez-faire* policies in particular).[14]

We conclude that a Keynesian theory that is built around rational expectations will be of an extremely hypothetical type in view of the numerous expectations formation schemes that can be applied by the economic agents in reality, which range from very naive extrapolations to highly sophisticated computer-based algorithmic procedures to forecast future events. In theory, because of analytical difficulties, one must represent such heterogeneous expectations formation processes as highly stylized ones where backward-looking procedures (of chartists) are for example represented by nested adaptive expectations and forward-looking procedures (of fundamentalists) by nested regressive expectation schemes. Numerically one can however exploit numerous actual and hypothetical expectations schemes like complicated charts used to interpret the past or forecasting procedures based on sophisticated macroeconometric techniques.

### Doubts about the rational expectations approach

On the basis of what has been discussed above, we would argue that the rational expectations approach, coupled with omnipotent forward-looking agent microfoundations and Walrasian market clearing, is a very doubtful axiomatic starting point for an applicable macrodynamic analysis. It represents a very cumbersome way to reproduce (or even understand) the factual behavior of actual economies.

We have argued that continuous time models are the more appropriate analytical tool as compared to over synchronized quarterly macro-models of the real-financial market interaction. We go on from this observation to corresponding disequilibrium adjustment processes in a matured, traditionally based AD–AS framework, as in Asada et al. (2010), where agents may have myopic model-consistent expectations (to simplify without significant loss of generality the analysis). We apply principal–agent structures on the macrodynamic level. If we are prepared to accept that economies may be locally repelling around their steady state position, but can generally be bounded by behavioral non-linearities when they depart by too much from their steady state, we might be able to find interesting new insights and policy conclusions not attainable within the New Consensus of mainstream macroeconomics. This movement towards the Keynesian paradigm, augmented by the presence of stochastic processes, on which the much more narrow Frisch paradigm is by and large focusing, may then be an alternative to deal with the challenges posed by the current crisis in macroeconomic thoughts as described in the statement of Paul Krugman at the beginning of this chapter.

## From DSGE to DSGD model building

The working hypothesis of this book – and its two planned companion volumes – is that there are alternatives to the standard macroeconomics prevalent in marcoeconomic graduate classes. We here pursue what we have called the Dynamic Stochastic General Disequilibrium (DSGD) approach. The DSGD approach will by contrast preserve the achievements of the old Neoclassical synthesis, and it will give the traditional Keynesian variant a matured and much more dominant role to play, in particular concerning the working of an advanced wage-price spiral embracing the labor and the goods markets and concerning the role of financial markets in this interaction. Viewed from this reconstruction of Keynesian macroeconomics, the Classical variant of the old Neoclassical synthesis becomes again what Keynes (1936) characterized it to be, namely a very special, though nevertheless limiting (equilibrium) case of a very general DSGD approach.

We base our investigation of this approach and of how Keynesian macroeconomics can be reconstructed, in a simplified way, on the following basic graphical representation and summary of its conceptual foundations. Figure 0.1 assumes that there is a fundamental causal nexus (or hierarchy) present in the interaction of the main markets of the macroeconomy which leads from the financial markets at the top of the hierarchy to the goods markets in the middle – based on the achieved valuation of the assets traded in the financial markets, the implied state of confidence and the term structure of interest rates – and from there to the labor markets at the bottom, which in turn depend on the effective demand that is realized in the market for goods. This viewpoint is fine from the perspective of dealing with short- and medium-run macroeconomic issues and problems, however we know that from the perspective of the long run (that is from the perspective of economic growth) that the labor market, productive knowledge and skills and productive potentials will play an important role in the long run performance of an economy. Or to state it even more succinctly, in the long run the supply side as well as the demand side are important.

Furthermore, the dominance of the financial market in the interrelationship of the main markets of the macroeconomy does not operate in isolation, but is surrounded by feedback channels leading from lower level markets to higher level ones. A typical example is given by the famous Keynes-effect, according to which money wage decreases can revive the economy if they lead to price level decreases and therefore to increases in real balances of the household sector, which induces

**Traditional Keynesian theory: summary**

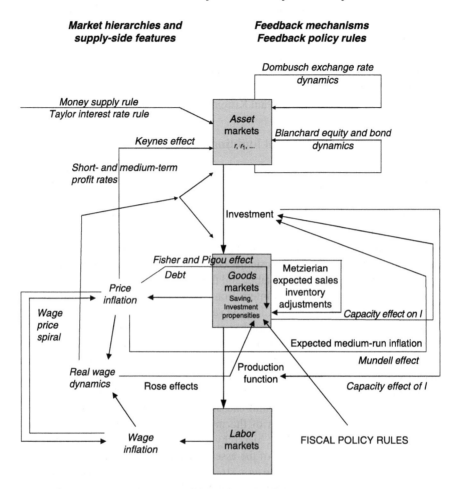

***Market hierarchies and
supply-side features***

***Feedback mechanisms
Feedback policy rules***

***How dominant is the downward influence? How strong are the repercussions?
How dominant are the supply-side dynamics?***

*Figure 0.1* Advanced Keynesian disequilibrium growth dynamics: graphical summary of
fairly sluggish or fairly fast, but never infinitely fast, feedback adjustment
mechanisms.

lower interest rates on the financial markets which in turn stimulate investment
and thus effective goods demand, leading finally to increases in employment and
thus to a check to further decreasing wages that is capable of moving the economy
back to its full employment level. This intricate chain of events is in fact needed
in Keynesian macroeconomics if the argument is made that adjusting money
wages will lead the economy towards such full employment positions, often
however being replaced by a grossly misleading short-cut, which looks only at the

market and price for labor as the ones being responsible for its disease and which is subject to a confusion of nominal with real wages, when it recommends wage reductions. Keynes' (1936) argument here was that the policy advice of lowering nominal wages is in fact a very illusory one – based on a narrow and erroneous understanding of the working of the institutions in advanced capitalist market economies – since it represents a long and painful process, which indeed can be circumvented and abbreviated by the proper choice of monetary policy measures.

Figure 0.1 summarizes the main feedback substructures between and within the three main markets of the macroeconomy and which we will investigate from many perspectives (in isolation as well as in their interaction) in our perspective for a "reconstruction of Keynesian macroeconomics". It will guide our model building strategy towards a more and more integrated Keynesian macroeconomics where the central macroeconomic markets will increasingly play the role as it is suggested by the above characterization of market hierarchies and the repercussions between them. At the bottom of the figure we also give a summary of the main questions to which we seek answers in the course of the investigation of this more and more refined approach to an analysis of fluctuating growth that is based on disequilibrium adjustment processes in the real and later on also in the financial markets of the economy, as suggested by the acronym DSGD.

Figure 0.1 first suggests to what extent the asset markets really dominate the outcome of the real/financial market interaction from a macroeconomic perspective. This requires that the dynamics of asset prices be linked to the stocks supplied and demanded on these markets by way of a macroeconomic portfolio approach. The stock markets are on this view primarily driven by the very short-term expectations of capital gains on bonds and equities, interspersed however with information from the real markets such as the profitability of firms, economic activity in general and the stance of fiscal and monetary policy. The financial markets determine internally the dynamics of asset prices and the changes in capital gains expectations that these dynamics imply. They are independent of the other markets to the extent they have become an end in themselves, where asset holders exchange their financial assets each day to a substantial and ever increasing degree as a result of the liberalization of financial markets and the financialization of the world economy.

In Figure 0.1 we show a downward causal market-nexus, leading from the financial markets just considered, via the implied investment decisions of firms and the resulting effective goods demand to a production-based labor market outcome that can be strong or weak, depending on the state of the goods market. This Keynesian downward causal nexus provides the background against which various repercussions from lower to higher markets in this hierarchy can be formulated and investigated.

Secondly, there is the question about what the various macroeconomic feedback mechanisms shown in Figure 0.1 add to the real/financial market interactions and to what extent they will contribute to or undermine, when working together, the local stability of the balanced growth path of the model. Clear candidates for destabilizing feedback channels are the Fisher debt deflation effect, but also the

Mundell real rate of interest channel by which inflationary expectations stimulate inflation in the boom. These accelerating processes maybe more destabilizing than similar ones on the quantity side of the goods market. The latter ones were introduced into the literature by Harrod's investment accelerator or Metzler's inventory accelerator mechanism. Yet all such feedback effects are important for macroeconomics and cannot be assumed away as is done in many currently standard macroeconomic approaches.

Thirdly, the dynamics of income distribution, as it finds expression in the wage–price spiral, has to be investigated, in particular in its role of shaping the long-run behavior of these dynamics with its Keynesian short-run regime. In this case there are possible scenarios depending on whether wages or prices react more strongly to changes in economic activity and whether aggregate demand is wage-led (increases with increases in the real wage) or profit-led (decreases when the real wage is rising). There is then, for example, the destabilizing case where real wages rise in the boom, which stimulates aggregate demand in the wage-led case whereby the rise in the real wage gains further impetus. In a profit-led regime, by contrast, this would lead to decreasing aggregate demand and thus to a break in further rises in real wages.

Finally, the perspective of our approach is of course to contribute to the analysis of policy issues which – due to the fact that we also want to treat medium- and long-run dynamics – is more oriented to the treatment of monetary or fiscal policy rules than to a treatment of the consequences of isolated fiscal or monetary policy actions that occur only at a particular point in time. In the general DSGD model the question will eventually be to what extent monetary policy should be oriented to what happens on the financial side of the economy rather than to the state of the business cycle, which should be left to countercyclical fiscal policy. When sufficiently coordinated by monetary as well as fiscal policy, which are assumed to be designed independently of the decisions of the government (which would then have narrower powers) this may then also be the way inflation could be controlled on the market for goods.

## Plan of the three volumes

The focus of our project is the detailed modeling and investigation of the disequilibrium adjustment processes characterizing the financial, the goods and the labor markets and their interaction. We consider such an attempt as providing "macrofoundations" which in our view have to precede "microfoundations", by first providing a detailed description of the envisaged more or less gradual reactions of the economy to observed discrepancies between demand and supply and the constraints and rationing processes that may be involved. These dynamic (stabilizing or destabilizing) feedback chains on one or between several markets of the DSGD macro-approach of course need to be supplemented by stochastic elements if they are to be applied to actual economies and specific periods in time. Yet in their theoretical understanding one has first to study their deterministic feedback structures and detailed working. We note in passing that shocks on the real markets may be less important than shocks that hit the financial markets – yet depending on the size of the shocks – since real shocks could have a slow impact on the level of macroeconomic activity, while changes in for example the asset market, interest rates, risk perception and credit spreads, can impact on investment and consumption behavior quickly and globally.

The first volume of our reconstruction of a Keynesian type of macroeconomics concerns partial model building, most notably the working of the labor market and the resulting wage-price spiral in its interaction with the price level dynamics on the market for goods, as embedded in a strictly Keynesian demand regime. We will however also analyze in Part I why the Keynesian goods market regime can be considered as the dominant one in the evolution of capitalist market economies, how it can be studied from the perspective of Steindl[15]and also from the perspective of endogenous growth. Empirical aspects of the wage-price spiral are investigated from various perspectives in Part IV. Moreover, important methodological issues are treated in Part I, for example the role of dimensional analysis in macroeconomic model building and the importance of continuous time modeling in this area. Last, but not least, there is the recurrent topic of the implications of the assumption of so-called rational expectations as compared to models with only myopic perfect foresight or model consistent expectations. We go on from there to the consideration of heterogeneous expectations which can range from very naive expectations formation processes to extremely sophisticated ones, but nevertheless still far from the "rational" type that is dominant in the current macroeconomics literature.

In the final chapter of Volume I we prepare the ground for the next volume in this series by considering for the first time an approach which not only integrates goods and labor market dynamics, but also financial markets, though here still from the perspective of a conventional type of LM-analysis or interest rate policy of the central bank (which makes money supply an accommodating variable). These integrated models correspond – from the formal perspective, but not with respect to their implications – to the New Keynesian structural model in a setting with both staggered wages and prices. It can therefore usefully be compared with this latter approach regarding its analytical, numerical and empirical implications. Apart from primarily stochastic Neo-Wicksellian mainstream DSGE theory, to which our three volumes seek to provide a detailed and rigorous alternative, there is also book available which provides an approach similar in spirit to the present one. We therefore refer the reader to Taylor (2004) if he or she wishes to read a work with the same broad focus, but written in a quite different way. There is also another excellent book, Aoki and Yoshikawa (2007), which is devoted to reconstructing macroeconomics. This book is however more formal in nature and it starts from statistical physics and combinatorial stochastic processes as the foundations of macroeconomic theory.

Volume II of our reconstruction of Keynesian macroeconomics will be devoted to the detailed analysis and comparison of the competing approaches (DSGE, DSGD) to Keynesian macroeconomics. It will also consider intermediate integrated models of the Keynes–Wicksell type in a one- and two-country setup. This intermediate case is characterized by supply driven real dynamics combined with a Wicksellian theory of inflation based on Keynesian demand discrepancies in the market for goods (the sole role for a Keynesian distinction between savings and investment schedules in this Wicksellian framework). In Part III of Volume II we use disequilibrium variants of the conventional AD–AS dynamics, that is models of the Dynamic Aggregate Demand–Dynamic Aggregate Supply (DAD–DAS) variety, to study our alternative to the New Keynesian model with staggered wage and price setting from the theoretical as well as the empirical perspective, and this also for single economies as well as for a two-country scenario.

The DAD–DAS structures that we employ are still partially of a reduced form type and thus semi-structural in design, since they use as short-cut a simple dynamic multiplier approach (which however can be wage led or profit led) to study the working of the market for goods in the context of the wage-price spiral and a monetary policy that attempts to control this spiral. The structural analog to these semi-structural approaches is given by the model we have called the Keynes–Metzler–Goodwin (KMG) growth model (see Chiarella and Flaschel (2000)) where sales expectations are confronted with Keynesian aggregate demand, so that unintended inventory changes result and on this basis their correction by means of an active inventory policy of firms, which was absent in models of the Keynes–Wicksell type.

The KMG approach is investigated in Volume II in a variety of ways, as a baseline model of the distributive cycle in a Keynesian environment, from the empirical perspective and from the perspective of the inertia term that is present in the wage–price spiral. It is extended to an endogenous treatment of the NAIRU rate of full employment, to small open economies and towards a treatment of endogenous growth. These investigations show that the baseline KMG approach can be fruitfully generalized in many directions and that it really constitutes a point of departure for the DSGD modeling approach we have in mind, which is simultaneously coherent and sophisticated enough in its treatment of the real markets of the economy, and this from the perspective of the demand side as well as from the supply side.

There is however still present a fundamental weakness or asymmetry in the KMG framework, given by the fact that it – like the baseline models of the New Keynesian variety – is heavily biased towards a detailed treatment of the real markets. It still confines the financial sector of the economy to a consideration of money market equilibrium (as in conventional advanced textbook approaches) or a Taylor type interest rate policy rule. The 2007–2009 crisis on the financial markets has however in particular revealed in a dramatic way that this is a fairly incomplete and unsatisfactory treatment of what has been designed as the core structure of the Keynesian approach to macroeconomics.

A macrodynamic model including the financial sector is still missing. In the final chapter of Volume II we therefore provide, as an outlook on Volume III, a more balanced treatment of the interaction between the real and the financial markets. We do so by adding a macroeconomic portfolio theory (as we have already sketched it above) to the KMG framework, extending it thereby, by including some Tobin portfolio ideas towards a KMGT(obin) modeling scenario with imperfect substitution between the financial assets. This is a significant extension of KMG based analysis, leading to a dynamical system with at least eight laws of motion, which can nevertheless be studied from the analytical perspective. In the concluding chapter of Volume II we solve this task however in a relatively tranquil setup for the financial markets, since we continue to assume that money is issued only by the central banks, that government deficits are financed by fixed price bonds throughout, and that firms' investment projects are financed solely by the issuing of new equities.

It remains the task of Volume III of our series to extend this situation to a treatment of further risky assets (besides equities). This is at first still done, as in simple LM approaches or Tobin portfolio equilibrium approaches, by assuming that asset prices always adjust such that asset markets are cleared at each moment in time. However, from the perspective of open economies we have to derive flow equations from such a stock approach to financial markets (which can be entered into the flow capital account of the balance of payments in a stock-flow consistent way).

We here make use of stock adjustment principles based on adjustment costs also on the financial markets of the economy. Desired stock adjustments will therefore also be somewhat gradual, as it is suggested from an empirical perspective, since there are also some adjustment costs on the financial markets, in particular when viewed from a continuous time perspective. This also implies that financial markets are subject to (fast) disequilibrium adjustment processes which will lead the financial markets to a full portfolio equilibrium over time when the gross substitute assumption is made, and when everything else (including capital gains expectations) is kept constant by way of a *ceteris paribus* clause. We thereby arrive for the first time at a complete description of a DSGD approach to Keynesian macrodynamics that will exhibit a variety of destabilizing feedback channels in the private sector of the economy. These will call for the introduction of new fiscal and monetary policy measures in order to keep the economy viable.

Extensions of the baseline DSGD model in Volume III will concern the addition of the term structure of interest rates and credit spreads by assuming the coexistence of fixed price bonds and perpetuities in the financing of government deficits. Moreover, we will also add a banking sector, in particular commercial banking with its endogenous credit and money creation from the perspective of traditional banking, as well as investment banking, and will discuss the return of the narrow banking idea, put forth in order to avoid in the future what has happened in commercial banking in the recent financial crisis, which, as some claim, the commercial banks have themselves triggered. These extensions of the baseline KMGT model also call for significant reforms in the conduct of monetary as well as fiscal policy.

In Part III of Volume III we provide a discussion of important mechanisms which are, on the one hand, responsible for the creation of financial bubbles, and on the other hand, for the establishment of busts in the real sector of the economy. We discuss what monetary policy can do in these situations when such regime changes occur. An important role is here played by Tobin's $q$ defined not only with respect to corporate stocks, but also corporate bonds and the implications that derive from such a distinction. We thus model boom–bust cycles and default risks in their interaction with asset prices. Various applications of these models are explored and investigated.

In Part IV of Volume III we make use of a simple completion of the Mundell–Fleming model of the open economy by means of a Tobin portfolio approach to analyze twin deficits and inflation dynamics. We consider fixed as well flexible exchange rate regimes and in the latter, the reasons for overshooting exchange rate dynamics. We extend this approach from limited national capital flows between domestic and foreign bonds to excessive international capital flows in the one country framework of a small open economy as well as in a two country framework representing, for example, the interaction of the US-economy and the Eurozone.

In a concluding chapter to the whole series we finally discuss fundamental reforms of labor market institutions in the baseline KMGT model of the DSGD research program, in order not only to address Minskyian processes of financial instability, but also reforms aimed at mitigating the distributive cycle, the wage-price spiral on which it is based, and the recurrent scenarios of high rates of unemployment that accompany business cycles in the busts.

This final chapter therefore argues that capital accumulation and financial markets may be stabilized by the proper choice of fiscal and monetary policy measures, but that an asset accumulation process that is really sustainable in a democratic society can only be achieved if the distributive problems on the real side of the economy can also be solved successfully, in the form of providing flexibility in production and in technical innovations, where however processes of social degradation through mass unemployment or low income work are avoided through appropriate labor market policies.

Lastly, we want to note that there is an important competing alternative to the explanation of business fluctuations of Keynesian type, which is not just a special case of the old Neoclassical Synthesis, but is based on von Hayek's work in particular, and is characterized by the following quotation from Lucas (1977):

> Why is it that, in capitalist economies, aggregate variables undergo repeated fluctuations about trend, all of essentially the same character? Prior to Keynes' General Theory, the resolution of this question was regarded as one of the main outstanding challenges to economic research, and attempts to meet this challenge were called business cycle theory. Moreover, among the interwar business cycle theorists, there was wide agreement as to what it would mean to solve this problem. To cite Hayek, as a leading example:

> > [T]he incorporation of cyclical phenomena into the system of economic equilibrium theory, with which they are in apparent contradiction, remains the crucial problem of Trade Cycle Theory;
> > By 'equilibrium theory' we here primarily understand the modern theory of the general interdependence of all economic quantities, which has been most perfectly expressed by the Lausanne School of theoretical economics. (Hayek 1933, pp.33–42)

A primary consequence of the Keynesian Revolution was the redirection of research effort away from this question onto the apparently simpler question of the determination of output at a point in time, taking history as given. A secondary consequence of this Revolution, due more to Tinbergen than to Keynes, was a rapid increase in the level of precision and explicitness with which aggregate economic theories were formulated. As a result, Keynesian macro-economics has benefited from several decades of methodological improvement whereas, from this technical point of view, the efforts of the business cycle theorists appear hopelessly outdated.

As outlined above, we do not at all agree with this view and with the described Hayekian alternative to Keynes' (1936) theory of the business cycle, and also not with the limited understanding Lucas' statement reveals of the coverage and substance of Keynes' (1936) General Theory, in particular when viewed from the experience of the financial meltdown of the years 2007–2009. Our three volumes are devoted to demonstrating this to the reader by way of a more and more advanced modeling of the interaction of the real with the financial markets that are both driven by disequilibrium adjustment processes, and macroeconomic feedback effects, with no obvious tendency to converge to temporary equilibrium positions or even to the steady state of the economy

# Part I

# Methodological issues

Macro-frequencies
and dimensions

# 1 Applicable macro is continuous time macro

## 1.1 Introduction

In this chapter, we reconsider the issue of the (non-) equivalence of period and continuous time analysis, first discussed in Flaschel et al. (2008, Ch.1). Period models – the now dominant model type in the macrodynamic literature – assume a single (uniformly applied) lag length for all markets, which therefore act in a completely synchronized manner. In view of this, we start in Section 1.2 from the methodological precept that period and continuous time representations of the same macrostructure should give rise to the same qualitative outcomes, in particular, that the qualitative results of period analysis should not depend on the length of the period, see Foley (1975) for an early statement of this precept, as well as Medio (1991) and Sims (1998) for related observations. A simple example where this is fulfilled is given by the conventional Solow growth model, here considered in Section 1.3, while all chaotic period dynamics of dimension less than 3 are in conflict with this precept, see however Medio (1991) for routes to chaos in such an environment.

A basic empirical fact moreover is that the actual data generating process in macroeconomics is by and large a daily one (and the data collection frequency is also much less than a year). This suggests that empirically oriented macromodels should be iterated with a short period length as far as actual processes are concerned and will then – we claim – in general provide the same answer as their continuous time analogues. Concerning expectations, the data collection process is however of importance and may give rise to certain (smaller) delays in the revision of expectations, which however may be overcome by the formulation of extrapolating expectation mechanisms and other ways by which agents smooth their expectation formation process. We do not expect here that this implies a major difference between period and continuous time analysis if appropriately modeled, a situation which may however radically change if proper delays, as they are for example considered in Invernizzi and Medio (1991), are taken into account.

We discuss in Section 1.4 a typical example from the literature (certainly not the only one), where chaos results from a "too" stable continuous time model when this model is reformulated as a "long-period" macro-model, then exhibiting a sufficient degree of locally destabilizing overshooting. Shortening the period lengths in such chaotic macro models, i.e., iterating them with a finer step size, removes on the one hand "chaos" from such model types, while it on the other hand (and at the same time) brings the model into closer contact with what happens in the data generating process of the real world.[1]

Macromodels can however give rise to complex dynamics in continuous time if they are sufficiently rich in their dynamical structure and dimension. We conclude from this result that the investigation of complex dynamics is of a more fundamental and relevant type when applied to higher dimensional continuous time macrodynamics, since such approaches avoid the mixture of locally destabilizing, strongly overshooting adjustment processes (which would converge in continuous time) with the dynamics as they are typical for the larger macro-models – with interacting real and financial markets – of the advanced macrodynamics literature.

## 1.2 The satellite nature of macroeconomic period models

Period analysis with a single period is now the dominant form for models in the macrodynamic literature and thus of interest in its own right, independently of the consideration of the existence of more complicated lags in more advanced macrosystems. Discrete time macro modeling is of course not restricted to the assumption of a uniform and synchronized period length between all economic activities, with which this chapter is concerned. We focus in this respect on the empirical fact that the actual *data generating process* in macroeconomics is of much finer step size than the corresponding *data collection frequency* available nowadays, also in the real markets of the economy, and that the latter process is nowadays also much finer than one year.[2] This suggests that empirically applicable period macromodels (using annualized data) should be iterated with a much finer frequency (approximately with step size between "1/365 year" and "1/52 year" with respect to the actual performance of economy) in order to increase the likelihood of generating results that are equivalent to the ones of their continuous time analogue.

These empirically applicable period models – which take account of the fact that macroeconomic (annualized) data are generally updated each day – will then not be able to give rise to chaotic dynamics in dimensions one and two, suggesting that the literature on such chaotic dynamics is of highly questionable empirical relevance (though mathematically often demanding and of interest from this point of view). To exemplify this we consider in this chapter a one-dimensional (1-D) non-linear dynamic model that is known to be globally asymptotically stable in continuous time and that has been used in a period framework to generate from its parameters a period doubling route to chaos.

Before doing so we however consider a simple case, the Solow growth model, where period and continuous analysis give qualitatively the same answer for any length of the period between zero and infinity. The clustering of production and investment activities at possibly very distant points in time thus does not raise in this case the question of which period length is the most appropriate one, though it may still be asked whether the assumed type of clustering of economic activities really makes sense from an applied macroeconomic point of view if periods longer than one month are considered.

In concluding, this chapter therefore proposes that continuous time modeling (or period modeling with a short period length) is the better choice to approach macrodynamical issues, in particular when compared to a period model where the length of the period remains unspecified, since it avoids the empirically uninterpretable situation of a uniform period length (with a length of one quarter, year or more) and with an artificial synchronization of economic decision making. If discrete time formulations (not period analysis) are used for macroeconomic model building they should represent averages over the day as the relevant time unit for *complete* models of the real-financial interaction on the macroeconomic level. The stated dominance of continuous time modeling (or quasi-continuous modeling with a period length of one day) not only simplifies significantly the stability analysis for macrodynamic model building, but also questions the relevance of period model attractors that differ from their continuous time analogue.

Chiarella and Flaschel (2000) argue that a fully specified Keynesian model of monetary growth exhibits at least the six state variables, namely wage share and labor intensity (the growth component), inflation and expected inflation (the medium-run component) and expected sales and actual inventories per unit of capital (the short-run dynamics), i.e., these models easily meet the 3-D requirement for the existence of strange attractors in continuous time. They can be used for detecting routes to complex dynamics without running into the danger of synthesizing basically continuous time ideas with radically synchronized (overshooting) discrete time adjustment processes (which when appropriately bounded produce "chaos" also in dimensions one or two). This suggests that the techniques developed for analyzing non-linear dynamical systems represent unquestionably a useful stock of knowledge, to be applied now (in macro-economics) to investigate strange attractors as they may come about in continuous time in high-order macrodynamics.

Continuous vs. discrete time modeling, in macroeconomics, was discussed extensively in the 1970s and 1980s, sometimes in very confusing ways and often by means of highly sophisticated, but through unnecessarily complicated mathematical apparatus. There are however some statements in the literature, old and new, which suggest that period analysis in macroeconomics, i.e. discrete time analysis where all economic agents are forced to act in a completely synchronized manner (with a time unit that is usually left unspecified) can be misleading from the formal as well as from the economic point of view. Foley (1975, p.310) in particular states:

> The arguments of this section are based on a methodological precept concerning macroeconomic period models: *No substantive prediction or explanation in a well-defined macroeconomic period model should depend on the real time length of the period.*

Such a statement has however been completely ignored in the numerous analytical and numerical investigations of complex or chaotic macrodynamics. Furthermore, from the view point of economic modeling, Sims (1998, p.318) states:

> The next several sections examine the behavior of a variety of models that differ mainly in how they model real and nominal stickiness ... They are formulated in continuous time to avoid the need to use the uninterpretable "one period" delays that plague the discrete time models in this literature.

Our interpretation here is that a macrodynamic analysis that is intended to consider real and financial markets simultaneously must consider period analysis with a very short time-unit ("one day"), if a uniform and synchronized period length is assumed (with averaging of what happened during the day). But then, following Tobin (1982), real markets cannot be considered in equilibrium all of the time. Instead gradual adjustment of wages, prices and quantities occurs in view of labor and goods markets imbalances for which moreover convergence to real market equilibria cannot automatically be assumed. Real market behavior is therefore to be based on gradual adjustment processes, as suggested in Chiarella and Flaschel (2000) and extended in Chiarella et al. (2005), and it can then be discussed whether, on this basis, financial markets should be modeled by equilibrium conditions (as Tobin (1982) proposes) or also by at least somewhat delayed responses as well, now to stock imbalances, both in short period analysis as well as in continuous time.

Such implications may be the outcome of a reconsideration of discrete vs. continuous time dynamics. The present chapter however focuses on a narrower point, namely, following Foley (1975), that discrete and continuous-time models should provide qualitatively the same results. This implies that a lot of mathematical simulations of typical macro-models should be evaluated as interesting and surely skillful, mathematical exercises, but as questionable from the point of view of their empirical relevance. Period models thus in general depend on their continuous time analogues for their results, if empirically meaningful, and thus exhibit, to use the language of US migration policy, only a "J2 status" (dependent on a J1 visitor with a work permit) in their macroeconomic implications.

## 1.3 1-D equivalence: the non-linear Solow model of economic growth

The Solow (1956) one-good model of economic growth is based on full employment throughout, with a natural rate of labor force growth that is exogenously given. The dynamics of Solovian growth are non-linear due to its use of a neoclassical production function. In the usual continuous time formulation it implies a monotonic one-dimensional transition towards its steady state solution for all initial values of its state variable capital-intensity. It can be varied in many ways, including differentiated saving habits, endogenous saving rates, endogenous technological change.

The Solow model of neoclassical economic growth is usually based on the following set of assumptions on the supply side of a closed macroeconomy. In the form that is presented below we still ignore capital stock depreciation and technical change for expositional reasons.

$$Y = F(K, L^d) \quad \text{the neoclassical production function} \tag{1.1}$$

$$S = sY, s = const. \quad \text{Harrod-type savings function} \tag{1.2}$$

$$\dot{K} = S \quad \text{capital stock growth driven by household savings decisions} \tag{1.3}$$

$$\dot{L} = nL, n = const. \quad \text{labor force growth} \tag{1.4}$$

$$L^d = L \quad \text{the full employment assumption} \tag{1.5}$$

$$\omega = F_L(K, L) \quad \text{the marginal productivity theory of employment.} \tag{1.6}$$

The notation in these equations is fairly standard. We here use $L^d$ to denote labor demand and $\omega = w/p$ to denote the real wage. Technology is described by means of a so-called neoclassical production function that exhibits constant returns to scale. There is only direct investment of savings in real capital formation, i.e., Say's Law is assumed to hold true in its most simple form:

$$I \equiv S = sY,$$

with savings being strictly proportional to output and income $Y$. Labor is growing at a given natural rate $n$ and is fully employed, i.e., this model simply bases economic growth on actual factor growth without any demand side restriction on the market for goods. The last of the above equations is only added to justify the full employment assumption and it does not play a role in the quantity dynamics to be considered below. These dynamics are obtained from the following reduced form representation of the above model:

$$\dot{K} = sF(K, L), \tag{1.7}$$

$$\dot{L} = nL. \tag{1.8}$$

Since the state variables of these dynamics exhibit an exponential trend the model is generally only analyzed in intensive form, i.e., in terms of the variable $k$. In intensive form the above Solow model reads:

$$\dot{k} = sF(k, 1) - nk = sf(k) - nk \tag{1.9}$$

and thus gives rise to a single differential equation in the state variable $k$ which is non-linear due to the strict concavity of the function $f$.

In the form of a period model with period length $h$ this form of the Solow model can be represented by

$$Y_{t+h} = hF(K_t, L_t) \tag{1.10}$$

$$S_{t+h} = sY_{t+h} \tag{1.11}$$

$$K_{t+h} = K_t + S_{t+h} \tag{1.12}$$

$$L_{t+h} = (1 + nh)L_t. \tag{1.13}$$

We note here that the literature generally sets $h$ equal to 1 and considers instead

$$Y_t = F(K_t, L_t)$$
$$S_t = sY_t$$
$$K_{t+1} = K_t + S_t$$
$$L_{t+1} = (1 + n)L_t,$$

i.e., it assumes that output and savings occur instantaneously and that there is a uniform gestation lag in investment only (that is synchronized over the whole set of firms). This however is misleading, since production $Y$ (a flow) grows the longer the stocks capital $K$ (the number of machines) and $L$ (the number of workers) are employed, i.e., output $Y$ must vary with $h$. This discrete time version of the model can be reduced to the two equations

$$K_{t+h} = K_t + shF(K_t, L_t) \tag{1.14}$$

$$L_{t+h} = (1 + nh)L_t, \tag{1.15}$$

which for $h = 1$ are identical to the ones implied by the case where the role of the period $h$ length is neglected. Using the identity $K_{t+h}/L_{t+h} = (K_{t+h}/L_t)(L_t/L_{t+h})$, this model can be reduced further to the state variable $k$ given by $k_t = K_t/L_t$ and then gives rise to:

$$k_{t+h} = (k_t + shf(k_t))/(1 + nh). \tag{1.16}$$

At first sight, this law of motion of the period version of the Solow model looks quite different compared to the one in continuous time

$$\dot{k} = sF(k, 1) - nk = sf(k) - nk$$

and its discretization by way of difference quotients

$$k_{t+h} = k_t + h(sf(k_t) - nk_t) = k_t + shf(k_t) - nhk_t.$$

Yet, since this last difference equation is (for small period lengths $h$) but an approximation to the continuous time case we have to check here whether this can also be stated with respect to $k_{t+h} = (k_t + shf(k_t))/(1 + nh)$, the law of motion of the period model. Indeed, this law of motion can be reformulated as

$$\frac{k_{t+h} - k_t}{h} = \frac{(k_t + shf(k_t))/(1+nh) - k_t}{h}$$
$$= \frac{(k_t - (1+nh)k_t + shf(k_t))}{(1+nh)h} = \frac{sf(k_t) - nk_t}{1+nh}.$$

For small period lengths $h$ this expression is close to the period analogue of the intensive form continuous time case, i.e., the original extensive form period model and the original extensive form continuous time model provide nearly the same dynamics on the intensive form level for small periods $h$. Yet, with respect to large period lengths, we have to compare the outcome of the continuous time case with the properties of the period case directly and not via the latter approximations.[3]

Moreover, all versions of the Solow model of this section share the same qualitative property of global monotonic convergence to the unique interior steady state of the model. This is exemplified by means of Figure 1.1 where the mapping $H$ of the period version of the Solow model is always strictly increasing and strictly concave and thus must cut the 45 degree line as shown in this figure if the Inada conditions are assumed to hold.[4] Note that the steady state, to be calculated from $k_o = (k_o + shf(k_o))/(1 + nh)$, is independent of the period length $h$.

We thus have two Solow growth model versions, using continuous time and period analysis respectively, that not only give rise to closely related reduced form dynamics, but that always share the same qualitative feature of not only convergence, but even monotonic convergence, independently of the period length that is assumed to underlie the period model. This period model may therefore assume as radical a clustering or bunching of economic activities, with huge amounts of idle time in between, but does give us the same qualitative results in a stricter sense than we demanded it to be the case in Section 1.2. The Solow growth model is therefore an ideal example for the fulfillment of Foley's (1975) quotation that we have given in Section 1.2. Nevertheless we would argue that iteration step size for this model type (with annualized capital–output ratios) should be chosen as small as one day, since in reality annualized output, investment etc. is changing every day due to the huge number of firm activities that are here aggregated.

One might however argue here that there are significant gestation lags in investment behavior in reality, between investment orders and actual production increases, and this is indeed a relevant observation. This idea was already put forward in Kalecki (1935) in an important "post-Keynesian" approach that even preceded the General Theory of Keynes (1936). But this does not question our above empirical observation on nearly continuous output and investment changes,

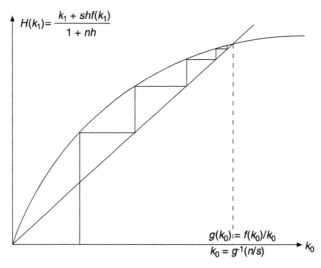

*Figure 1.1* Monotonic convergence in the *h*-period Solow growth model.

but only extends the (quasi-) continuous formulation of an empirically oriented Solow growth model towards its restatement as a delayed differential equation, a situation from which interesting results may be expected, but that is here beyond what can be treated in this chapter.[5]

In closing, we briefly observe that the ideal convergence properties of the Solow growth model get lost in discrete time when there is real wage rigidity as in the Goodwin (1967) growth cycle model, to be formalized by a real wage Phillips curve $\hat{\omega} = \beta_\omega (e - 1)$. We then get a synthesis of the Solow and the Goodwin model, see e.g. Flaschel (1993) for its investigation, and can recover the original Solow model as the limit case $\beta_\omega = \infty$ (if appropriately interpreted). In the continuous time formulation we get faster and faster convergence, at first cyclical and then monotonic, as the adjustment speed $\beta_\omega$ of real wages is increased, i.e., the Solow model is a meaningful limit case of the Goodwin–Solow model. Yet, for period modeling – where the increase in $\beta_\omega$ can be related to an increase in the period length $h$ – we get, since one eigen-value in the continuous version is approaching $-\infty$, sooner or later instability and thus a model that must be excluded from those that are of empirical relevance.

## 1.4 The emergence of "chaos" from a non-linear 1-D continuous time model?

In this section we investigate the paper by Brianzoni et al. (2007) and its results from the perspective of applicable macroeconomics and find that the model is misspecified from the perspective of economic theorizing as well as not applicable from the empirical point of view.[6]

### Differentiated saving habits and the Pasinetti paradox

We consider as in Brianzoni et al. (2007), in a Solovian growth context Kaldor's (1956, 1957) approach to growth via differentiated saving habits of workers and capitalists in continuous time. The continuous time version of the period model of Brianzoni et al. (2007) (see his equation 3), reads in this generalized Solovian growth context:

$$\hat{k} = \dot{k}/k = s_w w(k)/k + s_c r - (\delta + n), \quad w(k) = f(k) - f'(k)k, \quad r = f'(k),$$

which gives

$$\hat{k} = s_w a(k) + (s_c - s_w)f'(k) - (\delta + n), \quad a(k) = f(k)/k \tag{1.17}$$

with $a'(k) < 0$, $f''(k) < 0$. If the Kaldorian differentiated savings rate setup $0 \leq s_w < s_c \leq 1$ is assumed there then exists at most one interior steady state of this law of motion, since $\hat{k}'(k) < 0$ holds in this case. We assume that the function $f(.)$ and $\delta$, $n$ are chosen such that a steady state $k_o > 0$ exists.

The problem with this law of motion is however that it is an inconsistent one. Pasinetti (1962) was the first who demonstrated this. In other words, it simply runs counter to Say's law in such a supply side framework, since workers' savings is not matched by any goods demand from them, while capitalists consume and save (accumulate) in terms of the real one good model that is considered. The well-known and extensive debate about the so-called Pasinetti paradox of the 1960s gives a variety of further reasons why the Pasinetti extension of the Kaldorian growth law (1.17) is a compelling step in the further consideration of Kaldor's differentiated saving habits scenario, see for example Harcourt's (1972) section "Excuse me Professor Kaldor, but your slip is showing." Like capitalists, workers can here spend their savings only in terms of the one good assumed in this model type, i.e., they also accumulate capital according to the law of motion $\dot{K}_w = s_w(wL + rK_w)$, where $L$ denotes labor supply. This gives ($k_w = K_w/L$, $k_c = K_c/L = k - k_w$):

$$\hat{k} = s_w(w(k)/k + rk_w/k) + s_c rk_c/k - (\delta + n)$$

and thus implies a two-dimensional (2-D) system of differential equations (in growth rate formulation):

$$\dot{k} = s_w(w(k) + f'(k)(k - k_c)) + s_c rk_c - (\delta + n)k$$
$$= s_w f(k) + (s_c - s_w)f'(k)k_c - (\delta + n)k,$$
$$\hat{k}_c = s_c f(k) - (\delta + n).$$

These laws of motion simply take account of the fact that not all profits are distributed to capitalists as it was implicitly assumed in (1.17). The second equation provides the basis for the so-called Pasinetti paradox which states that the balanced growth path of this revised model is independent of the savings rate of workers $s_w$, and is characterized by the Cambridge equation $s_c r^* = \delta + n$ (in this Solovian extension of the model).

### Adding Beverton–Holt (1957) population growth

In order to get a non-linear dynamics of a more complex type Brianzoni et al. (2007) extend the above model of capital accumulation by endogenizing natural growth according to a law of motion of the Beverton and Holt (1957) type. In continuous time this law of motion reads, see Thieme (2003, p.42), when applied to the natural rate of growth:

$$\dot{n} = \left( \frac{\beta}{1 + \alpha n} - \mu \right) n, \quad n^* = \frac{\beta - \mu}{\alpha \mu}.$$

For reasons of simplicity we couple this law of motion with the Kaldor version Brianzoni et al. (2007) use in their paper in order to save one law of motion and to stay close to the mathematical model they are using.

$$\hat{k} = s_w a(k) + (s_c - s_w) f'(k) - (\delta + n), \tag{1.18}$$

$$\hat{n} = \frac{\beta}{1 + \alpha n} - \mu. \tag{1.19}$$

Using the auxiliary variables $\kappa = \ln k$, $v = \ln n$ one can transform this system into

$$\dot{\kappa} = s_w a(\exp \kappa) + (s_c - s_w) f'(\exp \kappa) - (\delta + n) = G(\kappa, v),$$

$$\dot{v} = \left( \frac{\beta}{1 + \alpha \exp v} - \mu \right) = H(v).$$

The Jacobian matrix of this system reads

$$J = \begin{pmatrix} G_\kappa & G_v \\ 0 & H_v \end{pmatrix}$$

$$= \begin{pmatrix} - & - \\ 0 & - \end{pmatrix}$$

in $\Re^2$, the image of the economic phase space under the performed logarithmic variable transformation. These dynamics fulfill the assumption of Olech's theorem on planar systems with a unique stationary state, see Chiarella et al. (2009, pp.477–478), i.e., its steady state is locally asymptotically stable, a feature that then also obviously holds for the original phase space as far as its economic part (the positive orthant of $\Re^2$) is concerned.

## The emergence of discrete time "chaos" from a 1-D continuous time model?

The period analog of the above continuous time model reads, see Brianzoni et al. (2007):

$$k_{t+1} = \frac{1}{1+n}[(1-\delta)k_t + s_w a(k_t) + (s_c - s_w)f'(k_t)k_t]. \tag{1.20}$$

This follows easily from the law for capital accumulation when it is introduced in extensive form (*L* the stock of labor):

$$\frac{K_{t+1}}{L_{t+1}} = \frac{L_t}{L_{t+1}}\left[(1-\delta)\frac{K_t}{L_t} + s_w w(k_t)\frac{L_t}{L_t} + s_c r(k_t)\frac{K_t}{L_t}\right].$$

The Beverton–Holt (1957) equation is easily rewritten as

$$n_{t+1} = n_t\left(\frac{\beta}{1+\alpha n_t} - \mu\right) + n_t \tag{1.21}$$

and delivers the equation used by Brianzoni et al. (2007) if $\mu = 1$, $r = \beta$, $\alpha = (r-1)/h$ is assumed. From an applied point of view the question however is how the time unit "1" is measured. In this respect the two parameters $\delta$, $n^* = h$ of the Brianzoni et al. (2007) model can be used to answer it. They use in their Figure 2.a as parameter values $h = 0.1$, $\delta = 0.4$ (in their notation). Assuming as crude estimates for depreciation and steady natural growth $h = 0.02 (= n^*)$, $\delta = 0.1$ for a period model with step size one year thus implies that the period length they are using is at least 4 years if not 5. They therefore use a period model with an extremely low frequency (and also couple this in their simulation with a production function that is nearly of the Leontief fixed proportions type. The model is therefore from an economic perspective a very "stiff" one where the coordination of savings with investment and natural growth occurs in a radically bunched form only every 4 years. The results depicted in their Figure 2 then simply mean that such a low frequency model is (though converging in continuous time) subject to radical overshooting in the period form, since it is – as the continuous model – adjusting into the right direction, but in a very exaggerated form.

However, in an empirically-oriented macrodynamic framework one must take note of the fact that the data generating process on the macrolevel is one with a very high frequency, since for example the annualized measure of national income (the data set) is changing every day when the reference period is moved one day forward. Period macromodels are thus high frequency macromodels that (even when the data collection process is only quarterly in frequency) must be iterated with a high frequency (small step size) at least when lower step sizes lead to qualitatively quite different outcomes as in Figure 2 of Brianzoni et al. (2007).

Parameters may have been estimated with quarterly data only (due to data availability), but the iteration procedure – by the Euler iteration procedure (with step size below 0.01) – must be chosen very small in which case the time-unit dependent parameters $\delta$, $h$ (their notation) will also be very small for each iteration step. From an applied perspective really nothing of the sort shown in the graphs of Brianzoni et al. (2007) is then likely to occur. This also holds – from a different perspective – for the choices of the parameters $s_w = 0.9$, $s_c = 0.2$ which simply will not be relevant for empirically oriented studies.

### *Labor supply and baby bunching*

There is still another problematic point to be mentioned when the paper of Brianzoni et al. (2007) is viewed from the perspective of applicable macroeconomics. The Beverton–Holt equation used above is normally specified in terms of population size (or population densities) of fish communities in a resource consumer framework. But in Brianzoni et al. (2007) the equation is used in growth rate form and applied to the reproduction rate of the working population. The way the level form can be transformed into a growth rate form is not discussed in the paper. But more seriously, we possibly have that certain fish populations may breed at one and the same time over the year (which would justify the unit 1 year as iteration step size). But with respect to human beings this is completely at odds with the facts since we have that annualized birth and mortality rates are changing on a daily basis and thus consisting of high frequency data and not occurring in the bunched or synchronized form the model of Brianzoni et al. (2007) is suggesting.

Brianzoni et al. (2007) call a constant growth rate of the working population "unrealistic", and suggest therewith that their approach to natural growth rates is more realistic. From our point of view, a macrodynamic model is not intended to explain the world for more than a century and therefore can be realistically modeled for Western capitalist economies with an (annualized) natural rate of growth close to zero (or even zero). The real issue concerning labor supply is not so much the reproduction rate of the population, but changes in the participation rate of the population and the occurrence of significant migration processes (which in this simple Solow–Kaldor framework are of course not present).

## 1.5 The linearized New Keynesian baseline model: global 2-D equivalence

Preparing the discussion of continuous versus period modeling of the NK model with both staggered wage and price setting, we finally consider in this section the New Keynesian baseline 2-D approach to macrodynamics. This baseline macrodynamic model is based on market clearing money wages and only gradually adjusting prices. In this choice of its baseline scenario it is therefore just the opposite case compared to the model of the old Neoclassical Synthesis of the 1970s, see the final chapter of this volume for details on this. We use this linear model here to show a case where continuous time and period models provide the same outcomes (see Chapter 7 for a related 4-D scenario). A non-linear 2-D example for non-equivalence of period and continuous analysis is given in Flaschel, Groh, Proeño and Semmler (2008, Ch.1).

We follow Walsh (2003, Ch.11.1) in the discrete time formulation of the New Keynesian dynamics which consists of three components. Its demand side is represented by a loglinear approximation to the representative household's Euler conditions for optimal consumption, giving rise to an expectational IS curve, where investment behavior of firms is not yet considered. Next, concerning its supply side, we have inflation adjustment occurring under the assumption of monopolistic competition, with individual firms adjusting prices in a staggered overlapping fashion. The third component, the monetary policy reaction function, is for the moment simply represented by an interest rate peg $i_o$ (at the steady state of the model). The first two components of the model thus are of the form (with steady state values $\pi_o = 0$, $Y_o = \bar{Y} = 1$):

$$\ln Y_t \overset{IS}{=} E_t \ln Y_{t+1} - \alpha_{yi}(i_t - E_t\pi_{t+1} - i_o) + u_t,$$

$$\pi_t \overset{PPC}{=} \beta E_t \pi_{t+1} + \beta_{py} \ln Y_t + \epsilon_t, \quad \pi_t = (p_t - p_{t-1})/p_{t-1}.$$

As in the Neoclassical Synthesis, stage I, the IS-curve depends on the expected real rate of interest. Furthermore, because of labor market clearing money wages, a price Phillips curve relates the currently observed rate of price inflation to the one expected for the next period and the currently given output gap.

We assume in these equations that the NAIRU output level is normalized to 1, and thus vanishes in a loglinear representation, and that the steady state rate of interest $i_o$ is given such that the steady state is inflation free. The steady state values of output and the inflation rate, $Y_o$, $\pi_o$, are thus simply given by 0, 0. Note that the rate of inflation $\pi_t$ is indexed in New Keynesian approaches by the endpoint of its reference period and thus defined by $\pi_t = (p_t - p_{t-1})/p_{t-1}$ in its relationship to the relevant price levels (which shows that the price level $p_t$ is a statically endogenous variable at the point in time $t$ and depending on the expected price level $p_{t+1}$).

In a deterministic framework these equations can be reformulated and rearranged as follows (using $y_t$ now for $\ln Y_t$):

$$y_{t+1} \overset{IS}{=} y_t + \alpha_{yi}(i_t - \pi_{t+1} - i_o),$$

$$\pi_{t+1} \overset{PPC}{=} (1/\beta)(\pi_t - \beta_{py} y_t).$$

Inserting the second equation into the first then finally gives in terms of first differences:

$$y_{t+1} - y_t \overset{IS}{=} \alpha_{yi}(i_t - i_o) - (\alpha_{yi}/\beta)(\pi_t - \beta_{py}y_t),$$

$$\pi_{t+1} - \pi_t \overset{PPC}{=} (1/\beta - 1)\pi_t - (\beta_{py}/\beta)y_t.$$

We stress that we have obtained thereby – as reduced form of the original dynamics – a linear first order system of difference equations that in principle can be solved in the conventional way by employing so-called predetermined values for the two endogenous variables of the model.

We now replace the difference quotients shown in this equation system by differential quotients, assuming that the thereby obtained mathematical model mirrors the features of the difference system in an adequate way. The change in the model is therefore a purely mathematical one and should not be interpreted as if a limit economy has been formulated and the period length of the model has shrunk to zero. We then obtain the autonomous linear 2-D dynamical continuous time system:[7]

$$\dot{y} \overset{IS}{=} \alpha_{yi}(i_t - i_o) - (\alpha_{yi}/\beta)\pi + (\beta_{py}\alpha_{yi}/\beta)y,$$

$$\dot{\pi} \overset{PPC}{=} (1/\beta - 1)\pi - (\beta_{py}/\beta)y.$$

It is straightforward to show – still assuming $i_t = i_o$ for the time being – that the steady state of the dynamics, $y_o = 0$, $\pi_o = 0$, is a saddlepoint. This however implies that the solution to these dynamics is indeterminate from a New Keynesian perspective, since we have two forward looking and thus non-predetermined variables in these IS–PC dynamics. Application of the jump variable technique to the two non-predetermined variables $y$, $\pi$ thus would not provide us with a unique convergent solution path, if only the boundedness condition is imposed on the myopic perfect foresight solutions that this model allows for. We thus have that the private sector when left to itself does not provide us with an unambiguous adjustment path to the steady state when some shock moves the economy out of its steady state position. Since the private sector of the economy thus does not provide us with a determinate reaction pattern outside the steady state, we may ask whether the addition of a more or less active monetary policy, in the form of a Taylor interest rate policy rule, can make the dynamics determinate, implying in particular that such a policy is indispensable for the proper operation of the economy.

To show that determinacy is possible if an interest rate policy rule is pursued by the central, bank we choose the rule considered in Walsh (2003, p.247) which is of a classical Taylor rule type:

$$i_t = i_o + \beta_{i\pi}\pi + \beta_{iy}y. \tag{1.22}$$

Adding this rule preserves the steady state of the economy and gives rise to the dynamics:

$$\dot{y} \overset{IS}{=} \alpha_{yi}(\beta_{i\pi}\pi + \beta_{iy}y) - (\alpha_{yi}/\beta)\pi + (\beta_{py}\alpha_{yi}/\beta)y, \tag{1.23}$$

$$\dot{\pi} \overset{PPC}{=} (1/\beta - 1)\pi - (\beta_{py}/\beta)y. \tag{1.24}$$

The Jacobian of these extended dynamics is given by:

$$J = \begin{pmatrix} \alpha_{yi}(\beta_{iy} + \beta_{py}/\beta) & \alpha_{yi}(\beta_{i\pi} - 1/\beta) \\ -\beta_{py}/\beta & 1/\beta - 1 \end{pmatrix}.$$

The trace of $J$ is always positive and determinant is given by:

$$|J| = (\alpha_{yi}/\beta)[(1 - \beta)\beta_{iy} + \beta_{py}(\beta_{i\pi} - 1)].$$

This latter quantity is positive if:

$$|J| > 0 \Leftrightarrow (1 - \beta)\beta_{iy} + \beta_{py}(\beta_{i\pi} - 1) > 0.$$

Furthermore both eigen-values must have positive real parts in this case. The result of this modification of the model therefore is that we can thereby enforce that the steady state becomes a source, either an unstable node or an unstable focus. In the language of New Keynesian economics and other related approaches this means that we have determinacy, since we have a uniquely determined bounded response of the system to all occurring shocks. In the presently considered situation it always places the system back onto its steady state position $y_o = 0$, $\pi_o = 0$, $i_o$.

The line separating determinacy from indeterminacy in the 2-D space of the policy parameters is according to the above given by:

$$\beta_{i\pi} = \frac{\beta - 1}{\beta_{py}}\beta_{iy} + 1.$$

We thus get the characterization of the parameter space shown in Figure 1.2.

We briefly note here that continuous time determinacy must always imply discrete time determinacy, but that the converse need not hold. In the present baseline case however, we have in the case of indeterminacy in the continuous time case a negative determinant and thus a saddle. Going back to the discrete time version then adds a 1 to the two eigen-values of the continuous time case. Since we have a positive determinant in the discrete time case there follows that both eigen-values must be positive then, but one of course smaller than, and the other larger than one. This shows (in)determinacy is equivalently measured by the two approaches.

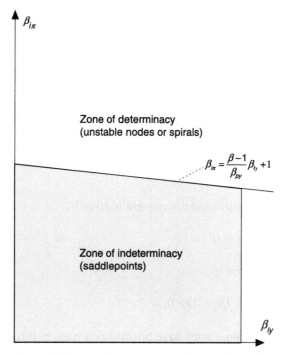

*Figure 1.2* Zones of determinate and indeterminate RE dynamics.

## 1.6 Conclusion

If there are lags in macroeconomic adjustment mechanisms they tend to be of a singular (unique) type, like investment gestation lags and are therefore not at all universal in nature. Such lags can be handled by delay-differential equations and thus by continuous time approaches. However, if pure period models, where everything is synchronized by a single uniform time length, are providing features that cannot be found in their continuous time analogue, then the high frequency nature of the macroeconomic data generating process clearly suggests that these period models are very problematic from the empirical point of view. They must be characterized as period models that are of a non-applicable type, since they are not robust with respect to variations of their iteration frequency (unless this frequency is made sufficiently large). In our view this also implies that period models that do not have a well defined continuous time analogue are also very questionable from the empirical perspective.

Significantly overshooting approaches to the generation of complex dynamics may be adequate in some (agrarian) cobweb cycle models, but certainly not on the macrodynamic level of whole advanced economies, where a yearly dating of activities may occur in book-keeping, but not in the macro-data generating process to which such economies give rise.

# 2 Walras' Law and the role of dimensional analysis in economics

## 2.1 Introduction

Starting from the basic article of May's (1970) and accelerated by an important contribution of Foley's (1975) there has been a confusing debate on period vs. continuous time models, on stocks vs. flows, and in particular on the formulation of Walras' Law in conventional continuous time macroeconomic models. Detailed analysis of these topics was provided – among others – by Turnovsky (1977a, 1977b), Drabicki and Takayama (1979), Buiter (1980), Jaeger (1983), and Hayakawa (1984). This discussion, embedded in the traditional (old) Neoclassical synthesis of Patinkin and others which was typically based on continuous time approaches, see Sargent (1987) for example, did not come to definite conclusions. Rather, it was simply replaced by the new Neoclassical Synthesis and its microfoundations, where models are mainly formulated from the perspective of period analysis. Building on and expanding the traditional Keynesian approach of Sargent (1987) and others however requires a return to this topic for which we will propose an easy solution in this chapter, in contrast to the complicated mathematics used by Turnovsky (1977a, b) and others in the conduct of this debate.

The quoted papers generally start from complicated specifications of the time structure implicitly underlying their conventional discrete time macro-models,[1] often making use subsequently of an incompletely specified and vaguely formulated limit process in order to derive and justify their version of a continuous time Walras' Law that is assumed to correspond to the given discrete time one. A typical conclusion within these approaches with respect to this Law then was that it necessarily gives rise to two constraints when transformed to continuous time [cf. e.g. Turnovsky (1977b, pp.52ff.) for such a statement and (2.1), (2.2) in the present chapter].

This chapter will show that such a conclusion is not justified at all. In this respect the chapter is in line with the assertions made in Jaeger (1983) and Hayakawa (1984). It, however, differs fundamentally from the method of proof chosen by these authors – which in our view still rely on incompletely specified and therefore again vaguely formulated limit considerations. In contrast, our approach will show that it is basically a matter of interpretation – and of a properly applied economic dimensional analysis – which together are sufficient to show that the period and the continuous time versions of Walras' Law can be formulated in a nearly identical way. We shall therefore show that the macroeconomic discussion of Walras' Law and its continuous time analog has been conducted by totally inadequate means[2] and that the solution to this problem is in fact mathematically trivial once its proper formulation has been established.

In the final section of this chapter we will show furthermore that the method we have applied to a discrete time as well as a continuous time version of Walras' Law of Flows can also be applied to the so-called Walras' Law of Stocks. We shall see in particular, that this latter law must be derived from quite different assumptions on the stylized time structure of the period model which has then to be used for the proper interpretation of this law. This time structure resembles that of cash-in-advance models which obviously is quite different from the well-known Hicksian "week" assumption that underlies the Walras' Law of Flows of conventional macro-models discussed in the main part of the chapter. The proposed reformulation of the time structure to be used for a correct presentation of Walras' Law of Stocks in discrete time, finally, will also show that this Law may have important consequences for the stylized representation of Keynes' own summary of the "causal nexus" within his macroeconomic theory.

In sum, this chapter will provide for the first time a transformation of (conventional) period into continuous time analysis that is complete, internally consistent and nevertheless mathematically trivial. Those who – quite naturally – will raise doubts about the solution presented here should, in our view, respond by presenting an alternative which must be at least as complete as the present one, in that it must be applied to the whole structure of the model and not only to a partial consideration of its budget constraints.

## 2.2 A standard macro-model and its proper dimensional interpretation

We shall utilize in the following the equilibrium part of a well-known Keynes–Wicksell monetary growth model as it is, e.g., formulated in Sargent (1987, Ch.II). This model is well-suited for our purposes, since, on the one hand, it is based on fairly standard macroeconomic relationships and since, on the other hand, it contains all the elements needed to show the importance of dimensional analysis for the proper understanding of such a model. Furthermore, the continuous time version of Walras' Law is discussed in Sargent (1987, Ch.II) for this model in the conventional way, an approach which we intend to falsify in this chapter. Finally, this model is also an important point of departure for the study of macroeconomic dynamics, cf. Sargent (1987, Ch.V) for example, where problems between period vs. continuous time representations are, of course, of particular significance.

Sargent's continuous time Keynes–Wicksell growth model starts from the following six equilibrium relationships:

$$Y = K^{\alpha} N^{1-\alpha}, \quad \alpha \in (0, 1), \tag{2.1}$$

$$w/\tilde{p} = (1 - \alpha) (K/N)^{\alpha}, \tag{2.2}$$

$$C = c(Y - \bar{T} - \delta K), \quad c \in (0,1), \tag{2.3}$$

$$I/K = i(\alpha(N/K)^{1-\alpha} - \delta - (r - \pi)) + n, \quad i > 0, \tag{2.4}$$

$$Y = C + I + \delta K + \bar{G}, \tag{2.5}$$

$$\bar{M} = k\tilde{p}Ye^{-\beta r}, \quad \beta > 0. \tag{2.6}$$

These equations describe the production function (Cobb–Douglas), the marginal productivity theory of wages, a simple type of consumption function, the investment function (based on rate of return differentials), goods market equilibrium (including depreciation and government expenditures), and money market equilibrium. Since the above notation is fairly familiar we shall not describe its details here (which indeed do not matter in our following arguments). The model is completed by Sargent (1987, pp.71ff.) in the conventional way by the twofold type of Walras' Law for continuous time models, i.e. (with fixed-price bonds *B* and thus $p_b = 1$):

$$B^d + M^d \equiv \bar{B} + \bar{M}(\equiv \bar{W}),^3 \tag{2.7}$$

the (stock) balance sheet constraint, and

$$Y^d - Y^s \equiv \dot{K} + \dot{M}/\tilde{p} + \dot{B}/\tilde{p} - S_p,^4 \tag{2.8}$$

which states that the excess aggregate demand for goods equals the excess flow supply for assets. According to Sargent (1987, p.73) this "is the form of Walras' Law of Flows implicit in the Keynesian model". Identity (2.7) justifies the fact that the market for bonds (and in Sargent's book also the market for equities) can be safely ignored. Identity (2.8) says that aggregate private savings must be assumed equal in sum to the new demand for assets, when the goods market is in equilibrium. It is therefore of the kind of a flow consistency requirement, that is assumed, but cannot be obtained by equilibrium equations, since the corresponding prices are already determined by the stock portfolio conditions.

We admit here that the latter type of approach (just assuming flow consistency, which is only corrected by subsequent portfolio stock reallocation decisions) is characteristic of the work this group of authors, and various further co-authors, have published in the past (see also Volume II of this trilogy). The present chapter is therefore an invitation not only to other authors, to reconsider such approaches, from the perspectives provided in this chapter. The assertions of this chapter must therefore be reflected further in future work on stock-flow consistency and stock-flow interactions as they are typical for Keynesian models of the real–financial market interactions. We, however, already claim here that the results obtained by such a discussion will help to clarify further the relationship between continuous time and period analysis, but will not result in significantly different outcomes of the possibly resulting respecification of macrodynamical models of the Keynesian variety. But this remains to be seen.

The above flow identity already shows some of the dynamic forces of Sargent's complete model of "Keynesian dynamics" (which, however, will not be treated in this chapter). We have chosen Sargent's continuous time model as point of departure – and not an arbitrary discrete time version of a macro-model – since the debate on period vs. continuous time analysis can, of course, only be conducted for models for which a continuous time version in fact exists.

Dimensional analysis, first of all, demands that equations should be dimensionally homogeneous [cf. De Jong (1967), the only detailed dimensional analysis for economics[5] that exists in the literature].[6] From this point of view, an equation like (2.1) does not make any sense at all, since $N$ does not have the dimension of goods [G]. It may be considered as an incompletely specified empirical law (where some parameters are not shown explicitly), and may be used in this way in econometric studies where the period is given and remains fixed, but from a theoretical viewpoint it is totally unacceptable in its dimensional inhomogeneity. Let us therefore reconsider this production function – and the whole model – in a theoretically sound *one-good world* and provide a completely specified version of it:

$$Y = A(c_k K)^\alpha (c_n N)^{1-\alpha},^7 \qquad (2.1')$$

$$w/\tilde{p} = (1-\alpha)Ac_n(c_k K/(c_n N))^\alpha, \qquad (2.2')$$

$$C = c(Y - \overline{T} - \delta K), \qquad (2.3')$$

$$I/K = i(\alpha Ac_k(c_n N/(c_k K))^{1-\alpha} - \delta - (r - \pi)) + n, \qquad (2.4')$$

$$Y = C + I + \delta K + \overline{G}, \qquad (2.5')$$

$$\overline{M} = k\tilde{p}Ye^{-\beta r}. \qquad (2.6')$$

The newly introduced parameters $c_k$, $c_n$ denote the characteristics of the basic production technology that must be assumed to underlie the assumed neoclassical macro-technology. Scale variations and the effects of factor substitution can then be expressed and measured in reference to this basic production technology. The parameter $c_n$ denotes labor productivity of this basic process per unit of time. We will employ the notation [G], [L], [T] and [M] to characterize the dimensions of "output" and "input", "labor", "time" and "money", respectively, and [1] for dimensionless constants [cf. again De Jong (1967) for details[8]]. The dimension of $c_n$ consequently is: $[GL^{-1}T^{-1}]$.[9] The parameter $c_n$ in front of N is the objective that any labor contract then attempts to regulate, but very often not in such a way that it can be considered as fixed, as is well-known. For the parameter $c_k$ we get $c_k[T^{-1}]$, because of our one-good assumption. The parameter A in equation (2.1') is thus a dimensional constant – which becomes useful if technological progress is to be considered and will be set equal to 1. In terms of dimensions, equation (2.1′) thus can be reduced to: $[GT^{-1}] = [GT^{-1}]^{\alpha}[GT^{-1}]^{1-\alpha}$, which now gives a dimensionally homogeneous and thus theoretically acceptable technology description.[10]

Our reformulation of (2.1′) has a very important implication for equation (2.2′). Calculating the dimension on the right-hand side of (2.2′) gives

$$[1][GL^{-1}T^{-1}]([GG^{-1}])^{\alpha} = [ML^{-1}(GM^{-1})T^{-1}] = [GL^{-1}T^{-1}]$$

which implies that *either the money wage w or the goods price $\tilde{p}$* on the left-hand side *must* include the dimension $[T]$ as a component (or as primary dimension). This, in our opinion, is a completely new aspect in the interpretation of wages $w$ or prices $\tilde{p}$ in continuous time models. And it will have striking consequences for the formulation of Walras' Law of Flows as we shall see in Section 2.4.

Equation (2.3′) poses no problems, because we have $c$ is of dimension $[1]$ and $\delta[T^{-1}]$. Since I/K has dimension $[T^{-1}]$ and since we have i[1], equation (2.4′)is also dimensionally homogeneous because the first term in square brackets has as dimension

$$[1][1][T^{-1}][GG^{-1}]^{1-\alpha} = [T^{-1}],$$

i.e., the same dimension as interest r, expected inflation $\pi$, and labor force growth n in this continuous time model. Equation (2.5′) is again not problematic. But with equation (2.6′) we now return to the astonishing fact already observed in the explanation of equation (2.2′). The first thing to note here is, that the expression $e^{-\beta r}$ necessarily implies that $\beta r$ *must* be a dimensional constant. Otherwise, a simple change in the measurement-unit of time would not be neutral in the theoretical framework here considered.[11] Since we have $r[T^{-1}]$, we get $\beta[T]$, i.e., a change in the time-unit used for the measurement of the time-rate of interest will change this parameter in the same proportion. From this we get – due to the fact that we have $Y[GT^{-1}]$ in a continuous time model (and $\bar{M}$ $[M]$) – that either $\tilde{p}$ *must* have the dimension $[MG^{-1}T^{-1}]$ or that we get for the cash-balance coefficient $k$ the dimension $[T]$ – the latter in conjunction with $w[ML^{-1}T^{-1}]$ (i.e., $wN[MT^{-1}]$) in view of equation (2.2′). It is not purely a matter of logic at this point, however, to choose between these two possibilities.[12]

Yet, in our opinion the continuous time framework – which is often preferred because of its analytical conveniences (not because of its ease of interpretation) – demands that the "goods price" $\tilde{p}$ *should* be viewed as being different from its discrete time analog. Properly interpreted, it in fact stands for the price *per unit of the time-rate of production*, i.e., it must have the dimension $[M]/[GT^{-1}] = [MTG^{-1}]$. It is thereby reformulated in a way which neutralizes the time dimension that is contained in the flow magnitude $Y[GT^{-1}]$ when its nominal counterpart $\tilde{p}Y$ is considered! This clarifies the question that remained with respect to equation (2.2′): it should be $\tilde{p}$ and not $w$ that has $[T]$ as a component- or primary-dimension in a continuous time setup.[13] We shall see in Section 2.4 that this choice is indeed the appropriate one when viewed from the perspective of a proper formulation of Walras' Law of Flows in continuous time.

## 2.3 Discrete time version and Walras' Law of Flows

In Foley (1975) the following methodological precept concerning macroeconomic period models is formulated:

> No substantive prediction or explanation in a well-defined macroeconomic model should depend on the real time length of the period.

For macrostatics and the accompanying comparative-static analysis it indeed should hold true, since it then basically says that the equilibrium part of a well-defined macro-model – and its comparative statics – should look the same in a discrete as well as in a continuous time framework.

In order to investigate this methodological postulate in a theoretically sound way we shall now consider the discrete time analog to the equations $(2.1')$–$(2.6')$. This is given by a straightforward extension of these equations by means of the period length $h$:

$$Yh = A(hc_kK)^\alpha (hc_nN)^{1-\alpha} = Ah(c_kK)^\alpha (c_nN)^{1-\alpha}, \tag{2.1''}$$

$$w/p = (1 - \alpha) Ahc_n(c_kK/(c_nN))^\alpha \quad (p = \tilde{p}/h!), \tag{2.2''}$$

$$Ch = c(Yh - \bar{T}h - \delta hK), \tag{2.3''}$$

$$Ih/K = i(\alpha Ahc_k(c_nN/(c_kK))^{1-\alpha} - \delta h - (rh - \pi h)) + nh, \tag{2.4''}$$

$$Yh = Ch + Ih + \delta hK + \bar{G}h, \tag{2.5''}$$

$$\bar{M} = kp(Yh)e^{(-\beta/h)(rh)} \quad (p = \tilde{p}/h!). \tag{2.6''}$$

The basic assumption underlying this discrete reformulation of our continuous time model is that all (continuous time) flow variables: $Y$, etc., remain constant over the assumed real time period $h$, the time length which separates Hicksian "Mondays" from each other, i.e., *the market period*. This basic assumption is appropriate if it is assumed that markets will be open only at time $t = 0, h, 2h$, etc., as it is suggested by the assumption of a "Hicksian week".

Equations $(2.1'')$–$(2.6'')$ are then straightforward reformulations of their continuous time analogs and have now to be interpreted as level magnitudes – obtained by multiplying all flows with the length $h$ of the Hicksian week and by taking into account that $\tilde{p}/h = p$ (dimension: $[MG^{-1}]$) holds, i.e., the goods price proper, is has to be used in valuing the output level $Yh[G]$.[14] Equations $(2.3'')$ – $(2.5'')$ are again not problematic, if one notes that the rate of depreciation $\delta h$, of interest $rh$, of inflation $\pi h$, and of labor force growth $nh$ are now dimensionless constants – due to the type of calculation $\Delta x)/x$ that is involved in their definition in discrete time. And equation (2.6'') is now also of a well-known type [we have $pYh[M] = \tilde{p}Y[M]$ and $(\beta/h)[1]$, $(rh)[1]$ in this discrete time setup].

Note that the expression $e^{(-\beta/h)(rh)}$ is the only exception to the rule that our behavioral relationships are assumed to be homogeneous of degree 1 with regard to length of the market period $h$, which makes sense since this expression derives from the momentary portfolio decision of asset holders. Note furthermore that the goods price $p$ will vary inversely with an isolated change in the market period $h$, as one should expect it in the light of an unchanged quantity of money $\bar{M}$ and the change in the institutional setup of the economy implied by the change in the length of the market period. In such a situation prices must, for example, double if the same amount of money is confronted with only ½ of the former output and when markets open twice as often than was the case before. This gives rise to the (at first perplexing) formulation that the price level $p$ depends on the length of the market period,[15] but not on the unit chosen for measuring physical time, while the opposite is the case for the goods price per rate of output $\tilde{p}$. A change in the period $h$ – as should be obvious – indeed means that a different economic environment is considered. We will express this fact by using the terms *h-economy*, *h/2-economy*, etc. in the following.

In discrete time there exists *a common acceptance* among macroeconomic theorists of the validity of the following macroeconomic version of Walras' Law of Flows (derived from sectoral budget constraints):[16]

$$p(Ch + Ih + \delta hK + \bar{G}h - Y^s h) + (B^d - \bar{B}) + (M^d - \bar{M}) \equiv 0 \qquad (2.7'')$$

[if the usual assumption $Y \equiv Y^s$ is made,[17] cf. again Turnovsky (1977b) with regard to this law]. There is thus *only one* aggregate identity in discrete time and – as already quoted from Turnovsky (1977b) – it is only in continuous time that it is generally believed that this identity must be split into two separate ones (because of the known dimensional difference that exists between stocks (such as $K$) and flows (such as $Y$) in continuous time. The following section will, however, show that this generally held opinion [exceptions are Jaeger (1983) and Hayakawa (1984)] is erroneous, that Walras' Law in continuous time is qualitatively of the same type as in discrete time models, and that there is no need for intricate mathematics to obtain such a result.

## 2.4 Walras' Law of Flows in continuous time

We have started in Section 2.2 from a well-defined (and well-known) continuous time model (which can be shown to exhibit a unique and economically meaningful solution) and have proposed a definite dimensional background for this model on the basis of which we then were able to formulate – in Section 2.3 – its discrete time analog for a market period of length $h$, i.e., an $h$-economy, in a straight-forward manner. Our comparison between discrete and continuous time showed that everything behaved as one would have expected from such a comparison – *yet with one important exception*. This exception is that the price-level used for both types of models is in fact not of the same type and dimension as it is generally believed, but rather we have relationship:

$$\tilde{p} = ph$$

when comparing the continuous time "goods price" $\tilde{p}$ with its discrete time analog $p$.

Dividing (2.1″)–(2.6″) by $h$ *transforms* the period model back to the continuous time one. And with respect to the commonly accepted identity (2.7″) there now follows that *we simply have to rewrite it* in the following straightforward manner:

$$\tilde{p}(C + I + \delta K + \overline{G} - Y^s) + (B^d - \overline{B}) + (M^d - \overline{M}) \equiv 0 \qquad (2.7')$$

in order to get its continuous time analog.[18]

Stocks and flows *can be summed also in continuous time* due to *the simple fact* that the "price-level" of continuous time models should be defined in a way such that this summation becomes meaningful from the perspective of dimensional analysis. Identity (2.7′) is the Walras' Law of Flows that corresponds to the discrete time version (2.7″) – and not identity (2.8) (and 2.7) as it is proposed in Sargent (1987)!

In our version, goods market equilibrium no longer implies – as in the case of (2.8) – that agents simply have to accept the new flow of money and bonds supplied by the government without any direct possibility to react to this new inflow (unless Sargent's open market operations of type $dM = -dB$ are considered). Such an impossibility – if it exists – should come about by explicitly formulated institutional reasons and not simply because of a questionable type of limit procedure. Furthermore, there is no longer any need to subdivide money supply into two components: $\overline{M}$, which is used for the formulation of money market equilibrium (that can be changed in an *ad hoc* fashion by $dM$), and $\dot{M}$, which does not have any influence on the present equilibrium situation. Again, if such differences exist they should be due to a particular choice of institutional circumstances (cf. Section 2.5 of this chapter) – which then necessarily will also concern and modify the discrete time version of the model that is used.

There is *no qualitative difference* between the equilibrium equations of the discrete and the continuous time version of our example model – *including Walras' Law*. Both models have the same solutions (up to multiplication by the factor $h$) – and will generate the same comparative-static results – i.e., *Foley's methodological postulate holds true for the general equilibrium part of Sargent's (as well as any other) macrodynamic model in a mathematically trivial way.* Equations (2.1′)–(2.7″) consequently are the mathematically correct time-rate formulation of the discrete time economic model (2.1″)–(2.7′). Differences between these two types of presentation of the same economic theory only appear when equations of motion (or the dynamic laws) are added to them [see Sargent (1987, Ch.V)) for the continuous case], which then give rise to either differential or difference equations. It is well-known that the resulting motions in phase space can differ dramatically between these two types of dynamic approaches (this is generally proved for $h = 1$ and models of a pronounced non-linear type). But this dynamic difference is by no means implausible, since it, of course, does matter whether an economy can reorganize itself in longer or shorter periods of time (or even in each moment of time).

We have presented in Section 2.2 two basic ways of taking account of the fact that the real wage of continuous time models must have the dimension $[T]$, since it is the marginal product per unit of time which is set equal to the real wage $w/\tilde{p}$ in the equation (2.2'). Choosing $\tilde{p}$ as the carrier of the time dimension, i.e., our solution to this problem implies the following list of benefits of this choice:

- No problems in obtaining Walras' Law of Flows for continuous time.
- No complicated (dubious) limit procedures to solve this task at some points in the discussion by $h \to 0$ and at other points by $1/h \to 0$.
- Our dimensional analysis allows for the addition of the term $w(N^d - N^s)$ to the aggregate constraint (2.7''), i.e., it also allows for a non-Keynesian version of Walras' Law of Flows in continuous time (which includes all four markets of our macro-model – as it would be the case in a continuous time version of a full market clearing approach).
- In our approach the cash-balance coefficient $k$ has dimension [1] also in continuous time, i.e., it is a pure percentage of the real income rate $Y$ that is held per unit of time as cash balances in the given $h$-economy.
- Comparing different $h$-economies in a "Gedankenexperiment" gives meaningful results with regard to the quantity theory of money.
- Our approach starts from a given $h$-economy, uses no limit procedure over $h$-economies to obtain the "0-economy" of continuous time, but instead only transforms the given equations in a mathematically trivial way so that differential equations can be used as an "approximation"[19] for the difference laws of motion of the given $h$-economy.
- As the final point we thereby arrive at the conclusion that taking a period model with Walras' Law of Flows as the starting point can only mean that we should transform it to continuous time in as neutral a way as possible, since we only want to use this new representation of the given economic structure to study its dynamical behavior by means of the more powerful tools of differential equations.

All these advantages of our approach will get lost if we choose the other alternative put forth in Section 2.2, i.e., $w[ML^{-1}T^{-1}]$ for solving the dimensional problem posed by equation (2.2'). And – in case this choice is nevertheless the preferred one – the task has still to be solved how the limit process over all equations of an $h$-economy with regard to the institutional parameter $h$ is correctly and completely performed – and interpreted. This problem has not yet been adequately answered in the literature which has started from such limit considerations.

## 2.5  Walras' Laws for Stocks and Flows

We have seen in Section 2.2 that it is mainly the so-called Walras' Law of Stocks which is used in continuous time analysis to eliminate one market from the full set of equilibrium conditions. On the other hand, it is generally accepted that the corresponding reduction to the equilibrium conditions that are explicitly shown has to be performed by means of Walras' Law of Flows in a discrete time model. Yet – as we have argued in this chapter – this is also the method that should be applied in continuous time as well. Does this imply that Walras' Law of Stocks has become redundant for the analysis of macroeconomic underemployment equilibria? Is it thus only the Walras' Law of Flows that we need to formulate in a consistent way in any macroeconomic setup that allows for the analysis of the dynamics of such equilibria?

This, in fact, is not the case. Walras' Law of Flows is the appropriate aggregate budget constraint if we believe that the flow of savings is so significant that it must be considered in order to allow for a realistic analysis of the stock market. If we believe that the opposite assumption gives the better approximation to reality, then it is of course Walras' Law of Stocks which is the more appropriate one. But employing this Law instead of the flow version in a way that is theoretically sound means that the standard assumption – or organizing idea – of a Hicksian week is no longer the correct way of modeling the market structure of an economy that gives rise to such a stock version of Walras' Law. Instead, such a macro-model now needs a structure which is similar to that of a cash-in-advance model, cf. e.g. Sargent (1988, p.158) for the description of such an approach.

The basic new assumption for a proper formulation of Walras' Law of Stocks is that there are now two trading sessions on Hicks' Monday – one security trading session "in the morning" and a "shopping session" – including past dividend collection – in "the afternoon". In contrast to this subdivision of the trading time – which now only allows for a certain sequence of market transactions – all prices are assumed to remain unchanged over the whole Monday (still a spot market approach). Such a model consequently implies the necessity of a sequential decision making and it is the proper organizing idea for theorizing in the case of the above second kind of empirically guided assumption on the importance of new savings for the coordination of stock markets. The "cash-in-advance approach" properly applied is therefore of great help in the understanding of certain types of macroeconomic reasoning and, as we shall see, also for a meaningful interpretation of the summary of the General Theory that is given in Keynes (1936, pp.247–249).

We have shown in this chapter that the use of Walras' Law of Flows is independent of the form of the analysis that is used – be it period or continuous time one. We shall now see that the same is true for Walras' Law of Stocks. We thus start again from a discrete macro-model, i.e., from the form that is the easier one to interpret. For the moment we shall only consider the budget constraints of the following three basic sectors of our economy, the private sector (index $p$), the government sector (index $g$), and banks (index $b$, only high-powered money). We use "$d$" for demand and "$s$" for supply, but otherwise the notation of the chapter in what follows. Since we are only considering one "Monday" we neglect the time index $t$ in the following.

On the "stock markets" – on Monday morning – we have the following three budget constraints for the given sectoral structure of our economy:

$$M_p^d - \overline{M}_p \equiv -(B_p^d - \overline{B}_p), \tag{2.9}$$

$$M_g^d - \overline{M}_g \equiv B_g^s - \overline{B}_g, \tag{2.10}$$

$$B_b^d - \overline{B}_b \equiv M_b^s - \overline{M}_b. \tag{2.11}$$

Furthermore we, of course, have the following two identities for the initial holdings of assets (where, e.g., $\overline{B}_p$ denotes the amount of government bonds held in the private sector):

$$\overline{M}_p + \overline{M}_g \equiv \overline{M}_b, \tag{2.12}$$

$$\overline{B}_p + \overline{B}_b \equiv \overline{B}_g. \tag{2.13}$$

By means of these identities we get by their summation and appropriate rearrangements the following form of a Walras' Law of Stocks:

$$M_{p+g}^d - M_b^s \equiv -(B_{p+b}^d - B_g^s). \tag{2.14}$$

Note here, that this Law is more precise than the continuous time formulation (2.7) in Section 2.2, in that it clearly states that the supply of new assets must be explicitly included in it. Open market operations are therefore part of the aggregate budget constraint that we have derived and are not excluded from this identity as in Sargent (1987, p.71) – where they are nevertheless present by the additional consideration of the infinitesimal operations of type $dM = -dB$ – which is quite different from the time rate of change formulation $\dot{M} = -\dot{B}$. It is obvious that the formulation $dM = -dB$ demands further explanation or refutation, which can only be done in a sound way from the perspective of discrete time analysis.

Turning now to the "afternoon session" we have to formulate for this new model the following additional budget constraints (setting $h = 1$ for simplicity):

$$pY^s + (1+\overline{r})\overline{B}_p + M_p^{noon} \equiv pC + pI + p\delta K + p\overline{T} + M_p^{eve}, \tag{2.15}$$

$$p\overline{T} + M_g^{noon} \equiv p\overline{G} + (1+\overline{r})\overline{B}_g + M_g^{eve}, \tag{2.16}$$

$$M^s - (1+\overline{r})\overline{B}_g \equiv M_b^{eve}. \tag{2.17}$$

With regard to these identities we, of course, have the following ex-post identity

$$M_p^{noon} + M_g^{noon} \equiv M_b^s. \tag{2.18}$$

These identities imply

$$M_p^{eve} + M_g^{eve} - M_b^{eve} \equiv pY^s - p(C + I + \delta K + \bar{G}). \tag{2.19}$$

This second aggregate budget constraint therefore states that Keynes' point of effective demand, i.e., goods market equilibrium – as it may be reached by the dynamic multiplier process – is realized if the private sector and the government sector exactly plan to hold that amount of money (for the next securities trading session) that remains when interest payments from the government sector to the bank have been deducted from the new supply of money [i.e., the monetary equivalent to the operations that are performed in the shopping session in equilibrium as well as in disequilibrium].

The above restructuring of the notion of a Hicksian week has surprising consequences for the presentation of the core of Keynes' theory. Instead of supporting the well-known Hicks apparatus of IS–LM analysis it in fact implies a chain of reasoning that is very similar to Keynes' own reasoning in his summary Chapter 18, cf. Keynes (1936, pp.247–249). The securities trading session in the morning determines – as in Keynes – the rate of interest, through portfolio demand equations which no longer contain income as an argument – in contrast to Sargent (1987) as well as many other approaches to the asset-market sub-sector of macro-models. On the basis of a given rate of interest for future loans – and given expectations on the proceeds of investment – the level of investment demand, in its simplest form, is then already given when the shopping session starts. Via the multiplier – here in its equilibrium formulation – the level of national income $Y$ is then determined in the shopping session which in turn implies a definite level of employment $N$ and of prices $p$ (if the level of money wages $w$ is given). This chain of events is identical to the "causal nexus" as it is explained in Keynes (1936), now only cast into the language of modern "cash-in-advance" approaches.

We note in passing, that such a time structure of the Hicksian "Monday" may lead to quite different results for the dynamics of the model (2.1′)–(2.7″); this model can now be solved explicitly and thus gives rise to an ordinary, i.e., explicit system of differential equations with regard to the dynamic laws of motion that are formulated in Sargent (1987, Ch.V).

Adding behavioral relationships (of the type of his Ch.V) to the above budget constraints should then give – as we have indicated above – a model which will look more Keynesian than the model (2.1″)–(2.6″) we have considered in Section 2.3. And the continuous time version of this model can be formulated in the same way as we have proposed it for model (2.1″)–(2.6″) in Section 2.4. Our concluding remarks directly apply to this reformulated model as well – which thereby is again transformed in a straightforward way into time rates of flows (instead of using discrete time levels). This again allows a description of the dynamics of this model in terms of differential instead of difference equations. We thus end up with the conclusion that there are two different types of economic models as far as the distinction between a Walras' Law of Flows and a Walras' Law of Stocks is concerned, independent of the type of mathematical analysis that is applied for their investigation (discrete or continuous time one). These two types of models, of course, will give rise in general to different comparative-static implications, a fact which then indeed is no longer astonishing.

Our discussion, see (2.14), immediately shows the superiority of the constraints (2.14) over Sargent's form of Walras' Law (2.1, 2.2). Open market operations are now explicitly included in the formulated aggregate constraints. The only question that remains – and that must be left unanswered in the present chapter – is whether we should treat the path of money supply in the continuous time version of this "cash-in-advance model" in a continuous or – to some extent – in a discontinuous fashion, which will allow for discontinuous jumps in this autonomous component.

## 2.6 Conclusions

Economists often prefer discrete time models simply because they are easier to interpret than their continuous time analogs. Nevertheless, one often wants to work with continuous time versions, because these versions are easier to handle from a mathematical point of view. This practice may be justified by arguments like the following:

- the length of the stylized market period (chosen to ease the formulation of the time structure of the economic behavior that is examined) is small relative to the time-unit for the measurement of the parameters of the macro-model,
- the non-linearities present in the model's formulation are not too pronounced, or
- it is hoped that the solutions of the continuous case will not be misleading with regard to the behavior of the original discrete time economic approach.

However, the interval $(0, h_{max})$ for which this might be true, of course, depends on the model in question. Secondly, its size – as well as the problem of the definition of *qualitatively equivalent behavior* of discrete time and continuous time dynamics – is a topic that needs a thorough analysis (of a fairly complex nature) which cannot be pursued any further in the present chapter.

Despite these open problems we can state, nevertheless, that it is the discrete time model (artificially) synchronized with respect to a given period of time which is generally the point of departure for macroeconomic model building, and that the continuous time reformulation is only introduced – assuming equivalence – to allow for more powerful instruments of analysis, as far as dynamical investigations are concerned. We have shown in this chapter that the continuous time case need not come about through an incompletely specified limit procedure, but by a simple process of substitution, which then prepares the original model for its dynamical investigation by means of differential instead of difference equations.

However, in view of the preceding chapter one may also argue that continuous time approaches are to be preferred over discrete (period based) ones, since the macroeconomic data generating process is characterized by such a high frequency that it makes period representations of structural macrodynamics superfluous.

What we have shown in this chapter, however, is the simple, and astonishing fact that no complicated mathematical manipulations are needed [as in, for example, Foley (1975) and Buiter (1980)], in order to obtain an equivalent specification of the equilibrium part – including asset market equilibria and budget constraints – of dynamic macroeconomic models in discrete and continuous time.

The discussion of stock-flow problems and continuous time vs. period analysis in macroeconomics has been further obscured by the introduction of the distinction between beginning-of-period and end-of-period equilibria. Viewed from the basic concepts underlying, e.g., Debreu's (1959) "Theory of Value" (see his notion of an "elementary interval") this distinction seems to imply that a different combination of spot-markets and futures-markets is considered in these two types of equilibria. However, macroeconomics in fact starts from the methodological device of a "Hicksian week" and thus from a pure spot-market approach in all of its standard formulations [with respect to the labor, the goods, and the credit market]. The distinction between the above two types of equilibria must therefore be rationalized in a different way in order to avoid any confusion which may result from the fact that the end of one period is always the beginning of the next one.

What we have analyzed in this chapter is the pure spot-market approach to the equilibrium part of a completely specified macroeconomic model. If one instead wants – because of empirical observations on the relative importance of stocks over the additions that go into them in each period of time – a Walras' Law of Stocks (such as (2.7)), then one should formulate it directly in discrete time – and justify it by explicit economic reasoning. Each Hicksian week – or elementary interval *à la* Debreu – then necessarily must consist of two points in time (on each Hicksian Monday) meaning that stock markets open first (at time $t_1$) and are already closed when the remaining markets are opened at $t_2$ (an "assets in advance approaches"). Such a sequential type of trading, however, has consequences for the behavior of economic agents which have not yet been thoroughly analyzed for the conventional type of macroeconomic model that we have considered in this chapter.

The main objective of the chapter is however to make macroeconomists aware of the importance of dimensional analysis for macroeconomics and not so much the determination of a specific solution to macroeconomic stock-flow consistency (which will still remain the subject of dispute in macroeconomic analysis). Dimensional analysis can detect errors in the specification and the derivation of macro-equations and it clearly shows that, for example, a Cobb–Douglas function may be easily specified from an empirical point of view, but nevertheless hard to justify from a theoretical perspective. The next chapter will provide another example of this type.

# 3    Lucas (1975)

## Too *ad hoc*?

### 3.1 Dimensional analysis and macroeconomic theorizing

Loglinear models are widely used in presentations of modern macroeconomics of both theoretical and empirical type. Yet, besides their uncomfortable feature of being of a somewhat cryptical nature as far as the economics they represent is concerned, there is also a real danger involved in their more or less precise formulation and application within economic theory. To exemplify this, we shall make use of a famous example from the macroeconomics literature, namely of R. Lucas' (1975) equilibrium model of the business cycle. Of course, if the following arguments are correct with respect to this model, there will exist numerous further examples – old and new – to which such an argument can be applied.

We shall show in this brief chapter that part of this model's structure is either formulated in a way that is inconsistent with the most basic requirements of dimensional analysis (if its equations are taken literally) or (if this is not accepted) that its implications do not prove anything on the true properties of the non-loglinear ghost-model that is underlying the employed loglinear equations. It follows that either some assumptions on the parameters of the loglinear model have to be reformulated in order to satisfy basic requirements of dimensional analysis or that the whole model must be established anew – with a very uncertain outcome on the validity of the claims made in Lucas' (1975) paper. These assertions will be considered in detail in Section 3.3. Before that we shall supply in Section 3.2 some elementary concepts from dimensional analysis as well as an economic example for their illustration.

### 3.2 Some basic aspects of dimensional analysis

There exists in the literature only one broad introduction into dimensional analysis for economists, namely the book of De Jong (1967). This publication is in many respects very helpful and informative, yet its economic applications – in our view – must be read with some care and sometimes need modification or correction as we shall show below by means of the example of a CES production function.

Let us note first of all that the proper definition of the *concept of dimension* is controversial, cf. for example De Jong (1967, pp.6ff) and Palacios (1964, pp.IXff.

and pp.35ff.). These difficulties, of course, cannot be the subject of this brief chapter. Instead we immediately start with an enumeration of the basic (primary) dimensions used in theoretical macroeconomics, in fact in one sector economies. These primary dimensions are in the notation of dimensional analysis: [G],[L],[M],[B],[T] and [1], where G stands for goods (output and input), L for labor (input), M for money, B for bonds, T for time and 1 for dimensionless entities.[1] These are basic units of macroeconomic theory, which can then be combined to give rise to further concepts such as, for example, labor productivity per unit of time $c_N$ which has the (so-called secondary) dimension $[GL^{-1}T^{-1}]$.

There are several fairly obvious postulates for a proper application of dimensional analysis as a test for sound theorizing and consistent modeling:[2]

- All truly theoretical models – such as Lucas' (1975) business cycle model – should only make use of equations which are dimensionally homogeneous.
- Dimensional constants – such as $c_N$, see our following discussion of the CES function – should be put equal to unity only if their existence is already well documented in the literature (which is not the case in this example).
- Equations containing logarithms, exponentials, and the like, can only employ dimensionless quantities as arguments in these functions, because of the transformation rules of dimensional analysis, cf. Palacios (1964, pp.52ff.) for details.

Let us consider the CES function as an illustration of the first two of these points. Fully specified it should read for a discrete time model as

$$Yh = A(hc_K K)^{-\alpha} + (hc_N N)^{-\alpha})^{-1/\alpha}, \qquad (3.1)$$

or as in the special case of a Cobb–Douglas production function,[3]

$$Yh = A(hc_K K)^{\alpha} ((hc_N N)^{1-\alpha}). \qquad (3.2)$$

We have already characterized the parameter $c_N$ used in these functions as having the dimension $[GL^{-1}T^{-1}]$, i.e., labor productivity per unit of time. The other important dimensional constant in the above equations is the corresponding productivity parameter of capital $c_K$ – but which due to our one-good assumption reduces in its dimension to $[T^{-1}]$ – measuring the flow of goods resulting from the usage of the stock of fixed capital goods (thus representing a time dependent input–output coefficient). These two dimensional constants characterize some sort of basic process behind our macro-technology with respect to which scale variations and factor substitution are then to be formulated and measured. The symbol $h$ denotes the length of the market period of the discrete time model and thus has [T] as its dimension. It is normally set equal to 1 (as, for example, in the Lucas model which we shall consider in the next section), a practice which sometimes creates significant confusion.

From the above we get as dimension for the secondary quantities $hc_K K$, $hc_N N$ in both cases simply the expression [G], which shows that equations (3.1), (3.2) are in fact dimensionally homogeneous:

$$[G] = [1] \cdot ([G]^{-\alpha} + [G]^{-\alpha})^{-1/\alpha} \quad \text{or} \quad [G] = [1] \cdot ([G]^{\alpha}[G]^{1-\alpha})$$

since the parameter A has dimension [1] and is only needed if technical progress is to be considered. By taking seriously the second postulate of our above list we have thus shown that the first postulate can be fulfilled for the most popular types of production functions in a meaningful way. This is generally not checked in the literature with the consequence that macroeconomic reasoning can sometimes be very confusing when the full dimensional content of the equations that are used is not made explicit as, for instance in the following conventional (dimensionally inconsistent) presentation of a CES functions as

$$Y = A(K^{-\alpha} + N^{-\alpha})^{-1/\alpha}, \tag{3.3}$$

which dimensionally does not make sense as it states that

$$[G] \overset{?}{=} A[1]([G]^{-\alpha} + [L]^{-\alpha})^{-1/\alpha}. \tag{3.4}$$

Of course all is well if the background is already well-understood, but unfortunately this is not yet the case in macroeconomics.

One could of course make the production function a dimensionally consistent function by assuming for the productivity parameters the situation

$$Yh = A[G]((hc_K[G]^{-1}K)^{-\alpha} + (hc_N[L]^{-1}N)^{-\alpha})^{-1/\alpha}. \tag{3.5}$$

We would however not consider this as an economically plausible solution of the problem of the dimensionality for macroeconomic production functions, since this only makes the terms below the exponents dimensionless and uses the parameter $A$ on the right-hand side to mechanically have the dimension [G].

In the case of production functions, which are not homogeneous of degree 1, dimensional analysis can also be of help in clarifying such situations. In the case of decreasing returns to the combined proportional use of capital and labor, dimensional analysis indicates that something is missing in the production function, say a limiting factor "land" which would make it again homogeneous of degree 1. This is meaningful in a one commodity model, without technical progress, since newly added firms should be of the same type as the ones already in existence. In the case of increasing returns to capital cum labor one must however be prepared to reflect such a situation from the perspective of technical change, for example by investigating or assuming how our productivity parameters (which are generally made invisible in the literature by setting them equal to one) are changed through technical change, for example by considering exogenous, disembodied forms of Harrodian, Hicksian or Solovian type. This simply adds – as usual – a dimensionless exponential term in front of the productivity parameters, depending on the type of technical change that is considered.

In order to demonstrate the importance of the third dot point above we now turn to the discussion (of part) of the business cycle model of Lucas (1975).

## 3.3 Log linear *ad hockeries*

In Lucas (1975) the following two demand functions for assets are postulated

$$k_{t+1} = \alpha_0 + \alpha_1 r_{kt} - \alpha_2 r_{mt} + \alpha_3 k_t, \tag{3.6}$$

$$m_{t+1} - p_t = \beta_0 - \beta_1 r_{kt} + \beta_2 r_{mt} + \beta_3 k_t. \tag{3.7}$$

The $\alpha$s and $\beta$s are assumed to be positive parameters and it is in particular assumed that $\alpha_3, \beta_3$ are less than unity. The equations (3.6), (3.7) are loglinear, so that here, the lowercase symbols $k_t, m_t, p_t$ stand for the log of the capital stock, money and prices at time $t$, while $r_{kt}, r_{mt}$ are the real rate of return on capital and money, respectively.

From the definition of the rates $r_{kt}$ and $r_{mt}$ in discrete time models (where the period length $h$ has to be applied again), it follows that these two magnitudes are dimensionless quantities. From the viewpoint of dimensional analysis we might as well neglect these two rates, since they (as well as $\alpha_0, \beta_0$) would in fact only appear as dimensionless factors $Q_1, Q_2$ (see (3.8) and (3.9) below) which we therefore set equal to one, on the right-hand side of the following non-logarithmic form of the equations (3.6), (3.7) (making use of uppercase symbols in this case):

$$K_{t+1} = Q_1 K_t^{\alpha_3}, \quad Q_1 = 1, \tag{3.8}$$

$$M_{t+1}/P_t = Q_2 K_t^{\beta_3}, \quad Q_2 = 1. \tag{3.9}$$

Our first postulate of dimensional analysis now implies that the parameters $\alpha_3, \beta_3$ *must* be equal to 1, and not less than one as assumed by Lucas. This revision of the model, however, seriously endangers its conclusions, cf. Lucas (1975, p.1136) for an example.

Of course one might argue that the constant terms can adjust to make the dimensions correct, however this approach is not in keeping with the spirit of dimensional analysis. For instance, in (3.8) and (3.9) the parameters $Q_1, Q_2$ are set equal to 1 but would exhibit the dimensions $[G]^{1-\alpha_3}$ and $[G]^{1-\beta_3}$, which would neutralize any conclusion drawn from the viewpoint of economic dimensional analysis.

The foregoing would imply that Lucas' economically meaningful, but *ad hoc*[4] specification of the following non-logarithmic type, taking the first dynamic demand equation as example:

$$K_{t+1} = A \exp(\alpha_1 r_{kt}) \exp(-\alpha_2 r_{mt}) K_t^{\alpha_3},$$

where the arguments in the exponential functions have dimension [1], can only be related to a function of the type $K_{t+1} = Q_1[G^{1-\alpha_3}]K_t^{\alpha_3}$ if $A = [G^{1-\alpha_3}]$ holds. From the perspective of dimensional analysis this then means that the parameter $A$ must have an economic interpretation, since it represents an economically measured magnitude. But what is the meaning of $A$ in the Lucas business cycle model?

By making use of a simplified theory of $r_{kt}$-determination, Lucas (1975, pp.1117–1118) furthermore derives from his full model a conjecture concerning the set of solution functions of his model. These functions read (when presented in non-logarithmic form):

$$K_{t+1} = e^{\pi_{10}} K_t^{\pi_{11}} M_t^{\pi_{12}}$$

$$P_t = e^{\pi_{20}} K_t^{\pi_{21}} M_t^{\pi_{22}}.$$

Dimensional analysis here implies that we must have $\pi_{11} = 1$, $\pi_{12} = 0$, $\pi_{21} = -1$, and $\pi_{22} = 1$, which differs significantly from the solutions given by Lucas (1975, p.1118).

One may raise the *objection* at this point that the equations (3.6), (3.7) are only loglinear approximations of the original demand equations which – according to Lucas – are to be derived from an infinite-horizon maximization problem. The latter consequently need not necessarily be of the form (3.8), (3.9). Yet this objection provides no real way out of the dimensional inconsistency of the Lucas model, since it is very questionable that a local approximation can differ significantly in its dimensional structure from the original one.

Lucas' (1975) agents use equations (3.6), (3.7) to form rational expectations (see his p.1117). Their behavior thus has to be of the following kind. First they solve their infinite horizon problem. In a second step, seeing the complexity of their optimal solution, agents decide that they will be better off when using a loglinear approximation to the proper solution they have successfully calculated. They take instead of their proper demand functions $f$ a set of functions which are given by the linear part of the composed function ln ∘ $f$ ∘ exp calculated at the logarithm *of the equilibrium point* $x_0$ of the state variables[5] of the complete economic model. They then form their forward-oriented expectations in this loglinear setup. It is very questionable that this is a meaningful description of household behavior. Note also that the proper solution for the local approximation is found by two boundary conditions: a given initial value of the capital stock *and* the condition that real balances remain bounded away from zero and from infinity. The latter condition is, however, a global condition which need not approximate *the* solution of the proper economic (ghost) model underlying this local approximation. Such local approximations may be quite useless for a discussion of rational expectation solutions in the originally given, economically correct counterpart.

We consequently arrive at the conclusion that loglinear *approximations* are not admissible in the context of Lucas' equilibrium model of the business cycle. The 'approximation argument' is thus not a good line of defense against our earlier arguments where the Lucas model was taken as an economic one.

There is, however, one observation made in Lucas' article (on p.1117) which might be useful for a proper economic modeling of the proposed dynamic model. For completeness, says Lucas on this page, the log of beginning-of-period real balances, $m_t - p_t$, should also appear on the right sides of our equations (3.1), (3.2). In a corresponding footnote he proposes to add a term $\alpha_4(m_t - p_t)$ to the right of (3.1) and $\beta_4(m_t - p_t)$ to the right of (3.2). Applying again dimensional analysis we get by this type of reasoning (instead of our former result that $\alpha_3, \beta_3$ must be equal to 1) now as side-conditions that $\alpha_3 + \alpha_4 = 1$ and $\beta_3 + \beta_4 = 1$.

This is the kind of model that should have been investigated in Lucas (1975) of which he says that it is (without noting these two extra conditions) poorly understood by him.

Accepting this as a fact, what then is the value of an analysis which distorts dynamic economic equations to at least make highly complex mathematical investigations possible in order to obtain something of a purely mathematical nature?

### 3.4 Conclusions

Loglinear approximations are a standard tool for *local* macrodynamic analysis, just like ordinary linearization. When taken literally they suggest multiplicative exponential expressions for the nonlogarithmic variables (which therefore must be dimensionless from the viewpoint of dimensional analysis) and power functions for logarithmic variables (which poses restrictions on the powers when their basis is not of dimension [1]).

One may of course argue that these restrictions are only valid ones in the true model and not in its loglinear representation, but this implies that the approximation is qualitatively seen in a significantly different way from the equations of the true model. One may alternatively associate all missing dimensions with the constant term of non-logarithmic approximation. However, this makes dimensional analysis fairly superfluous. Moreover, it also incorporates economic meaning to a parameter, the origin of which is left unexplained.

In the Lucas (1975) paper, the proper solution to all these problems is however an easy one. The arbitrary omission of real balances from the right-hand side of his difference equations needs to be reversed. If the model is represented in this detruncated, loglinear form we however still face the problem that the coefficients in front of the log-state variables must sum to one in each equation.

We conjecture, that there exist numerous loglinear approaches in the literature which – because of the arguments put forward in this chapter – need careful reexamination with regard to the validity of their assertions.

# Part II

# Model-consistent forecasts, determinacy and the rational expectations school

# 4   Price flexibility and instability
## Tobin (1975) reconsidered[1]

## 4.1 Introduction

Keynesian economics is often said to be founded on wage (and possibly also price) rigidities. Correspondingly, these "imperfections" are taken as the primary cause for unemployment. Especially Tobin has shown that this need not necessarily be true. So, in a well-known article Tobin (1975) he incorporates dynamic adjustments of money wages and the price level into a simple macroeconomic framework. In combination with, specifically, adjustments of inflationary expectations they constitute a dynamic process whose stability properties are then to be investigated. It is found that under certain conditions the full employment equilibrium may well turn out to be unstable. Quoting from Tobin (1989, p.18), his conclusion in this regard is:

> I regarded my article [i.e., Tobin (1975)] as supporting Keynes's intuition that price and wage flexibility are bad for real stability. I wanted to shake the profession off its conventional interpretation of Keynesian economics, according to which unemployment arises only because of a dubious assertion of wage and price rigidity. I wanted to recall and reinforce the second strand of Keynes's argument, according to which unemployment is attributable to inadequate real demand, a deficiency that flexibility will not remedy.[2]

In this chapter we wish to reconsider the stability issue in Tobin's approach. Our main concern is that in Tobin's specification wage and price dynamics are virtually indistinguishable. In order to pave the way for a more detailed discussion of the consequences of wage and price flexibility, we find it important to put forward separate adjustment equations for the two variables. Thus, new insights can be gained into the different impact of highly flexible prices and wages on the local stability of the equilibrium. In particular, it will be discovered that the destabilizing potential of price flexibility in this context is greater than that of flexible money wages.

The chapter is divided into five sections and one appendix. After elucidating the main stabilizing and destabilizing feedback mechanisms, Section 4.2 discusses the central building blocks of the Tobin (1975) model and introduces our modification of the wage-price dynamics. It also points out a close resemblance to a monetary growth model advanced by Sargent (1979) and Sargent (1987, Ch.V). Section 4.3 presents a local stability analysis of the full model, where inflationary expectations are supposed to be formed adaptively. Section 4.4 deals with the case of myopic perfect foresight of price inflation. Apart from the wider acceptance of this hypothesis, it clarifies that it is not imperfect expectations (alone) which are to blame for the instability results. Section 4.5 contains some concluding remarks. The proofs of the mathematical propositions are relegated to an appendix.

## 4.2  Basic features of an extended Tobin model

In the Tobin (1975) model, two main feedback loops can be identified, whose theoretical significance goes far beyond the particular specifications adopted there. The first chain of feedback effects has the Keynes effect as its basic ingredient, the second relies on the Mundell effect. According to the Keynes effect, a rise in the price level decreases real money balances and raises the nominal rate of interest on the bond market. This reduces investment expenditures as well as output and employment. When reactions on the labor market are represented by a Phillips curve mechanism, a fall in money wages occurs. If, furthermore, prices are closely linked to the wage bill the price level will decline, too.[3] A similar argument applies to changes of the price level, i.e., to the rate of inflation. In sum, we have a negative feedback loop in prices or inflation, for that matter, which acts as a stabilizer.[4]

By contrast, the Mundell effect contributes to a destabilizing feedback loop. It presupposes that investment is influenced by the real rate of interest (rather than the nominal one). Thus, a rise in anticipated price inflation has an expansionary effect on demand and output.[5] Through the same channels as sketched in the previous paragraph, this increases the current rate of inflation. If this evolution results in rising expectations about future inflation, a positive feedback loop comes into being. It is also easily conceivable that the speed at which expected inflation adjusts to the recent figures of realized inflation plays an important role in the relative strength of this destabilizing feedback chain.

Tobin (1975) makes his point by means of an elementary model consisting of the dynamic multiplier process, a natural rate-based Phillips curve for price inflation, and the standard form of an adaptive mechanism of inflationary expectations. This so-called Wicksell–Keynes–Phillips (WKP) model has, therefore, three dynamic variables, whose evolution is governed by three differential equations. These are output $Y$, the price level $p$, and the expected rate of inflation $\pi$. Let $Y_p^d$, $Y_\pi^d$ denote the partial derivatives of aggregate demand with respect to $p$ and $\pi$, and let $\beta_\pi$ represent the speed at which $\pi$ adjusts to $\hat{p} = \dot{p}/p$ (a dot over a variable denotes its time derivative, a caret its growth rate). Then the stabilizing influence of the Keynes effect ($Y_p^d < 0$) and the destabilizing influence of the Mundell effect ($Y_\pi^d > 0$) as well as of the adjustment speed $\beta_\pi$

are neatly reflected in one of the necessary conditions for local stability (ibid., p.199),

$$\beta_\pi Y_\pi^d < -p Y_p^d. \tag{4.1}$$

In particular, it is immediately seen that the equilibrium is unstable if, in the presence of a positive Mundell effect, adaptive expectations are close to the case of myopic perfect foresight (to which corresponds $\beta_\pi = \infty$). Note that instability can prevail irrespective of the parameters characterizing the adjustments on the goods and the labor market.[6]

Considering the model in greater detail, we should like to point out Tobin's assumption that product and labor markets are condensed in one sector, so that wage and price dynamics are virtually indistinguishable. Conceptually, it is money wages that, in a Phillips curve-like manner, respond to output and employment. Tobin's specification of this law nevertheless refers to changes in the price level,

$$\hat{p} = \dot{p}/p = \beta_p(Y - \bar{Y}) + \pi \tag{4.2}$$

($\bar{Y}$ being the exogenously given "natural" output that corresponds to the level of full, or normal employment $\bar{N}$). The use of (4.2) can be justified by the straightforward pricing rule of a constant markup over wage unit costs, which firms are supposed to follow in every instant of time.[7] The interpretation given by Tobin, however, cannot be maintained. He postulates (ibid., p.198) that prices are determined by marginal variable costs, i.e., $p = w/F_N$ ($w$ is the money wage rate, $F$ the production function, $F_N$ its partial derivative with respect to labor). The reason for rejecting this background story is that it would imply $\hat{p} = \hat{w} - (F_{NN}/F_N).\dot{N}$ which differs from the price Phillips curve (4.2) by the accelerating term:

$$-(F_{NN}/F_N).\dot{N} > 0.$$

More important than this interpretational aspect, in our view, is a certain asymmetric treatment of prices and wages. Whereas nominal wages are supposed to react with some lag to excess labor supply, which using the above "Okun gap" $Y - \bar{Y}$ may provisionally be written down as (cf. Tobin 1975, p.198)

$$\hat{w} = \beta_w(Y - \bar{Y}) + \pi, \qquad 0 < \beta_w < \infty, \tag{4.3}$$

prices are thought to be perfectly flexible and to adjust instantaneously such as to satisfy the marginal productivity equation (or some similar principle).[8] This device precludes deeper insights into the different consequences for stability of high or low speeds of wage *as well as* price adjustments, an issue Tobin has been concerned with in various verbal discussions (Tobin 1975, 1980, 1989).

In the present context it seems to be more natural to put price and wage adjustments on an equal footing. Including the marginal productivity principle alluded to by Tobin, this means that prices adjust to marginal wage cost at a finite speed $\beta_p$, so that $\dot{p} = \beta_p(w/F_N - p)$ or[9]

$$\hat{p} = \beta_p(w/(pF_N) - 1), \qquad 0 < \beta_p < \infty. \tag{4.4}$$

After thus setting the stage, it is interesting to compare Tobin's (1975) approach with a monetary growth model developed by Sargent in his macroeconomic textbook (Sargent 1979; Sargent 1987, Ch.V). He designs it with a view to demonstrating some of the hypotheses or assertions that were advanced by Milton Friedman in his 1968 presidential address. The most fundamental assertion is, of course, that of the asymptotic stability of the steady state (in the absence of stochastic perturbations). Sargent's analysis of his dynamic process, however, is incomplete in that he assumes, but does not prove, asymptotic stability. As a matter of fact, it is shown in Franke (1992b) that his stability optimism is generally unwarranted: the system changes from being locally convergent to locally divergent if the adaptive expectations of inflation become sufficiently fast.

Though it has not been noticed in the reception of the two models by Sargent and Tobin, there is a close conceptual relationship between them once we abstract from growth and the capacity effect of fixed investment in Sargent's model. Apart from an explicit representation of the LM-part and the components of aggregate demand, the differences are the following:

- Sargent adopts an expectations-augmented wage Phillips curve (with the employment rate as its main argument).
- He explicitly incorporates the marginal productivity principle to determine the price level.
- He works with an IS-equation, that is, the multiplier is supposed to work out with infinite speed.

The third point should be of minor importance since Tobin's critical stability condition (4.1) makes no reference to the goods market and the efficiency of the multiplier. The first two points are the direct formalization of Tobin's verbal presentation. Seen from this perspective, it may come no longer as a surprise that the Sargent model may be unstable. Although the mathematical treatment is quite involved,[10] the basic stability and instability arguments are the same as in Tobin's model.

It follows from this discussion that our modification (4.3) and (4.4) of the wage-price dynamics can also be viewed as a direct generalization of the Sargent model;[11] the justification is, of course, the same as sketched above. So, in the next section these two adjustment equations are combined with the other elements of the two models, where our specification will be somewhat closer to Sargent's than to Tobin's approach. We will thus, in particular, be able to see that sluggish prices are stabilizing, and that high price flexibility may be more damaging for stability than wage flexibility.

## 4.3 The case of adaptive expectations

Abstracting from growth and the endogenous evolution of fixed capital, the model we wish to investigate can be formulated in terms of the level variables. Correspondingly, let the capital stock $K = \bar{K}$ and the volume of full, or normal, employment $N = \bar{N}$ be given. Since we likewise neglect inflation in the long-run, the money supply may be exogenously fixed at $M = \bar{M}$. Letting $r$ denote the nominal rate of interest, the model is then described by the following set of short-run equilibrium conditions and dynamic adjustment rules

$$Y = C(Y) + I(Y - wN/p - (r - \pi)\bar{K}),\ 0 < C' < 1,\ I' > 0 \tag{4.5}$$

$$\bar{M} = pm(Y, r),\ m_Y > 0,\ m_r < 0 \tag{4.6}$$

$$Y = F(N, \bar{K}) \tag{4.7}$$

$$\hat{w} = \beta_w(N - \bar{N} - 1) + \pi,\ 0 < \beta_w < \infty \tag{4.8}$$

$$\hat{p} = \beta_p(w - (pF_N) - 1),\ 0 < \beta_p < \infty \tag{4.9}$$

$$\dot{\pi} = \beta_\pi(\hat{p} - \pi),\ 0 < \beta_\pi < \infty. \tag{4.10}$$

Equations (4.5) and (4.6) assume continuous clearing of the goods and money markets. They constitute the IS–LM part of the model, where the temporary equilibrium is brought about by variations in output $Y$ and the interest rate $r$. Nothing has to be said on consumption demand $C = C(Y)$ (which here includes government expenditures) and the demand for real balances $m = m(Y, r)$. When deciding on investment, firms compare their rate of profit $(pY - wN)/p\bar{K}$ with the alternative real rate of return on bond holding, $r - \pi$.[12] On usual Keynesian grounds, the marginal propensity to consume is supposed to fall short of unity.[13] By inverting the production function, the demand for labor is determined by equation (4.7). It is assumed that firms are not rationed in this respect.

Equations (4.8)–(4.10) represent the dynamic part, where linear adjustments are fully sufficient for our limited purpose of studying local stability. Equation (4.9) rewrites (4.4) in the previous section, equation (4.8) directly follows Sargent and replaces the Okun gap in (4.3) with the deviations of the employment rate from its normal level, which is set at 100 percent. Equation (4.10) finally formulates the conventional adaptive expectations of inflation. This hypothesis is employed both in Tobin (1975) and Sargent (1987, Ch.V.1). In sum, equations (4.5)–(4.10) can most easily be perceived of as a modification of the Sargent model: the latter is simplified by removing growth and the capacity effect of net investment, and it is generalized by allowing for a finite speed at which firms seek to adjust product prices to marginal variable costs (going to the limit, $\beta_p \to \infty$, would reestablish the Sargent model).[14] The dynamic variables of system (4.5)–(4.10) are the real wage rate $\omega := w/p$, the price level $p$, and expected inflation $\pi$. They determine the IS–LM equilibria of $Y = Y(\omega, p, \pi)$ and $r = r(\omega, p, \pi)$.

It is a routine exercise to verify the following reaction pattern in the partial derivatives, which can of course be explained by the usual textbook stories,

$$Y_\omega < 0 \quad Y_p < 0 \quad Y_\pi < 0$$
$$r_\omega < 0 \quad r_p < 0 \quad r_\pi < 0.$$

Next, define

$$\phi = \phi(\omega, p, \pi) := 1/F_N(N(\omega, p, \pi))$$

as the reciprocal of the marginal product of labor, the volume of employment $N = N(\omega, p, \pi)$ being determined by the IS–LM equilibrium output. Clearly, $N$ and $\phi$ respond in the same way to changes in $\omega$, $p$ and $\pi$ as the production level $Y$. Subtracting (4.9) from (4.8), the dynamics is then compactly represented by the three differential equations

$$\dot{\omega} = \beta_w \omega \left[ N(\omega, p, \pi)/\bar{N} - 1 \right] + \pi - \beta_p \left[ \omega\phi(\omega, p, \pi) - 1 \right], \tag{4.12}$$

$$\dot{p} = \beta_p p \left[ \omega\phi(\omega, p, \pi) - 1 \right], \tag{4.13}$$

$$\dot{\pi} = \beta_\pi \left[ \beta_p(\omega\phi(\omega, p, \pi) - 1) - \pi \right]. \tag{4.14}$$

Under standard assumptions, processes (4.12)–(4.14) has a unique stationary point $(\omega^*, p^*, \pi^*)$. It is given by $\pi^* = 0$, $\omega^* = F_N(\bar{N}, \bar{K})$, $N^* = \bar{N}$, $Y^* = F(\bar{N}, \bar{K})$. The steady state rate of interest $r^*$ can subsequently be derived from the IS-equation (4.5) and $p^*$ from the LM-equation (4.6) (which, however, is only a purely formal procedure).

Computing the Jacobian and examining the Routh–Hurwitz conditions of the three-dimensional (3-D) system (4.12)–(4.14), the following statements on its local stability behavior can be made. It goes without saying that all variables are evaluated at their equilibrium values.

***Proposition 1***

(a)   *A necessary condition for local asymptotic stability of the stationary state of processes (4.12)–(4.14) is the inequality*

$$\beta_\pi Y_\pi < -pY_p - (\beta_\pi/\beta_w), (\backslash F_{NN} \backslash F_N), pY_p - (\beta_\pi/\beta_p), \omega Y_\omega. \tag{4.15}$$

*It is satisfied if $\beta_p < -wN/pK$.*

(b)   *The equilibrium is locally asymptotically stable if the price adjustment speed $\beta_p$ is sufficiently low. The benchmark value of $\beta_p$*

*below which stability is ensured is bounded away from zero for variations of the parameter $\beta_\pi$.*

(c) *In the presence of $|Y_\omega| < p|Y_p| + F_N/|F_{NN}|$, the equilibrium is locally asymptotically stable if $\beta_\pi$ is small enough. In general, however, neither arbitrarily small values of $\beta_\pi$ nor of $\beta_w$ may be sufficient to bring about stability.*

(d) *Define $\beta_o := \dfrac{F_N^2 \left(|m_r|(1-C') + m_Y I'\right)}{|F_{NN}| \, \|m_r| \, |I'}$ and suppose that $\beta_p > \beta_o$.*

*Then the equilibrium is unstable for all $\beta_\pi$ sufficiently large. On the other hand, if $\beta_\pi > -\left(F_N/|F_{NN}| - |Y_\omega| + p|Y_p|\right)/Y_\pi$ then the equilibrium is unstable for all values of $\beta_p$ sufficiently large.*

The necessary condition in the first part of the proposition is the counterpart of Tobin's critical condition (4.1) (mathematically, it derives from the same Routh–Hurwitz term). Inequality (4.1) contained the information that the equilibrium is unstable if the Mundell effect, as represented by the IS–LM multiplier $Y_\pi > 0$, is sufficiently strong relative to the Keynes effect, which is captured by $Y_p < 0$. Alternatively, it directly showed that instability could be brought about by fast speeds of adjustment $\beta_\pi$ of adaptive expectations of inflation. In contrast, these terms may not be capable of violating condition (4.15), namely, if $\beta_p$ falls short of the product of the wage share and the output–capital ratio, $\beta_p < wN/pK = (wN/pY)(Y/K)$.

The latter observation is a first hint at the central role of the speed $\beta_p$ at which firms seek to close the gap between marginal cost and current prices. Its significance is clearly brought to the fore in part (b), which states that sufficiently sluggish prices can always stabilize the economy. In a certain sense, this is even independent of the adjustments of inflationary expectations. A high degree of price flexibility, on the other hand, may be detrimental to stability – at least if $\beta_\pi$ exceeds a certain threshold value (see part (d)). It should be pointed out that, in general, similar arguments do not hold true for the wage adjustment speed $\beta_w$ in the Phillips curve.

Part (c) and (d) of Proposition 1 also provide conditions under which the parameter $\beta_\pi$ has a similar impact on stability as the variations of $\beta_p$. $\beta_\pi$ would then have the same property as in the Sargent model (mentioned in Section 4.2 above) where, loosely speaking, $\beta_p = \infty$ is underlying. The interplay of the two coefficients $\beta_p$ and $\beta_\pi$ can best be seen from the inequality $\beta_p > \beta_o$ (or $\beta_p < \beta_o$, respectively). This condition determines if there is an "overreaction" of prices in response to changes in expected inflation, i.e., if $\partial \hat{p}/\partial \pi > 1$ in equation (4.13) (otherwise $\partial \hat{p}/\partial \pi < 1$). It can consequently give rise to centrifugal (centripetal) forces in the adjustments of $\pi$ since $\partial \hat{p}/\partial \pi > 1$ ($<1$) renders the own derivative $\partial \hat{\pi}/\partial \pi$ positive (negative) in (4.14). In particular, if $\beta_\pi$ is raised to sufficiently high levels then this destabilizing power would dominate the other feedback effects. Analytically, the positive 33-entry in the Jacobian $J$ of (4.12)–(4.14) would be preponderant in the trace of $J$, so that the stationary state becomes unstable. As the computation of $J$ in the appendix shows, these tendencies are somewhat counteracted by highly flexible (not sticky! ) money wages, but their influence can always be outweighed by the deflationary or inflationary self-reference of $\pi$.

We may summarize that the potentially destabilizing force of the Mundell effect could be constrained in two ways. On the one hand (under the additional condition given in part (c)), by slow adjustments of expected inflation, even if the actual rate of inflation displays larger fluctuations owing to a high value of $\beta_p$. On the other hand, fast adjustments speeds $\beta_\pi$ would do no harm if a small $\beta_p$ puts a curb on price reactions.

The next proposition is concerned with a disposition of our economy to exhibit oscillatory motions. Consider to this end a rising price adjustment speed $\beta_p$ and let $\beta_p^H$ denote a benchmark value at which the dynamics changes from being locally convergent to locally divergent. When $\beta_p$ passes $\beta_p^H$, some eigen-value of the Jacobian $J$ of (4.12)–(4.14) crosses the imaginary axis in the complex plane. Since the proof of Proposition 1 shows that the determinant of $J$ is always negative, it is not a real eigen-value but a pair of conjugate complex eigen-values. This phenomenon is the key condition for a Hopf-bifurcation to occur (therefore the superscript $H$). For a certain range of parameter values of $\beta_p$ close to $\beta_p^H$, this analytical tool allows us to establish the existence of periodic orbits. That is, the loss of stability that we find as firms adjust prices faster to their marginal wage costs is associated with the emergence of persistent but bounded cyclical variations in the variables of system (4.12)–(4.14). A similar reasoning applies if $\beta_\pi$ is chosen as a bifurcation parameter. Before stating the Hopf-bifurcation result, Proposition 2 provides a condition that guarantees the uniqueness of $\beta_p^H$, i.e., it rules out a 'reswitching' of local stability as $\beta_p$ varies from zero to infinity.

### Proposition 2

*Suppose that the reaction coefficients $\beta_w$ and $\beta_\pi$ satisfy*

$$\beta_w < \frac{|F_{NN}|}{F_N} \frac{pY_p}{Y_\pi}, \beta_\pi > \frac{F_N/|F_{NN}|-|Y_\omega|+p|Y_p|}{Y_\pi},$$

*i.e., money wages are sufficiently sluggish and adaptive expectations are sufficiently fast. Then there exists a benchmark value $\beta_p^H$ of the price adjustment speed such that the equilibrium of system (4.12)–(4.14) is locally asymptotically stable if $\beta_p < \beta_p^H$, and it is unstable if $\beta_p > \beta_p^H$. Furthermore, there exists a function $\varepsilon \mapsto \beta_p(\varepsilon)$ with the following property:*

(a)  *for all sufficiently small $\varepsilon > 0$ there is a non-degenerate periodic orbit generated by system (4.12)–(4.14) with respect to $\beta_p = \beta_p(\varepsilon)$;*

(b)  *$\beta_p(\varepsilon) \to \beta_p^H$ and the corresponding periodic orbits collapse to the stationary point of that system as $\varepsilon \to 0$.*

It has, however, to be noted that the proposition contains no information as to whether the periodic orbits are repelling or attracting. Mathematical conditions exist to tell which case prevails. Unfortunately, they depend on higher-order non-linear terms in the Taylor expansion of the right-hand side of (4.12)–(4.14) and are so complicated that they would not be accessible to an economic interpretation. The proposition is also essentially local in its nature, and we do not exactly know what happens to the periodic orbits when the deviations of a rising $\beta_p$ from the bifurcation value $\beta_p^H$ get larger. So, Proposition 2 provides a first step to study the oscillatory tendencies inherent in our economy, but it cannot take the place of a careful inquiry into the global dynamics.[15]

Tobin (1975, p.200) has claimed that the case $\beta_\pi = 0$ is always stable, while the other extreme, $\beta_\pi = \infty$ (that is, $\pi = \hat{p}$), is necessarily unstable. It has already been shown that the first claim need not be true in the present economy. Of more interest, however, is the second conjecture (which cannot be proved within the Tobin model itself since according to (4.2), this supposition would fix actual output at its full employment level). The case of myopic perfect foresight of inflation is the subject of the next section, where also an extended model of the Tobin variety will be considered.

## 4.4 The case of myopic perfect foresight

In this section an infinite adjustment speed of inflationary expectations, $\beta_\pi = \infty$, is assumed, which is tantamount to the supposition $\pi = \hat{p}$. In the IS equation (4.5), therefore, $\pi$ has to be replaced with the actual rate of inflation $\hat{p}$ as given in equation (4.9), giving $\hat{p} = \beta_p \ (w/(pF_N \ (N, \ \bar{K})) - 1)$. This means that output, employment, and current inflation are determined simultaneously from the goods market equilibrium condition, whereas in the adaptive expectations (AE) economy the IS–LM volume of employment has been determined independently of $\hat{p}$ (and $\pi$ was historically given). To formalize the clearing of goods and financial markets and the concurrent price formation under perfect foresight (PF) of inflation, let $N = N(Y)$ be the inverse production function, i.e., the inverse of the mapping $N \mapsto F(N, \ \bar{K})$, and define[16]

$$\phi = \phi(Y): = 1/F_N(N \ (Y), \ \bar{K}).$$

Obviously, $N' = dN/dY > 0$ and $\phi' = d\phi/dY > 0$. With respect to a given price level $p$ and a given real wage rate $\omega$, the temporary equilibrium part is then represented by

$$Y = C(Y) + I(Y - \omega N(Y) - r\bar{K} + \beta_p(\omega\phi \ (Y) - 1)\bar{K}), \tag{4.16}$$

$$\bar{M} = pm(Y, r). \tag{4.17}$$

It should be pointed out that the Mundell effect can now no longer be considered under the usual *ceteris paribus* assumption. It is, however, incorporated in the feedback effects that give rise to the impact multiplier $Y_p$ and, in this sense, is combined with the Keynes effect. In fact, the Mundell term $\pi = \hat{p} = \beta_p(\omega\phi(Y) - 1)$ provides another channel for output $Y$ to enter the investment function.

Since inflation is positively related to output, the *overall* marginal propensity to spend out of current income will exceed unity if the price adjustment speed $\beta_p$ is sufficiently high. Correspondingly, the thus defined IS-curve may have a positive slope and be even steeper than the LM-curve. It is easily verified that this would change the familiar negative sign of $Y_p$. In such a situation the Mundell effect may be said to dominate the Keynes effect.

The sign of $Y_p$ has an important bearing on the stability of the adjustment process of $\omega$ and $p$. Denoting the temporary equilibrium output by $Y = Y(\omega, p)$, the differential equations read

$$\dot{\omega} = \beta_w\,\omega\left[N\left(Y(\omega, p)\right)/\bar{N} - 1\right], \tag{4.18}$$

$$\dot{p} = \beta_p\,p\left[\omega\phi\left(Y(\omega, p)\right) - 1\right]. \tag{4.19}$$

In comparison to the economy with adaptive expectations in equations (4.12)–(4.14), the present dynamic system not only saves the state variable $\pi$, but also the equation for the real wage is much simpler (since with $\pi = \hat{p}$ we have a real wage Phillips curve in (4.8)). The main results of the IS–LM analysis and the local behavior of (4.18), (4.19) are collected in the next proposition.

### Proposition 3

Let $\beta_o$ be defined as in Proposition 1(d) and put $\beta_1 := wN/pK$. Then the following statements hold.

(a)   If $\beta_p < \beta_o$ the combined Keynes–Mundell effect causes $Y_p < 0$ for the output solution of (4.16), (4.17), while $Y_p > 0$ if $\beta_p > \beta_o$.

(b)   The equilibrium point of processes (4.18), (4.19) is locally asymptotically stable if $\beta_p < \min\{\beta_o, \beta_1\}$, and it is a saddlepoint if $\beta_p < \beta_o$.

(c)   The equilibrium is also locally asymptotically stable if $\beta_1 < \beta_p < \beta_o$ and $\beta_w$ is sufficiently small. On the other hand, if $\beta_w$ is sufficiently large then the equilibrium is locally repelling for $\beta_1 < \beta_p < \beta_o$, and the system undergoes a Hopf-bifurcation at $\beta_p = \beta_p^H = \beta_1$.

The proposition shows that dominance of the Mundell effect over the Keynes effect, as specified by $Y_p > 0$, is sufficient to destabilize the economy, whereas the dominance of the Keynes effect, $Y_p < 0$, definitely favors stability. These phenomena are connected with the price adjustment speed $\beta_p$. The myopic PF economy shares the property with the AE economy that the equilibrium is locally asymptotically stable provided that price adjustments are sufficiently sluggish, and it is in any case unstable if $\beta_p$ exceeds the benchmark value that has already played a decisive role in Proposition 1(d). It may also be noted that the salient condition $Y_p < 0$ amounts to $\partial Y/\partial M > 0$, i.e., expansionary monetary policy works as expected. Thus, monetary policy is efficient if the economy is stable (it may not be needed then), and it is counter-productive if instability prevails.

Despite the close analogy to Proposition 1(*b*) and (*d*) there is, however, a difference when under variations of $\beta_p$ the system switches from stability to instability. In the AE economy such a structural change always (not only under the conditions of Proposition 2) gives rise to a Hopf-bifurcation and its periodic motions. In the present case, this happens only if $\beta_o > \beta_1$; the bifurcation is of a different type if $\beta_o < \beta_1$.

We can sum up as the most important result that, contrary to Tobin's view mentioned above, even a PF economy can be stable — if only price reactions are not too fast in order to close a gap to the marginal wage costs.[17] The wage adjustment speed $\beta_w$, on the other hand, can mostly be neglected in discussing the stability issue. There is only one exception where sufficiently sluggish (flexible) money wages are capable of stabilizing (destabilizing) the economy, namely, if $\beta_1 < \beta_o$ and $\beta_p$ is contained in the interval $(\beta_1, \beta_o)$.

As another facet of the Tobin–Sargent framework we return to Tobin' (1975) original formulation and employ a dynamic multiplier within the present setting of delayed price adjustments and myopic perfect foresight of inflation.[18] With respect to a finite output adjustment speed $\beta_Y > 0$, the evolution of the economy is described by

$$\dot{Y} = \beta_Y \left[ C(Y) + I\left[ Y - \omega N(Y) - r(Y,p)\bar{K} + \beta_p(\omega\phi(Y) - 1)\bar{K} \right] - Y \right], \quad (4.20)$$

$$\dot{\omega} = \beta_w \omega \left[ N(Y)/\bar{N} - 1 \right], \quad (4.21)$$

$$\dot{p} = \beta_p p \left[ \omega\phi(Y) - 1 \right], \quad (4.22)$$

where $r = r(Y, p)$ is the LM-rate of interest determined by (4.17). Proposition 4 shows that the previous stability and instability properties of the parameters $\beta_p$ and $\beta_w$ are essentially maintained. The new adjustment coefficient $\beta_Y$ has no bearing on stability if $\beta_p$ exceeds the same threshold value as in Proposition 3. On the other hand, the stabilizing effect of low price adjustment speeds can be destroyed by sufficiently slow reactions of producers to excess demand or supply. Incidentally, the same is possible in Tobin's (1975) model (cf. the proof of Proposition 4). Apart from that, system (4.20)–(4.22) again widens the scope for a Hopf-bifurcation.

### Proposition 4

*Making reference to $\beta_o$ and $\beta_1$ defined in Proposition 1(d) and 3, respectively, the following statements hold.*

(a) *The equilibrium point of processes (4.20)–(4.22) is locally asymptotically stable if $\beta_p$ is sufficiently small, whereas it is unstable if $\beta_p > \beta_o$.*

(b)   With respect to a given price adjustment speed $\beta_p < \beta_o$, local asymptotic stability prevails if $\beta_w$ is sufficiently small. Large values of $\beta_w$ destabilize the equilibrium (at least) if $\beta_1 < \beta_p < \beta_o$.

(c)   With respect to a given $\beta_p < \min\{\beta_o, \beta_1\}$, the equilibrium is locally asymptotically stable if $\beta_Y$ is sufficiently large, but it becomes unstable if $\beta_Y$ is small.

(d)   Whenever upon variations of $\beta_p$ the system switches from stability to instability, a Hopf-bifurcation occurs.

Lastly, a remark may be added concerning low adjustment speeds $\beta_Y$. If one wants to pinpoint a focal reason for economic instability in the efforts of firms to smooth production, as expressed by low values of $\beta_Y$, then goods market equilibrium must be taken more seriously and (if rationing schemes are to be avoided) inventories have to be introduced. Since Metzler's discussion of inventory cycles it is known that the interplay between gross demand, output, and desired and actual inventory investment may then generate new destabilizing forces.[19]

## 4.5 Conclusion

Starting out from the, as it turned out, closely related macrodynamic models of Tobin (1975) and Sargent (1979, Ch.V.1), several variants of these two prototype economies have been considered. Our central modification concerned the formation of goods prices. The assumption that they instantaneously adjust to the marginal wage costs was dropped and replaced with the behavioral rule that in each market period firms seek to close the gap between actual prices and marginal costs only partially. The most notable versions are summarized in the form of Table 4.1, where the differences between the models are expressed in terms of the adjustment speeds $\beta_x$, $x = w, p, \pi, Y$. Finite coefficients are indicated by the symbol itself, while prevalence of an equilibrium condition is designated by the infinity sign. $\beta_p = \infty$ means that prices are continuously equal to marginal costs, $\beta\pi = \infty$ signifies myopic perfect foresight of inflation ($\pi = \hat{p}$), and $\beta_Y = \infty$ stands for IS-equilibrium. $\beta_w$ refers to the wage Phillips curve.[20] As they are named, Model 1 was treated as our basic case in Section 4.3, Models 2 and 3 were presented in Section 4.4. Analysis of the variant where all four adjustment speeds

*Table 4.1* Variants of Tobin (1975) models

|  | Tobin | Sargent | Model 1 | Model 2 | Model 3 | Model 4 |
|---|---|---|---|---|---|---|
| $\dot{Y}$ | $\beta_Y$ | $\infty$ | $\infty$ | $\infty$ | $\beta_Y$ | $\beta_Y$ |
| $\hat{w}$ | $\beta_w$ | $\beta_w$ | $\beta_w$ | $\beta_w$ | $\beta_w$ | $\beta_w$ |
| $\hat{p}$ | $\infty$ | $\infty$ | $\beta_p$ | $\beta_p$ | $\beta_p$ | $\beta_p$ |
| $\dot{\pi}$ | $\beta_\pi$ | $\beta_\pi$ | $\beta_\pi$ | $\infty$ | $\infty$ | $\beta_\pi$ |

are of finite order was bypassed here because of its higher complexity, although we expressed our believe that it would not add anything essentially new to the other stability findings (cf. fn.17).

Our main result is that the "imperfections" of price adjustments have a significant stabilizing potential, at least as far as the local stability of the equilibrium position is concerned. A sufficient degree of price stickiness in Models 1, 2 and 3 can always achieve local asymptotic stability. The basic reason we have identified as being responsible for this result is that the stabilizing Keynes effect then dominates the destabilizing Mundell effect. Wage adjustments, in contrast, are less forceful: they may have the same property over a limited range of, especially, the price adjustment speed, but not generally so. Destabilization, on the other hand, can be brought about by highly flexible prices and fast adjustments of expected inflation towards the current rate of inflation. Above certain threshold values of the reaction coefficients, either feature is sufficient to make the Mundell effect dominate over the Keynes effect. Again, money wages share this property only over a limited set of parameters. These characteristics also provide a better understanding of the destabilization tendencies that were found in Tobin's and Sargent's models with their infinitely fast price adjustments (see Franke (1992b) for the analysis of the Sargent model).

The fact that the modifications across our three model variants leave the results regarding the price adjustment speed basically unaffected leads us to expect that our characterization of the impact of price flexibility on dynamic stability may prove to be fairly robust under further modifications and generalizations of the present modeling framework. At least, this aspect of the macroeconomic consequences of the price setting behavior of firms should not be neglected when discussing the likely effects of high or low price flexibility.

## Appendix: mathematical proofs

In all proofs, it is assumed for notational simplicity that the levels $\bar{N}$ and $\bar{K}$ are normalized at unity.

### *Proof of proposition 1*

The Jacobian $J$ of processes (4.12)–(4.14) evaluated at the equilibrium point is given by

$$
\begin{bmatrix}
\omega\left(\beta_w N_\omega - \beta_p(\phi + \omega\phi_\omega)\right) & \omega\left(\beta_w N_p - \beta_p \omega\phi_p\right) & \omega\left(\beta_w N_\pi + 1 - \beta_p \omega\phi_\pi\right) \\
\beta_p\, p(\phi + \omega\phi_\omega) & \beta_p\, p\omega\phi_p & \beta_p\, p\omega\phi_\pi \\
\beta_\pi \beta_p(\phi + \omega\phi_\omega) & \beta_\pi \beta_p \omega\phi_p & \beta_\pi\left(\beta_p \omega\phi_\pi - 1\right)
\end{bmatrix}.
$$

From this the Routh–Hurwitz terms can be computed as follows ($J_i$ are the second-order principal minors),

$$a_1 = -\text{trace } J = -J_{11} - J_{22} - J_{33}$$
$$= \beta_w \,\omega\, |N_\omega| + \beta_p\, (\phi - \omega|\phi_\omega| + \omega p|\phi_p|) + \beta_\pi\, (1 - \beta_p\, \omega\phi_\pi),$$
$$a_2 = J_1 + J_2 + J_3 = \beta_w \beta_p\, p|N_p| + \beta_\pi \beta_p\, p\omega|\phi_p|$$
$$+ \beta_w \beta_\pi\, \omega(|N_\omega| - \beta_p\, \phi N_\pi),$$
$$a_3 = -\det J = \beta_\pi \beta_p \beta_w\, p|N_p| = \beta_\pi J_1,$$
$$b = a_1 a_2 - a_3 = (-J_{11} - J_{22})\,(J_1 + J_2 + J_3)$$
$$+ \beta_\pi\, (1 - \beta_p\, \omega\phi_\pi)\,(J_2 + J_3) - \beta_\pi \beta_p\, \omega\phi_\pi\, J_1.$$

The necessary and sufficient conditions for all eigen-values of $J$ to have negative real parts are

$$a_1 > 0, \qquad a_2 > 0, \qquad a_3 > 0, \qquad b > 0.$$

To demonstrate the first part of the proposition note first that $N_x = Y_x/F_N$ and $\phi_x = \gamma Y_x/F_N$, where $\gamma := |F_{NN}|/F_N^2$ and $x = \omega, p, \pi$. Condition (4.15) follows from dividing the condition $a_2 > 0$ by $\beta_w \beta_p/F_N$ and rearranging the resulting terms appropriately (using $\omega = F_N$). On the other hand, $a_2 > 0$ is in any case satisfied if $\beta_p < -N_\omega/(\phi N_\pi) = -\omega Y_\omega/Y_\pi = -\omega I' \bar{N}/(-I'\bar{K}) = w\bar{N}/p\bar{K}$, where the equalities are established by the formulae of the IS–LM comparative-statics.

The proof of part (b) begins with the observation that $a_3 > 0$ is always fulfilled and that $J_1, J_2 > 0$. Furthermore, there exists a positive number $\tilde{\beta}_p$ such that $\beta_p < \tilde{\beta}_p$ implies the following inequalities: (i) $-J_{11} - J_{22} > \beta_w\, \omega|N_\omega|/2$; (ii) $1 - \beta_p\, \omega\phi_\pi > 0$; (iii) $J_3 > \beta_\pi \beta_w\, \omega|N_\omega|/2$; (iv) $(\beta_w \omega N_\omega)^2/4 > \beta_p\, \omega\phi_\pi\, J_1$. $\beta_p$ is independent of the size of $\beta_\pi$. $\beta_p < \tilde{\beta}_p$ then ensures $a_1 > 0$ by (i) and (ii), $a_2 > 0$ by (iii), and lastly $a_1 a_2 - a_3 > J_3(-J_{11} - J_{22}) - \beta_\pi \beta_p\, \omega\phi_\pi\, J_1 > \beta_\pi[(\beta_w \omega N_\omega)^2/4 - \beta_p \omega\phi_\pi\, J_1] > 0$ by (ii)–(iv).

The proof of part (c) is based on the fact that the inequality given, which is equivalent to $\phi - \omega|\phi_\omega| + \omega p|\phi_p| > 0$, makes it possible to render $a_1$ positive by choosing $\beta_\pi$ sufficiently small. The same holds true for $a_2$. Both $a_1$ and $a_2$ are bounded away from zero as $\beta_\pi \to 0$. Thus also $b = a_1 a_2 - a_3 > 0$ as $\beta_\pi$ approaches zero. It is easily seen that in general this kind of argument does not go through.

As regards part (d) we first assert that $\beta_o$ is equal to $F_N^2/(|F_{NN}|Y_\pi)$ (it is a routine matter to verify this). The inequality $\beta_p > F_N^2/(|F_{NN}|Y_\pi)$, in turn, is equivalent to $1 - \beta_p\, \omega\phi_\pi < 0$. Hence, rising values of $\beta_\pi$ will eventually violate the first Routh–Hurwitz condition $a_1 > 0$. Similarly, the inequality for $\beta_\pi$ is equivalent to $\phi - \omega \mid \phi_\omega \mid + \omega p \mid \phi_p \mid -\beta_\pi \omega \phi_\pi < 0$, so that sufficiently large $\beta_p$ lead to $a_1 < 0$.

### *Proof of proposition 2*

Using the relationships for $N_x$ and $\phi_x$ that were pointed out in the preceding proof, it is easily verified that the first condition implies $\beta_p \beta_\pi [p\omega \mid \phi_p \mid -\beta_w \omega \phi N_\pi]$ $> 0$, and the second $\beta_p [\phi - \omega \mid \phi_\omega \mid + \omega p \mid \phi_p \mid -\beta_\pi \omega \phi_\pi] < 0$. Hence, $a_1$ is linearly increasing, and $a_2$ is linearly decreasing in $\beta_p$ (actually, the condition on $\beta_w$ is stronger than necessary to obtain this result). Moreover, $a_3$ is linearly increasing, so that $b$ is a quadratic function of $\beta_p$. Since the quadratic term has a negative coefficient, and it has already been established that $b > 0$ when $\beta_p = 0$, the function $b = b(\beta_p)$ has exactly one positive root $\beta_p^H$. $a_3 > 0$ implies that the product $a_1 a_2$ is positive at this point. As we know that $a_1$ is positive for all $\beta_p > 0$, $a_2$ must be positive too. From this we can conclude that all Routh–Hurwitz terms $a_1, a_2, a_3, b$ are positive if $0 < \beta_p < \beta_p^H$, which completes the proof of the first part of the proposition.

As concerns the Hopf-bifurcation, it has already been observed in the text that the Jacobian has two purely imaginary eigen-values at $\beta_p^H$. The other conditions for the dynamics to undergo a Hopf-bifurcation are: (*a*) the equilibrium is independent of $\beta_p$; (*b*) the functions of the RHS of (4.12)–(4.14) are continuously differentiable; (*c*) the Jacobian is continuous; (*d*) for all $\beta_p$ near but not equal to $\beta_p^H$, no eigen-value has zero real part (cf. Theorem A in Alexander and York 1978, pp.263–266). (*a*)–(*c*) are obvious while (*d*) follows from Orlando's formula for the eigen-values $\lambda_i$ (see Gantmacher 1959, p.197), which here reads $b = (\lambda_1 + \lambda_2)(\lambda_2 + \lambda_3)(\lambda_1 + \lambda_3)$, and the fact that $\beta_p^H$ is a (locally) unique root of $b$.

### *Proof of proposition 3*

The comparative-static exercise for (4.16)(4.17) yields $Y_\omega = \mid m_r \mid I'(\beta_p \phi \bar{K} - \bar{N})/\Omega$ and $Y_p = -I'\bar{M}/\Omega$, where $\Omega := p^2 [\mid m_r \mid (1 - C' - \beta_p I' \mid F_{NN} \mid /F_N^2) + m_Y I']$. Part (*a*) follows directly from the observation that $\Omega > 0$ if and only if $\beta_p < \beta_o$.

To study the stability of system (4.18), (4.19) consider the Jacobian

$$J = \begin{bmatrix} \beta_w \omega N'Y_\omega & \beta_w \omega N'Y_p \\ \beta_p p(\phi + \omega \phi' Y_\omega) & \beta_p p\omega \phi' Y_p \end{bmatrix}.$$

The determinant is given by $\det J = -\beta_w \beta_p pN'Y_p$. Thus, $\det J < 0$ if $\beta p > \beta o$, which implies saddlepoint instability, and $\det J > 0$ if $\beta_p < \beta_o$. To demonstrate the other statements of part (*b*) and (*c*) it suffices to note that $\beta_p \phi \bar{K} - \bar{N} < 0$ is equivalent to $\beta_p < \beta_1$, so that, in particular, $Y_\omega < 0$ if $\beta_p < \beta_1$ together with $\beta_p < \beta_o$, and $Y_\omega > 0$ if $\beta_1 < \beta_p < \beta_o$ (while $\det J$ is still positive then).

## Proof of proposition 4

The Jacobian of the dynamics (4.20)–(4.22) is given by

$$
J = \begin{bmatrix}
-\beta_Y(1-C'+r_Y I' - \beta_p \omega\phi'I') & -\beta_Y r_p I' & \beta_Y I'(\beta_p\phi\bar{K}-\bar{N}) \\
\beta_p p\omega\phi' & 0 & \beta_p p\phi \\
\beta_w \omega N' & 0 & 0
\end{bmatrix}.
$$

The matrix, by the way, has the same structure as the Jacobian obtained in the original Tobin (1975, p.199, equation (3.3.)) model. Taking account of the LM-derivative $r_Y = -m_Y/m_r$, the corresponding Routh–Hurwitz terms are (cf. the proof of Proposition 1),

$$a_1 = \beta_Y(1-C'+m_Y I'/|m_r|-\beta_p \,|\,F_{NN}\,|\,I'\,/\,F_N^2) = \beta_Y\tilde{a}_1$$
$$a_2 = \beta_Y I'(-\beta_w\,\omega N'(\beta_p\,\phi\bar{K}-\bar{N})+\beta_p p\omega\phi'r_p) = \beta_Y I'\tilde{a}_2$$
$$a_3 = \beta_Y\,\beta_w\,\beta_p\,pr_p\,N'I' = \beta_Y\,I'\beta_w\,\beta_p\,\tilde{a}_3$$
$$b = \beta_Y I'(\beta_Y\,\tilde{a}_1\,\tilde{a}_2 - \beta_w\,\beta_p\,\tilde{a}_3).$$

$a_3$ is always positive since $r_p > 0$. $a_1$ is negative (positive) if $\beta_p > \beta_o$ ($\beta_p < \beta_o$). $\beta_p\,\phi\bar{K}-\bar{N}$ is positive (negative) if $\beta_p > \beta_1$ ($\beta_p < \beta_1$). The latter implies that $a_2$ becomes negative if $\beta_p > \beta_1$ and $\beta_w$ is sufficiently large. The observations of $a_1 < 0$ and $a_2 < 0$ prove the instability statements with respect to variations of $\beta_p$ and $\beta_w$.

Suppose next that $\tilde{a}_1 > 0$ as well as $\tilde{a}_2 > 0$ (which, in particular, is ensured by $\beta_p < \beta_o$, $\beta_p < \beta_1$). Then $b > 0$ if $\beta_p$ tends to zero ($\tilde{a}_1$ and $\tilde{a}_2$ are bounded away from zero then) or if $\beta_Y$ is sufficiently large. On the other hand, $b < 0$ comes about if $\beta_Y$ gets small. Finally, all Routh–Hurwitz conditions are also satisfied if $\beta_p < \beta_o$ and $\beta_w$ is so small that $a_2 > 0$ and, subsequently, $b > 0$.

The proof of part (*d*) is similar as in Proposition 2.

# 5 Stock market driven multiplier dynamics

## A reconsideration

### 5.1 The Blanchard (1981) model reconsidered

In this chapter we reconsider a macrodynamic model of Blanchard, see Chiarella et al. (2009, Ch.2) for its recent reinvestigation, which integrates output and stock market dynamics in a fundamental way.[1] We add budget equations (and their implications) to all sectors of the economy, as well as capital accumulation and growth (but not yet proper wage–price dynamics). We obtain a model of the real–financial interaction with quite different steady state characteristics as compared to the Blanchard approach. We furthermore allow for somewhat sluggish adjustments of share prices and capital gains expectations in place of perfect substitutes and perfect foresight. Instead of the originally only 2-D dynamics we now obtain a 4-D dynamical system with two real and two financial variables and specific stability properties. However, by setting certain secondary expressions equal to their trend values, we can regain the mathematical form of the original 2-D dynamics of Blanchard type. This form is now based on variables that allow for stationarity when estimated. It permits the estimations of the model to get information about the magnitude of its adjustment speeds, the size of which is crucial for the stability or instability of this dynamical system.

### 5.2 Adding growth: the point of departure for empirical analysis

Conventional Keynesian analysis of the short run generally combines multiplier analysis, in static or dynamic terms, with a money market based determination of the nominal rate of interest, which interacts with the goods market by way of interest dependent investment behavior and output dependent transaction balances. This standard model ignores the fact that investment financing has a long-term orientation, and should thus not be based solely on the money market rate of interest which is clearly of short-term nature. Furthermore, if all income generated accrues to households and if households do not hold real capital directly, one needs another financial instrument, namely equities, by which the income of firms is distributed to the households. It is therefore clearly desirable to extend the narrow financial framework of conventional IS–LM analysis, by assuming, besides money and short-term bonds, further financial assets such as long-term bonds and equities.

Such an important extension of the IS–LM approach has been provided (in still simple terms) by Blanchard (1981), with emphasis on the dynamic interaction of output with stock market prices by way of their impact on the investment behavior of firms. Long-term bonds are also considered in his analysis, but do not interact with the real side of the dynamics. In building on the real and stock market interactions proposed by Blanchard (1981) we will therefore only briefly consider the adjustment process on the market for bonds, but not use these dynamics in the model studied in this chapter. Blanchard and Fischer (1989) do make investment behavior instead dependent on the long-term rate of interest and thus study the interaction of output and the market for long-term bonds (but they ignore the stock market). Letting investment depend on both stock market prices and long-term interest rates is, of course, the next step suggested by this type of analysis which however has not been investigated so far and which we also leave for future research.

The short-run real–financial interaction studied in Blanchard (1981) is, therefore, in a significant way richer than that of the conventional IS–LM type. This analysis combines the dynamic multiplier process with adjustments in four financial markets and thus three rates of return: the short-term rate of interest, the rate of return on long-term bonds (which includes capital gains, besides interest payments) and the rate of return on equities (which also includes capital gains, besides dividend payments). The resulting real–financial interaction is therefore built on four important macroeconomic feedback chains as they are graphically represented in Figures 5.1–5.4.

The dynamic multiplier process is known to be stabilizing when the marginal propensity to spend is less than one, as it is assumed in Blanchard (1981). It is however an incomplete description of quantity adjustments on the goods market, since it considers goods market disequilibrium but neglects what happens to inventories. The Metzlerian sales-inventory dynamics, as shown in Figure 5.1, would remedy this deficiency, but it would also add one further law of motion to the dynamics which must be left here for future research. The Metzler process is known to be stable if, in particular, inventory adjustment is sufficiently sluggish and would then – we conjecture – not change significantly the analysis that follows if it is integrated into it. Figure 5.1 shows the way in which the dynamic multiplier approach simplifies the Metzlerian dynamics on the market for goods by the arrow leading from top-right to bottom-left.

Also known to be stabilizing is the conventional Keynes-effect, by which declining wage and price levels lower the short-term rate of interest which, sooner or later, should increase investment and aggregate demand and thus via the multiplier process also output and employment, see Figure 5.2. The quantity adjustment accompanying the nominal adjustments of the Keynes-effect is shown in Figure 5.1 as the discussed short-cut of its full representation as a Metzlerian output and inventory adjustment process. Generally, traditional Keynesian macrodynamics of AS–AD type is based on these two stable processes, where

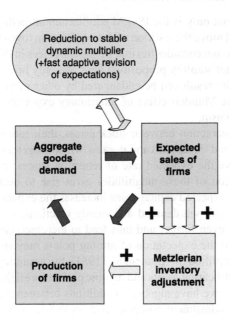

*Figure 5.1* The stable dynamic multiplier process as a short-cut for a stable Metzlerian inventory mechanism.

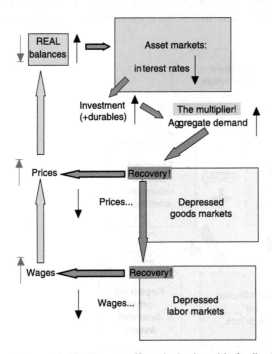

*Figure 5.2* The Keynes-effect, the basic stable feedback effect between real and financial markets.

the view is supported that not only is the IS–LM equilibrium attracting, but the wage-price adjustments will move the position of this equilibrium towards the full employment position. We do not consider flexible wages and prices in this chapter and thus do not test this latter stability proposition here. We only briefly want to point out that such a stability result can be endangered by other macrodynamic feedback chains such as the Mundell effect of inflationary expectations or the Fisher debt deflation mechanism.

Next, we consider the interaction between stock prices, their rate of change (the actual capital gains), and expected capital gains which, together with the dividend rate of return, give the expected rate of return on shares. It is easily explained that the interaction of these magnitudes gives rise to destabilizing forces, since an increase in expected capital gains increases the expected rate of return on stocks which should, via demand and supply reactions, increase the growth rate of share prices even further and thus lead to increased capital gain expectations and so on until the expectation of turning points may stop such a spiral. This process is simplified in Blanchard (1981) by assuming perfect substitution between interest-bearing assets and myopic perfect foresight for stock price dynamics. In this case we have algebraic conditions between the rates of returns in place of dynamic adjustment processes and get saddlepoint instability which however is turned into stability by applying the so-called jump variable technique. Indirectly, the instability depicted in Figure 5.3 is present also in the Blanchard (1981) limit case. It is however overcome by assuming that asset prices are always on the stable manifold of the resulting saddlepoint dynamics. We will

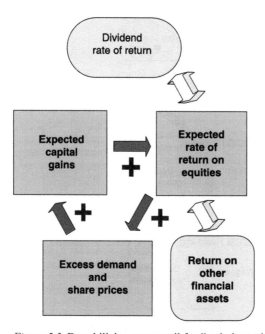

*Figure 5.3* Destabilizing or tranquil feedback dynamics on the stock market?

investigate in this chapter the less perfect adjustment of asset prices shown in Figure 5.3 and will therefore not consider the jump variable technique as a proper representation of asset market behavior.

What has been stated on stock market behavior also holds for the adjustment processes characterizing the market for long-term bonds and is thus not repeated here. This market does not really play a role in Blanchard (1981) nor will it in our subsequent reformulation of this analysis (see also Appendix I to this chapter). Such an analysis is given in Blanchard and Fischer (1989) in their study of the dynamics of demand in their Chapter 10.[2]

In the present chapter we reconsider the short-run dynamics investigated by Blanchard (1981) by assuming more or less sluggish adjustment of share prices and to some extent also of expected capital gains in the place of his perfect substitute and perfect foresight assumptions. We add moreover budget equations of households, firms and the government, and their implications in particular for steady state positions, as well as capital accumulation and growth. Yet here we do not yet deal with proper wage-price dynamics, and thus a proper long-run perspective to the Blanchard approach to output, interest and stock market dynamics.[3] In place of the originally only 2-D dynamics (of output and Tobin's *q*) we thereby obtain a fully interdependent 4-D dynamical system with two real (output and real balances) and two financial variables (Tobin's *q* and share price expectations), where the former are expressed in per unit of capital form. However, by setting certain secondary expressions equal to their trend or average values, we

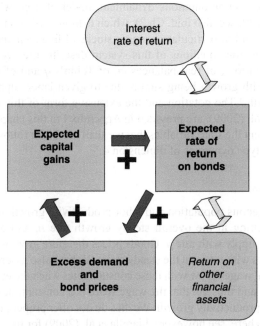

*Figure 5.4* Destabilizing or tranquil feedback dynamics
on the market for long-term bonds?

can regain the mathematical form of the original 2-D dynamics of Blanchard type, yet now expressed in intensive form variables that can be predicted to exhibit stationarity, at least from a very long-run perspective.

In Section 5.2 we present the full model directly in intensive form. The original or extensive form of the model, including all budget equations, is provided in Appendix I of this chapter and discussed in detail in Chiarella et al. (2009). Section 5.3 presents propositions on the steady state solution of the 4-D dynamics and their stability features and also considers briefly the limit limit case of perfect substitutes and myopic perfect foresight. In Section 5.4 we then simplify the full dynamics in such a way that in fact the original form of the Blanchard (1981) dynamics can be regained and be characterized by propositions that are closely related to the ones of the full 4-D dynamics. This simple reformulation of the Blanchard output and stock market dynamics by means of variables that are characterized by stationarity in their time series representation is further reformulated in the final section of the chapter and in Appendix II. This is undertaken in order to obtain representations of these dynamics that allow for growth, but are reduced in such a way that empirical estimates in particular for the average behavior of stock market adjustment speeds and capital gains expectations, the sizes of which are crucial for the stability of the dynamics, should be obtainable.

## 5.3 The model in intensive form

We start from the 4-D autonomous dynamical model of a growing economy Chiarella et al. (2009; see also ibid. Ch.2), which exhibits fully consistent stock–flow relationships and in particular changing stocks of financial and real assets. The following dynamic equations of this system describe the evolution of the output to capital ratio $y$, of real balances $m$, of Tobin's $q$ and of capital gains expectations $\epsilon$, with growth being simply due to given labor supply and labor productivity growth.[4] The notation and the extensive form of this model, taken from Chiarella et al. (2009), are provided in Appendix I to this chapter.

Let us first present the state variables that we shall use in the following analysis of our Blanchard-type dynamics of dimension 4.

### *The state variables*

We consider exogenous population and labor productivity growth of the Harrod neutral type, resulting in the overall steady growth rate $n$, and assume given growth in money supply with rate $\mu$. Goods prices therefore grow with rate $\mu - n$ and nominal wages with rate $\mu$ in the steady state. We here also assume that goods prices and nominal wages grow with these constant rates when the economy is not at its steady state, and thus get that the wage share is a constant, due to what has been assumed for productivity growth. We thus do not offer proper laws of motion for these variables here, see however Chiarella et al. (2009) for their introduction into a model of the considered type. We express the state variables output and real balances in per unit of capital form, $y$, $m$, in order to get dynamics with stationary long-run solutions throughout. Due to what has been assumed for money supply and the price level, the variable $m$ mirrors the fluctuations in the capital stock in a one to one fashion, since everything else in this expression has been reduced to trend growth here. The state variables are

$y = Y/K$    the output to capital ratio,

$m = M/(pK)$    real balances per unit of capital,

$q = p_e E/(pK)$    Tobin's average $q$,

$\epsilon = \hat{p}_e^e$    capital gains expectations.

The model, and its notation, from which these intensive form variables and their laws of motion are deduced is presented in Appendix I of this chapter. Due to space limitations we do not comment on this model here, but immediately progress to the implied laws of motion for the above listed state variables, their interior steady state solution and their stability features.

## The laws of motion

The model presented and analyzed in Chiarella et al. (2009; see also Appendix I of the present chapter), slightly extended in order to include productivity growth and steady state inflation, implies the following intensive form dynamics which we at first represent in condensed definitional form solely.[5]

$$\dot{y} = \beta_y (y^d - y) + ny - \hat{K}y$$
$$\hat{m} = \hat{M} - (\hat{K} + \hat{p}) = -\hat{K} + n,$$
$$\hat{q} = \hat{p}_e + \hat{E} - (\hat{K} + \hat{p}) = \hat{p}_e + \frac{1-q}{q}\hat{K} - (\mu - n)$$
$$\dot{\epsilon} = \beta_\epsilon (\hat{p}_e - \epsilon).$$

Inserting the laws of motion for output, capital, equities and share prices and inserting the definition of aggregate demand per unit of capital, see the appendix, we then arrive at a 4-D autonomous non-linear system of differential equations, as shown in equations (5.1)–(5.4). Note that some of the steady state values of the dynamics are employed as point of reference in the laws of motion, by way of an appropriate Taylor approximation, and that these laws of motion are still formulated as linear as possible, by the same reasoning, in order to concentrate the analysis on their unavoidable or intrinsic non-linearities.

$$\dot{y} = \beta_y(c(y - \delta - t) + i(q - 1) + \delta + n + g - y) - i(q - 1)y, \tag{5.1}$$

$$\hat{m} = -i(q - 1), \tag{5.2}$$

$$\hat{q} = \beta_{p_e}\left(\frac{(1-v)y-\delta}{q} + \epsilon - (r_0 + \frac{ky-m}{h_1})\right) + k_{p_e}\epsilon + (1-k_{p_e})\epsilon_0$$

$$+ \frac{1-q}{q}(i(q-1)+n) - (\mu-n),$$  (5.3)

$$\dot{\epsilon} = \beta_{\epsilon}[(\beta_{p_e}\left(\frac{(1-v)y-\delta}{q} + \epsilon - \left(r_0 + \frac{ky-m}{h_1}\right)\right) - (1-k_{p_e})(\epsilon - (r_o)].$$  (5.4)

The law of motion (5.1) describes the evolution of the output to capital ratio which is driven by excess demand (with $c \in (0, 1)$ per unit of capital in the market for goods, subject to the adjustment speed $\beta_y$, but diminished by an expression that takes account of the growth of the denominator of the output to capital ratio, i.e., the rate of investment ($I/K = i(q-1) + n$). Note that the trend term $n$ is also part of the dynamics of output adjustments on the extensive form level, since growth must be accounted for there too, and thus cancels in the intensive form of the dynamics. Depreciation, taxes (net of interest), trend growth of the capital stock and government expenditures: $\delta, t, n, g$, are all given constants. Consumption depends linearly on disposable income, $y - \delta - t$, and net investment, apart from trend growth, responds to Tobin's $q$, i.e. more precisely, its deviation from the long-run value of this ratio here given by 1.[6]

The second law of motion describes the evolution of real balances per unit of capital which is given by the (negative of the) fluctuating component $i(q-1)$ of net investment, since the difference of the growth rate of the money supply and the trend rate of real growth summed with the rate of trend inflation is exactly zero.

Tobin's $q = p_e E/(pK)$, in the third law of motion, is driven, via adjusting share prices $p_e$, by the nominal rate of return differential between stocks and short-term bonds, which is given by $\frac{(1-v)y-\delta}{q} + \epsilon - \left(r_0 + \frac{ky-m}{h_1}\right)$, i.e., the difference between dividend return $(1 - v)y - \delta$ per unit of capital, equal to the rate of profit of firms, divided by Tobin's $q$ and augmented by capital gains expectations $\epsilon$, and the nominal rate of interest $r_0 + \frac{ky-m}{h_1}$ on short-term bonds which is based on a standard (linear) money demand equation and the assumption of money market equilibrium.[7] The speed of adjustment of the growth rate of share price $p_e$ and thus indirectly of Tobin's $q$ is given by $\beta_{p_e}$. The resulting expression is augmented by an accelerator term $k_{p_e}\epsilon + (1-k_{p_e})\epsilon_0$ as in the theory of price inflation, which is here however also partly based on long-run expectations $\epsilon_o$ of capital gains which in the present model are equal to the long-run rate of inflation. Finally, the growth rate of the stock of equities has to be added to the dynamics of share prices and the growth of the capital stock to be deducted (and also the rate of price inflation) in order to satisfy the definition of the growth rate of $q = p_e E/(pK)$, with $\hat{E}q = \hat{K}$

due to the budget equation of firms: $p_e \dot{E} = p\dot{K}$, which assumes that all investment expenditure is equity financed in our model.

The difference between the growth law for share prices just described and the expression for expected capital gains $\epsilon$ finally determines, in the fourth law of motion, the evolution of these expectations in an adaptive fashion. This law of motion could be augmented easily by a regressive expectations formation process, and thus be based on heterogeneous expectations formation, which however would not change the dynamics of the model very much. The discussed four laws of motion are basically fairly direct consequences of the extensive form equations provided in Appendix I.

This system of four laws of motion can be estimated if it can be assumed as an approximation that wage and price inflation are basically determined by money supply growth and trend growth in the real part of the economy. The question however remains how such a model can be extended and estimated when the economy under investigation is not close to the steady state, see in this case Chiarella et al. (2009) for the inclusion of wage and price dynamics into such an approach.

We stress that the limit case, considered in Blanchard (1981) on a less complete level, since the law of motion for real balances is disregarded, is given by assuming $\beta_q, \beta_\epsilon = \infty$, i.e., by assuming perfect substitutes and myopic perfect foresight and $\mu = n = 0$.

## 5.4 Steady state and stability analysis

With regard to steady states of the dynamics we have the following proposition. Note that this proposition is very different from the steady state analysis presented in Blanchard (1981), where zero, one or two meaningful steady state solutions are indeed possible depending on the parameters of the model.

### Proposition 1

*The interior steady state of the laws of motion (5.1)–(5.4) is uniquely determined and given by:*

$$q_0 = 1$$

$$m_0 = ky_0$$

$$z_0 = \mu - n$$

$$y_0 = \frac{1}{1-c}(\delta + n + g - c(\delta + t))$$

$$r_0 = (1-v)y_0 - \delta.$$

In contrast to Blanchard (1981) who has not considered budget equations, capital accumulation or decumulation, we thus no longer have the possibility of no or two steady state solutions. In our model, the capital accumulation equation enforces a unique and really stationary solution for Tobin's $q$; see also Chiarella et al. (2009) for such a long-run reformulation of the short-run approach to output and stock market dynamics. Note also that income distribution is still kept fixed and that supply side considerations on the market for labor and for goods are still excluded; see however Chiarella et al. (2009) for an inclusion of these aspects of an integrated growth dynamics. Note finally that our analysis does not depend on the distinction of bad and goods news cases as in Blanchard (1981).

### Proposition 2 (tranquil stock market adjustments)

*Assume $\beta_y > y$, $h_1 < k/(1-v)$, $\beta_{p_e} < 1 - k_{p_e}$. The steady state of the 4-D dynamics (5.1)–(5.4) is locally asymptotically stable for all $\beta_\epsilon$ sufficiently large.*

See Chiarella et al. (2009) for a proof of this proposition where also further stability propositions are provided. Taken together these propositions imply that convergence to the interior steady state will be given for all adjustment speeds of capital gain expectations if the above three conditions on $\beta_y, h_1, \beta_{p_e}$ hold, representing sufficiently strong dynamic multiplier dynamics, a strong Keynes-effect and share price dynamics that are sufficiently tranquil.

### Proposition 3 (accelerating stock market dynamics)

*Assume $\beta_{p_e} > 1 - k_{p_e}$. Then: The local stability found in the preceding proposition 2 gets lost by way of a Hopf-bifurcation if $\beta_\epsilon$ is sufficiently large (but is regained again for $\beta_\epsilon$ sufficiently small).*

See Chiarella et al. (2009) for a proof of this proposition. Less tranquil stock market dynamics of the assumed kind can thus always be made divergent by making the speed of adjustment of capital gain expectations sufficiently large. Based on Propositions 2 and 3 we conceive the behavior of the stock market to be governed by phase diagram switching (repeated changes between tranquil periods and periods of cumulative instability), with fast adaptive expectations in both cases. These expectations are close to rational expectations in tranquil situations (Proposition 2), since we then have convergence of real and financial variables to the steady state and thus the possibility of fast adaptive processes to catch up with reality. In periods of cumulative instability and rapid divergence away from the steady state (Proposition 3) we have a less perfect working of the adaptive expectations mechanism, but assume that sooner or later a switch back to tranquil asset market behavior will occur due to the added expectation of turning points, a reduction in the trading volume and thus in the adjustment speed on the stock market. We do not consider this regime switching or phase diagram switching method here any further, but refer the reader for the details implied by Propositions 2 and 3 to Chiarella et al. (2009). In the next section we shall instead make use of a simpler threshold mechanism that also keeps the dynamics within economically meaningful bounds when the steady state is surrounded by destabilizing forces.

We note finally that the feedback mechanism employed in these dynamics are basically a combination of the Keynes-effect, as it derives from the conventional LM curve here employed, and a financial accelerator mechanism based on the interaction of share price and capital gains expectations dynamics, which become the dominant mechanisms under the conditions stated in Proposition 3. There is, by contrast, on the real side of the dynamics, a stable dynamic multiplier process, but not yet Rose (1967) type stabilizing or destabilizing real wage rate dynamics, Metzlerian type inventory accelerator or a Mundell-effect based on the destabilizing interaction between inflationary expectations, aggregate demand and output dynamics and actual inflation.

### *The special case of myopic perfect foresight and perfect substitutes*

The special case of perfect foresight ($\beta_\epsilon = \infty$) considered in Blanchard (1981) in the present model gives rise to the dynamics shown below. Here we take $\mu = n$ for simplicity.

$$\dot{y} = \beta_y (c(y - \delta - t) + i(q - 1) + \delta + n + g - y) - i(q - 1)y, \tag{5.5}$$

$$\hat{m} = - i(q - 1), \tag{5.6}$$

$$\hat{q} = \frac{1}{1 - \beta_{p_e} - k_{p_e}} \beta_{p_e} (\frac{(1-v)y - \delta}{q} - (r_0 + \frac{ky - m}{h_1})) + \frac{1-q}{q}(i(q-1) + n). \tag{5.7}$$

Note that the distinction between $\hat{p}_e$ and $\hat{q}$ must be taken care of appropriately in the derivation of the third law of motion. Note also that the steady state solution of these dynamics is identical to the one of the 4-D system, the variable $\epsilon$ being disregarded now as a separate variable of the dynamics. Note finally that this special case allows for a phase diagram switching technique as well, now simply by assuming that the parameter in front of the law of motion for $q$ switches back and forth between positive and negative values and thus between tranquil markets where $\beta_{p_e} > 1 - k_{p_e}$ holds and activated ones where the there is divergence away from the steady state.

Assuming bonds and equities as perfect substitutes in addition ($\beta_{p_e} = \infty$) implies furthermore the following special case of the above 3-D dynamics (due to $\hat{q} = \hat{p}_e + \hat{E} - \hat{K}$):

$$\dot{y} = \beta_y (c(y - \delta - t) + i(q - 1) + \delta + n + g - y) - i(q - 1)y, \tag{5.8}$$

$$\hat{m} = - i(q - 1), \tag{5.9}$$

$$\hat{q} = r_0 + \frac{ky - m}{h_1} - \frac{(1-v)y - \delta}{q} + \frac{1-q}{q}(i(q-1) + n). \tag{5.10}$$

This is the 3-D analog to the 2-D system considered in Blanchard (1981), with new growth-dependent terms in the output and $q$ dynamics and with an additional law of motion for real balances per unit of capital now. This limit case is however significantly different from what we considered beforehand, since it only allows for a positive feedback of $q$ on its rate of change and thus no longer for tranquil periods that can limit an explosive motion of stock prices should this motion become too extreme. Therefore, a quite different technique has been developed here in order to stabilize the dynamics, namely the so-called jump variable technique by which all explosive motions are simply ignored through a unique and instantaneous adjustment of so-called non-predetermined variables, here share prices $p_e$ or Tobin's $q$, to the stable manifold of the dynamics. We do not go into a discussion of the meaningfulness of this technique here, but refer the reader instead to Chiarella et al. (2000b) in this respect.[8]

## 5.5 Simplifying the output growth–stock market interaction

As the model has been formulated above we have already assumed that goods prices rise with $\mu - n$ and that the wage share is constant, based on the assumptions that wages rise with inflation and productivity growth. This allowed us to ignore effects of income distribution in aggregate demand in particular. We now assume in addition that:

- $\hat{K} = n$ holds, that is we ignore the cyclical component in the evolution of the capital stock. We get from this assumption that the term $-i(q - 1)$ is removed from (5.1) and also that $m$ can be considered a given magnitude from now on, i.e., the law of motion (5.2) can be discarded from the dynamics.

- $\hat{E} = \hat{K}$ holds, that is we ignore quantity effects in the development of Tobin's $q$. This assumption removes the term $\hat{E} - \hat{K} = \frac{1-q}{q}\hat{K}$ from the third law of motion.

- $\kappa_{p_e} = 0$ for reasons of simplicity. This removes the capital gains accelerator from the third law of motion and also the trend term in the rate of inflation (which is equal to $\epsilon_o$ in size).

We thus now ignore fluctuations in the growth rate of the capital stock due to the term $i(q - 1)$, in addition to the assumption of no fluctuations in the rate of price and wage inflation, and the assumption of a constant money supply growth, i.e., we also regard real balances per unit of capital $m = M/(pK)$ a given magnitude (fixed at its steady state value) just as the wage share $v = (w/p)/x$, $x$ being the current state of labor productivity.

As stated, the assumptions, taken together, remove the expressions that are appended in the intensive form from the Blanchard (1981) type approach to economic growth and thus move the short-run and the long-run formulations closer to each other. Note that the law of motion for Tobin's $q$ is now in fact reduced to a law of motion for real stock prices $p_e/p$. The assumption $\kappa_{p_e} = 0$ furthermore removes $\epsilon_o = \mu - n$ from the law of motion for $q$. In sum we therefore get that terms referring to fluctuating stock evolutions are suppressed and the law of motion for real balances per unit of capital replaced by a given value for this stock magnitude. We therefore obtain a dynamical system that concentrates in principle on the same variables and laws of motion as the one used in the short-run model of Chiarella et al. (2009) with its delayed share price and capital gain expectations adjustments, with the sole difference that certain quantities (output and the value of the stock) are now expressed in per unit of capital form and in simple real terms, respectively.

Based on empirical reasoning we finally add a risk premium $\xi$ to the comparison of interest and equity returns used in the equation describing the share price dynamics and thus in sum get as dynamics the following system of differential equations.[9]

$$\dot{y} = \beta_y(c(y - \delta - t) + i(q - 1) + \delta + n + g - y), \tag{5.11}$$

$$\hat{q} = \beta_{p_e}\left(\frac{(1-v)y - \delta}{q} + \epsilon - \left(r_0 + \frac{ky - m}{h_1}\right)\right) + \xi, v, m \text{ given} \tag{5.12}$$

$$\dot{\epsilon} = \beta_\epsilon\left(\beta_{p_e}\left[\frac{(1-v)y - \delta}{q} + \epsilon - \left(r_0 + \frac{ky - m}{h_1} + \xi\right) - (\epsilon - \epsilon_0)\right]\right). \tag{5.13}$$

The resulting dynamical model is formally of the same type as the short-term one analyzed in Chiarella et al. (2000b) and closely related to the one of Blanchard (1981). The stability and instability propositions we derived in this chapter, and in Chiarella et al. (2009), thus here apply as well. However, we regard the present model as an approximation of the 4-D full dynamics now, where fluctuations of certain variables around their trend value are ignored.

Furthermore, the model will probably be applied to situations not necessarily close to its steady states, as they are determined in Chiarella et al. (2009), nor close to the steady state of the full 4-D dynamics considered above, at least as far as the evolution of the output to capital ratio may be concerned. It is, however, in principle possible, see Chiarella et al. (2009), to formulate a full-fledged version of the model which (besides fluctuating capital and equity stock) exhibits fluctuating labor intensity, real wages and inflation (as well as inflationary expectations). Yet in order to stay close to the Blanchard-type model, estimated in Chiarella et al. (2002), we reserve such a complete growth perspective for future considerations and estimation of the parameters of a real–financial interaction of the Blanchard (1981) type.

## 5.6 Stability analysis

We now investigate the stability of the reduced dynamics (5.11)–(5.13) from the perspective of the results achieved for the full 4-D dynamics.

### Proposition 4

*For the dynamics (5.11)–(5.13) there holds:*

1. *Assume* $r_o = (1-v)y_o - \delta + \epsilon_o - \xi$, $m = m_o = ky_0$ *with respect to the steady state value of y, to be determined on this basis. The* **steady state** *of the dynamics (5.11)–(5.13) is uniquely determined and* **the same** *as the one we considered in proposition 1 (up to the addition of the parameter $\xi$ in the present formulation of the dynamics).*

2. *Assume that $h_1 < k/(1-v)$ holds. The steady state of the dynamics (5.11)–(5.13) is* **locally asymptotically stable** *for all $\beta_\epsilon$ if $\beta_{p_e} < 1$ holds.*

3. *In the case $\beta_{p_e} > 1$ the* **local asymptotic stability** *of assertion 4.2 (which is given for $\beta_\epsilon$ sufficiently small)* **gets lost** *at a value $\beta_\epsilon^H$*

   *below $\beta_\epsilon = \dfrac{\beta_y(1-c)+r_0}{\beta_{p_e}-1}$ in a cyclical fashion by way of a Hopf-bifurcation.*

4. *After the loss of stability we will have one negative real eigen-value and two with positive real parts for all $\beta_\epsilon > \beta_\epsilon^H$, i.e., there is* **no reswitching** *back to local asymptotic stability in the considered dynamics.*

Note that 4.1 is a proposition that restores the steady state of the full 4-D dynamics also for the approximate situation here under consideration and thus avoids – by means of an appropriate positioning of the LM curve – the complex steady state situation of the original Blanchard approach, reconsidered in Chiarella et al. (2009) in slightly more general terms.

We thus here avoid non-uniqueness of steady state positions and can also show that the resulting steady state position is indeed attracting if the stock market responds sufficiently sluggishly to the possibility of rate of return differentials in the financial markets of the model, at least when the positive interest rate effect of output changes dominates the one on the dividend payments of firms. This holds for all speeds of adjustment of capital gains expectations and thus also in the limit case of myopic perfect foresight. By contrast, speeds of adjustment on the stock market larger than the threshold value 1 will give rise to a steady state that is (presumably globally) repelling if capital gains expectation formation is sufficiently fast.

Note here however that there is still stability for $\beta_{p_e} > 1$ if expectations are adjusting sufficiently slowly, since the determinant of the Jacobian of the 3-D dynamics at the steady state is always negative and since the situation $\beta_\epsilon = 0$ is easily shown to exhibit two eigen-values with negative real parts and one which is zero. Due to the sign of the 3-D determinant, the zero eigen-value must turn positive for small increases of the parameter $\beta_e$ without change in the stability characteristics of the other two eigen-values. There is thus always a positive value for the Hopf-bifurcation point $\beta_e^H$ of Proposition 3.

### *Proof of Proposition 1*

On the basis of the values assumed for $r_o$, $m_o$ we get from eqn. (5.12) $q_o = 1$ and thus from eqn. (5.11) that the postulated value of $y_o$ (and only this one) indeed sets this dynamic equal to zero Since (5.12) is already shown to be zero, we finally get from (5.13) that $\epsilon = \epsilon_0$ must hold true.

### *Proof of Proposition 2*

It is easy to show (by subtracting the second from the third row, which does not change the entry $J_{33}$) that the determinant of the Jacobian $J$ of the dynamics at the steady state is negative, since it is thereby shown to be the product of the upper principal minor $(J_{11}J_{22} - J_{12}J_{21})$ of order two with the entry $J_{33}$. Due the assumption on the parameter $h_1$ we know that this minor must be positive, while $J_{33}$ is negative if $\beta_{p_e} < 1$ holds true. The other two principal minors of order two are always positive, while all elements forming the trace of $J$ are negative. The coefficients $a_1$, $a_2$, $a_3$ of the Routh–Hurwitz polynomial are thus all positive, and also $a_1 a_2 - a_3$, since $a_3$ is among the products that determine the value of $a_1 a_2$. According to the Routh–Hurwitz Theorem[10] we therefore get the local asymptotic stability asserted in proposition 4.3.

### *Proof of Proposition 3*

When we assume $\beta_{p_e} > 1$ the Jacobian $J$, which was (qualitatively) given by

$$J = \begin{pmatrix} J_{11} & J_{12} & J_{13} \\ J_{21} & J_{22} & J_{23} \\ J_{31} & J_{32} & J_{33} \end{pmatrix} = \begin{pmatrix} - & + & 0 \\ - & - & + \\ - & - & - \end{pmatrix},$$

is changed to a positive value for $J_{33}$, given by $\beta_e(\beta_{p_e} - 1)$. This entry can be made as large as possible without changing the other elements in the trace of $J$. Trace $J$ can therefore be made positive, which overturns the most basic of the Routh–Hurwitz conditions for local asymptotic stability. Since $\det J < 0$ holds under all circumstances, there must therefore exist a first positive value of the parameter $\beta_e$ where the system loses its stability by way of a Hopf-bifurcation (if the speed condition of the Hopf-bifurcation theorem is fulfilled, which it will be).[11] It is furthermore easy to show that both $a_1 = -\text{trace } J$ and $a_2$ are linear function of $\beta_e$ with a negative coefficient in front of this parameter. The product $a_1 a_2$ viewed as a function of $\beta_e$ is therefore a polynomial of degree 2 with a positive coefficient in front of $\beta_e^2$ which is characterized by the graphical features shown in Figure 5.5, since it must have zeros to the right of the vertical axis.

We see that $a_1 a_2 (\beta_e)$ is positive for small $\beta_e$ and must cut the horizontal axis together with either *trace J* or $a_2$ as shown. The order in which the trace of *J* and the sum of principal minors of order two $a_2$ cut the horizontal axis may however be just the opposite. Yet, this does not really matter, since the Hopf-bifurcation must occur when $b = a_1 a_2 - a_3$ becomes zero, i.e., when the linear function det *J* cuts the $a_1 a_2$ curve (as shown) which must be the case before the zeros of the polynomial $a_1 a_2$ occur. This proves assertion 4.3.

### *Proof of Proposition 4*

Obvious from Figure 5.5. This concludes the proof of proposition 4.

We conjecture, which of course can be checked by means of numerical simulations solely, that there is always a large basin of attraction within which all trajectories will converge to the steady state here considered. In the opposite case, where the steady state is locally unstable, the dynamics will generally be totally unstable as well, i.e., the dynamics are then diverging away from the steady state without bound.

In such a case it is natural to assume that speeds of adjustment in the market for shares become smaller than 1 once the system has departed to a sufficient degree from the steady state solution, due to the view that agents will react more cautiously in such a situation, reducing the volume of transactions on the stock market and thus increasing the stability of the adjustment processes on this market. Speeds of adjustment are thus assumed to become less than 1 far away from the steady state which implies that the system then moves back into the direction of the steady state making the dynamic system a bounded and thus a viable one if this happens.

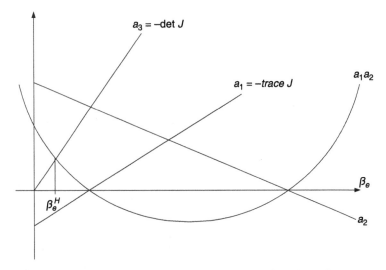

*Figure 5.5* A graphical characterization of the Hopf-bifurcation point.

A simple example of such bounded dynamics is provided by the following modification of the dynamics (5.11)–(5.13) (which we use as a simplification of the phase diagram switching methodology briefly considered in Section 5.2 of this chapter).[12]

$$\dot{y} = \beta_y (c(y - \delta - t) + i(q - 1) + \delta + n + g - y), \tag{5.14}$$

$$\hat{q} = \beta_{p_e} \{ c_0 \ tanh \ [c_1 \frac{(1-v)y-\delta}{q} + \epsilon - (r_0 + \frac{ky-m}{h_1} + \xi))] \}, \tag{5.15}$$

$$\dot{\epsilon} = \beta_\epsilon (\beta_{p_e} \{ c_0 \ tanh \ [c_1 \frac{(1-v)\ y-\delta}{q} + \epsilon$$

$$- (r_0 + \frac{ky-m}{h_1} + \xi))] \} - (\epsilon - \epsilon_o )), \tag{5.16}$$

where the expression $X = c_0 \ tanh \ [c_1 (\frac{(1-v)y-\delta}{q} + \epsilon - (r_0 + \frac{ky-m}{h_1} + \xi))]$ is to be interpreted as excess demand $X$ (limited by $-c_0$ and $c_0$) which in turn is driving share prices $p_e$ with speed $\beta_{p_e}$. Such a modification of the dynamics (5.11)–(5.13) should make them globally bounded and indeed viable from the economic point of view in the case where the steady state is a repeller. We leave this point again for later numerical simulations of these dynamics.[13]

Let us return however to the only intrinsically non-linear form of the dynamics, the system (5.11)–(5.13). The model to be estimated[14] on the basis of this approximation of the full 4-D dynamics (which suppresses the fluctuations in $K$, $E$, $m$ and the accelerator term in the share price dynamics) thus reads in the parameters to be estimated:

$$\dot{y} = \beta_y (-a_y y + b_y q + c_y), \tag{5.17}$$

$$\hat{q} = \beta_{p_e} ((a_\pi y - c_\pi)/q + \epsilon - (a_m y - b_m m + c_m)), \tag{5.18}$$

$$\dot{\epsilon} = \beta_\epsilon (\beta_{p_e} ((a_\pi y - c_\pi)/q + \epsilon - (a_m y - b_m m + c_m)) - (\epsilon - \epsilon_o )). \tag{5.19}$$

This is the core dynamics[15] of the Blanchard real–financial interaction between the output to capital ratio $y$, Tobin's $q$ and capital gains expectations, to be augmented later on again by the additional aspects we have removed here from the dynamics. In formal terms this system is identical to the short-run version of the Blanchard model, though of a growing nature now as far as extensive form variables are concerned. Depending on the length of the period that to be investigated there may be a trend in the evolution of the data $y = Y/K$ and $q = const \cdot p_e/p$ used for the estimation that has to be taken care of. Furthermore, the unobservable variable $\epsilon$ has to be substituted by observable magnitudes to allow estimation of the model, see Appendix II in this regard. Finally, the model has to be transferred to a discrete time representation by means of the Euler method which basically replaces differential quotients by difference quotients in a straightforward way. Theory suggests that all parameters $a$, $b$, $c$, etc. in the above dynamics should be positive when estimated.

## 5.7 Conclusions

We have considered in this chapter an extension of the Blanchard (1981) approach to output dynamics, the stock market and interest rates that integrated the budget equation of firms and the implications of investment for capital stock growth, but continued to use two other of his simplifications. These simplifications concerned the use of dynamic multiplier analysis in the place of a fully developed Metzlerian inventory accelerator mechanism and the assumption that only stock market dynamics, but not yet long-term interest rates, influence the investment behavior of firms.[16] The investigated dynamics therefore integrated stable multiplier dynamics, a stabilizing Keynes effect and potentially destabilizing stock market dynamics, a situation that gives rise to (in) stability of the jump-variable type when married with the assumptions of perfect asset substitution and myopic perfect foresight. Relaxing these two assumptions, however, we could show various propositions on local asymptotic stability and instability that can be used as foundation for the phase diagram switching methodology introduced in Chiarella et al. (2000b).

Our main interest in the present chapter, however, was to simplify the obtained 4-D growth dynamics by appropriate assumptions of secondary order such that the dynamic format of the Blanchard (1981) model as employed in Chiarella et al. (2002) could be recovered, now however on the basis of variables which allow for long-run stationarity. In this way the chapter provided an alternative approach to the one used in Chiarella et al. (2002) and should be made the subject of the same type of empirical analysis as performed there. Finally, our growth framework guaranteed, in contrast to the Blanchard model and its reformulation in Chiarella et al. (2002), that there was only one interior steady state of the obtained reduced 3-D dynamics. This steady state exhibited stability characteristics which resembled the general 4-D dynamics from which this chapter started.

## Appendix I: model equations

The following equations describe aggregate demand, disposable income, the savings of households, the government and firms as well as aggregate savings, fiscal policy rules (government expenditure and taxation rules), the laws of motion of output and share prices, money market equilibrium, including the definition of the steady state rate of interest, capital gain expectations, capital accumulation, the new issue of equities according to the budget equation of firms, Tobin's average $q$ and given labor and capital productivity indices.

$$Y^d = cY^D + (i(q-1)+\delta+n)K + G \qquad (5.20)$$

$$Y^D = Y - \delta K + rB/p - T = \omega L^d + \Pi + rB/p - T \qquad (5.21)$$

$$\Pi = (1-v)Y - \delta K$$

$$S_p = (1-c)Y^D = (\dot{M} + \dot{B} + p_e\dot{E})/p, \ \dot{M} = \bar{\mu}M \tag{5.22}$$

$$-S_g = G + rB/p - T = (\dot{M} + \dot{B})/p, \quad \dot{M} = \bar{\mu}M \tag{5.23}$$

$$S_f = 0 \tag{5.24}$$

$$S = S_p + S_q + S_g = p_e\dot{E}/p = I \tag{5.25}$$

$$G/K = \text{const} = g \tag{5.26}$$

$$T/K = t + rB/(pK), \quad t = \text{const} \tag{5.27}$$

$$\dot{Y} = \beta_y(Y^d - Y) + nY \tag{5.28}$$

$$\hat{p}_e = \beta_{p_e}\left(\frac{(1-v)pY - \delta pK}{p_eE} + \epsilon - r\right) + \kappa_{p_e}\epsilon + (1 - \kappa_{p_e})\epsilon_o \tag{5.29}$$

$$M = kpY + h_1(r_0 - r)pK \tag{5.30}$$

$$r_0 = (1-v)\left(\frac{Y}{K}\right)_0 - \delta + \epsilon_o$$

$$\left(\frac{Y}{K}\right)_0 = y_0 = \frac{1}{1-c}(g + \delta + n - c(t + \delta))$$

$$\dot{\epsilon} = \beta_e(\hat{p}_e - \epsilon) \tag{5.31}$$

$$\hat{K} = I/K = i(q-1) + n \tag{5.32}$$

$$\dot{E} = pI/p_e \tag{5.33}$$

$$q = p_eE/(pK) \tag{5.34}$$

$$x = Y/L^d = \text{const} \tag{5.35}$$

$$y^p = Y^p/K = \text{const.} \tag{5.36}$$

## Appendix II: substituting unobservables through observables

To allow for an estimation of the dynamics (5.17)–(5.19):[17]

$$\dot{y} = \beta_y(-a_y y + b_y q + c_y), \quad y = Y/K$$

$$\hat{q} = \beta_{p_e}((a_\pi y - c_\pi)/q + \epsilon - (a_m y - b_m m + c_m + \xi)), \quad q = \text{const} \cdot p_e/p$$

$$\dot{\epsilon} = \beta_\epsilon(\beta_{p_e}((a_\pi y - c_\pi)/q + \epsilon - (a_m y - b_m m + c_m + \xi)) - (\epsilon - \epsilon_o))$$

we have to reformulate this system such that the unobservable variable $\epsilon$ is removed from explicit consideration. To this end we introduce the new state variable $\varepsilon = \hat{q}$ and solve the law of motion for $q$ with respect to the expectational variable $\epsilon$. This gives

$$\epsilon = \varepsilon/\beta_{p_e} + r(y) + \xi - \rho(y)/q.$$

By differentiating this equation with respect to time we furthermore get

$$\dot{\epsilon} = \dot{\varepsilon}/\beta_{p_e} + r'(y)\dot{y} - \rho'(y)\dot{y}/q + (\rho(y)/q)\varepsilon.$$

These two equations can be inserted into the law of motion for capital gains expectations

$$\dot{\epsilon} = \beta_\epsilon(\varepsilon - (\epsilon - \epsilon_o))$$

and give rise to

$$\dot{\varepsilon} = \beta_\epsilon((\beta_{p_e} - 1)\varepsilon + \beta_{p_e}(\rho(y)/q - r(y) - \xi) + \beta_{p_e}\epsilon_o)$$
$$+ \beta_{p_e}(\rho'(y)\dot{y}/q - (\rho(y)/q)\varepsilon - r'(y)\dot{y}).$$

Inserting now the law of motion for $y$:

$$\dot{y} = \beta_y(-a_y y + b_y q + c_y)$$

into this last equations provides us finally with a differential equation for $\varepsilon$ which depends on $y$, $q$, $\varepsilon$ and thus on observable magnitudes throughout. Taken together we thus have transformed the laws of motion to be estimated into a system of three autonomous differential equation of order 1 in the state variables $y$, $q$, $\varepsilon$ with $\dot{\varepsilon}$ as derived above and with

$$\dot{y} = \beta_y(-a_y y + b_y q + c_y), \quad \hat{q} = \varepsilon$$

as the other two laws of motion. We note that the law of motion for $q$ is now much simpler in outlook, but this at the cost of third dynamical equation which now contains all the complexities of the dynamics.

# 6 Inflation and perfect foresight
## Implications of non-linearity

## 6.1 Introduction

Prior to the publication of Sargent and Wallace (1973), monetary growth models with perfect foresight were plagued by a well-known instability problem.[1] The problem may be seen most clearly in the simplest case in which output and the real rate of interest are treated as exogenous and the money supply is held constant. In this case, under the assumption that movements in the price level are continuous, a model of price dynamics in which money market equilibrium depends negatively on inflationary expectations, and in which perfect foresight and continuous market clearing are assumed, gives rise to a unique steady state equilibrium which is globally unstable. The following log linear specification for the demand for real balances is used by Sargent and Wallace to illustrate the point:

$$\ln\left(\frac{M}{P}\right) = \alpha\pi, \ \alpha < 0 \tag{6.1}$$

where $M$ denotes the stock of money, $P$ the price level, and $\pi$ the expected rate of inflation. If it is assumed that the relation (6.1) holds continuously, and that expectations are characterized by perfect foresight, then (6.1) may be written as:

$$\dot{p} = (1/\alpha)[m - p]$$

where lower case letters denote logarithms. Since $\alpha$ is negative, this one-dimensional linear differential equation implies global instability of its steady state: a slight perturbation away from equilibrium triggers a process of ever-accelerating inflation or deflation, if it is assumed that the price level moves continuously in the face of shocks to the money supply. We have the paradoxical result that a sudden *increase* in the money supply sets off an ever-accelerating *deflation*. Likewise, a downward shift in the money supply leads to accelerating inflation.

These properties are both counter-intuitive and counter-factual. Sargent and Wallace (1973) proposed a solution to the problem by relaxing the assumption that prices move continuously in the face of a monetary shock and adding the assumption that "the public expects that, if *m* were to be constant over time, a process of ever-accelerating inflation or deflation would eventually come to an end, if only in the very remote future" (p.1045). If this terminal condition is to be satisfied, then the only response of the economy to a monetary shock is an instantaneous *jump* in the price level to restore money market equilibrium. By thus imposing a terminal condition on the price dynamics and relaxing the continuity assumption, Sargent and Wallace were able to obtain a solution to the instability problem. Gray and Turnovsky (1979) took the argument a step further, exploiting the saddlepoint property of a two dimensional differential equation system to argue that in response to a shock displacing the equilibrium, the (discontinuous) price variable jumps to the stable manifold of the new system, and the trajectory subsequently converges gradually to the new steady state equilibrium. Again the justification offered for the jump is that in its absence, the saddlepoint property of the equilibrium would imply that trajectories not originating on the stable manifold would lead eventually to the violation of the condition that "the long-run level of the real money stock is strictly positive and finite" (p.650). This *jump variable* technique, based on the postulate that prices move discontinuously in response to shocks, has since become a standard practice in macroeconomic modeling, so much so that the attempt to rationalize it by reference to some possibly remote future is not even deemed necessary in contemporary work.[2]

The basic issues and the merits of this approach have been summarized recently in Turnovsky (1995, Ch.3) and thus need not be repeated here. In his chapter, Turnovsky however also states that rational expectations or myopic perfect foresight models need not necessarily lead to such a result.

> Rather, it is the combination of rational expectations *and* continuous market clearance that gives rise to this phenomenon. It is possible to restore stability (in the traditional sense) by coupling the assumption of rational expectations with sluggish adjustment in the money market.
>
> (Turnovsky 1995, p.76)

To show this, Turnovsky (1995, p.76) extends the model (2) by allowing for a sluggishly adjusting price level and finds as stability condition – directly analogous to the Cagan condition of the adaptive expectations case – that the product of the semi-elasticity of the demand for money times the adjustment speed of the price level must be less than 1. He concludes that "the rationale for jumps in the price level ... lose some of their force" thereby.

It is important to recognize here that the original justification for the jump-variable technique is only valid for *linear* models, where local instability is sufficient to ensure that all trajectories not originating on a stable manifold will eventually become unbounded. Non-linear models do not have this feature in general: all trajectories may be bounded even if there is a unique locally unstable equilibrium. Furthermore the above conclusion of Turnovsky on the implications of myopic perfect foresight in the presence of a gradually adjusting price level are also based on loglinearity (and eigen-value calculations) solely.

It will be argued below that a modification of Turnovsky's (1995, p.76) loglinear disequilibrium model to allow for non-linear money demand provides a dramatically different and, in our view, more satisfactory solution to the instability problem. First, it is shown as in Turnovsky (1995) that without continuous market clearing, the instability of price dynamics is not guaranteed, and that a sufficiently sluggish adjustment of prices can give rise to a globally stable price dynamics. Second, it is argued that even if the price dynamics are locally unstable, a suitable non-linear specification for money demand, motivated by portfolio considerations as in Chiarella (1990), is sufficient to ensure that trajectories always remain bounded. The price dynamics converges in this case to a stable limit cycle and are characterized – if adjustment of the price level becomes very fast – by so-called *relaxation oscillations*.

With bounded trajectories, the terminal conditions invoked by Sargent and Wallace are neither necessary to ensure boundedness of trajectories, nor justified by reference to a remote future. In the non-linear disequilibrium model considered here, the response of the economy to a shock in the money supply is a jump in *inflation* and not in prices. Prices move continuously at all times. Moreover, if the shock to the money supply is sufficiently large, then an increase in *m* is shown unambiguously to *raise* the rate of inflation in the short run while a decrease unambiguously lowers inflation. These results are both intuitively and empirically appealing.

## 6.2 Non-linear money demand and inflation

To introduce the possibility of non-linear money demand into the model of Turnovsky (1995, p.76), equation (6.1) may be rewritten as:

$$\ln\left(\frac{M}{P}\right) = \alpha(\pi).$$

The function $\alpha : \mathcal{R} \to \mathcal{R}$ is assumed to be continuously differentiable at all points. This function is linear in Sargent and Wallace (1973) and Turnovsky (1995), whereas in Chiarella (1990) its is assumed to be non-linear, satisfying the properties:

*Assumption 1*

$\alpha(0) = 0$, $\alpha' < 0$, $\lim_{\pi \to \infty} \alpha(\pi) = -l > -\infty$, *and*

$\lim_{\pi \to -\infty} \alpha(\pi) = u < \infty$, *where l and u are positive constants.*

The non-linear specification is justified by Chiarella on the basis of portfolio considerations, which place bounds on the extent to which agents can economize on (or accumulate) real balances even when the price level is expected to change very rapidly. Note that the assumption $\alpha(0) = 0$ is made without loss of generality, since units of measurement for $P$ may be chosen such that the demand for real balances equals unity whenever the expected rate of inflation is zero. To allow for disequilibrium in the money market, the rate of change of prices is made to depend on the excess demand for real balances in the following way:

$$\dot{p} = b_p[m - p - \alpha(\pi)]. \tag{6.2}$$

The above specification is used by Chiarella (1986), and is the non-linear equivalent of the adjustment process which appears in Goldman (1972) and Turnovsky (1995); see also Flaschel (1993). Imposing the perfect foresight condition, the following equation is obtained:[3]

$$\dot{p} = b_p[m - p - \alpha(\dot{p})]. \tag{6.3}$$

Unlike the linear case studied by Sargent and Wallace, relation (6.3) does not admit an explicit solution expressing $\dot{p}$ in terms of $p$. In order to examine the dynamics that are implicitly defined by this relation, we first represent prices as a function of the rate of inflation by rearranging (6.3) as follows:

$$p = f(\dot{p}) = m - \alpha(\dot{p}) - \dot{p}/b_p. \tag{6.4}$$

The function $f: \mathcal{R} \rightarrow \mathcal{R}$ is continuously differentiable at all points, since $\alpha(\cdot)$ is. In addition, it satisfies the following properties:

### Lemma 1

*Suppose Assumption 1 holds. Then:*

1. $\lim_{x \rightarrow \infty} f(x) = -\infty = -\lim_{x \rightarrow -\infty} f(x),$

2. $f'(0) > 0 \ (< 0)$ *if and only if* $|\alpha'(0)| > 1/b_p \ m(|\alpha'(0)| < 1/b_p).$

Hence $f(\cdot)$ has a negative slope at points sufficiently distant from the origin, and has a negative slope at the origin if and only if the effect of inflation on the demand for real balances in equilibrium (as measured by $|\alpha'(0)|$) is sufficiently weak relative to the reciprocal of the speed $b_p$ at which prices respond to money market disequilibrium. Alternatively, if price adjustment is sufficiently rapid, or if the effect of inflation on desired real balances is sufficiently strong, then the function $f(\cdot)$ is upward sloping at the origin. It is convenient for expositional purposes to impose the following further restrictions on $\alpha(\cdot)$:

### Assumption 2

$\alpha''(\dot{p}) < 0 \ (> 0)$ *whenever* $\dot{p} < 0 \ (> 0).$

This assumption states simply that the effect of changes in inflation on desired real balances ($|\alpha'(\dot{p})|$) is lower at higher rates of inflation or deflation. In other words, a given change in inflation has a greater effect on desired real balances when it occurs at low levels of inflation or deflation than otherwise. This assumption allows us to illustrate the price dynamics geometrically, since it ensures that the function $f(\cdot)$ is either monotonic decreasing, or has exactly two turning points:

## Lemma 2

*Suppose Assumptions 1 and 2 hold.*
*If $f'(0) < 0$ then $f'(x) < 0$ for all $x \in \Re$.*
*If $f'(0) > 0$ then there exist $a, b \in \Re$ such that $a < 0 < b$, $f'(x) > 0$ for all $x \in (a, b)$, $f'(x) < 0$ for all $x < a$, and $f'(x) < 0$ for all $x > b$.*

## Proof

Under Assumption 2, $\alpha''(\dot{p}) < 0 \ (> 0)$ whenever $\dot{p} < 0 \ (> 0)$ as required. Then $|\alpha'(\dot{p})|$ declines monotonically as $\dot{p}$ moves away from the origin. Observe further that $\lim_{x \to \infty} \alpha'(x) = \lim_{x \to -\infty} \alpha'(x) = 0$ as a consequence of the boundedness conditions on $f$ stated in Lemma 1. At any turning point of $f(\dot{p})$, it must be the case that $|\alpha'(\dot{p})| = 1/b_p$. If $f'(0) < 0$, then $|\alpha'(0)| < 1/b_p$ from part (b) of the Lemma, so that $|\alpha'| < 1/b_p$ everywhere and there can be no turning point. If $f'(0) > 0$, then $|\alpha'(0)| > 1/b_p$. Since $\lim_{x \to \infty} \alpha'(x) = \lim_{x \to \infty} \alpha'(x) = 0$ and $|\alpha'(\dot{p})|$ declines monotonically as $\dot{p}$ moves away from the origin, there must be exactly two turning points in this case, one on either side of the origin. Let these points be denoted by $a$ and $b$ respectively. Then continuity of $f(\cdot)$ in conjunction with part (a) of the Lemma ensures that there is a maximum at $b$ and a minimum at $a$.

Lemma 2 distinguishes between two cases, which are illustrated in Figure 6.1. When $f'(0) < 0$, the function $f'(\cdot)$ is monotonic decreasing, and the dynamics implicit in the equation (6.4) may be determined in a straightforward manner:

## Proposition 1

*Suppose Assumptions 1 and 2 hold. If $|\alpha'(0)| < 1/b_p$, then relation (6.4) implicitly defines a differential equation $\dot{p} = f^{-1}(p)$ with a unique equilibrium at $p = m$ that is globally asymptotically stable.*

If price adjustments are sufficiently rapid so that $|\alpha'(0)| < 1/b_p$, the function $f(\cdot)$ defined in (6.4) will no longer be invertible, and $\dot{p}$ is no longer uniquely determined at all values of $p$. In order to make the dynamics determinate, relation (6.4) must be augmented by some further assumption. The following assumption is accordingly made:

## Assumption 3

*The price level $p(t)$ is everywhere continuous, and the rate of inflation $\dot{p}(t)$ is continuous except at points where the function $f$ is noninvertible (points B and D in Figure 6.1).*

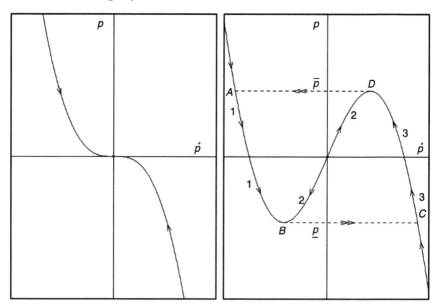

*Figure 6.1* Price dynamics and perfect foresight: some scenarios.

The assumption of continuity in price movements stands in sharp contrast to the assumption of *discontinuity* in price movements that characterizes the jump-variable technique. Without continuity in price movements, there would be points in time at which the inflation rate is infinite. This is both counterfactual and methodologically unappealing. Even when price movements are extremely rapid there is a dynamic adjustment process by means of which prices move from one position to another and the stability of this process needs to be established independently. It is for this reason that price level continuity was a standard assumption prior to Sargent and Wallace (1973). The continuity assumption led to absurd results (global instability) only because it was imposed on a *linear* model, as we establish below. In the Sargent/Wallace solution to the global instability problem, the centrifugal forces driving prices away from the steady state were effectively removed by assuming that the system was always at the point of rest, even when this point itself was displaced by a monetary shock.

This assumption on the continuity and smoothness of price movements makes the price dynamics determinate even in the locally unstable case:

### Proposition 2

> *Suppose Assumptions 1–3 hold. If $|\alpha'(0)| > 1/b_p$, then the unique equilibrium at $p = m$ is locally unstable, and for all initial conditions $p_0 \neq m$ trajectories satisfying (6.4) converge to a unique limit cycle.*

This scenario is illustrated on the right-hand side of Figure 6.1. The system is now characterized by three differential equations defined over the domains $[\underline{p},\infty)$, $[\underline{p}, \overline{p}]$, and $(-\infty, \overline{p}]$ respectively (denoted *1*, *2* and *3* in the figure). For $p < \underline{p}$ the system must be in state *3* with prices rising and for $p > \overline{p}$ the system must be in state *1* with prices falling. The limiting trajectory is characterized by the cycle *ABCD* which involves *jumps* in $\dot{p}$ between *BC* and *DA*. Note that the jumps are in the rate of inflation and not in the price level. Price movements are continuous at all times, although the time series of prices is not differentiable at all points. Even if the equilibrium is locally unstable, therefore, all trajectories remain bounded. If the differential equation *2* is valid at some point in time (for instance due to a small displacement from the steady state), then $p$ moves towards either $\underline{p}$ or $\overline{p}$. At $\underline{p}$ ($\overline{p}$) the dynamical law switches to state *3 (1)* and future movements lie on the unique limit cycle.

To summarize, the dynamics defined by equation (6.4) are characterized by a unique equilibrium at $p = m$. The local stability of this equilibrium depends on the sign of $f'(0)$. As a direct consequence of Lemma 1, the equilibrium will be stable (unstable) provided that the slope $|a'(0)|$ is less (greater) than $1/b_p$. For any given function $a(\cdot)$, therefore, the unique equilibrium will be *stable* if the speed of price adjustment as measured by $b_p$ is sufficiently *slow*. If, on the other hand, price adjustment is sufficiently *fast*, all trajectories originating at other than the equilibrium point converge to a unique attracting periodic orbit.

## 6.3 Monetary shocks and the emergence of relaxation oscillations

Having defined the model and examined its stability properties, we turn to the important question of how the economy responds to an unanticipated monetary shock. As above, the assumption that price movements are always continuous is maintained. In the stable case, depicted on the left side of Figure 6.1, the effects are easy to trace. An unanticipated upward shift in the money supply shifts the entire schedule $f(p)$ upwards so that the current price is below its equilibrium value. In order to maintain consistency with perfect foresight as well as continuity of the price level, there has to be an upward shift in the *rate of inflation* $\dot{p}$. The inflation drives the price towards its new equilibrium over time, and slows as the equilibrium is approached. The case of a downward movement in the money supply is analogous, setting off a deflation which drives the price to its new (lower) equilibrium level.

### *Proposition 3*

*Suppose Assumptions 1–3 hold, that $|a'(0)| < 1/b_p$, and that the economy is initially at the unique, globally asymptotically stable equilibrium. Then an unanticipated upward (downward) shift in the money supply leads to an upward (downward) shift in the rate of inflation.*

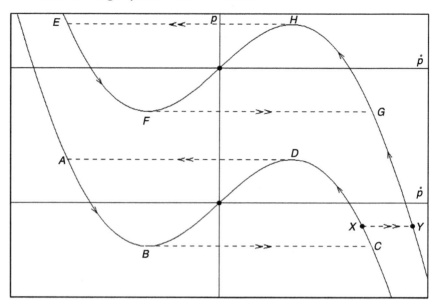

*Figure 6.2* Effect of an unanticipated monetary shock.

The case in which the equilibrium with constant prices is locally unstable is less straightforward. Consider first a shift in the money supply that is sufficiently large, so that the lower turning point of the new schedule is above the upper turning point of the old schedule. This is the case depicted in Figure 6.2, where the old limiting trajectory is *ABCD* while the new (post-shift) attractor is *EFGH*. The result of such a shift in the money supply is exactly the same as in the case of a stable equilibrium: there is an upward jump in the rate of inflation. This is depicted in the figure as a jump from the point *X* on the old schedule to the point *Y* on the new one. However, the argument applies irrespective of which point on the attractor *ABCD* the economy is at when the money supply shift occurs, since price continuity and perfect foresight can only be maintained with an unambiguous shift of $\dot{p}$ to the right, that is, by an unambiguous rise in inflation. This inflation drives the price upward over time until the new attractor *EFGH* is reached, after which the relaxation oscillations resume. Note that the long-run effect of the money supply rise is a higher average price level, while the short-run effect is a rise in the rate of inflation. Again no jumps in prices are required. The case of a downward shift in the money stock, if sufficiently large, leads unambiguously to a deflation, and in the long-run to a lower average price level, again without requiring discontinuous price movements. This may be stated as:

### Proposition 4

> *Suppose Assumptions 1–3 hold, that $|\alpha'(0)| > 1/b_p$, and that the economy is initially on the unique, globally attracting limit cycle. Then*

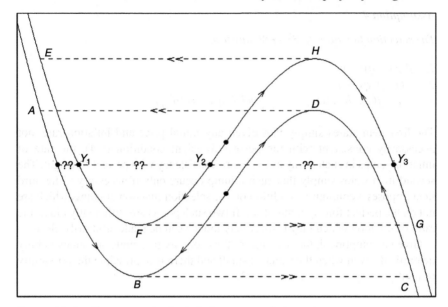

*Figure 6.3* Small monetary shocks: inflation response indeterminacy.

> *a sufficiently large unanticipated upward (downward) shift in the money supply leads to an upward (downward) shift in the rate of inflation.*

Finally, consider the case in which the monetary shock is small, so that there is more than one possible change in the rate of inflation which could restore consistency with the perfect foresight condition (6.4). This is the case illustrated in Figure 6.3. If the economy is initially at state $X$ and is subject to an upward shift in the money supply, there are three possible responses which can restore consistency with perfect foresight without requiring jumps in prices. These are shown as $Y_1$, $Y_2$, and $Y_3$ in the figure. In this particular case all three possibilities require an upward shift in inflation, but it is easy to see that this need not always be the case. If the monetary shock is sufficiently small, it may give rise to either an inflationary or a deflationary response under perfect foresight when the equilibrium is locally unstable.

The indeterminacy arises because whenever the economy is not on the manifold defined by relation (6.4), there are up to three possible ways of getting there by appropriate jumps in the rate of inflation. In order to choose among these possibilities, it is necessary to specify a *selection criterion* which associates with any point $(p, q)$ in $\Re^2$, a *unique* point $\dot{p}$ such that $(p, \dot{p})$ lies on the manifold defined by (6.4). Alternatively, given any price level and inflation rate (not necessarily on the perfect foresight manifold), there is a unique point on the manifold to which the rate of inflation jumps. Define this function as $\psi(p, q)$. We assume the following:

**Assumption 4**

*The selection function* $\psi: \mathfrak{R}^2 \to \mathfrak{R}$ *satisfies:*

1. $f(\psi\,(p,\,q)) = p$.
2. $\psi(f\,(q),\,q) = q$.
3. *If* $p \neq f(q)$, *then* $\lim_{(p',\,q') \to (p,\,q)} \psi\,(p',\,q') = \psi\,(p,\,q)$.

The first item states simply that given any initial price and inflation rate, not necessarily consistent with the perfect foresight condition (6.4), the rate of inflation jumps in such a way as to restore consistency with perfect foresight. The second item states simply that such a jump occurs only if necessary.[4] The third item imposes a continuity condition on the selection function at points which are not on the perfect foresight manifold: If two such points are sufficiently close, the rates of inflation which they respectively induce can be made arbitrarily close.

Given assumption 4, the response of the economy to a monetary shock is fully determinate even when the shock is small and there is in principle the possibility of multiple responses as in Figure 6.3.

**Proposition 5**

*Suppose Assumptions 1–4 hold. Then an unanticipated upward (downward) shift in the money supply leads to an upward (downward) shift in the rate of inflation.*

The reason this holds is because of the assumed continuity of the rate of inflation in the instantaneous out-of-equilibrium state which an unanticipated monetary shock induces. Since large upward shifts in the money supply *must* give rise to an inflationary response by Proposition 4, this must also be the case for slightly smaller shifts, by continuity, and so on even for very small shocks. In terms of Figure 6.3, an upward shift in the money supply with the economy initially at $X$ causes a movement to $Y_3$, which corresponds to higher inflation. The case of monetary contraction is analogous. In terms of Figure 6.3, with the economy initially at $Y_1$, a reduction in money supply leads to a deflationary leftward shift to $X$ rather than an inflationary shift to the right. Though the latter possibility would be entirely consistent with perfect foresight, it is inconsistent with the continuity condition in Assumption 4 above.[5]

## 6.4 Monetary growth and inflation

The model so far has been based on the assumption that the long-run rate of monetary growth, and hence the long-run rate of inflation, is zero. If this were not the case, then equation (6.2) would imply persistent money market disequilibrium even in the steady state when $\dot{m} = \dot{p} = \pi = \mu > 0$. In order to generalize the framework to allow for persistent monetary growth, consider the following specification:

$$\dot{p} = b_p[m - p - \alpha(\pi)] + \eta\pi + (1-\eta)\pi_a \qquad (6.5)$$

where $\pi$ is the expected short-run rate of inflation as before, and $\pi_a$ is the average or long-run rate of inflation. The rate of change of current prices is therefore assumed to depend not simply on the extent of current money market disequilibrium, but also on a weighted average of expectations regarding short- and long-term inflation rates, with the weight being represented by $\eta \in [0,1]$. Unlike the specification (6.2), which is restricted to the case of a fixed money supply, the above relation is consistent with steady state monetary growth at any fixed rate $\mu$. Specifically, along the steady state path, $\hat{M} = \dot{m} = \dot{p} = \pi = \mu$, with equilibrium real balances being given by $\alpha(\mu)$. Assume the following simple money supply rule:

$$\dot{m} = \mu.$$

In addition, assume that short-run expectations are characterized by myopic perfect foresight, so that $\pi = \dot{p}$. This occurs as the limiting case of the following adaptive expectation revision rule:

$$\dot{\pi} = \beta_\pi(\dot{p} - \pi)$$

as the parameter $\beta_\pi$ tends to infinity. Assume further that the expected long-run rate of inflation is equal to the steady state inflation rate so that $\pi_a = \mu$. This again is a special case of the following expectation revision rule, referred to as *asymptotically rational expectations* by Stein (1982):

$$\dot{\pi}_a = \beta_a(\mu - \pi_a)$$

as the parameter $\beta_a$ tends to infinity. Substituting $\pi = \dot{p}$ and $\pi_a = \mu$ in (6.5) yields:

$$\dot{p} = b_p[m - p - \alpha(\dot{p})] + \eta\dot{p} + (1-\eta)\mu.$$

Defining $p_m = p - m$, the above equation implies:

$$\dot{p}_m = \tilde{\beta}_p(-p_m - \alpha(\dot{p}_m + \mu)),$$

where $\tilde{\beta}_p = \beta_p/(1-\eta)$.

This equation must be used in the place of equation (3) to generalize – without change in substance – the results we have obtained for a stationary money supply to the case where money supply is growing at the constant rate $\mu$. Note however that the size of the limit cycles we obtain thereby will depend on the size of the parameter $\eta$; they will become the larger the closer this parameter is to 1. Note also that the inclusion of the $\pi_a$ term into the price dynamics (5) allows for a simple inclusion of anticipated monetary shocks into our framework if the value of $\pi_a$ depends on them (through its dependence on the growth rate of the money supply $\mu$ as was suggested above).

## 6.5 Conclusions

The main purpose of this chapter has been to make three points. First, the dynamic instability problem in monetary growth models which gave rise to the ingenious device of the jump variable technique may be solved in a very different manner by appealing to plausible non-linearities in monetary demand. Second, the presence of such non-linearities gives rise to bounded trajectories even when the unique equilibrium is locally unstable. This feature brings into question the backward induction arguments that are commonly advanced in support of the jump-variable technique. Third, monetary shocks in the non-linear model cause discontinuous shifts not in prices but in the rate of inflation. This result is both more plausible and more intuitive than the discontinuous price movements that arise in models based on the jump variable technique.

One shortcoming of the simple framework developed here for a new treatment of monetary growth is that it deals with anticipated shocks only in a preliminary way. This is because the demand for money is made to depend only on current inflation, so that the influence of long-term forecasts (which may be shifted by announcements of future policy) does not play a role there. In order to take adequate account of such effects, it is necessary to model money demand in a more sophisticated and explicitly forward looking manner. This is beyond the scope of the present methodological chapter.

# 7 Determinacy in the New-Keynesian sticky wage/price model

## 7.1 Introduction

A basic extension of the standard New-Keynesian model, which is constituted by a (purely) forward-looking price Phillips curve, a dynamic IS equation and a monetary policy rule, is concerned with an integration of labor markets. Introducing imperfect competition and staggered nominal wage setting in these markets, they can be treated in an analogous way to the goods markets; see Erceg et al. (2000), Woodford (2003, Ch.6), or Galí (2008, Ch.6). In its reduced form, the model now contains four dynamic variables: output gap, price inflation and wage inflation on the one hand, which are non-predetermined variables, and the real wage gap on the other hand, which is a predetermined variable.

As the model is formulated in discrete time, uniqueness of a stationary equilibrium requires that three eigen-values of a suitable $4 \times 4$ matrix lie outside, and one inside the unit circle. From the numerical investigations to be found in the literature one can infer that this determinacy causes no problems once a modified Taylor principle is satisfied, which says that the central bank adjusts the nominal interest rate more than one-for-one in response to variations in any arbitrarily weighted average of price and wage inflation (Galí 2008, p.128). A mathematical proof supporting this numerical knowledge is, however, not available. It also seems hard to achieve in general, given that already the conditions for all four eigen-values to lie on either side of the unit circle are fairly complicated (see Samuelson's or the Cohn–Schur conditions compiled in Gandolfo (2009, Sec.7.4)).

Prospects of analytical tractability appear to improve if the model were conceived in continuous time, so that three eigen-values of suitable matrix would have to lie in the right half of the complex plane and the fourth one in the left half. An *a priori* preference for continuous time on the basis of mathematical reasons fits in with a methodological precept that was put forward by Duncan Foley several decades ago: *"No substantive prediction or explanation of a well-defined macroeconomic period model should depend on the real time length of the period"* (Foley 1975, p.310; his emphasis). Accordingly, the length of the period should be retained as an explicit variable in the mathematical formulation of a period model, and it is to be made sure that it is possible to find meaningful limiting forms of the equations as the period goes to zero. And Foley goes on to state, "In my view, this procedure should be routinely applied as a test that any period model is consistent and well formed where no particular calendar time is specified as the natural period" (ibid., p.311).

In this chapter[1] we follow Foley's maxim and reformulate the sticky wages and prices model as a high-frequency economy with an explicit period of arbitrary length. We will thus confirm that the model indeed passes the test of remaining well-defined as the period shrinks to zero, or the frequency of the agents' (nevertheless staggered) decision-making tends to infinity. It will subsequently be possible to study the four eigen-values of the Jacobian matrix that constitutes the model's continuous time counterpart. Determinacy in this case carries over to the discrete time framework at least if the period length is sufficiently short, and it is in this sense that we can derive conditions for determinacy in the period model. As a matter of fact, they essentially amount to the modified Taylor principle mentioned above.

The chapter extends previous work on the same subject by Flaschel, Groh, Proaño and Semmler (2008) in two ways. First, in their study the high-frequency economy is still formulated in a fairly *ad hoc* manner, whereas it is now rigorously derived from Galí's original model and its structural parameters.[2] The second issue appears rather technical but must nevertheless be treated for completeness. Curiously enough, the determinacy proposition in Flaschel, Franke and Proaño (2008) presupposes a strictly positive output gap coefficient ($\phi_y$) in the central bank's interest rate reaction function. Although the aforementioned 3:1 distribution of the eigen-values will be expected to be preserved if $\phi_y$ approaches zero, this is no general principle. Unfortunately, an inequality relationship in the mathematical proof is no longer valid, and cannot be easily restored, if $\phi_y = 0$ is admitted. The proof that is here presented must therefore, in a major part, follow different lines. In exchange, so to speak, the reasoning becomes less specific to certain favorable conditions in the Jacobian matrix and the basic arguments come out more clearly. Also their potential application to other determinacy problems can be better indicated in this way, so that the present method of proof may be also of some wider interest.

The remainder of the chapter is organized as followed. The next section reiterates the key equations of the New-Keynesian period model. Section 7.3 discusses the general framework for the eigen-value relationships between the high-frequency and continuous time economies. Section 7.4 presents the reformulation of the original model with a variable period, while the determinacy proposition together with an outline of the method of proof is contained in Section 7.5. The mathematical elaboration itself is relegated to an appendix. Section 7.6 gives some numerical evidence of how variations of the period length may affect the determinacy threshold of the sum of the two policy coefficients on wage and price inflation. Section 7.7 concludes.

## 7.2 The period model

The presentation of the key equations of the New-Keynesian model follows Galí (2008, Ch.6). In the main we also adopt his notation, except that we avoid using a tilde. Thus, let $y_t$ be the output gap in period $t$, i.e. the percentage deviation of output from its natural level, and $\omega_t$ the real wage gap, which is the difference between the (log of the) real wage rate and the (log of the) natural real wage. Price and wage inflation are denoted by $\pi_t^p$ and $\pi_t^w$, respectively, the nominal rate of interest is $i_t$ and the natural interest rate $r_t^n$ (they are explicitly supposed to be quarterly rates; cf. Galí, p.52, fn.6). If in addition $u_t$ and $v_t$ designate the model's two exogenous components, Galí's equations (15), (17)–(20) on pp.126f can be reproduced as follows:

$$\pi_t^w = \beta\, E_t[\pi_{t+1}^w] + \kappa_w\, y_t - \lambda_w \omega_t, \tag{7.1}$$

$$\pi_t^p = \beta\, E_t[\pi_{t+1}^p] + \kappa_p\, y_t + \lambda_p \omega_t, \tag{7.2}$$

$$y_t = E_t[y_{t+1}] - \frac{1}{\sigma}\,(i_t - E_t[\pi_{t+1}^p] - r_t^n), \tag{7.3}$$

$$i_t = \rho + \phi_p\, \pi_t^p + \phi_w\, \pi_t^w + \phi_y\, y_t + v_t, \tag{7.4}$$

$$\omega_t = \omega_{t-1} + \pi_t^w - \pi_t^p - u_t. \tag{7.5}$$

All coefficients are constant and positive, apart from the policy coefficients in (7.4), some of which may also attain zero values. The coefficient $\rho$ can be interpreted as the household's discount rate, from which $\beta$ derives as $\ln \beta = -\rho$ (Galí 2008, p.18).

Effectively, the two exogenous variables in the dynamics are $z_{1,t} := v_t - (r_t^n - \rho)$ and $z_{2,t} = u_t$. If the system is to have a solution satisfying $y_t = \pi_t^p = \pi_t^w = 0$ for all $t$, then $z_{1,t}$ and $z_{2,t}$ must vanish (Galí, pp.127f). Assuming this for the rest of the chapter, we are left with the four dynamic variables $x_t := (\pi_t^w, \pi_t^p, y_t, \omega_{t-1})'$. Plugging (7.4) into (7.3) and solving these four equations for the expected values of $x_{t+1}$, the system can be transformed into the representation,

$$E_t[x_{t+1}] = A x_t, \tag{7.6}$$

where $A$ is a suitable $4 \times 4$ matrix. The non-predetermined variables of the model are $\pi_t^w$, $\pi_t^p$ and $y_t$, while the real wage gap $\omega_{t-1}$ of the previous quarter is a predetermined variable. Hence determinacy requires that the matrix $A$ has three eigen-values outside, and one inside, the unit circle.[3] As a result of his numerical analysis, Galí (p.128) asserts that a sufficient (albeit not necessary) condition for this to prevail is the inequality,

$$\phi_w + \phi_p > 1. \tag{7.7}$$

Accordingly, determinacy is guaranteed if the central bank adjusts the nominal interest rate more than one-for-one in response to variations in any arbitrarily weighted average of price and wage inflation. Equation (7.7) is thus an extended version of the famous Taylor principle.

## 7.3 Determinacy and the concept of a variable period length

Let us now consider Foley's axiom mentioned in the introduction, though still at a general level. Given a fixed a time unit, we will refer to a dynamic system as an *h*-economy if its period has length *h*. To make the results comparable across different values of *h*, the variables in $x_t$ have to be expressed in terms of the time unit. In the present case this means that the inflation rates have to be "quarterized", if the underlying time unit continues to be a quarter: $\pi_t^w = (w_t - w_{t-h})/h$ and $\pi_t^p = (p_t - p_{t-h})/h$ for the log wages $w_t$ and prices $p_t$ (the output gap as a ratio of two flow magnitudes and the real wage gap have no time dimension).

Transforming a quarterly model into an *h*-economy would be straightforward if $E_t[x_{t+1}] = x_{t+1}$ holds true in (7.6) and the right-hand side represents a linear partial adjustment mechanism for each variable. The matrix $A$ can then be decomposed into $A = I + J$ (*I* the identity matrix) and the adjustments in the *h*-economy become $x_{t+h} = x_t + h J x_t$. In the limit $h \to 0$ a differential equations system is obtained, $\dot{x} = Jx$, whose basic dynamic properties are characterized by the eigen-values of the matrix $J$. Provided no eigen-value is zero or lies on the imaginary axis, these properties will carry over to the discrete time *h*-economy, at least if *h* is sufficiently small.

Things are a bit more involved for the present New-Keynesian model. Here the influence of *h* will be of a non-linear nature and the matrix $J = (A - I)/h$ from (7.6) is itself dependent on *h*. This gives us $J = J(h)$ and

$$E_t[x_{t+h}] = [I + h J(h)]x_t. \tag{7.8}$$

It will furthermore be established that the matrices $J(h)$ converge to some finite matrix $J^o$ as *h* tends to zero. Under $E_t[x_{t+h}] = x_{t+h}$, the limit would be well-defined if $Ix_t$ is brought to the left-hand side in (7.8) and the resulting equation divided by *h*. Hence the "continuous time matrix" $J^o$ should contain all the relevant information about the qualitative behavior of the discrete time system (7.8) if *h* is small enough. In the present context we are interested in the number of stable and unstable eigen-values in $J^o$ and $[I + hJ(h)]$, respectively. The precise relationship between the two is stated in the following Lemma.

### *Lemma*

Let $h \mapsto J(h)$ be a continuous function of $n \times n$ matrices defined on an interval $[0, \varepsilon]$ for some $\varepsilon > 0$. Suppose k eigen-values of $J^o := J(0)$ have positive, and $n - k$ eigen-values have negative real parts. Then there is a positive number $\bar{h}$ such that for all $0 < h < \bar{h}$ the matrix $[I + hJ(h)]$ has k eigen-values of $J^o$ inside, and $n - k$ eigen-values outside, the unit circle.

**Proof**

It is immediate that if $\mu(h)$ is an eigen-value of $J(h)$, then $1 + h\mu(h)$ is an eigen-value of $[I + hJ(h)]$. Let $\mu_o = -a_o \pm ib_o$ be an eigen-value of $J^o$ with $a_o > 0, b_o \geq 0$, and let $\mu(h) = -a(h) \pm ib(h)$ be the eigen-values of $J(h)$ that converge to $\mu_o$ as $h \to 0$. Then for $h$ sufficiently small we have $|1 + h\mu(h)|^2 =$
$$[1 - ha(h)]^2 + h^2 b^2(h) < (1 - ha_o/2)^2 + 2h^2 b_o^2 = 1 - h[a_o - h(a_o^2/4 + 2b_o^2)].$$

Clearly, there exists some $\bar{h} > 0$ such that the last term in square brackets is positive for $h < \bar{h}$, which says that for all these $h$ the eigen-values $[1 + h\mu(h)]$ are inside the unit circle. On the other hand, it is obvious that if an eigen-value $\mu_o = a_o \pm ib_o$ of $J^o$ has a positive real part $a_o$, then $|1 + h\mu(h)| > 1$ for all $\mu(h)$ close to $\mu_o$.

Taking $J(h) \to J^o$ for granted as $h$ approaches zero, the main significance of the Lemma lies in the fact that it is usually much easier to derive the number of eigen-values of the matrix $J^o$ that are in the left and right half of the complex plane, respectively, than the number of eigen-values of $[I + hJ(h)]$ that are inside and outside the unit circle, whether $h$ is small or $h = 1$ as in the original economy.

## 7.4 Reformulation of the model with a variable period length

After presenting the general idea of the $h$-economies and expressing our hopes for its benefits in the determinacy analysis, we now have to come to terms with our specific model and introduce a period of arbitrary length $h$ in its structural relationships. Our final aim is to write these high-frequency economies in the reduced form of (7.8) with its constituent matrix $J(h)$. The single steps are straightforward though a bit tedious. In the limit $h \to 0$, however, a handsome matrix $J^o = J(0)$ will be obtained.

We begin with the equation for the real wage gap. With the assumption $u_t = z_{2,t} = 0$ mentioned above, which means that the natural real wage is constant, (7.5) becomes $\omega_t = \omega_{t-h} + (w_t - p_t) - (w_{t-h} - p_{t-h}) = \omega_{t-h} + h[(w_t - w_{t-h})/h - (p_t - p_{t-h})/h]$, or

$$\omega_t = \omega_{t-h} + h(\pi_t^w - \pi_t^p). \tag{7.9}$$

Consider next the Taylor rule in (7.4). Given that in the quarterly model the interest rate $i_t$ corresponds to the log of the gross yield on bonds purchased in $t$ and maturing in $t + 1$ (Galí 2008, pp.16, 18), $hi_t$ corresponds to the log of the gross yield when these bonds are maturing in $t + h$. The household's rate for discounting periods of length $h$ is $h\rho$, and similarly so for the component $v_t$ (see the specification of $z_{1,t}$ in Section 7.2). In the $h$-economy, the Taylor rule thus reads $hi_t = h\rho + \phi_p(p_t - p_{t-h}) + \phi_w(w_t - w_{t-h}) + h\phi_y y_t + hv_t$. Retranslated into quarterly magnitudes we obtain

$$i_t = \rho + \phi_p \pi_t^p + \phi_w \pi_t^w + \phi_y y_t + v_t. \tag{7.10}$$

Before we turn to the counterparts of (7.1)–(7.3) in the *h*-economy, we have to have a look at the structural parameters entering these equations or their composed coefficients $\kappa_w$, $\lambda_w$, $\kappa_p$, $\lambda_p$, respectively. The latter are given by

$$\kappa_w = a_w \lambda_w \qquad\qquad\qquad \kappa_p = a_p \lambda_p$$

$$a_w = \sigma + \phi/(1-\alpha) \qquad\qquad a_p = \alpha/(1-\alpha) \qquad\qquad (7.11)$$

$$\lambda_w = \frac{(1-\theta_w)(1-\beta\theta_w)}{\theta_w}\frac{1}{1+\phi\varepsilon_w} \qquad \lambda_p = \frac{(1-\theta_p)(1-\beta\theta_p)}{\theta_p}\frac{1-\alpha}{1-\alpha+\alpha\varepsilon_p}$$

(cf. Galí 2008, pp.121, 125f). All of these parameters are specified as positive numbers, where the following ones are independent of the length of the period: $\alpha$ is the exponent on labor in the production function ($\alpha < 1$, p.18 in Galí); $\sigma$ and $\phi$ are the intertemporal elasticities in the household's utility function that refer to present and future consumption and labor, respectively (p.17);[4] $\varepsilon_p$ is the household's elasticity of substitution among the differentiated consumption goods (pp.41f, 122); and $\varepsilon_w$ is the firms' elasticity of substitution among the varieties of labor inputs (p.120).

The parameter $\beta$ serves to discount the household's intertemporal utility and so changes with the length of the period. When instead of a quarter this parameter applies to a period of length $h$, it may be denoted as $\beta(h)$. Since the discount rate for a period of length $h$ is $h\rho$ and the quarterly coefficient $\beta = \beta(1)$ was already said to be related to the quarterly discount rate by $\ln \beta = -\rho$, or equivalently $\beta = 1/(1 + \rho)$,[5] the coefficient $\beta(h)$ is determined by

$$\beta(h) = 1/(1+h\rho). \qquad\qquad (7.12)$$

The two remaining parameters $\theta_w$ and $\theta_p$ have a time dimension, too. $(1 - \theta_w)$ is the fraction of households/unions that reoptimize their posted nominal wage within a given quarter, while the rest $\theta_w$ of them post the wage of the previous quarter (Galí, p.122). Likewise, $(1-\theta_p)$ is the fraction of firms that in this period reset their price, and the rest $\theta_p$ does not (pp.43, 47, 121).

The parameter $\theta_w(h)$ appropriate for the *h*-economy is obtained from the observation that in a period of length $h$ the fraction of reoptimizing households will be $h(1-\theta_w)$. This gives us $\theta_w(h) = 1 - h(1-\theta_w)$. Using (7.12), the term $(1-\beta\theta_w)$ in (7.11) now reads $1 - \beta(h)\theta_w(h) = 1 - [1 - h(1-\theta_w)]/(1+h\rho) = h(1+\rho-\theta_w)/(1+h\rho)$. In this way the first fraction in the definition of $\lambda_w$ in (7.11) becomes $[1-\theta_w(h)][1-\beta(h)\theta_w(h)]/\theta_w(h) = h(1-\theta_w)h(1+\rho-\theta_w)[1-h(1-\theta_w)](1+h\rho)$. The same reasoning applies to $\theta_p(h)$ and the first fraction in the definition of $\lambda_p$ in (7.11). The coefficients $\lambda_w(h)$ and $\lambda_p(h)$ adjusted to the *h*-economy can thus be written as

$$\lambda_w(h) = h^2\beta_w(h), \qquad \beta_w(h) := \frac{(1-\theta_w)(1+\rho-\theta_w)}{[1-h(1-\theta_w)](1+h\rho)}\frac{1}{1+\phi\varepsilon_w}$$

$$\lambda_p(h) = h^2\beta_p(h), \qquad \beta_p(h) := \frac{(1-\theta_p)(1+\rho-\theta_p)}{[1-h(1-\theta_p)](1+h\rho)}\frac{1-\alpha}{1-\alpha+\alpha\varepsilon_p}. \qquad (7.13)$$

If the period-dependent parameters $\beta$, $\theta_w$ and $\theta_p$ in the model are suitably adjusted, then all of the agents' optimization procedures go through unaltered. This means that we can directly refer to the Phillips curve and the dynamic IS equation as they are formulated in (7.1)–(7.3); we only have to replace the coefficients $\beta$, $\lambda_w$, $\lambda_p$ with $\beta(h)$, $\lambda_w(h)$, $\lambda_p(h)$, and $\kappa_w$, $\kappa_p$ with $\kappa_w(h) = a_w\lambda_w(h)$, $\kappa_p(h) = a_p\lambda_p(h)$, respectively.

So, to begin with, let us reconsider the wage Phillips curve (7.1) in the context of an $h$-economy. Employing (7.11) and (7.13) we here get $w_t - w_{t-h} = \beta(h)E_t$ $[w_{t+h} - w_t] + a_w\lambda_w(h)y_t - \lambda_w(h)_t = \beta(h)E_t[w_{t+h} - w_t] + h^2[a_w\beta_w(h)\,y_t - \beta_w(h)\omega_t]$. Dividing through by $h$ to express the wage inflation rates as quarterly magnitudes, $\pi_t^w = (w_t - w_{t-h})/h$, solving for the expected values and using (7.12) as well as (7.9) yields $E_t[\pi_{t+h}^w] = (1+h\rho)\{\pi_t^w - h[a_w\beta_w(h)y_t - \beta_w(h)(\omega_{t-h} + h(\pi_t^w - \pi_t^p))]\}$. Expected price inflation can be treated in the same way. It is then convenient to define

$$j_{ww}(h) = \rho + h(1+h\rho)\beta_w(h) \qquad j_{wp}(h) = -h(1+h\rho)\beta_w(h)$$

$$j_{wy}(h) = -(1+h\rho)a_w\,\beta_w(h) \qquad j_{w\omega}(h) = (1+h\rho)\beta_w(h)$$

$$j_{pw}(h) = -h(1+h\rho)\beta_p(h) \qquad j_{pp}(h) = \rho + h(1+h\rho)\beta_p(h)$$

$$j_{py}(h) = -(1+h\rho)a_p\,\beta_p(h) \qquad j_{p\omega}(h) = -(1+h\rho)\beta_p(h) \qquad (7.14)$$

and write the reduced form of the expected inflation rates as

$$E_t[\pi_{t+h}^w] = \pi_t^w + h[\,j_{ww}(h)\pi_t^w + j_{wp}(h)\pi_t^p + j_{wy}(h)y_t + j_{w\omega}(h)\,\omega_{t-h}], \qquad (7.15)$$

$$E_t[\pi_{t+h}^p] = \pi_t^p + h[\,j_{pw}(h)\pi_t^w + j_{pp}(h)\pi_t^p + j_{py}(h)y_t + j_{p\omega}(h)\omega_{t-h}]. \qquad (7.16)$$

Regarding the output gap, use (7.10) to obtain the counterpart of the dynamic IS curve (7.3) in the $h$-economy, solved for the expectational variable, as $E_t[y_{t+h}] = y_t + (h/\sigma)(\rho + \phi_p\pi_t^p + \phi_w\pi_t^w + \phi_y y_t + v_t - E_t[\pi_{t+h}^p] - r_t^n)$. The magnitudes $\rho$, $v_t$ and $r_t^n$ cancel out if $z_{1,t} = 0$ from Section 7.2 is taken into account. Substituting (7.16) and defining

$$j_{yw}(h) = [\phi_w - hj_{pw}(h)]/\sigma \qquad j_{yp}(h) = [\phi_p - 1 - hj_{pp}(h)]/\sigma$$

$$j_{yy}(h) = [\phi_y - hj_{py}(h)]/\sigma \qquad j_{y\omega}(h) = -h\,j_{p\omega}(h)/\sigma \qquad (7.17)$$

the output equation can be written as

$$E_t[y_{t+h}] = y_t + h[\,j_{yw}(h)\pi_t^w + j_{yp}(h)\pi_t^p + j_{yy}(h)\,y_t + j_{y\omega}(h)\omega_{t-h}]. \qquad (7.18)$$

Lastly, put

$$j_{\omega w} = 1 \qquad j_{\omega p} = -1 \qquad j_{\omega y} = j_{\omega \omega} = 0 \tag{7.19}$$

and adjust the identity for the real wage gap (7.9) to the present notation (apart from the reference of these coefficients to $h$, which is here obsolete),

$$E_t[\omega_t] = \omega_{t-h} + h[\, j_{\omega w} \pi_t^w + j_{\omega p} \pi_t^p + j_{\omega y} y_t + j_{\omega \omega} \omega_{t-h}]. \tag{7.20}$$

With equations (7.15), (7.16), (7.18), (7.20) and the corresponding definition of the coefficients $j_{kl}$ ($k, \ell = w, p, y, \omega$), we have achieved our goal to write the $h$-economy version of the model compactly as in (7.8), $E_t[x_{t+h}] = [I + hJ(h)]x_t$. Thus we are ready to apply the Lemma from the previous section. It only remains to make explicit that the limit of the matrices $J(h)$ exists. In fact, from (7.14), (7.17), (7.19), (7.9) we obtain:

$$J^o = J(0) = \begin{bmatrix} \rho & 0 & -a_w \beta_w & \beta_w \\ 0 & \rho & -a_p \beta_p & -\beta_p \\ \phi_w/\sigma & (\phi_p - 1)/\sigma & \phi_y/\sigma & 0 \\ 1 & -1 & 0 & 0 \end{bmatrix} \tag{7.21}$$

with:

$$\beta_w = \beta_w(0) = (1 - \theta_w)(1 + \rho - \theta_w)/(1 + \phi \varepsilon_w),$$
$$\beta_p = \beta_p(0) = (1 - \theta_p)(1 + \rho - \theta_p)(1 - \alpha)/(1 - \alpha + \alpha \varepsilon_p).$$

In contrast to the unwieldy general discrete time matrices $J(1)$ or $J(h)$ in (7.8), the limit matrix $J^o$ seems to offer some scope for an analytical treatment of the determinacy problem. This will be the upshot of the chapter in the next section.

## 7.5 The determinacy proposition

According to the Lemma, for determinacy in the $h$-economies it has to be shown that the limit matrix $J^o$ in (7.21) has one real and negative eigen-value and three eigen-values with positive real parts. The following two assumptions will prove sufficient to ensure this.

*Assumption 1*

$$\phi_w + \phi_p > 1 - \frac{\rho \phi_y (\beta_w + \beta_p)}{\beta_w \beta_p (a_w + a_p)},$$

where $a_w$, $a_p$, $\hat{\beta}_w$, $\hat{\beta}_p$ are defined in (7.11) and (7.21), respectively.

***Assumption 2***

Either $\phi_y = 0$ or $\rho^2 \le \beta_w + \beta_p$ *(or both).*

The first assumption is a relaxed version of the Taylor principle stated in (7.7). Just as in the Galí (2008, p.130, figure 6.2) illustration of the determinacy frontier, a positive policy coefficient on the output gap allows a (slight) weakening of the condition that the sum of the two inflation coefficients exceed unity. The assumption will also turn out to be a necessary condition for determinacy, at least in $h$-economies with a short period length $h$ (if we disregard equality in Assumption 1, in which case the Lemma fails to apply).[6]

The inequality in Assumption 2 is a convenient condition to determine the sign of a partial derivative in the proof; see (7.25) below. However, neither the condition for the sign nor the sign itself are necessarily needed in the mathematical argument. Nevertheless, since a typical value of the quarterly discount rate is $\rho = 0.01$ and so $\rho^2$ is extremely small, this inequality can be safely taken for granted and there is no need to seek for further (more tedious) refinements. In fact, with the numerical parameters that we will employ from the literature below, we get $\beta_w = 0.009$ and $\beta_p = 0.029$.

***Proposition 1***

1. *If the inequality in Assumption 1 is reversed, then an h-economy as it was developed above, and compactly summarized by (7.8), exhibits indeterminacy for (at least) all h sufficiently small.*

2. *Let Assumptions 1 and 2 be satisfied. Then the steady state of the h-economy is determinate (at least) if the period length h is sufficiently short.*

The hard work to do is, of course, the proof of the determinacy part of the proposition, that is, a demonstration of the 3:1 structure in the four eigen-values of $J^o$. To give a short outline of our approach, the proof begins with assigning zero values to two selected parameters. They are easily seen to give rise to a negative and a positive eigen-value, and to two eigen-values on the imaginary axis. In a second step, the Implicit Function Theorem is employed to show that the real parts of the latter two become positive as one of these parameters slightly increases. The third step makes sure that upon further increases of the two parameters toward their originally given values, none of the eigen-values can change the sign of its real part. The precise mathematical arguments in these three steps are given in the appendix.

## 7.6 Determinacy under a variable period length

In this section we study determinacy under variations of the period length $h$, which may then no longer appear "sufficiently small" as supposed by the proposition. To this end let $\phi_{wp}^*(h)$ denote the critical value of the sum of the wage and price policy coefficients $\phi_w + \phi_p$ at which, given $h$, the steady state of (7.8) becomes determinate as $\phi_w + \phi_p$ increases from zero.[7] Then, taking Assumption 2 for granted, the proposition and the Lemma tell us that $\phi_{wp}^*(h)$ converges toward the right-hand side of Assumption 1 as $h$ tends to zero, which may be written as $\phi_{wp}^*(0)$. Attempts to check this numerically will, however, face an intrinsic problem. While usually a procedure computing eigen-values with a precision of, say, five significant digits will be considered fully satisfactory, this error is no longer negligible if, at a given small value of $h$, one of the eigen-values of the matrix $[I + hJ(h)]$ in (7.8) is, for example, computed as 0.99995 and thus said to be stable, although it is actually unstable with a true value of 1.00001. As a consequence, the numerical computations yield somewhat distorted values for the determinacy threshold $\phi_{wp}^*(h)$.

In fact, in a battery of numerical explorations in which we let $h$ tend to zero, $\phi_{wp}^*(h)$ was typically found to converge to a value distinctly larger than $\phi_{wp}^*(0)$. Nevertheless, in all of these cases the limit was still consistently below unity, even for very small values of the policy coefficient $\phi_y$ (recall that $\phi_{wp}^*(0)$, the right-hand side in Assumption 1, tends to unity from below as $\phi_y$ approaches zero). Hence for small values of $h$, the pure Taylor principle $\phi_w + \phi_p > 1$ was always sufficient to ensure numerical determinacy.

On the other hand, the rigorous mathematical formulation of the determinacy part of the proposition is limited to sufficiently short period lengths $h$ and so must leave it open whether for longer periods, up to $h = 1$, determinacy would require stronger or weaker conditions. This problem has to be investigated by numerical methods anyway. To this end we take up the numerical example discussed in Galí (2008, pp.52, 129). The values of the structural parameters that will remain constant, or for which we only consider two alternative values as in the case of $\phi_y$, are given in Table 7.1.[8] Note that the first value of $\phi_y$ is Taylor's original value for the policy coefficient on the output gap, which is here divided by 4 since Galí uses a quarter as his underlying time unit.

Given the period length $h$ and one of the values for $\phi_y$ together with the other parameters in Table 7.1, we can compute the determinacy threshold $\phi_{wp}^*(h)$ by way of a suitable iteration mechanism (basically a *regula falsi* procedure). Drawing the threshold as a function of $h$ over the interval [0.01, 1.00], the two graphs in Figure 7.1 are obtained; one for $\phi_y = 0.5/4 = 0.125$ and the other for $\phi_y = 2/4 = 0.500$. The diagram illustrates that the condition for determinacy is steadily relaxed as the period length increases up to a quarter, $h = 1$. It may be added that in both of the cases here depicted, the computed values of $\phi_{wp}^*(h)$ are still persistently above

*Table 7.1* Galí's numerical parameter scenario

| $\rho$ | $\alpha$ | $\phi$ | $\sigma$ | $\varepsilon_p$ | $\varepsilon_w$ | $\theta_p$ | $\theta_w$ | $\phi_y$ |
|---|---|---|---|---|---|---|---|---|
| 0.01 | 2/3 | 1 | 1 | 6 | 6 | 2/3 | 3/4 | 0.5/4 or 2/4 |

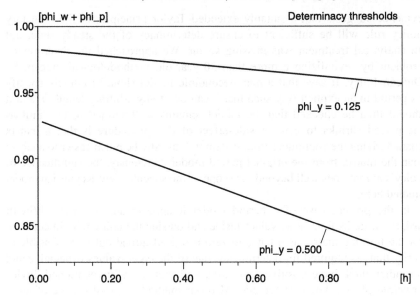

*Figure 7.1* Determinacy thresholds $\phi_{wp}^*(h)$ under variations of the period length $h$.

the theoretical threshold $\phi_{wp}^*(0)$, which is 0.9406 for $\phi_y = 0.125$ and 0.7623 for $\phi_y = 0.500$.

There are obviously values of $\phi_w + \phi_p$ such that the economy is indeterminate at high frequencies ($h$ close to zero) and determinate at sufficiently low frequencies. This is a similar phenomenon to the "paradox" (as he calls it) that was obtained by Hintermaier (2005) in a standard real business cycle model augmented by externalities in production. However, while his numerical calibration is a widely accepted benchmark in the literature, here very special values of the policy coefficients are needed to produce the paradox, which also contradict common sense on sound monetary policy. Thus, at least with respect to determinacy issues under a variable period length, the present version of the New-Keynesian model with sticky wages and prices appears to be well-behaved.

## 7.7 Conclusions

The chapter may be viewed as a small yet interesting contribution to the literature on the determinacy properties of forward-looking macro models. Specifically, it takes up a standard version of the New-Keynesian period model that integrates goods and labor markets by designing imperfect competition and staggered price and wage setting in an analogous manner. The model can be reduced to a dynamic system in four variables, one of which is predetermined and the other three are so-called jump variables. Numerical evidence suggests that a suitably extended Taylor principle for the monetary policy rule will be sufficient to ensure determinacy of the steady state, but an analytical treatment was missing so far. We approached the determinacy problem by revitalizing a more than 30-year-old methodological precept by Duncan Foley. It says that a macroeconomic model should routinely specify its period in an explicit way such that it can be of any arbitrary length $h$, and it should then be checked that the model remains well-defined in the limit as the period shrinks to zero. A side-effect of this procedure is that a matrix characterizing the continuous time system will usually be much easier to analyze than the matrix from the original period model. Obviously, the significance of Foley's axiom goes well beyond the scope of the specific New-Keynesian model studied here.

In the present case of a period model it appears an extremely difficult task to locate its four eigen-values inside and outside the unit circle. In contrast, for the limiting matrix as $h$ tends to zero it indeed turned out to be feasible to verify that, as required for determinacy, one of the eigen-values is negative and the other three have positive real parts, and that the aforementioned Taylor principle plays a key role for this. Also our method of proof can be of more general interest. The proof begins with a special set of the parameters that gives rise to one positive and one negative eigen-value, while the other two eigen-values are on the imaginary axis. Using the Implicit Function Theorem it is then shown that the latter two are moving into the positive half of the complex plane as one of the modified parameters slightly increases. A final step makes sure that upon further variations of the modified parameters toward their original values, none of the eigen-values can hit the imaginary axis again. We may thus hope that similar methods and ideas will prove fruitful for other dynamic systems of dimension three, four or perhaps even five if it comes to a mathematical analysis of their stability or determinacy.

## Appendix: proof of the proposition

For the analysis of the eigen-value structure of the matrix $J^o$ in (7.21) we need the coefficients in its characteristic equation, $\lambda^4 + A_1\lambda^3 + A_2\lambda^2 + A_3\lambda + A_4 = 0$[9]. With the notation $\eta := 1/\sigma$ to avoid fractions, they result as follows (e.g., see Murata, 1977, p.14):

$$A_1 = -\text{trace } J^o = -2(\rho + \eta\phi_y)$$

$$A_2 = \text{sum of the principal second-order minors of } J^o$$

$$= \begin{vmatrix} \rho & 0 \\ 0 & \rho \end{vmatrix} + \begin{vmatrix} \rho & -\alpha_\omega\beta_w \\ \eta\phi_w & \eta\phi_y \end{vmatrix} + \begin{vmatrix} \rho & \beta_w \\ 1 & 0 \end{vmatrix} +$$

$$\begin{vmatrix} \rho & -a_p\beta_p \\ \eta(\phi_p-1) & \eta\phi_y \end{vmatrix} + \begin{vmatrix} \rho & -\beta_p \\ -1 & 0 \end{vmatrix} + \begin{vmatrix} \eta\phi_y & 0 \\ 0 & 0 \end{vmatrix}$$

$$= \rho(2\eta\phi_y + \rho) - [1 - \eta\phi_w a_w]\beta_w - [1 - \eta(\phi_p-1)a_p]\beta_p$$

$A_3 = -$ (sum of the principal third-order minors of $J^o$)

$$= -\begin{vmatrix} \rho & 0 & -a_w\beta_w \\ 0 & \rho & -a_p\beta_p \\ \eta\phi_w & \eta(\phi_p-1) & \eta\phi_y \end{vmatrix} - \begin{vmatrix} \rho & 0 & \beta_w \\ 0 & \rho & -\beta_p \\ 1 & -1 & 0 \end{vmatrix}$$

$$- \begin{vmatrix} \rho & -a_w\beta_w & \beta_w \\ \eta\phi_w & \eta\phi_y & 0 \\ 1 & 0 & 0 \end{vmatrix} - \begin{vmatrix} \rho & -a_p\beta_p & -\beta_p \\ \eta(\phi_p-1) & \eta\phi_y & 0 \\ -1 & 0 & 0 \end{vmatrix}$$

$$= \eta\phi_y(\beta_w+\beta_p-\rho^2)+\rho[(1-\eta\phi_w a_w)\beta_w+(1-\eta(\phi_p-1)a_p)\beta_p]$$

$$A_4 = \det J^o = -\eta[\rho\phi_y(\beta_w+\beta_p)+(\phi_w+\phi_p-1)(a_w+a_p)\beta_w\beta_p].$$

The first part of the proposition is easily verified by making use of the relationship $A_4 = \det J^o = \lambda_1\lambda_2\lambda_3\lambda_4$ for the four eigen-values of $J^o$. Recalling that for determinacy three eigen-values must have positive real parts and one must be negative, it suffices to note that the strict violation of Assumption 1 is equivalent to $A_4 > 0$, and that a positive sign of the determinant implies an even number of eigen-values with positive real parts.

In the proof of the second part of the proposition, the coefficients $\rho$ and $\phi_y$ are treated as variable. Their given values may therefore be marked as $\rho^*$ and $\phi_y^*$. We also distinguish the two cases that the expression in $[1 - \eta\phi_w a_w]\beta_w + [1 - \eta(\phi_p-1)a_p]\beta_p$ in $A_2$ and $A_3$ is zero or nonzero, respectively. The proof begins with the normal nonzero case.

In a first step, put $\rho = \phi_y = 0$. Then $A_1 = A_3 = 0$, $A_2 \neq 0$ and, with Assumption 1, $A_4 < 0$. The characteristic equation thus reduces to $\lambda^4 + A_2\lambda^2 + A_4 = 0$. The quadratic equation that results from replacing $\lambda^2$ with $\mu$ has two real solutions $\mu_{1,2}$, one of which is positive and the other negative. Hence (from $\mu_1 > 0$) one eigen-value $\lambda$ is a positive and one a negative real number, and (from $\mu_2 < 0$) the remaining two are a pair of purely complex eigen-values. In the next step we want to show that this pair moves into the right half of the complex plane when now $\rho$ is slightly increased above zero. As the signs of the other two real eigen-values are preserved, this intermediate step will achieve the desired structure of the eigen-values.

For this purpose, write a complex eigen-value of $J^o$ as $\lambda = \alpha + \beta i$ and compute $\lambda^2 = (\alpha^2 - \beta^2) + 2\alpha\beta i$, $\lambda^3 = \alpha(\alpha^2 - 3\beta^2) + \beta(3\alpha^2 - \beta^2)i$, $\lambda^4 = (\alpha^2 - \beta^2)^2 - 4\alpha^2\beta^2 + 4\alpha\beta(\alpha^2 - \beta^2)i$. The characteristic equation can be decomposed into its real and imaginary component as follows,

$$(\alpha^2 - \beta^2)^2 - 4\alpha^2\beta^2 + A_1\alpha(\alpha^2 - 3\beta^2) + A_2(\alpha^2 - \beta^2) + A_3\alpha + A_4 = 0$$

$$4\alpha\beta(\alpha^2 - \beta^2) + A_1\beta(3\alpha^2 - \beta^2) + 2A_2\alpha\beta + A_3\beta = 0. \qquad (7.22)$$

In the special situation where $\alpha = 0$, we obtain two relationships that will prove useful further below,

$$\beta^2 - A_2 = -A_4 / \beta^2 > 0 - A_1 \beta^2 + A_3 = 0. \tag{7.23}$$

Conceiving the composite terms $A_j$ as functions of $\rho$ and (later) $\phi_y$, the two equations in (7.22) may be more compactly written as,

$$F_1(\alpha, \beta; \rho, \phi_y) = 0$$
$$F_2(\alpha, \beta; \rho, \phi_y) = 0. \tag{7.24}$$

Equation (7.24) is a typical example for an application of the Implicit Function Theorem in its 2-D version: $\alpha$ and $\beta$ are two endogenous real variables that vary with the exogenous variables $\rho$ and $\phi_y$ in order to reestablish equality in (7.24), which may be expressed as $\alpha = \alpha \,(\rho, \phi_y)$, $\beta = \beta(\rho, \phi_y)$. Furthermore we have a base solution $\alpha(0, 0) = 0$, $\beta(0, 0) > 0$ for $\rho = \phi_y = 0$. The theorem, then, gives us a formula to compute the partial derivative of the real part $\alpha = \alpha(\rho, \phi_y)$ at this point with respect to $\rho$, which should turn out to be positive.

Entering the formula will be all of the partial derivatives of the two function $F_1$ and $F_2$. Denote them as $F_{j\gamma} = \partial F_j / \partial \gamma$ for $j = 1, 2$, $\gamma = \alpha, \beta, \rho, \phi$, where in order to avoid stacked indices let here $\phi$ stand for $\phi_y$. Likewise write $A_{j\rho} = \partial A_j / \partial \rho$ and $A_{j\phi} = \partial A_j / \partial \phi_y$ for $j$ 1, 2, 3, 4. Generally at a point at which $\alpha = 0$, we can, in particular, use (7.23) to compute the derivatives and their signs:

$$F_{1\alpha} = 2\beta^2 (2\rho + \eta \phi_y) \ge 0 \qquad F_{2\alpha} = -2\beta^2 (2\beta^2 - A_2) < 0$$
$$F_{1\beta} = 2\beta(2\beta^2 - A_2) > 0 \qquad F_{2\beta} = 2\beta^2 (2\rho + \eta \phi_y) \ge 0$$
$$F_{1\rho} = -2\beta^2 (\rho + \eta \phi_y) \le 0 \qquad F_{2\rho} = \beta(\rho^2 + 2\beta^2 - A_2) > 0$$
$$F_{1\phi} = -\eta\rho(2\beta^2 + \beta_w + \beta_p) < 0 \qquad F_{2\phi} = \eta\beta(2\beta^2 + \beta_w + \beta_p - \rho^2) > 0. \tag{7.25}$$

In the computation of $F_{2\rho}$ it has also been exploited that $A_{3\rho} = -2\eta\phi_y \rho + [1 - \eta\phi_w a_w]\beta_w + [1 - \eta \,(\phi_p - 1)a_p]\beta_p$ equals $\rho^2 - A_2$. The positive sign of $F_{2\phi}$ is ensured by Assumption 2.

After these preparations we can take the real part of an eigen-value $\lambda = \lambda(\rho, \phi_y) = \alpha(\rho, \phi_y) + \beta(\rho, \phi_y)i$ and differentiate it with respect to $\rho$. The formula from the Implicit Function Theorem reads,

$$\frac{\partial \alpha(\rho, \phi_y)}{\partial \rho} = \frac{-F_{2\beta} F_{1\rho} + F_{1\beta} F_{2\rho}}{F_{1\alpha} F_{2\beta} - F_{1\beta} F_{2\alpha}}. \tag{7.26}$$

Equation (7.25) ascertains that both the numerator and denominator are unambiguously positive. This holds for all nonnegative values of $p$ and $\phi_y$ and thus, in particular, at the point $\rho = 0$ and $\phi_y = 0$. The positive derivative in (7.26) proves the claim that at $\phi_y = 0$ and for $\rho$ sufficiently small (but positive), one eigen-value of $J^o$ is negative and the other three have positive real parts.

It next has to be shown that at a further rise of $\rho$ up to the given value $\rho^*$, none of the eigen-values can hit the imaginary axis or even move from one half-plane into the other. Suppose this happens at some value $\tilde{\rho} > 0$. Owing to $A_4 = \det J^o \neq 0$ there must be again a pair of purely imaginary eigen-values, for which $\alpha(\tilde{\rho}, 0) = 0$. Furthermore, since there is only a single eigen-value with a negative real part, the partial derivative $\partial\alpha(\tilde{\rho}, 0)/\partial\rho$ must be negative or zero. This, however, contradicts the fact that (7.25) has just been found to be strictly positive at all $\rho$ and $\phi$ that would entail $\alpha(\rho, 0) = 0$. Hence the desired 3:1 eigen-value structure also prevails at $\rho = \rho^*$ and $\phi_y = 0$.

For the case of a positive coefficient on the output gap it remains to verify that the eigen-value structure is preserved if now $\phi_y$ rises from zero to the given value $\phi_y^*$. The argument is completely analogous to the previous paragraph. In computing the partial derivative $\partial\alpha(\rho^*, \phi_y)/\partial\phi_y$ we only have to replace $F_{1\rho}$ and $F_{2\rho}$ in (7.26) with $F_{1\phi}$ and $F_{2\phi}$ and observe with (7.25) that this does not change the sign of the numerator. Hence $\partial\alpha(\rho^*, \phi_y)/\partial\phi_y > 0$ for all values of $\phi_y$, which implies that the variations of $\phi_y$ cannot change the signs of the real parts of the four eigen-values, either.

Finally, consider the special case c, $C := [1 - \eta\phi_w a_w]\beta_w + [1 - \eta(\phi_p - 1)a_p]\beta_p = 0$. Here the above method of proof fails to apply since $A_2 = 0$ at the very beginning. Instead, we now treat $\eta$ as a variable coefficient and mark its given value as $\eta^*$. Since $C = C(\eta) \neq 0$ for $\eta \neq \eta^*$, we know that for all these $\eta$ the real parts of the corresponding eigen-values have the desired 3:1 structure. The rest of the proof makes sure that at $\eta = \eta^*$ this property does not possibly get lost.

Suppose to the contrary that some eigen-value changes the sign of its real part at $\eta^*$. Then by virtue of $\det J^o \neq 0$ there must be a pair $\lambda_{1,2} = \pm i\beta$ of purely complex eigen-values at this value. Since for $\eta \neq \eta^*$ the other two eigen-values are real and of opposite sign, $\lambda_3 < 0 < \lambda_4$ (say) also holds true at $\eta = \eta^*$. To check the consistency of this situation, we refer to the following two identities between the coefficients in the characteristic polynomial and the four eigen-values of $J^o$,[10]

$$A_1 = -\lambda_1 - \lambda_2 - \lambda_3 - \lambda_4$$
$$A_3 = -\lambda_1\lambda_2\lambda_3 - \lambda_1\lambda_2\lambda_4 - \lambda_1\lambda_3\lambda_4 - \lambda_2\lambda_3\lambda_4.$$

Since $A_1 < 0$ $\lambda_1 + \lambda_2 = 0$, the first equation implies $\lambda_3 + \lambda_4 > 0$. The second equation yields $A_3 = -\lambda_1\lambda_2(\lambda_3 + \lambda_4) - (\lambda_1 + \lambda_2)\lambda_3\lambda_4 = i^2\beta^2(\lambda_3 + \lambda_4)$, which ays that $A_3$ is negative. With $C(\eta^*) = 0$, on the other hand, $A_3$ is here given by $A_3 = \eta^*\phi_y(\beta_w + \beta_p - \rho^2)$. Since according to Assumption 2 this expression is nonnegative, we have a contradiction, that is, $\lambda_{1,2} = \pm i\beta$ at $\eta = \eta^*$ is impossible.

# Part III

# Macroeconomic adjustment processes

Theory

# 8   Disequilibrium growth theory with insider–outsider effects

## 8.1 Introduction

In an interesting paper, Ito (1980) has applied the non-Walrasian regime switching methodology to the Solovian neoclassical growth model. He there discussed in detail the occurrence of full employment, overemployment and underemployment and the different dynamical systems these possible regimes (to be "patched up") give rise to. We shall show in this chapter, however, that nothing of this sort really characterizes Solovian growth with sluggishly adjusting, non market clearing real wages if one basic extension of this model is considered as relevant and assumed: the existence of over- or under-time work of the workforce within the firms (the insiders). This simple extension of the 2-D dynamical systems considered in Ito (1980) (by one dimension) gives the dynamics a completely new outlook, described by the interaction of two employment cycles as in Goodwin (1967), one for insiders and one for outsiders, where the actual employment of the insiders is governed by the marginal productivity rule (or more generally by the size of the capital stock), while the outside rate of employment follows the inside rate of employment with a time delay.

We show through this extension,[1] augmented by smooth factor substitution and endogenous growth in later sections of the chapter, that there is then only one regime possible – the classical regime of capital shortage – in the global dynamics of such a Solovian model with varying rates of inside and outside employment. Furthermore and more importantly, this 3-D extension of the Solow model implies asymptotic stability for many parameter constellations of the model. If locally unstable, it allows – under simple additional non-linearites – for global stability in an economically meaningful domain with or without absolute full employment on the external labor market, but with no regime switches on the internal market. A different extension of neoclassical growth with fluctuating employment rates thus makes the non-Walrasian methodology basically redundant and allows for new assertions on local as well as global stability. We stress that at least the first of these assertions applies to non-Walrasian macrodynamics in general and thus provides a way out of the complicated phase diagram analysis generally suggested by this approach.[2]

## 8.2 The case of fixed proportions in production

We start with the case of given output–capital and output–labor ratios, $x = Y/K$, $y = Y/L$, where we use $Y$ for denoting the output level and $K, L$ for the capital stock and the stock of labor. In such a situation, the Ito model is basically of the Goodwin (1967) growth cycle type,[3] if we neglect its regime switching aspect for the moment. We therefore start with a brief representation of this very basic model of cyclical growth which will be extended in various ways in this chapter, including variable inside employment, substitution and endogenously generated technical change.

The Goodwin (1967) growth cycle model is based on two laws of motions, one for real wages $\omega$ and one for the rate of employment $e = L^w/L^s$. We here denote by $L^w$ the employment level and by $L^s$ labor supply, where the latter is assumed to grow at the given natural rate $n = \dot{L}^s/L^s$. We denote the rate of growth of a variable $z$ by $\hat{z}(= \dot{z}/z)$. Standard growth rate formulae then imply for the rate of growth of the employment rate $\hat{e}$, on the basis of the assumed fixed proportions technology, the general expression $\hat{e} = \hat{L} - n = \hat{Y} - n = \hat{K} - n$, i.e., this growth rate is determined in its endogenous evolution by the growth rate of the capital stock in this classical world of full capacity growth. The Goodwin model assumes that the growth rate of the capital stock, $\hat{K}$, is determined by savings out of profits per unit of capital, which gives rise to $\hat{K} = s_c x(1 - \omega/y)$ if we assume a given rate of savings $s_c$ out of profits, since $\omega/y$ is the share of wages and therefore $x(1 - \omega/y)$ the rate of profit due to our above definitions of $y, x$. We thus get that the growth rate of the employment rate solely depends on real wages which gives one of the two laws of motion of the Goodwin (1967) model (still neglecting technical change here, see Section 8.6 in this regard). Assuming in addition a real wage Phillips curve, as it can be derived from a conventional money-wage Phillips curve by assuming myopic perfect foresight, here based on a "natural" rate hypothesis in addition, provides the other law of motion of this growth cycle model, which in sum thus reads:

$$\hat{\omega} = \beta_w(e - \bar{e}), \ \beta_w > 0, \tag{8.1}$$

$$\hat{e} = s_c x(1 - \omega/y) - n, \tag{8.2}$$

where $\bar{e} = const \in (0, 1)$ denotes the "natural" rate of employment of the Goodwin model.[4] This "cross-dual" dynamics, where the level of $\omega$ induces changes in $e$ and the level of $e$ changes of $\omega$, with its well-known prey–predator implications and interpretation, represents our point of departure for an alternative analysis of the situations of under- and over-employment in a growth context that completely bypasses the regime switching methodology of Ito's (1980) and the non-Walrasian approach to macrodynamics.

In the place of Ito's (1980) assumption that there is a switch to a new type of dynamics when the labor market reaches the full employment ceiling (which due to our assumption of a "natural" rate of employment $\bar{e} < 1$ does not occur at the steady state as in Ito's model), we assume as further flexibility in the production process of the economy the possibility of overemployment of the employed workforce in such cases. In the above model, we have the employment function $L = xK/y$ due to the assumption of fixed proportions in production. We assume for the time being that there is no limit with respect to available overtime work. We then have that firms can always produce what they want to produce by choosing an appropriate internal rate of employment $u^w = L/L^w$ of the labor force $L^w$ they employ.

Based on this internal rate of employment $u^w$, we assume next that firms adjust their labor force by recruiting new laborers from the external labor market as follows:

$$\dot{L}^w = \beta_l(L - L^w) + nL^w, \text{ or equivalently: } \hat{L}^w = \beta_l(u^w - 1) + n. \tag{8.3}$$

This law of motion states that the workforce $L^w$ of firms is enlarged or reduced in a growing economy according to the difference between the actual employment $L$ of the employed, $L^w$, and the normal employment of the workforce of firms, also measured for simplicity by $L^w$, plus a term that reflects trend growth $n$. This employment policy of course comes to an end when the external labor market is exhausted (to be considered in Section 8.4). This however is generally not accompanied by a limit to further production due to the above distinction between actual employment $L$ and normal employment $L^w$.

Since $L \neq L^w$ is now possible, the Phillips curve (8.1) should be reformulated as follows:

$$\hat{w} = \beta_{w_1}(e - \bar{e}) + \beta_{w_2}(u^w - 1), \quad e = L^w/L^s, u^w = L/L^w \tag{8.4}$$

to take account of the impact of the over- or underemployment of the employed on wage formation. This is our new formulation of the first differential equation of the Goodwin model (8.1), (8.2). The second law of motion, for the internal rate of employment $u^w$, is according to equation (8.3) given by:

$$\hat{u}^w = \hat{L} - \hat{L}^w = \hat{K}^w - \hat{L}^w = s_c x(1 - \omega/y) - \beta_l(u^w - 1) - n \tag{8.5}$$

while the one for the external rate of employment $e$ is given by

$$\hat{e} = \hat{L}^w - \hat{L}^s = \beta_l(u^w - 1) \tag{8.6}$$

due to the role the rate $u^w$ plays in the employment policy of firms. The differential equations (8.4), (8.5) and (8.6) constitute our augmented Goodwin model, now with variable inside and outside employment rates. Note that this model is a linear model up to its use of growth rates in the place of simple time derivatives.

### Proposition 1

1.  The dynamical system (8.4)–(8.6) has a unique interior steady state given by:

$$\omega_0 = y(1 - \frac{n}{s_c x}) > 0, \; u_0^w = 1, \; e_0 = \bar{e}$$

    if $s_c x > n$ holds.
2.  This steady state is locally asymptotically stable if and only if $\beta_{w_2} > \beta_{w_1} \bar{e}$ holds.

3.  At the value $\beta_{w_2}^H = \beta_{w_1} \bar{e}$ of the parameter $\beta_{w_2}$ there occurs a Hopf-bifurcation of either subcritical, supercritical or degenerate type.

### Proof of Proposition 1

See the appendix.

The concept of a Hopf-bifurcation is explained in detail in Wiggins (1990) and has been thoroughly discussed in the case of a Tobin type growth model in Benhabib and Miyao (1981). We here only briefly state that the obtained (generally non-degenerate) Hopf-bifurcations imply either the loss of a stable corridor and the death of an unstable limit cycle as the Hopf-bifurcation value is approached or the birth of a stable periodic motion after the bifurcation point has been passed. The center-type stability of the Goodwin (1967) growth cycle is thus in particular made a locally implosive dynamics if inside workers dominate the real wage bargain and an explosive one in the opposite situation (at least locally). In the explosive case we have to add – as in Ito (1980) – the condition $e \leq 1$ to the model. We shall later on also assume – and motivate – that the growth rate of the labor supply will increase appropriately as the overemployment within firms becomes higher and higher which will take pressure from the labor market and thus help to avoid labor supply bottlenecks. This will lead us to bounded dynamics, but in the present situation still one where the share of profits $1 - \omega/y$ may fall below zero – which is not meaningful. We therefore add in a next step, as in Ito (1980), smooth factor substitution and the neoclassical theory of employment before we come to the discussion of global constraints from the side of labor supply and their implications.

   Before closing this section let us stress that the above extension of the Goodwin (1967) growth cycle model is now based on two interacting cycles: the usual outsider cycle (which can be isolated by assuming $\beta_l \approx \infty$, $\beta_{w_2} = 0$ and which might be called the "US case" of the model) and a new insider cycle (which can be isolated by $\beta_l = 0, \beta_{w_2} = 0$, the "Japanese case" of the model). The astonishing thing is that the interaction of these two Goodwin cycles contributes to the stability of the general model, i.e., the presence of both variable inside employment with strong wage claim effects and the assumed lagged adjustment of outside employment produces convergence to the steady state in a Goodwin growth cycle setup. A first explanation of this may be seen in the fact that equation (8.6) inserted into equation (8.4) adds a derivative term to the postulated Phillips curve (8.4) which is known to be stabilizing. Note that this derivative term is already contained in Phillips (1958) original article and gave rise there to the explanation of so-called Phillips loops.

## 8.3 Smooth factor substitution

In the case of a neoclassical production function (with the usual properties) and the marginal productivity theory of the rate of employment

$$Y = F(K,L) \text{ and } \omega = F_L(K,L) \tag{8.7}$$

we have to recalculate $\hat{K}$ and on this basis the law of motion for the variable $u^w$.

Denoting by $k$ the actual capital intensity $K/L$ we know from the Solow model of neoclassical growth that (8.7) gives rise to

$$y = f(k), x = f(k)/k, \ \omega = f(k) - f'(k)k = g(k)$$

for the now endogenous output–input ratios of the preceding section. For the function $g$ there furthermore holds

$$g'(k) = f'(k) - f'(k) - f'(k)k = -f''(k)k > 0,$$

i.e., the function $g$ is strictly increasing (due to decreasing marginal products of labor). We denote by $k = k(\omega)$ the inverse of $g$ and by $\varepsilon(\omega) = k'(\omega)\omega/k(\omega) > 0$ the elasticity of this function $k$. On the basis of these equations we then get:

$$\hat{L} = \hat{K} - \hat{k} = s_c x(1 - \omega/y) - \varepsilon(\omega)\hat{\omega} = s_c f'(k(\omega)) - (\omega)\hat{\omega}.$$

This expression is now to be used in equation (8.5) in the place of only $s_c x(1 - \omega/y)$ in order to describe the dynamics of inside employment $u^w = L/L^w$ under neoclassical factor substitution and the neoclassical theory of employment. This, however, is the only change in the dynamical system (8.4)–(8.6) if such substitution is included.

*Proposition 2*

1.  *The interior steady state of the dynamical system (8.4)–(8.6) with smooth factor substitution is of the same type as before, but now with an endogenous determination of $y_o = f(k_o), x_o = f(k_o)/k_o$ and $k_o = k(\omega_o)$, where $\omega_o$ is given by the solution of the equation n/ $s_c = f'(k(\omega_o))$).*
2.  *This steady state is locally asymptotically stable if $\beta_{w_2} > \beta_{w_1}\bar{e} - \delta$ holds for some suitably chosen $\delta > 0$. The size of $\delta$ can be chosen the larger, the larger the terms $\varepsilon(\omega), \beta_1, \beta_{w_2}$ become.*

**Proof of Proposition 2**

See the appendix.

*Remark*

As the expression for the Routh–Hurwitz condition $a_1 a_2 - a_3 > 0$ in the proof shows, stability is indeed significantly increased by the inclusion of smooth factor substitution and the neoclassical theory of employment.

## 8.4 Effective supply constraints?

Having extended the Goodwin growth cycle approach by inside–outside labor market effects married with Solovian economic growth we now come to a specification of the bounds that can limit the evolution of such an economy. To do so, let us assume as an example that overtime work of the employed workforce $L^w$ is legally restricted to $L^w$, i.e. overtime work supplied by a person can be (and will be) at most as large as the normal working time of this person, i.e., we impose the inequality $L \le 2 L^w$ or $u^w \le 2$. Furthermore: $e \le 1$ must hold true as in the Ito (1980) model, due to the external labor market constraint. Finally, the rate of profit $x(1 - \omega/y)$ should be positive at all times.

Summarizing, our dynamical system with smooth factor substitution then reads, including the bounds $\omega < y, u^w \le 2, e \le 1$:

$$\hat{w} = \beta_{w_1}(e - \bar{e}) + \beta_{w_2}(u^w - 1), \tag{8.8}$$

$$\hat{u}^w = s_c f'(k(\omega)) - \in (\omega)[\beta_{w_1}(e - \bar{e}) + \beta_{w_2}(u^w - 1)] - \beta_l(u^w - 1) - n, \tag{8.9}$$

$$\hat{e} = \beta_l(u^w - 1). \tag{8.10}$$

The above constraints represent all constraints that are needed from the perspective of non-Walrasian disequilibrium growth theory. Note here that $\omega, u^w, e > 0$ is automatically ensured (in finite time) due to the growth rate formulation of the model, but that this does not yet exclude that limit points of trajectories which start in the positive orthant may lie on the boundary of it. This however is another topic that is not related to our questioning of the validity of the regime switching methodology of Ito (1980) and others, which is the topic of this chapter.

Note here first that the viability condition $\omega < y$ (a positive profit share) is always fulfilled, since

$$\omega = f(k) - f'(k)k < f(k)$$

holds at all times in the Solow model.

Next we consider the condition $u^w \le 2$. In order to guarantee that this condition holds true at each moment in time we make the following simple additional assumption on the growth rate $n$ of labor supply:

$$n = n(u^w), \quad n' \geq 0, n(2) = \infty.$$

This assumption states that the growth rate of labor supply increases when overtime work increases, up to infinity, when the legal barrier $u^w = 2$ is approached (in a continuous time framework!), due to rapid changes in the participation rate of households, due to the influx of labor from rural surroundings and also due to migration from other parts of the world. Note that all these changes may be due solely to workers' decision making, but they may also be due to systematic efforts of the firms. Firms surely will attempt to recruit new labor force in case of significant labor shortage by influencing in particular the labor supply decisions of those households that so far were not part of the external labor market of the economy. In short, if labor tends to become the short side of the market, firms in market economies find ways to push up the growth rate of the labor supply sufficiently to avoid absolute supply bottlenecks. There may be many microeconomic aspects of the points just mentioned that deserve more detailed discussion. Our basic argument here however simply is that macroeconomic dynamics has to take account of these possibilities and flexibilities in the behavior of households and firms even on a preliminary level, instead of discussing the hypothetical consequences of hard constraints that have never existed in this form in developed market economies.[5]

With respect to the third restriction $e \leq 1$ it is possible, but not necessary, to assume that firms must reduce recruiting efforts on the "traditional" labor market when the upper bound on the external employment rate is approached,[6] increasing instead their activities for recruiting new workers as just discussed. In fact this constraint can become binding in the hard way, without any supply consequences as long as firm can use the internal labor market for more employment and production (which they always can if the above assumption on the rate $n$ holds).

## Proposition 3

1.   The dynamical system (8.8)–(8.10) with smooth factor substitution and supply constraints exhibits the domain $(0, \infty) \times (0, 2) \times (0, 1]$ as invariant subset which it thus cannot leave.
2.   The classical regime of non-Walrasian disequilibrium analysis is the only regime that is possible in this domain, i.e., $\omega = F_L(K, L)$ holds true at all times.

## Proof of Proposition 3

See the appendix.

Adding three simple extrinsic non-linearities to the linear growth model of Section 8.2 is thus sufficient to imply that there is no need for supply constraints as in non-Walrasian disequilibrium (growth) dynamics in order to keep such a dynamical system economically viable, in particular in the case where local asymptotic stability (see Proposition 2) does not hold. The numerical properties of the dynamics considered in Proposition 3 will be briefly discussed in the following section.

**8.5 Numerical features of the dynamics**

In order to investigate the dynamics (8.8)–(8.10) from the numerical point of view we choose a CES-representation of the assumed neoclassical production function which in intensive form is given by:

$$y = f(k) = \gamma[ak^{-\eta} + (1-a)]^{-1/\eta} \tag{8.11}$$

with $\alpha \in (0,1), \eta \in (-1,\infty)$ (and with $\rho = 1/(1+\eta)$ the constant elasticity of substitution of this function). We assume $\gamma = 1$ for simplicity. This CES production function implies the following equations as background for our system (8.8)–(8.10):

$$f'(k) = a[a + (1-a)k^{\eta}]^{-(1+\eta)/\eta}$$
$$\omega(k) = f(k) - f'(k)k = (1-a)[ak^{-\eta} + (1-a)]^{-(1+\eta)/\eta}$$
$$k(\omega) = ([\frac{\omega}{1-a}]^{-\eta/(1+n)} - (1-a)]/a)^{-1/\eta}$$
$$\varepsilon(\omega) = \frac{1}{1+\eta} \frac{1}{1-(1-a)\left(\dfrac{\omega}{1-a}\right)^{\eta/(1+\eta)}}.$$

It gives rise to the following formulae for the steady state values of capital intensity and the real wage (on the basis of the expression obtained for $\omega(k)$ and $f'(k)[= n/s_c]$):

$$k_o = ([(\frac{n/s_c}{a})^{-\eta/(1+\eta)} - a]/(1-a))^{1/\eta},$$
$$\omega_o = (1-a)[ak_o^{-\eta} + (1-a)]^{-(1+\eta)/\eta}.$$

Note here that CES functions do not fulfill the Inada conditions for neoclassical production functions which means that there will not always exist a steady state solution with respect to the parameters $n$, $s_c$, $a$.

The numerical analysis of the dynamics with this type of production function gives rise to the following observations:

- The steady state of the dynamics appears to be globally asymptotically stable with respect to all initial values in the domain described in Proposition 3 for much larger parameter sets than those characterized by assertion 2, in Proposition 3.
- If locally unstable, the dynamics are however generally bounded and economically viable without hitting the full employment ceiling $e = 1$ (unless

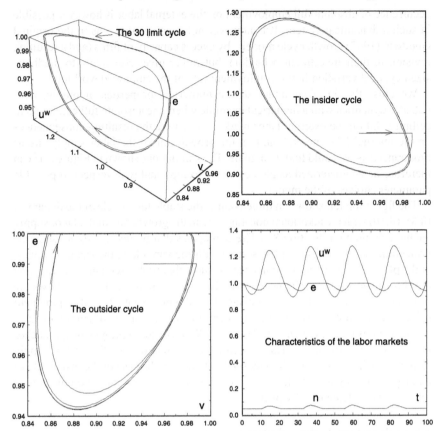

*Figure 8.1* A limit cycle and the full employment ceiling.

the NAIRU rate $\bar{e}$ is chosen very close to it). This result seems to be due to the fact that the profitability bound (based on marginal productivity theory and neoclassical use of smooth factor substitution) represents a very strong mechanism in the creation of the boundedness of the dynamics.

- If the full employment ceiling $e = 1$ is indeed hit by the trajectories of the dynamics this generally happens in conjunction with overtime work of approximately 20 percent, which – depending on the exact formulation of the natural growth rate effect – is accompanied only by small increases in the growth rate of labor supply.
- If locally explosive, the considered 3-D dynamics is generally fairly simple – giving rise to a unique stable limit cycle solely – but not to more complex types of attractors which are possible in such a setup due to the dimension of the dynamics.

In sum we can therefore state that the combination of Solovian growth with insider and outsider growth cycles is generally already sufficient to imply global stability in an economically meaningful domain of the resulting dynamics. The occurrence of absolute full employment on the external labor is however possible in such a dynamical system. It is however not accompanied – as in the original Goodwin (1967) growth cycle model – by excess capacity of firms (and a resulting revision in their investment behavior), but rather gives rise solely to medium-sized cyclical variation in the employment rate of the employed workforce.

We close this brief summary of the numerical properties of our insider–outsider dynamics with a numerical example where the absolute full employment ceiling is hit on the external labor market and where the resulting consequences on the internal labor market, and on the growth rate of the labor supply, are as pronounced as we could find them to be. The simulations shown in Figure 8.1[7] can therefore be characterized as already fairly exceptional with respect to possible parameter choices of the model.

The figure top left shows, in dimension 3, the stable limit cycle of the dynamics (8.8)–(8.10) with the additional non-linearity in the growth rate of the labor supply we have assumed in Section 8.4. The two cycles that border this figure show its projection into the adjacent planes, now with the variable $u$, the share of wages, in the place of $\omega$, the real wage in order to show that profits remain positive along the shown cycle (and on the way to it). The figure bottom right finally shows the time series for the outside and inside rate of employment (with the full employment ceiling for the first rate sometimes in operation and with a rate of employment of inside workers that stays below 130 percent). When inside employment approaches this level it is furthermore clearly visible that the rate of growth of labor supply responds to this as assumed in Section 8.4, but, as in the case of the inside rate of employment, only in a moderate way in order to satisfy the labor volume and its rate of growth demanded by firms.

## 8.6 Endogenous technical change

In this section of the chapter we investigate to what extent our analysis of cyclical growth will change when modern discussions of the endogeneity of technical change and growth is taken into account. There exist various possibilities in the literature to model endogenous technical change, see in particular Barro and Sala-i Martin (1995), Aghion and Howitt (1998). We here follow Barro and Sala-i Martin (1995, Ch.4), see also Ziesemer (1995, p.17), and use as representation of such technical change an approach based on Uzawa (1965) and Romer (1986), and synthesized by Lucas (1988). Other representations of endogenous change will not significantly alter the conclusions of this section which serves the purpose of illustrating the implications of an integration of the production of technological change into the extended growth cycle model of this chapter.

The Uzawa–Romer–Lucas approach to endogenous technical change can be described by means of the following two equations, characterizing the productive activities of firms:

$$\hat{A} = \eta L_2^w / L^w, \quad \eta > 0, \quad \text{the research unit,} \tag{8.12}$$

$$Y = K^\beta (AL_1)^{1-\beta} A^\xi, \quad \xi > 0, \quad \text{the production unit.} \tag{8.13}$$

The employed workforce $L^w = L_1^w + L_2^w$ is now split between the production of output (8.13), described by a Cobb–Douglas production function with productivity measure $A$, augmented by the Romer externality $A^\xi$, and the production of productivity growth as described by equation (8.12). Note that we do not consider over- or undertime work in the research sector, but as before in the production unit, where hours worked, $L_1$ can deviate as before from the normal employment $L_1^w$ of the there employed workforce due to the pace of capital accumulation. We denote the ratio $L_2^w / L_1^w$, the allocation of the workforce within the firm, by $h$ which implies for the ratio $L_2^w / L^w$ the expression $h/(1 + h)$.

The production function (8.13) can be easily reformulated as follows:

$$Y = K^\beta (A^{\frac{1-\beta+\xi}{1-\beta}} L_1)^{1-\beta} = K^\beta (BL_1)^{1-\beta}.$$

It shows in this way that it is of the usual type (with Harrod neutral technical change), yet with a growth rate $\hat{B}$ of the aggregate productivity index $B$ that exceeds the growth rate of the individual productivity index $\hat{A}$ of the firms, due to the Romer externality $\xi: \hat{B} = (1 + \xi/(1 - \beta))\hat{A}$.

We will apply this approach to technical change to the fixed proportions section of this chapter, and leave the case of smooth factor substitution for future investigation.[8] In the place of (8.12), (8.13) this gives rise to the following representation of produced productivity growth:

$$\hat{A} = \eta \frac{h}{1+h},$$

$$Y = \min\{xK, AL_1 A^\xi\} = \min\{xK, A^{1+\xi} L_1\} = \min\{xK, yL_1\},$$

where, as in Section 8.2, the symbol $y = Y/L_1$ denotes labor productivity on the aggregate level, whose rate of growth is given by $\hat{y} = (1+\xi)\hat{A} = (1+\xi)\eta \frac{h}{1+h}$. Let us consider $h$ as a given parameter for the moment.

The equations constituting the model of section 8.2, adjusted to the purposes of the present section, read:

$$\hat{w} = \beta_{w_1}(e - \bar{e}) + \beta_{w_2}(u_1^w - 1) + \hat{y}, \tag{8.14}$$

$$e = \frac{L_1^w + L_2^w}{L^s} = (1+h)e_1, \quad e_1 = \frac{L_1^w}{L^s}, $$

$$\hat{L}_1^w = \beta_l(u_1^w - 1) + n, \quad u_1^w = \frac{L_1}{L_1^w}, \tag{8.15}$$

$$\hat{K} = s_c x(1 - \omega/y). \tag{8.16}$$

The employment policy of firms (8.15), is based in this formulation on their production unit and there on the degree of over- or undertime work $L_1$ performed by production workers $L_1^w$ (while employment in the research unit is given by $L_2^w = hL_1^w$ in each moment of time). Wage claims are now made in view of labor productivity growth $\hat{y}$ which augments the real wage Phillips curve of Section 8.2 in a straightforward way, see (8.15). There are thus only minor adjustments needed in these two equations of the dynamics in order to include produced productivity growth and the allocation of the workforce of firms into them. There is no change in the third equation (8.16), which again gives the growth rate of the capital stock on the basis of the savings that are made out of profits.

In the presence of technical change we have to use the share of wages $u = \omega/y$ in the place of real wages as state variable of the model. Furthermore, the dynamical equations must be reduced to expressions concerning the production unit solely in order to get an autonomous system of differential equations in the case of produced productivity growth $(h > 0)$. This is easily done and gives rise to the following system of differential equations ($e \leq 1, u_1^w \leq 2$ again):

$$\hat{u} = \beta_{w_1}((1+h)e_1 - \bar{e}) + \beta_{w_2}(u_1^w - 1), \tag{8.17}$$

$$\hat{u}_1^w = \hat{K} - \hat{y} - \hat{L}^w$$
$$= s_c x(1-u) - \beta_l(u_1^w - 1) - (n + (1+\xi)\eta \frac{h}{1+h}), \tag{8.18}$$

$$\hat{e}_1 = \beta_l(u_1^w - 1). \tag{8.19}$$

This system is of exactly the same type as the dynamical system considered in Section 8.2. It thus gives rise to the same proposition as in this section. However, technical change, though produced by firms, is still basically of an exogenous nature here and thus demands in a next step the endogenization of the parameter $h$ in order to arrive at a model which generates growth endogenously. In view of this necessity we propose as law of motion for the labor allocation ratio $h$

$$\dot{h} = \beta_h((\hat{K} - \hat{y}) - n)$$
$$= \beta_h(s_c x(1-u) - (n + (1+\xi)\eta \frac{h}{1+h})), \tag{8.20}$$

where we interpret the expression $\hat{K} - \hat{y}$ as growth rate of labor demand, calculated by firms on the basis of their investment decisions concerning output and productivity increases. This rate is contrasted with the growth rate of labor supply available to fill this gap between capital stock and productivity growth. Firms therefore increase their efforts in raising labor productivity in the case of insufficient growth in the labor supply and vice versa. This is of course only a first step into the direction of endogenously generated technical change. Further extensions could for example concern the role of income distribution, but must be left for future reconsideration in this chapter.

For the extended dynamics (8.17)–(8.20) we get in place of Proposition 1:

**Proposition 4**

1. *The dynamical system (8.17)–(8.20) exhibits a ray, parameterized by $h \in (0, \infty)$, of interior steady state solutions, given by:*

$$u_o = 1 - \frac{n + (1+\xi)\eta \dfrac{h}{1+h}}{s_c x}, \quad u_{10}^w = 1, \quad e_{10} = \frac{\bar{e}}{1+h}$$

*if the parameters of the model are chosen such that* $\dfrac{n + (1+\xi)\eta}{s_c x} < 1$

*holds.*

2. *These steady states are locally asymptotically stable in all cases where the dynamics of Section 8.2 or the one for a given h are locally asymptotically stable, i.e., endogenous technical change increases the parameter domain where local asymptotic stability prevails, combined with zero-root hysteresis now, since one of the eigenvalues of the linear part of the dynamics must be zero throughout.*

3. *If not locally asymptotically stable, which is the case if $\beta_h$ is sufficiently small and $\beta_{w_1}$ sufficiently large,[9] the system can be made locally asymptotically stable, again by way of a Hopf-bifurcation, if the parameter $\beta_h$ is made sufficiently large.*

**Proof of Proposition 4**

See the appendix.

We thus in sum have that endogenous technical change and growth (with rate $(1+\xi)\eta \dfrac{h}{1+h}$) is easily integrated into the growth cycle model of this chapter, adds to its stability, preserves its cyclical characteristics (at least to some extent) and most importantly, makes the generation of technical change and growth path-dependent, since shocks to its orbits will cause convergence to a different steady state position, due to the zero-root hysteresis now present in the dynamics. Furthermore, the steady state wage share now depends negatively on the parameters that characterize long-run productivity growth (including the size of $h$ that determines the allocation of workers to production and research activities). Of course, further investigations and extensions of the considered dynamics which add the effects of income distribution on the generation of technical change, the role of substitution in production, extensions of the model from the global point of view as considered in section 8.4 should follow, but cannot be approached here due to space limitations.[10]

## 8.7 Conclusions

We have shown in this chapter that the non-Walrasian reconsideration of the Solow growth model by Ito (1980) which studies situations of over- and under-employment, caused by a sluggish real wage dynamics, by means of differential inequalities or "patched-up" dynamical systems, is misleading as there is indeed no regime-switching of this type close to or farther away from the Solovian steady state. Taking the possibility of over- (and under-) time work of the workforce of firms into account instead gives rise to an ordinary three-dimensional dynamics of Solow–Goodwin type with no regime switching at all, i.e., with the classical regime holding throughout.

  Increasing the range of the adjustment possibilities that a market economy allows for therefore removes the non-smooth reaction patterns as assumed in non-Walrasian fix price theory which are thus only due to implausible rigidities in the assumed structure of the economy. Furthermore and perhaps more importantly, we have also shown that it is not difficult to design non-linearities in the adjustment behavior of such an economy which not only globally prevent the occurrence of hard constraints on the output of firms, but which in fact produce a viable and basically smooth economic dynamics under all circumstances. Such a viability demonstration is generally not an easy task in the case of three dimensional dynamical systems.

  These conclusions not only apply to the neoclassical disequilibrium growth theory of Ito (1980), but also to Keynesian growth models of Picard (1983), Solow and Stiglitz (1968), as well as many others, as shown in Flaschel (1999), Chiarella et al. (2000b, Ch.4). They are also valid when endogenous growth is included in such model types as shown in Section 8.6 for the situation considered in section 2. Consequently, though non-Walrasian economics has made us aware of the importance of supply-side constraints for Keynesian growth dynamics, it has vastly overstated the possibility of regime switches in such a setup due to its reliance on rigidities that do not really exist in market economies. Patching different dynamics together is therefore not a big issue in the macrodynamic analysis of market economies.

## Appendix: mathematical proofs

### *Proof of proposition 1*

1. Obvious (and as in the original Goodwin (1967) model).
  2. The Jacobian of (8.4), (8.5), (8.6) at the steady state is given by

$$J = \begin{pmatrix} 0 & \beta_{w_2}\omega_0 & \beta_{w_1}\omega_0 \\ -s_c x/y & -\beta_l & 0 \\ 0 & \beta_l e_0 & 0 \end{pmatrix}.$$

Therefore, $-a_1 = \text{trace } J = -\beta_l < 0$ and $-a_3 = \det J = -\beta_{w_1}\omega_0 s_c x/y \beta_l e_0 < 0$. For $a_2$ (the sum of the principal minors) we get $a_2 = \beta_{w_2}\omega_0 s_c x/y > 0$. According to the

Routh–Hurwitz conditions, see Gantmacher (1971), we have to consider the positivity of $a_1 a_2 - a_3$ in addition:

$$a_1 a_2 - a_3 = \beta_l \omega_0 s_c (x/y) \; (\beta_{w_2} - \beta_{w_1} \bar{e}_0).$$

Hence $a_1 a_2 - a_3 > 0$ if and only if $\beta_{w_2} > \beta_{w_1} \bar{e}_0$. The assertion of a Hopf-bifurcation at $\beta_{w_2} = \beta_{w_1} \bar{e}_0$ is then proved by means of the above expression for $a_1 a_2 - a_3$. as in Benhabib and Miyao (1981).

3. As in Benhabib and Miyao (1981), due to the above expression for the coefficient $a_1 a_2 - a_3$.

## *Proof of proposition 2*

The Jacobian of the dynamics with substitution is given (at the steady state) by the following matrix:

$$J = \begin{pmatrix} 0 & \beta_{w_2} \omega_0 & \beta_{w_1} \omega_0 \\ -1/k(\omega_0) & -\beta_l - \in \beta_{w_2} & - \in \beta_{w_1} \\ 0 & \beta_l e_0 & 0 \end{pmatrix}$$

since the expression

$$r(\omega) = x(1 - \omega/y) = \frac{f(k(\omega))}{k(\omega)} \; (1 - \frac{\omega}{f(k(\omega))})$$

that now defines the rate of profit of the economy has the derivative $r'(\omega) = -1/k(\omega)$:

$$r'(\omega) = \frac{f'(k(\omega))k'(\omega)k(\omega) - f(k(\omega))k'(\omega)}{k(\omega)^2} - \frac{k(\omega) - \omega k'(\omega)}{k(\omega)^2}$$

$$= \frac{k'(\omega)[f'(k(\omega))k(\omega) - f(k(\omega)) + \omega]}{k(\omega)^2} - \frac{1}{k(\omega)} = -\frac{1}{k(\omega)}$$

because of $f(\omega) - f'(k(\omega))k(\omega) = \omega$. There follows $e_0 = \bar{e}$:

$$a_1 = \beta_l + \in \beta_{w_2} > 0$$

$$a_2 = \beta_{w_2} \omega_0 / k(\omega_0) + \beta_l e_0 \in \beta_{w_1} > 0$$

$$a_3 = \beta_l e_0 \beta_{w_1} \omega_0 / k(\omega_0) > 0$$

$$a_1 a_2 - a_3 = \beta_l^2 e_0 \in \beta_{w_1} + \in \beta_{w_2}^2 \omega_0 / k(\omega_0)$$

$$+ \in^2 \beta_{w_2} \beta_l e_0 \beta_{w_1} + \beta_l \omega_0 / k(\omega_0)[\beta_{w_2} - e_0 \beta_{w_1}].$$

*Proof of proposition 3*

The assumption made on the function $n = n(u^w)$ implies:

$$\hat{u}^w < 0 \text{ close to } u^w = 2,$$

i.e., the state variable $u^w$ cannot approach this border. Furthermore, $e \le 1$ holds by assumption, while $\omega < y$ has already been shown to be the simple consequence of the marginal productivity theory of employment.

*Proof of proposition 4*

1. Setting (8.17)–(8.20) equal to zero gives only three independent equations for the four state variables $u, u_1^w, e_1, h$, from which the shown steady state solutions are then easily obtained.

2. Inspection of the laws of motion (8.17)–(8.20) shows that the fourth law can be obtained form the second and the third in the following way: $\dot{h} = \beta_h \hat{u}_1^w + \beta_h \hat{e}_1$. This implies that the determinant of the linear part of the system must be zero throughout, implying that one eigen-value must always be zero, and it implies also the following algebraic relationship between the three state variables shown: $h = \beta_h \ln u_1^w + \beta_h \ln e_1 + const$. This relationship can be inserted into (8.17)–(8.19), thereby giving rise to an autonomous three dimensional dynamic system in the remaining state variables $u, u_1^w, e_1$. These reduced dynamics must remain locally asymptotically stable if it was locally asymptotically stable for $h = const.$, as will be shown below, which due to the relationship $h = \beta_h \ln u_1^w + \beta_h \ln e_1 + const$ shows that it will in particular converge to $h = \beta_h \ln e_1 + const.$ It will thus exhibit shock-dependence with respect to the value of $h$ the system will converge to. The Jacobian of this system at the steady state is given by the sum of the Jacobian of the system without *endogenous* technical change

$$J = \begin{pmatrix} 0 & \beta_{w_2} u_0 & \beta_{w_1}(1+h)u_0 \\ -s_c x & -\beta_l & 0 \\ 0 & \beta_l e_{10} & 0 \end{pmatrix}$$

and new terms as they derive from the above algebraic relationship for $h$:

$$H = \begin{pmatrix} 0 & \beta_{w_1}\beta_h e_{10} u_0 & \beta_{w_1}\beta_h u_0 \\ 0 & -k_h \beta_h & -k_h \beta_h / e_{10} \\ 0 & 0 & 0 \end{pmatrix}$$

with $k_h = (1+\xi)\eta \dfrac{h}{(1+h)^2}$. Recalculating the expressions for $a_1, a_2, a_3$ in the proof of Proposition 1 for this extended Jacobian then shows that the addition of the matrix $H$ to the original Jacobian $J$ used to prove Proposition 1 will increase all of the coefficients $a_1, a_2, a_3$ of the Routh–Hurwitz polynomial, and this by the summation of positive terms throughout. Furthermore, since $a_3$ is solely augmented by the expression $-J_{21} J_{32} \beta_{w_1} \beta_h u_o$ and $a_1 a_2$ in particular by $-J_{22}(-J_{21} \beta_{w_1} \beta_h e_{10} u_o)$, and since $J_{32} = \beta_l e_{10} = -J_{22} e_{10}$ holds, we get that also $b$ is increased through the addition of the matrix $H$. The stability conditions of the Routh–Hurwitz theorem are thus all improved when exogenous technical change (a given $h$) is extended by (8.20) in order to allow endogenous technical change.

3. On the basis of what has been shown in part 2 of the proof we know that $a_1 a_2 - a_3$ is a quadratic function of $\beta_h$ with only positive terms in front of the $\beta_h's$. Since stability can only get lost via a negative term in $a_1 a_2 - a_3$, we thus get that such instability can always be removed again by making the parameter $\beta_h$ sufficiently large. Such switches from stability to instability and back to stability can only occur via Hopf-bifurcations as the reduction of the 4-D dynamics to a 3-D dynamics in part 2 of the proof immediately implies.

# 9 The dominance of Keynesian regimes in non-Walrasian growth

## 9.1 Introduction

Non-Walrasian macroeconomics has provided many significant contributions to macrostatics as reviewed recently in Benassy (1993). There are however fewer contributions of this approach to the theory of business fluctuations and only very few to the theory of economic growth (in real or monetary economies). There is indeed only one footnote in Benassy (1993) with respect to these important areas of macroeconomics, which (though it does not mentioning all important contributions in this area) nevertheless provides the correct impression that there is not much to say about the non-Walrasian modeling of monetary growth.

The explanation for this theoretical deficit in non-Walrasian macrodynamics is not difficult to provide if one looks at the papers in Hénin and Michel (1982) for example. Regime switching scenarios, as they are investigated thoroughly in non-Walrasian statical analysis of general economic interdependence and the spill-over of disequilibria between markets, can be managed in the static context, but become nearly untractable in the analysis of macroeconomic fluctuations and growth in monetary economies. This holds in particular if the considered dynamics are no longer planar ones, due to laws of motion for real wages, real money balances, factor endowments, and more.

In this respect the paper by Picard (1983) has made significant progress since it provides a monetary growth model of non-Walrasian type with its typical switches of regimes (Keynesian or classical unemployment and repressed inflation), giving rise to 3-D dynamics in the above named variables which, however, are not easy to analyze as the long appendixes containing the proofs of Picard's (1983) propositions show.

The present chapter[1] shows in this regard that this analysis – and the model formulation on which it is based – can be considerably simplified if some basic aspects in the formulation of wage–price dynamics in the macrodynamical literature are taken into account, i.e., the facts (for which various rationalizations may be offered) that wages and prices start rising before the level of absolute full employment in the labor market and absolute capacity utilization within firms has been reached. These simple additions to the wage–price module, which are used here as an example solely, suffice to show that the environment of the steady state of such models of monetary growth is completely Keynesian, with no regime switching to classical unemployment or repressed inflation. The dynamics around the steady state is thereby radically simplified and propositions as in Picard (1983) are then easily proved and extended.

We conclude that macroeconomic applications of the non-Walrasian approach are predominantly Keynesian in nature and thus do not need the heavy machinery of non-linear differential inequalities for most of its propositions.

## 9.2  The Picard model of non-Walrasian growth

In order to show this, this chapter only reconsiders the dynamics of the disequilibrium growth model presented in Picard (1983), of course, on the basis of the temporary (dis)equilibrium positions provided in this article. We therefore do not repeat the determination of these positions here, but simply note that they are classified in Picard (1983), as is typical for non-Walrasian approaches, into Keynesian unemployment, classical unemployment and repressed inflation, here with respect to the two statically exogenous (but dynamically endogenous) variables real balances per unit of labor $m$ and full employment capital intensity $k = K/L$. Of course, this classification into three regimes in the $m, k$ state space is based on assumptions made on households', firms' and the government's behavior, including fully specified budget restrictions, and it makes use of the parameters $c, d$ the marginal propensities to consume out of income and wealth, respectively, $\tau, \mu$, the income tax rate and the growth rate of the money supply, and $y^p = Y^p/K$, $x = Y/L^d$, the potential output–capital ratio $y^p$ and actual output–employment ratio or labor productivity $x$. We thus have here the assumption of a fixed proportions technology in particular and on this basis straightforward expressions for the rate of capacity utilization of firms, $u = Y/Y^p$ and for the rate of employment, $e = L^d/L = Y/(xL)$ in terms of actual output $Y$.

Concerning the laws of motion of the economy, Picard (1983) assumes two specific types of Phillips curves, one for money wages $w$ and one for the price level $p$, based on demand–pull as well as cost–push considerations of the following form ($\omega = w/p$ the real wage and $\tilde{\omega}$ a given target real wage of workers):

$$\hat{w} = \beta_{w_1}\left(\frac{\tilde{L}^d - L}{\tilde{L}^d}\right) + \beta_{w_2}(\tilde{\omega} - \omega) + \kappa_w \pi, \quad \hat{p} = \beta_p\left(\frac{\tilde{Y}^d - \check{Y}}{\tilde{Y}^d}\right) + \kappa_p \pi$$

with positive $\beta$'s as adjustment speeds and both $\kappa_w$ and $\kappa_p$ in the interval $[0, 1]$. In these equations we denote by $\tilde{Y}^d$ the unconstrained demand for goods $\tilde{Y}^d = C + I + G$, and make in addition use of the expressions $\tilde{L}^d = \min\{\tilde{Y}^d/x, Y^p/x\}$, $\check{Y} = \min\{Y^p, xL\}$, denoting the minimum labor demand (when aggregate demand $\tilde{Y}^d$ and potential output $Y^p$ are taken into account as constraining labor demand) and the minimum production when potential output and the full employment output act as constraints on production [for $\omega = w/p < x$]. The above two magnitudes are called effective labor demand and the effective supply of goods in Picard (1983).

For capital stock growth we have on the basis of the investment function assumed in Picard (1983):

$$\hat{K} = i_1 \, \bar{Y}/K + i_2(x - \omega), \quad \omega < x$$

and $\dot{K} = 0$ for $\omega \geq x$, while labor supply $L$ grows at the exogenously given rate $n$.

These three laws of motion imply the following non-linear autonomous dynamical system in the intensive form variables $\omega = w/p$, $m = M/(pL)$ and $k = K/L$ if expected inflation $\pi$ is fixed at the steady state value of the rate inflation $\mu - n = \hat{M} - \hat{L}$. For simplicity we assume $\mu = n$ in the following.

$$\hat{\omega} = \beta_{w_1}\left(\frac{\tilde{L}^d - L}{\tilde{L}^d}\right) + \beta_{w_2}(\tilde{\omega} - \omega) - \beta_p\left(\frac{\tilde{Y}^d - \check{Y}}{\tilde{Y}^d}\right), \tag{9.1}$$

$$\hat{m} = -\beta_p\left(\frac{\tilde{Y}^d - \check{Y}}{\tilde{Y}^d}\right), \tag{9.2}$$

$$\hat{k} = i_1 \, \bar{Y}/K + i_2(x - \omega) - n, \tag{9.3}$$

with

$$\frac{\tilde{L}^d - L}{\tilde{L}^d} = \frac{\tilde{l}^d - 1}{\tilde{l}^d}, \qquad \frac{\tilde{Y}^d - Y}{\tilde{Y}^d} = \frac{\tilde{y}^d - \check{y}}{\tilde{y}^d}, \qquad \frac{\bar{Y}}{K} = \frac{\bar{y}}{k},$$

where all variables have been transformed to intensive form by dividing through labor supply $L$.

Since $\check{y} = \min\{y^p k, x\}$, $\bar{y} = \min\{\tilde{y}^d, x\}$, $\tilde{l}^d = \min\{\tilde{y}^d/x, y^p k/x\}$ and $y = \min\{\tilde{y}^d, \check{y}\}$, $l^d = y/x$ there remains $\tilde{y}^d$ to be calculated. In the Keynesian regime one gets for this variable from Picard (1983):

$$\tilde{y}^d = \frac{1}{1 - c(1 - \tau) - \tau}(d + \mu)m = f^1(m),$$

which can be interpreted as a Keynesian multiplier, while $\tilde{y}^d$ is given in the Classical regime by

$$\tilde{y}^d = (c(1 - \tau) + \tau)y^p k + (d + \mu)m = f^2(k, m)$$

and in the regime of repressed inflation by

$$\tilde{y}^d = (c(1 - \tau) + \tau)x + (d + \mu)m = f^3(m).$$

This shows that the above dynamical system can indeed be reduced to the three state variables $\omega$, $m$ and $k$.

## 9.3 Analysis of the model

This dynamical system is not easy to treat with respect to steady state determination and stability analysis and gives rise to fairly complicated propositions in Picard (1983) which we do not reconsider here due to space limitations. Summing up this type of disequilibrium theory of monetary growth we here simply state that its richness of implication and difficult proofs derive from the numerous possible regimes it allows for (in fact there are two further subregimes in each of three regimes we have considered above), and that it represents a complete model of monetary growth with a very complicated dynamical structure due to the many differential inequalities that have to be considered in general.

In contrast to this we shall demonstrate in the following that a basic modification of this disequilibrium growth model, which is closer to the description of a market economy than the model of Picard, will be much simpler to treat from the viewpoint of dynamical systems (steady state and stability analysis) due to the fact that this revised model of monetary growth of a market economy is not subject to switching regimes and will not allow for the establishment of Classical unemployment or repressed inflation around its steady state. Therefore much of the effort that has gone into the analysis of laws of motions based on differential inequalities can simply be avoided by paying attention to the fact that market economies have a variety of mechanisms and flexibilities (of which only one example will be analyzed here) that allow them to avoid the rationing of consumers, or investors or the government on the macro-economic level.

The most basic critique of the considered non-Walrasian dynamics is that its two Phillips-curves for money wages and the price level are misspecified with respect to the actual working of market economies.

Whatever microeconomic motivation is offered in the literature for the NAIRU rate of employment $\bar{e}$, it is generally agreed on the macrolevel that money wages are subject to an upward pressure before everybody in the workforce is employed. One explanation for this aggregate occurrence is that there are asymmetries in the adjustment of money wages.[2] Our interest here solely are the macroeconomic consequences of such a situation in a non-Walrasian setup. The obvious and necessary change thus is[3]

$$\hat{w} = \beta_w \left( \frac{\tilde{L}^d - \bar{e}L}{\tilde{L}^d} \right) + \beta_{w_2}(\tilde{\omega} - \omega), \quad \bar{e} \in (0,1), \tilde{L}^d = \min\{\tilde{Y}^d/x, \bar{u}Y^P/x\}.$$

Likewise, the price level starts rising before either the capacity constraint or the labor supply constraint becomes binding, i.e., the law for price dynamics should be modified as follows:[4]

$$\hat{p} = \beta_p \left( \frac{\tilde{Y}^d - \check{Y}}{\tilde{Y}^d} \right), \quad \check{Y} = \min\{\bar{u}Y^p, \bar{e}Lx\}, \ \bar{u} \in (0,1).$$

Finally, firms should now use $\overline{\overline{Y}} = \min\{\tilde{Y}^d, \bar{e}Lx\}$ in the place of $\overline{Y} = \min\{\tilde{Y}^d, Lx\}$ as the capacity constraint for their investment decisions which gives $\hat{k} = i_1(\overline{\overline{Y}}/K) + i_2(x - \omega) - n$ as third law of motion.

Up to the use of $\check{Y}, \overline{\overline{Y}}, \bar{e}L$ in place of $\check{Y}, \overline{Y}$ and $L$ in the dynamical system (1)–(3) the model is the same as before.

## Proposition 1

1. The unique interior steady state of the revised dynamical system

$$\hat{\omega} = \beta_{w_1} \left( \frac{\tilde{L}^d - L\bar{e}}{\tilde{L}^d} \right) + \beta_{w_2} (\tilde{\omega} - \omega) - \beta_p \left( \frac{\tilde{Y}^d - \check{Y}}{\tilde{Y}^d} \right), \tag{9.4}$$

$$\hat{m} = -\beta_p \left( \frac{\tilde{Y}^d - \check{Y}}{\tilde{Y}^d} \right), \tag{9.5}$$

$$\hat{k} = i_1 \left( \overline{\overline{Y}}/K \right) + i_2 (x - \omega) - n \tag{9.6}$$

is given by

$$\omega_0 = \tilde{\omega}, \quad m_0 = \frac{(1 - c(1 - \tau) - \tau)x\bar{e}}{d + \mu}, \quad k_0 = \frac{x\bar{e}}{y^p \bar{u}},$$

if we assume that $\tilde{\omega} = \bar{\omega}$ holds, where $\bar{\omega}$ given by the balanced growth condition $i_1\bar{u}y^p + i_2(x - \bar{\omega}) = n$.

2. At this steady state we have

$$\tilde{Y}^d = \bar{u}Y^p = \bar{e}Lx < \min\{Y^p, xL\},$$

i.e., this steady state always belongs to the region of Keynesian unemployment.

3. This assertion also holds true for all steady states belonging to a target real wage $\tilde{\omega}$ in a neighborhood of $\bar{\omega}$.

## Proof of Proposition 1

The proof of this proposition is based on the following simple observations:

A. Setting $\hat{m} = 0 \ (m \neq 0)$ implies $\tilde{Y}^d = \check{Y} = \min\{\bar{u}Y^p, \bar{e}Lx\}$.

B. In the case $\tilde{Y}^d = \bar{u}Y^p \leq \bar{e}Lx$ we then get $\overline{\overline{Y}} = \bar{u}Y^p = \tilde{Y}^d$, i.e., $\omega_0 = \bar{\omega} = \tilde{\omega}$. Therefore: $\bar{e}L = \min\{\tilde{Y}^d/x, Y^p/x\}$ because of $\hat{\omega} = 0 \ (\omega \neq 0)$, i.e., $\tilde{Y}^d = x\bar{e}L$ or in sum

$$\tilde{Y}^d = x\bar{e}L = \bar{u}Y^p.$$

Since we are thus always in the Keynesian regime we have

$$\tilde{y}^d = x\bar{e} = \frac{1}{1-c(1-\tau)-\tau}(d+\mu) = m_0$$

as equation for $m_0$ and

$$x\bar{e} = \bar{u}y^p k_0$$

as equation for $k_0$ $[=x\bar{e}/(\bar{u}y^p)]$.

C. In the other case $\tilde{Y}^d = \bar{e}Lx = \overline{\overline{Y}} \le \bar{u}Y^p$ (see 1.), we have $\tilde{y}\bar{e} = x\bar{e} \le \bar{u}y^p$. We therefore again get $\omega_0 \le \bar{\omega}$ and thus $\tilde{L}^d \le L\bar{e}$ or min $\{\tilde{Y}^d/x, \bar{u}Y^p/x\} \le L\bar{e}$. Thus

$$\tilde{y}^d = x\bar{e} = \bar{u}y^p.$$

Therefore $\omega_0 = \bar{\omega}$ and $m_0$, $k_0$ are determined as in the preceding case 2.

We thus get that $Y = \tilde{Y}^d$ must always hold true in the neighborhood of the steady state and $L^d = \tilde{Y}^d/x$, i.e., employment is always demand determined sufficiently close to the steady state. The $KU$-regime is therefore the only relevant one at least in the vicinity of the steady state solution of the dynamical system (9.4)–(9.6).

*Remark*

This result on the dominance of the Keynesian regime can be made much stronger if overtime work of insiders, smooth factor substitution, excessive production (with respect to the profit maximizing output) in order to satisfy customers' demand and inventories are taken into account as in Chiarella et al. (2000b) Flaschel (2000).

## 9.4 Modifications of the model

Instead of pursuing this line of approach further, we further reexamine the dynamical laws for $\hat{w}$ and $\hat{p}$ with respect to their meaningfulness. Since we have the Keynesian demand regime ($Y = \tilde{Y}^d$) close to the steady state we get for $\tilde{L}^d/L$ the expression min$\{e, \bar{u}y^p k/x\}$ with $e = L^d/L = Y/(xL)$ the actual rate of employment. But how does the expression $\bar{u}y^p k/x$ influence money–wage dynamics as proposed by the expression

$$\beta_{w_1}\left(\frac{\tilde{L}^d - \bar{e}L}{\tilde{L}^d}\right)$$

in the above money-wage Phillips curve? Furthermore, why this choice of a denominator? In our view it is sufficient to use (as is customary):

$$\beta_{w_1}\left(\frac{e-\bar{e}}{\bar{e}}\right) = \beta_{w_1}\left(e/\bar{e}-1\right), e = L^d/L$$

in place of the above expression in order to describe the demand pull component of the dynamics of money wages. Similarly (again because of $Y = \tilde{Y}^d$):

$$\beta_p\left(\frac{\tilde{Y}^d - \min\{\bar{u}Y^p, \bar{e}Lx\}}{\tilde{Y}^d}\right) = \beta_p\left(\frac{u - \min\{\bar{u}, \bar{e}x/(y^p k)\}}{u}\right).$$

But why $\bar{e}x/(y^p k)$ and $u$ in the denominator of this expression? Again the term

$$\beta_p\left(\frac{u-\bar{e}}{\bar{u}}\right) = \beta_p\left(\frac{u}{\bar{u}}-1\right)$$

is fully sufficient to express the demand pull component, now in the market for goods. Taken together, the dynamical system (9.4)–(9.6) should therefore be rewritten as

$$\hat{\omega} = \beta_{w_1}\left(e/\bar{e}-1\right) + \beta_{w_2}\left(\hat{\omega}-\omega\right) - \beta_p\left(u/\bar{u}-1\right), \tag{9.7}$$

$$\hat{m} = -\beta_p\left(u/\bar{u}-1\right), \tag{9.8}$$

$$\hat{k} = i_1 y_p u + i_2\left(x-\omega\right), \tag{9.9}$$

since $Y^d = Y$, $L^d = Y/x$ are the relevant expressions for the actual position of the economy, below or above $\bar{e}L$ and $\bar{u}Y^p$, but below $L$ and $Y^p$ $(e = \tilde{Y}^d/(xL) = \tilde{y}^d/x, u = \tilde{Y}^d/Y^p = \tilde{y}^d/(y^p k))$.

*Remark*

The interior steady state of the system (9.7)–(9.9) is the same as for the system (9.4)–(9.6), with $e_o$ below $\bar{e}$ if $\tilde{\omega} > \bar{\omega}$ holds true.

*Proposition 2*

1.  *The steady state of the dynamical system (9.7)–(9.9) is locally asymptotically stable if $\beta_{w_1} < \beta_p$ holds true.*[5]
2.  *The steady state of the dynamical system (9.7)–(9.9) loses its stability in a cyclical fashion at the unique Hopf-bifurcation point:*

$$\beta_{w_1}^H = \frac{a_1 a_2}{\beta_p i_2 (e'/\bar{e})(-u_k/\bar{u})\omega_o m_o k_o}$$

*through the birth of a stable or the death of an unstable limit cycle of or periodic orbit.*[6]

**Proof of Proposition 2**

1. Due to the prevalence of the Keynesian regime around the steady state we have

$$\tilde{y}^d(m) = y = \frac{1}{1 - c(1 - \tau) - \tau}(d + \mu)m$$

for $e = L^d/L = Y/(xL) = y/x$ and $u = Y/Y^p = y/(y^p k)$. Hence, $e = e(m)$, $e' > 0$ and $u = u(m, k)$, $u_m > 0$, $u_k < 0$.

According to the Routh–Hurwitz conditions, see Benhabib and Miyao (1981), one has to show

$$a_1 = -\text{trace } J > 0, \quad a_3 = -\det J > 0, \quad a_1 a_2 - a_3 > 0 \quad (a_2 > 0)$$

where $J$ is the Jacobian of the above dynamical system at the steady state and where $a_2$ is given by the sum of principal minors of this matrix.

It is easy to show that $\det J < 0$ must hold, since linearly dependent expressions can be removed from $J$ without altering its determinant which simplifies the calculation of this determinant significantly. Thus:

$$a_3 = -\det J = \beta_{w_1}\beta_p i_2 (e'/\bar{e})(-u_k/\bar{u})\omega_o m_o k_o > 0.$$

Quite obviously, also

$$a_1 = -\text{trace } J = \beta_{w_2}\omega_0 + \beta_p(u_m/\bar{e})m_0 + i_1 y_p(-u_k)k_0 > 0.$$

Furthermore, we also immediately get:

$$a_2 = \beta_{w_2}\beta_p(u_m/\bar{u})\omega_o m_o + \beta_{w_2} i_2 y^p(-u_k)\omega_o k_o + \beta_p i_2(-u_k/\bar{u})\omega_o k_o.$$

Due to $e(m) = \tilde{y}^d(m)/x, u(m, k) = \tilde{y}^d(m)/(y^p k)$ we finally get (by setting the positive $\beta_{w_2}$ – terms all equal to zero)

$$a_1 a_2 - a_3 > \beta_p i_2(-u_k/\bar{u})\omega_o m_o k_o \tilde{y}^{d'}(m_o)(\beta_p - \beta_{w_1}),$$

since $i_1 y^p(-u_k)k_o > 0$ and $y^p \bar{u} k_o = x\bar{e}$  [$\bar{u}Y^p = x\bar{e}L$] at the steady state.

2. Since the parameter $\beta_{w_1}$ only appears in the determinant of the Jacobian $J$ the calculation of the Hopf-bifurcation point is an easy task, since it is characterized by $b = a_1 a_2 - a_3 = 0$, the only stability condition which can change its sign in the present situation. Furthermore, the value of $b$ is a linear (negatively sloped) function of the parameter $\beta_{w_1}$ which implies as in Benhabib and Miyao

(1981) that the eigen-values cross the imaginary axis with positive speed and thus allows the application of the Hopf-bifurcation theorem as in Benhabib and Miyao (1981).

We thus have that price flexibility that is larger than wage flexibility (with respect to demand pull components) is good for economic stability, which is not too surprising due to the assumed Pigou- or real balance-effect on aggregate demand. Furthermore, this stability is increased through increases in the parameter $\beta_{w_2}$, since this adjustment parameter only appears in $a_1 a_2$ and there always with positive signs as the above calculations have shown. We therefore have definite reasons to expect that the local asymptotic stability result holds also for $\beta_p \ll \beta_{w_1}$ if (e.g.) $\beta_{w2}$ is chosen sufficiently high. Nevertheless, there is a limit to this stability result if the parameter $\beta_{w_1}$ is made sufficiently large (all others held constant), where the stability of the system then gets lost in a cyclical fashion.

## 9.5 Conclusions

We have shown in this chapter that non-Walrasian approaches to monetary growth can be transformed into a special case of Keynesian monetary growth at least in the vicinity of the steady state. Regime switches arbitrarily close to the steady state of market economies is neither empirically plausible nor analytically convincing, since they are based on too many rigidities in contrast to the many flexible adjustment procedures that are imaginable for developed market economies. Thus, for example, the situation of repressed inflation will only happen far off the steady state, if overtime work of the workforce of firms is properly taken into account, see Chiarella et al. (2000b, Ch.3), Flaschel (2000). The classical regime furthermore is much less likely if account is taken of smooth factor substitution and of the fact that firms will temporarily serve their customers, in a Keynesian environment (where firms are not price-takers), beyond the point where prices equal marginal costs, unless their inventories are exhausted, see Flaschel (1999) for the occurrence of such situations and their likelihood. The barriers to serving aggregate demand for goods are thus much less rigid than assumed in non-Walrasian macroeconomics.

# 10 Steindlian models of growth and stagnation

## 10.1 Introduction

Steindl explained the depression in the interwar period by the inability of the economy "to adjust to low growth rates because its saving propensity is adapted to a high one" (Steindl 1979, p.1). The argument was laid out in Steindl (1952). In the process of capitalist development, he argued, previously competitive industries become oligopolized. This change in competitive conditions puts upward pressure on the profit margin and makes the profit margin less responsive to changes in demand conditions. An increase in the profit margin may provide the trigger for reduced demand and a reduction in growth rates; the insensitivity of the margin to lower demand and the emergence of unwanted excess capacity potentially turn the downturn into secular depression or stagnation. The economy, in his terminology, becomes "mature", where maturity is defined "as the state in which the economy and its profit function are adjusted to the high growth rates of earlier stages of capitalist development, while those high growth rates no longer obtain" (Steindl 1979, p.7).

The post-war economy was revitalized and experienced a golden age with near full employment and high growth rates from the 1950s to around 1970. This golden age, in Steindl's view, was explained by a combination of expansionary policy (large increases in the government sector in all OECD countries), an acceleration of R&D stimulated by the cold war, increased cooperation between western countries, and the potential for technological catch-up in both Europe and Japan. The stimulus from these factors, he argued, was temporary, and other influences also contributed to a re-assertion of stagnationist tendencies in the 1970s. Steindl singles out, in particular, an increasing trend of personal saving and "a changed attitude of governments towards full employment and growth" (1979, p.12). This latter influence, which is seen as "the most striking feature of the new economic climate" (1979, p.12), is explained in terms of a Kaleckian political cycle "as a reaction against the long period of full employment and growth which has strengthened the economic position of workers and the power of the trade unions, and has led to demands for workers' participation" (pp.12–13). Writing in 1979, Steindl therefore expected "low growth for some time to come".

It is beyond the scope of this chapter[1] to attempt an empirically based evaluation of Steindl's theory.[2] Our aim is more modest and almost entirely theoretical. Steindl's contributions to an understanding of capitalist growth and stagnation have been highly influential but re-reading his original studies, we have been struck by the fact that important aspects of his argument appear to have been left out of subsequent models. In this chapter we try to clarify the connection between a "standard Steindlian model" and Steindl's own analysis. Secondly, and more importantly, we extend the standard model to include some of the aspects of his analysis that have been left out.

Most Steindlian models focus on the product market and treat the markup as exogenous. We outline a standard model of this kind in Section 10.2. Unlike Steindl's (1952) own model, which is set up as mixed difference-differential equations and which has multiple steady growth solutions, the standard model is cast entirely in continuous time and has a unique steady growth solution. In some respects the standard model does a good job of capturing Steindl's argument, and the switch to a continuous time setting simplifies the analysis enormously. However, the standard model also has weaknesses, both on its own terms and from an exegetical perspective. One weakness is the use of an exogenous markup. This assumption clashes with Steindl's verbal analysis of how "elastic profit margins" tend to eliminate undesired excess capacity in competitive industries and how the "growth of the monopolistic type of industry may lead to a fundamental change in the working of the economy: bringing about greater inelasticity of profit margins" (1952, p.ix). A second weakness concerns the specification of the long-run investment function. The standard model differs from Steindl's own specification in this respect and there are, we shall argue, problems with the standard model as well as with Steindl's own analysis.

Section 10.3 presents a reformulation of the standard model which addresses the two weaknesses. The reformulation, first, introduces Steindlian movements in the markup. Thus, we assume that the markup will be rising when actual capacity utilization exceeds desired utilization. Other models exist, of course, in which the mark-up changes endogenously, but in these models the determination of the changes is rather different. Dutt (1984), for instance, relates changes in the markup to the rate of growth of the economy while Sawyer (1995) allows the *level* of the markup to depend on the rate of utilization (as indeed did Kalecki (1954)). Although still different, the specifications in Taylor (1985) and Lavoie (1995) which relate changes of the markup to the profit rate come closer to the Steindlian position.

Our second extension of the standard model concerns the investment function. We respecify this function to allow for a distinction between the short-run and the long-run sensitivity of the accumulation rate to changes in utilization. This distinction – central to models in a Harrodian tradition and discussed at some length in Skott (1989a) – is included in Steindl's formal 1952 model as well as in Dutt's (1995) more recent formalization of Steindl's theory. Our specification of the function in this chapter is much simpler than Steindl's and more general than Dutt's.

Both of the extensions in Section 10.3 find support in Steindl's writing. The main contribution of the section, however, is not exegetical. It lies in the analysis of a system that combines an unstable accumulation dynamics with a stabilizing Steindlian markup dynamics. We show that (i) if the re-formulated investment function is used in the standard model without markup dynamics, the steady growth path is likely to become unstable, (ii) that the markup dynamics has a stabilizing influence and (iii) that the combined model may, but need not, produce a stable steady-growth path. In the stable case, increasing oligopolization leads to a decline in both the rate of growth and the utilization of capital but, paradoxically, to a fall in the share of profits. Thus, the stable case leaves intact some but not all of key results of the standard model.

In Section 10.4 we go beyond the analysis of the product market. Both financial and labor markets play important roles in Steindl's verbal argument; financial markets because of Steindl's emphasis on internal finance and changes in household saving, and labor markets because Steindl regarded prolonged full employment in the 1950's and 1960s as a key factor behind the subsequent stagnation. Financial extensions of the standard model have been explored by Dutt (1995) and in this chapter we make no attempt to pursue this aspect of Steindl's analysis. Our emphasis, instead, is on the labor market.

A labor market has been introduced into Steindlian models by Dutt (1992), among others. Our specification, however, differs substantially from his. Following Steindl's (1979) argument we let the rate of employment affect firms' investment decisions and show that the implications of this extended model for the effects of increased oligopolization are largely in line with Steindl's predictions, at least for a range of parameter values. Dutt, by contrast, considers the influence of the rate of employment on wage inflation. He assumes that firms' pricing decisions fail to neutralize these nominal changes in the wage. Thus, the labor market enters his model because of its effects on (the rate of change of) the markup. This mechanism is akin to the one in Goodwin (1967) and other models in which a real wage Phillips curve generates a rising real wage and a falling markup when employment is high. It should be noted, however, that if one assumes that the employment and utilization rates move together and can be represented by the same variable, a real wage Phillips curve implies an inverse relation between utilization and the change in the markup – the opposite of the Steindlian assumption.[3] The chapter closes, in Section 10.5, with some conclusions and remarks on future work.

## 10.2 Steindl and the standard model

### *A standard model in continuous time*

We consider a closed economy without public sector. Output is produced using two inputs, labor and capital, and the production function has fixed coefficients. It would be straightforward to include Harrod-neutral technical change but we leave out this element to simplify the exposition. It is assumed that firms retain a proportion $s_f$ of profits and distribute the rest to households in the form of interest payments and dividends, and that there is a uniform saving rate $s$ out of distributed incomes, including wages.[4] Investment is positively related to the rate of utilization of the capital stock and may also depend positively on retained earnings. Algebraically, the (net) investment and saving functions are given by

$$\frac{I}{K} = a + m(u-1) + bs_f \pi \frac{u}{k}, \tag{10.1}$$

$$\frac{S}{K} = s_f \pi \frac{u}{k} + s(1 - \pi + (1 - s_f)\pi)\frac{u}{k} = s(\pi)\frac{u}{k}, \tag{10.2}$$

where $I$, $S$ and $K$ denote investment, saving and the capital stock, $k$ is the capital–output ratio at the desired utilization rate (normalized to one), $u$ the actual utilization rate and $\pi$ the share of profits in income ($u/k$ and $\pi u/k$ thus define the actual output–capital ratio and the profit rate). Note here that it is customary in the Post-Keynesian literature to use $\pi$ to denote the profit share (and thus not the rate of inflation as it is generally the case in this book). The average saving rate out of income is $s(\pi) = s_f (1 - s)\pi + s$. All variables are contemporaneous, and the parameters $m$, $b$, $s_f$ and $s$ are positive.

The equilibrium condition for the product market can be written

$$a + m(u - 1) + b\frac{s_f}{k}\pi u = \frac{u}{k}[s_f(1 - s)\pi + s] = \frac{s(\pi)}{k}u. \tag{10.3}$$

This equation determines the rate of capacity utilization $u$ as a function of the profit share $\pi$. The profit share itself is determined by an exogenously given markup on unit labor cost ($\pi = (\beta - 1)/\beta$ where $\beta$ is the markup).

Solving equation (10.3) for $u$ we get

$$u = \frac{k(a - m)}{s + s_f(1 - s - b)\pi - mk}. \tag{10.4}$$

Using standard assumptions for the adjustment process, the stability of this short-run equilibrium requires that investment be less sensitive than saving to variations in output; that is, $mk + bs_f \pi < s(\pi)$. When this "Keynesian stability condition" is imposed, the constant $a$ in the accumulation function must satisfy the restriction $a > m$ in order for the model to produce a positive rate of utilization.

Equations (10.1)–(10.4) give rise to Bhaduri and Marglin (1990a) possibilities of exhilarationist or stagnationist outcomes. Assuming that the Keynesian stability condition holds, an increase in the profit share will lead to a decline in utilization if the "Robinsonian stability condition" $0 < [s_f(1 - s - b)]$ is satisfied; a reversal of this Robinsonian condition implies that $u$ will rise with $\pi$ and thus will fall with increases in the real wage.[5] The effects on growth are ambiguous. Differentiating $g = \dfrac{s(\pi)}{k} u(\pi)$ with respect to $\pi$, we get

$$\frac{\partial g}{\partial \pi} = \frac{u}{k}\left[ s(\pi)\frac{-s_f(1-s-b)}{s+s_f(1-s-b)\pi - mk} + s_f(1-s) \right]$$

$$= \frac{us_f}{k}\frac{sb-(1-s)mk}{s+s_f(1-s-b)\pi - mk}.$$

Hence, if both the Keynesian short-run stability condition and the Robinsonian stability condition are met, an increase in the profit share will have a negative impact on growth if

$$sb < (1-s)mk.$$

This ambiguous conclusion mirrors the results in Steindl (1952). Thus, Steindl (1952, 9.224) finds that a rise in the markup depresses growth if the direct effect of the profit share on investment is small relative to the effect of utilization on investment, a condition which is similar to the condition above.

Overall, a linear model with a constant term in the investment function and parameter restrictions that ensure Keynesian and Robinsonian stability might appear to capture the spirit of Steindl's argument. It is not surprising therefore that following early contributions by Rowthorn (1981) and Dutt (1984) and subsequent work by, among others, Taylor (1985), Sawyer (1985) and Bhaduri and Marglin (1990a), a model along these lines has become the standard formalization of the Kalecki–Steindl theory.

The rest of this section examines the relation between the standard model and Steindl's (1952) formalization in greater detail. Readers with no interest in this relation may skip directly to Section 10.3.

### The 1952 argument

Steindl's formal model of an economy with variable utilization (Steindl 1952, pp.211–228) is cast in terms of mixed difference-differential equations. The key investment equation (equation (39), p.213) can be written

$$I_{t+\theta} = \gamma_1 \dot{C}_t + \gamma_2 (C_t - g_0 K_t) + m (kY_t - u_0 K_t), \tag{10.5}$$

where $\theta$ is a discrete investment lag, $k$ is the ratio of the stock of capital to productive capacity and $u_0$ the desired utilization rate; the impact of financing conditions are captured by the retained earnings $\dot{C}$ and the stock of "entrepreneurs' capital" $C$; $g_0$ is the inverse of the desired gearing ratio and the parameters $\gamma_1, \gamma_2$ and $m$ are all positive.[6] Using assumptions similar to those of the standard model concerning the determination of retained earnings and personal saving, Steindl derives a dynamic equation for the evolution of the capital stock,

$$\ddot{K}_{t+\theta} - L\ddot{K}_t + M\dot{K}_t + NK_t = 0, \tag{10.6}$$

where the composite parameters $L$, $M$ and $N$ can be expressed in terms of the underlying parameters of the functions describing investment and saving.

To solve equation (10.6), Steindl assumes that the equation represents "a long-run model of moving averages" (p.227) and that long-run movements may plausibly be described by exponential trends determined by the real roots of (10.6). Thus, implicitly it is assumed that the initial conditions (i.e. the trajectory of the system over a time interval corresponding to the discrete lag $\theta$) can be written

$$K(t) = \sum c_i \exp \rho_i t, \tag{10.7}$$

where $c_i$ is constant and $\rho_i$ represents the real roots of the characteristic equation

$$\rho^2 \exp(\theta\rho) - L\rho^2 + M\rho + N = 0. \tag{10.8}$$

Given these initial conditions, the full solution to equation (10.6) also takes the form (10.7).

The next step is to find the real roots of (10.8). It turns out that in order to get any positive roots, additional restrictions on the parameter values have to be introduced. These restrictions *reverse* the Keynesian stability condition in the standard model. Thus using the notation of the standard model, Steindl's necessary condition for positive roots (p.219) is that

$$\frac{mk + b\pi s_f}{s(\pi)} > 1,$$

which is the condition for Keynesian *instability* in the standard model.

Assuming that positive roots exist, the equation will have three real roots and the movements of the capital stock can be described by

$$K(t) = c_1 e^{\rho_1 t} + c_2 e^{\rho_2 t} + c_3 e^{\rho_3 t},$$

where $\rho_1 < 0 < \rho_2 < \rho_3$. Asymptotically, the largest of the three roots dominates the movements in $K$ and, Steindl concludes, the capital stock must therefore grow asymptotically at the high rate $\rho_3$.[7]

The comparative statics of the steady growth path associated with $\rho_3$ can now be examined. From a Steindlian perspective, the effects of increasing oligopolization are particularly interesting. Increasing oligopolization is associated with an upward shif of the profit function (that is, the markup).[8] This shift, Steindl finds, produces a decline in the rate of growth, as long as the expansionary financial effects on investment (represented by the parameters $\gamma_1$ and $\gamma_2$ in equation (10.5)) are weak relative to the effect of utilization (represented by $mk$ in equation (10.5)). This condition seems plausible, and the results are strengthened if the rise in the degree of monopoly also leads to increased fears of excess capacity in the industry and a corresponding increase in the desired utilization rate $u_0$.[9] Thus, the model appears to support Steindl's central conclusion:

> On the basis of the present model it is thus possible to demonstrate that the development of monopoly may bring about a decline in the rate of growth of capital. I believe that this is, in fact, the main explanation of the decline in the rate of growth which has been going on in the United States from the end of the last century. (p.225)

Unfortunately, the empirical application of the model raises difficulties, and Steindl is refreshingly forthright and clear about these difficulties. He points out that "if plausible values are given to the structural coefficients . . . then it appears that the limiting rate of growth thus obtained is very big" (p.226). This problem is serious since it implies that it "is difficult to explain, on the basis of my model, moderate rates of growth, such as has been observed in the history of capitalism" and "either the model requires modifications in important respects in order to be realistic, or else, it follows that an exponential trend in the strict mathematical sense is not a proper description of long-run growth" (p.226).

The complex nature of mixed systems of differential equations with discrete lags makes it difficult to ascertain the reasons for this empirical anomaly in the model. The reasons become clearer if one considers a simplified version of the model in a discrete time setting.

## A simplified 1952 model

We set $I_{t+1} = m(kY_t - K_t)$, where (to simplify notation) the desired utilization rate has been normalized to unity and $k$ is the capital–output ratio at the desired rate of capital utilization. Aside from the switch to a pure discrete time system, equation (10.9) differs from (10.5) by leaving out the effects of retained earnings and the gearing ratio on accumulation. These effects, it may be recalled, were assumed small relative to the effects of the utilization rate, and it simplifies matters to leave them out altogether.

Combining equation (10.9) with (a discrete time version of) the saving function (10.2), the equilibrium condition $I = S$ implies that

$$\frac{I_t}{K_t} = m\frac{K_{t-1}}{K_t}(u_{t-1} - 1)$$

$$= m\frac{1}{1 + \frac{s(\pi)}{k}u_{t-1}}(u_{t-1} - 1) = s(\pi)\frac{Y_t}{K_t} = \frac{s(\pi)}{k}u_t = \frac{S_t}{K_t},$$

or

$$u_t = \frac{mk}{s(\pi)} \left( \frac{u_{t-1} - 1}{1 + \frac{s(\pi)}{k} u_{t-1}} \right),$$

(10.9)

where $u_t = kY_t/K_t$ is the actual rate of utilization. It is readily seen (see Appendix I) that generically this difference equation has either no stationary point or two stationary points. Furthermore, the existence of stationary points requires (as a necessary condition), that

$$\frac{mk}{s(\pi)} > 1.$$

In the case with two stationary points, the high equilibrium is locally stable; the low is unstable. Qualitatively, these conclusions mirror Steindl's results: positive steady growth rates require that the ratio of $mk$ to the average saving rate is sufficiently high.

The outcome is illustrated in Figure 10.1 which uses the parameter values $m = 0.2$, $k = 2$, $s(\pi) = 0.1$. Using (10.10) and Figure 10.1, it is readily seen that a rise in the saving rate $s(\pi)$ (associated with an increase in profit share) generates a shift in the expression on the right-hand side of (10.10) and a decline of the stable solution for $u$. The growth rate $su/k$ also suffers. To see this, note that the growth rate can be written

$$g = \frac{s(\pi)u}{k} = m \left( \frac{\frac{s(\pi)u}{s(\pi)} - 1}{1 + \frac{s(\pi)}{k} u} \right) = m \left( \frac{\frac{gk}{s(\pi)} - 1}{1 + g} \right).$$

The existence of two solutions for the utilization rate implies that this equation in $g$ will also have two solutions; graphically the picture is similar to Figure 10.1. The expression on the extreme right-hand side of the equation is decreasing in $s(\pi)$, and it follows that a rise in $s(\pi)$ leads to a decline in the high solution for $g$.

The stability of the high solutions for $u$ and $g$ may suggest that these, rather than the low and unstable solutions, are the relevant ones. This indeed is the reasoning that guided Steindl's analysis. But consider the special case where the sensitivity $m$ of investment to changes in utilization goes to infinity. The stable solution goes to infinity as $m \to \infty$ and we get a unique, unstable $u$ solution: $u^* = 1$. For finite values of $m$, a high and locally stable solution may exist, but Steindl's problem re-emerges in this simplified setup: for plausible parameter values, the high solution becomes unreasonably high and, as a corollary, the growth rate also becomes too high.[10]

The reason for this problem is transparent in the simplified version. The stable equilibrium owes its existence to the non-linearity on the right-hand side of (10.10). This non-linearity is quite weak, especially for realistic, small values of

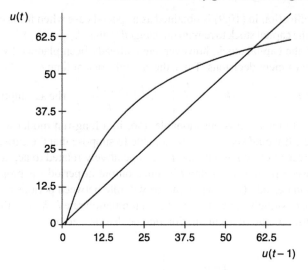

*Figure 10.1* The two stationary solutions.

$s(\pi)$. Hence, the high equilibrium value necessarily becomes large. In Figure 10.1, for instance, the high equilibrium yields a utilization rate of over 58, with desired utilization normalized at unity. Since it is hard to envisage an economy that experiences steady growth with utilization significantly above the desired rate, these observations indicate the empirical and theoretical irrelevance of the high solution.

In support of this conclusion, it should be noted that the economic logic behind the specific non-linearity in equation (10.10) is difficult to justify. It arises because the investment function (10.9) imposes a lag: it is investment at time $t + 1$ rather than at time $t$ that is determined in period $t$. The existence of this lag may be reasonable, but it would seem plausible to suppose that when they form their investment plans, firms take into account expected changes in output as well as the changes in the capital stock that are already in the pipeline. Thus, we may want to respecify the investment function as

$$I_{t+1} = g^e_{t+1} K^e_{t+1} + m(kY^e_{t+1} - K^e_{t+1})$$

or

$$\frac{I_{t+1}}{K^e_{t+1}} = g^e_{t+1} + m\left(\frac{kY^e_{t+1}}{K^e_{t+1}} - 1\right),$$

where $g^e_{t+1}$ is the expected growth rate of demand between periods $t + 1$ and $t + 2$ (when period $(t + 1)$ investment enters service as part of the productive capital stock) and where $K^e_{t+1}$ and $Y^e_{t+1}$ denote the expected values of the capital stock and the level of output in period $t + 1$.

The specification in (10.9) is obtained as a special case when firms expect both output and the capital stock to remain unchanged so that $K_{t+1}^e = K_t$, $Y_{t+1}^e = Y_t$, $g^e = 0$. Changes in the capital stock, however, have already been planned by past – and known – investment decisions. Thus, the capital stock at time $t + 1$ should also be known and $K_{t+1}^e = K_{t+1} = K_t\left(1 + \dfrac{I_t}{K_t}\right) = K_t\left(1 + \dfrac{s(\pi)}{k}u_t\right)$. The assumption of static output expectations seems questionable, too, in a long-run model with positive growth rates. It would seem more reasonable to suppose that the expected output growth between period $t$ and period $t + 1$ is positively related to actual growth in output between periods $t - 1$ and $t$.[11] Since output at period $t$ is proportional to investment in period $t$ ($I_t = s(\pi)Y_t$), the growth rate between periods $t - 1$ and $t$, in turn, will be positively dependent on the accumulation rate $I_t/K_t$. Combining these observations, the rate of accumulation maybe determined by

$$\frac{I_{t+1}}{K_{t+1}} = g_{t+1}^e + m\left(u_t \frac{1 + g_t^e}{1 + \dfrac{s(\pi)}{k}u_t} - 1\right)$$

$$g_t^e = f\left(\frac{s(\pi)}{k}u_t, z\right).$$

where $z$ captures other influences on expected output growth. If, as a simple benchmark, $f\left(\dfrac{s(\pi)}{k}u, z\right) = \dfrac{s(\pi)}{k}u$ and the growth rates further into the future – between $t + 1$ and $t + 2$ – are treated as a constant, we have $g_{t+1}^e = a$ and

$$\frac{I_{t+1}}{K_{t+1}} = a + m\,(u_t - 1). \tag{10.10}$$

Using the specification (10.11), the equilibrium condition $I = S$ yields

$$u_t = \frac{k}{s(\pi)}[a + m(u_{t-1} - 1)]. \tag{10.11}$$

The non-linearity now is gone and there is a unique stationary solution. If we impose Steindl's parameter restriction, $mk > s(\pi)$, this solution is unstable, and an increase in the saving rate raises the equilibrium solutions for both utilization and the growth rate.

The assumptions underlying (10.11) are, we would argue, at least as plausible as the ones underlying (10.10). Of course, one may reject both sets of simplifying assumptions. In a more general specification, however, $u_t$ may become either convex or concave in $u_{t-1}$. Convexity – which may arise when $(1 + g_t^e)/(1 + I_t/K_t)$

is increasing in $u_t$ – seems as likely as concavity, and convexity rules out a high and locally stable solution.

These conclusions (the irrelevance of the high equilibrium and the instability of the low solution) may seem at odds with the general tenor of Steindl's argument. His vision of long-term stagnation would appear to require a stable equilibrium with slow growth and/or high unemployment. In order to achieve this outcome, the sensitivity of investment to variations in utilization needs to be reduced. Indeed, this is what happens through the back door at the high equilibrium in the non-linear case depicted in Figure 10.1: a first-order Taylor approximation of the reduced-form relation between the rate of accumulation and the lagged value of the utilization rate around the high equilibrium has a positive constant and a small coefficient on utilization. As a result, the Keynesian stability condition is satisfied at the high solution.

Having rejected Steindl's high solution, a unique and stable steady-growth solution can be obtained by using (10.11) instead of (10.10). All that is required is a reversal of the parameter restriction $mk/s(\pi) > 1$. Moreover, using $a \approx s(\pi)/k$, it is possible to ensure that the steady-growth value of the utilization rate will be in the neighborhood of one, thus avoiding the anomaly of excessive utilization and growth rates. The lag in the investment function, finally, is of no real importance in the stable case; the long-run results would be the same with a contemporaneous formulation.

Putting together these conclusions, our analysis of the weaknesses of Steindl's own formalization leads us, it might seem, to the simple and transparent formulation of the standard model.

## 10.3 A core model of the product market

### *Two shortcomings*

Although the standard model replicates key Steindlian conclusions, its assumptions violate Steindl's verbal argument in some respects. Two areas of conflict seem particularly prominent.

The first area concerns the specification of the accumulation function. The standard model assumes that the long-run sensitivity of investment to changes in utilization is small. This imposition of the Keynesian stability condition on the long-run investment and saving functions violates Steindl's (1952, p.219) own parameter restrictions.[12] Steindl's verbal argument also amounts to a rejection of the stability condition. On p.123, for instance, he argues that

> [i]f the entrepreneur finds himself with more excess capacity than he wants to hold . . . he will be strongly discouraged from undertaking any expansion. This discouragement will be even stronger if he knows that such an unusual degree of excess capacity is fairly general in his industry.

The destabilizing implications of this argument are clearly stated (p.123): "The individual entrepreneur may think that by reducing investment he will cure his excess capacity, but in fact for industry as a whole this strategy has only the effect of making excess capacity even greater." Similar statements about the cumulative process arising from the interaction between investment and utilization can be found throughout Chapters 9–10 (e.g. p.115 and pp.135–137), and in Chapter 12 (pp.174–175; italics in original) Steindl goes out of his way to argue that "a *cumulative* process, with the trend rate of accumulation decreasing more and more" was avoided in the late-nineteenth and early-twentieth centuries only because "the fall in the profit rate was largely compensated by the cheapening of the terms on which share finance could be obtained". Disregarding questions of exegetical accuracy, the specification of the accumulation function in the standard model seems questionable. There are two separate but closely related issues. The relative insensitivity of investment, first, is plausible in the short run. But changes in utilization may have lagged effects on investment, and a weak impact effect (which is required for the stability of the short-run Keynesian equilibrium) does not guarantee that the long-term effects of a sustained increase in utilization will be weak, too. Thus, the standard model can be criticized because of its offhand extension to the long run of a restriction – the insensitivity of investment to fluctuations in the utilization rate – that is perfectly reasonable for the short run.[13] From a long-run perspective, second, the specification of the accumulation function seems implausible. Like Steindl, we find it hard to conceive of a steady growth path where firms are content to accumulate at a constant rate if, along this path, they have significantly more (or less) excess capacity than they desire. Thus, if the desired rate of utilization were constant, the long-run accumulation function should be (almost) perfectly elastic at this desired rate. Managerial constraints or other bottlenecks may make it difficult or costly to expand at high rates and the desired utilization rate, consequently, may not be constant. Instead, it may depend, inter alia, on the share of profits and the rate of accumulation. This complication may modify the analysis and affect some conclusions. Within the relevant range of steady-growth solutions for the rates of accumulation and utilization, however, we find it implausible to assume that the long-run accumulation function will be anything but highly elastic with respect to the rate of utilization.[14]

The second area of conflict between the standard model and Steindl's analysis concerns the determination of the markup. In his verbal discussion Steindl devoted a lot of attention to the influence of demand on the markup. He did not succeed, however, in developing a formal model which incorporated the possibility of adjustments in both the profit margin and the rate of utilization. Instead, he set up two distinct models: one with constant utilization and a flexible "profit function" (that is, a flexible markup) and the other with variable utilization rates but a fixed markup. He considered neither of these models fully satisfactory: the first was deficient since "the underlying hypothesis of a prompt re-establishment of a given degree of utilization is not realistic" but the second was not realistic either since "in reality there may be some adjustment of the profit function" (p.211). Thus, "the actual behavior of the system will probably be somewhere in between the two extreme cases" (p.212). These concerns are reiterated in Steindl's comments on the results of the second model (p.228):

The profit function which I assumed constant in my long run model should not really be so. In reality there will be a certain elasticity of the profit margins, that is the profit function will depend on the degree of utilization (a high utilization shifting it upwards, and a low utilization downwards). My mathematical model does not include this complication, and it is in this respect poorer than the verbal exposition of the theory in the earlier chapters.

The movements in the markup (which in our simple version is identical to the profit share) will be strong in competitive regimes. The transition to oligopolistic regimes weakens the adjustment mechanism, but according to Steindl a tendency remains for the markup to rise (resp. fall) when utilization is above (resp. below) the desired level.[15] Thus, we see no justification for assuming a fixed markup in Steindlian models of growth and stagnation.[16]

Of course, even if a fixed markup cannot be attributed to Steindl, one might still view this assumption as a reasonable representation of real-world pricing. It is beyond the scope of the present chapter to consider this question in any detail. It should be noted, however, that at the micro level there is evidence of significant variability in prices and markups. A study by Levy et al. (1997), for instance, found that a sample of US supermarkets changed an average of 16 percent of their prices every week and that most of these changes were unrelated to cost changes. Thus, Steindl's model might err by attributing too little rather than too much flexibility to the markup. An alternative, Marshallian approach reverses the adjustment speeds of output and the profit margin. Using this approach, Skott (1989a, b) treats the profit margin as a fast variable and output as a gradually adjusting state variable.

In the remainder of this section we address the two areas of conflict between Steindl's own analysis and the standard model. We extend the standard model by adding dynamic equations to describe induced shifts in both the markup and the accumulation function. The implications of these shifts and their interactions will be examined in subsection 10.3.4. First, however, the two types of dynamic adjustment are considered separately in the next two subsections.

### *Markup dynamics*

The endogenous movements in the profit share can be captured by the following price equation:

$$\hat{p} = f(u, \pi) + \hat{w}^e; f_u > 0, f_\pi \leq 0, f(u,0) > 0, f(u,1) < 0,$$

where $\hat{p} = \dot{p}/p$ is the rate of inflation and $\hat{w}^e$ the expected rate of wage inflation. The equation describes the effects of the utilization rate and the profit share on the (expected) change in the markup: firms set prices so that $\hat{p} > \hat{w}^e$ if they want to raise the markup. Utilization reflects current demand in the product market relative to firms' capacity and, according to Steindl, high utilization gives firms an incentive to raise the markup, that is, the partial with respect to $u$ is positive. The non-positive effect of the current profit share is included because it seems reasonable to assume that, although the markup may be flexible, firms will always aim for a profit share between zero and one. This property is ensured by the restrictions that $f(u, 0) > 0$ and $f(u, 1) < 0$ for any value of the utilization rate.

The price equation can be viewed as an expectations-augmented price Phillips curve which relates price inflation to deviations of actual from desired utilization rather than to conditions in the labor market.[17] We assume that the rate of wage inflation is correctly anticipated by firms $(\hat{w}^e = \hat{w})$. The rate of wage inflation therefore has no impact on changes in the markup and the share of profits. As in other simple Keynesian models, moreover, aggregate demand is invariant with respect to changes in both the level and the rate of change of the money wage. Thus, for present purposes there is no need to specify a wage Phillips curve.

Using $\hat{w}^e = \hat{w}$ the price Phillips curve implies that

$$\dot{\pi} = -\frac{d}{dt}\left(\frac{w\,L}{p\,Y}\right) = -\frac{w\,L}{p\,Y}(\hat{w} - \hat{p}) = (1 - \pi)f(u, \pi). \tag{10.12}$$

Combining equation (10.13) with the equilibrium condition for the product market, equation (10.4), the result is a first-order differential equation in $\pi$,[18]

$$\dot{\pi} = (1 - \pi)f(u(\pi), \pi) = \phi(\pi); \quad \phi(0) > 0; \; \phi(\pi) < 0 \text{ for } \bar{\pi} < \pi < 1. \tag{10.13}$$

This equation has at least one locally stable stationary solution between zero and one. Uniqueness is ensured if the Robinsonian stability condition is met, since in this case $\phi'(\pi) < 0$. If the Robinsonian stability condition fails to be satisfied, the derivative of $\phi$ cannot be unambiguously signed, and there may be multiple solutions. Even with multiple solutions, we still get convergence of the profit share to a stationary point but initial conditions will determine which one. Using (10.4), it follows that $u \to u(\pi^*)$ if $\pi \to \pi^*$.

The comparative statics are straightforward. At a locally stable stationary point:

- A marginal upward shift in the investment function (a rise in $a$) leads to an increase in both $u^*$ and $\pi^*$. The growth rate also increases.
- A marginal increase in the saving propensity $s$ leads to a decline in both $u^*$ and $\pi^*$, and the growth rate also suffers.
- A marginal weakening of competition (an upward shift in the $f$-function) leads to an increase in $\pi^*$. Utilization falls if the Robinsonian stability condition is met, and the growth effects of weaker competition and higher profit margins are ambiguous, as in the standard model.

### Accumulation dynamics

The combination of a low short-run but high long-run sensitivity of investment to changes in utilization can be captured by introducing dynamic adjustments in the constant term $a$ in the investment function. These changes in $a$ are related to the discrepancy between actual and desired utilization but, in accordance with our discussion in Section 10.2, we allow for the possibility that the desired rate of utilization may depend on both profitability and the growth rate. Thus, let

$$\dot{a} = h(u, \pi, g); \quad h_u > 0, h_\pi \geq 0, h_g \leq 0, \tag{10.14}$$

where $g$ is the current rate of accumulation and desired utilization is defined implicitly by the stationarity condition, $h(u, \pi, g) = 0$.

The formulation in (10.1) and (10.14) generalizes the approach used by, among others, Dutt (1995). Dutt takes actual accumulation $g$ as predetermined at each moment while the desired accumulation rate is determined by utilization and profitability (as well as the gearing ratio, a variable that we have left out). The change in $g$ is assumed proportional to the difference between desired and actual accumulation. Thus,

$$\dot{g} = \theta(g^d(u, \pi) - g).$$

Setting $m = b = 0$ in the accumulation function (10.1), Dutt's specification emerges as a special case of equations (10.1) and (10.14).

Combining (10.1), (10.4) and (10.16) – and treating $\pi$ as constant – we get a one-dimensional differential equation for the movements in "animal spirits",

$$\dot{a} = h(u(a, \pi), \pi, g(a, \pi)) = \psi(a).$$

The sign of $\psi'$ is ambiguous: both utilization and accumulation depend positively on the value of $a$, and the net feedback from $a$ to the rate of change in $a$ therefore depends on the partial derivatives $h_u$ and $h_g$ that describe the relative strength of the effects of $u$ and $g$. In principle there could be multiple stationary points (or no stationary points), and even in the case of a unique stationary point the stability properties are undetermined. But since, as argued above, the effects of utilization are likely to be strong and the negative feedback effects from changes in the growth rate weak within the relevant range, the most likely outcome is one with a unique, unstable stationary point.

As a simple example, consider the Harrodian case in which desired utilization is exogenously given and constant, that is $h_\pi \equiv h_g \equiv 0$. Normalizing desired utilization at unity and assuming that the change in $a$ is proportional to the difference between actual and desired utilization, the shift in $a$ is given by

$$\dot{a} = \lambda(u - 1); \quad \lambda > 0.$$

Substituting for $u$, we get

$$\dot{a} = \lambda \left( \frac{k(a - m)}{s + s_f(1 - s - b)\pi - mk} - 1 \right). \tag{10.15}$$

This equation has a unique, unstable stationary solution

$$a = \frac{s + s_f(1 - s - b)\pi - mk}{k} - m.$$

The warranted growth rate at the associated (unstable) growth path is given by the standard Harrodian expression $g = \frac{s(\pi)}{k}$. This growth rate is a continuous-time analogue to the empirically relevant, unstable solution in Steindl's model.

Comparative statics can be readily derived. Consider, for instance, the effect of a change in the saving rate $s$. Returning to the general specification (10.14), we have $da/ds = -h_u u_s/\phi'$. Since $h_u > 0$ and $u_s < 0$, it follows that an increase in the saving rate has a negative effect on $a$ if the stationary point is locally stable ($\phi' < 0$) but positive if the stationary point is unstable. The sign of $da/ds$ in turn influences the effect of changes in the saving rate on the rate of growth since, using (10.15), we have

$$\frac{dg}{ds} = \frac{mk + bs_f \pi}{k} u_s + \left(1 + \frac{mk + bs_f \pi}{k} u_a\right) \frac{da}{ds}.$$

In the unstable case the comparative statics are interesting insofar as one has some indication that forces outside the model keep the economy near the steady growth path. Policy intervention or feedback effects from the labor market may play this role. The next subsection, however, considers an alternative, Steindlian mechanism: the stabilizing influence of induced changes of the markup.

### Combining markup and accumulation dynamics

Using equations (10.1), (10.4) and (10.13)–(10.14), we get a 2-D system of differential equations in $a$ and $\pi$:

$$\dot{a} = h\left(u\left(a, \pi\right), \pi, g(a, \pi)\right) = H(a, \pi); \ H_a > 0, \tag{10.16}$$

$$\dot{\pi} = (1 - \pi) f\left(u\left(a, \pi\right), \pi\right) = G(a, \pi); \ G_a > 0, G_\pi < 0. \tag{10.17}$$

The properties of this system depend on the functions $H$ and $G$. We assume that both the Keynesian and the Robinsonian stability conditions are met so that $u_\pi < 0$. Hence,

$$G_a = (1 - \pi) f_u u_a > 0, \tag{10.18}$$

$$G_\pi = (1 - \pi)(f_u u_\pi + f_\pi) - f$$

$$= (1 - \pi)(f_u u_\pi + f_\pi) < 0 \text{ at a stationary point with } \dot{\pi} = f = 0. \tag{10.19}$$

Turning to the partial derivatives of $H$, we have

$$H_a = h_u u_a + h_g g_a > 0,$$ (10.20)

$$H_\pi = h_u u_\pi + h_\pi + h_g g_\pi.$$ (10.21)

The first term in the expression for $H_a$ is positive and the second negative. In line with the discussion in the subsection "Accumulation dynamics", however, we assume that the first term will dominate and that the pure accumulation dynamics is destabilizing; that is, we consider the case in which $H_a > 0$. The partial $H_\pi$, on the other hand, is difficult to sign on either theoretical or empirical grounds. As a result, qualitatively diverse dynamic scenarios are possible.

In terms of the reduced forms $H$ and $G$, the Jacobian of the system is given by

$$J(a, \pi) = \begin{pmatrix} H_a & H_\pi \\ G_a & G_\pi \end{pmatrix}$$

and the stationary point is locally stable if (evaluated at the stationary point) we have

$$\det J = H_a G_\pi - G_a H_\pi > 0$$

$$\operatorname{tr} J = H_a + G_\pi < 0.$$

Saddlepoint instability is obtained if $\det J < 0$, and the system generates an unstable node or focus if $\det J > 0$ but $\operatorname{tr} J < 0$.

In Appendix II we illustrate these possibilities. One case allows for a stable steady growth path and generates roughly Steindlian results. This case demonstrates that a system which has an unstable equilibrium when the markup is exogenous may be stabilized by endogenous changes in the markup, provided the adjustments of the markup are sufficiently fast. A second case (also based on assumptions that seem plausible a priori) implies saddlepoint instability. This case shows that fast adjustment in the markup may not suffice to stabilize the system. Both cases are characterized using assumptions concerning the underlying functions $f$, $g$ and $h$.[19]

The phase diagram in Figure 10.2 depicts the dynamics when the system (10.17)–(10.18) generates a node or a focus and, assuming stability, the figure can be used to examine the effects of changes in competition. According to Steindl, a decline in competition puts upward pressure on the markup and, secondly, leads to a decline in the adjustment speed of the markup. The first effect corresponds to an upward shift in the Phillips curve (the $f$-function) while the second can be parameterized by introducing a multiplicative constant $\mu$ in the equation for the

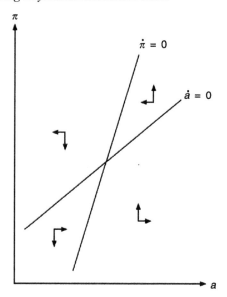

*Figure 10.2* Stabilizing markup dynamics.

change in the profit share. Thus, the effects of changes in the degree of competition can be captured by re-writing equation (10.18) as

$$\dot{\pi} = (1 - \pi)\mu[f(u(a, \pi), \pi) + v] = G(a, \pi; \mu, v).$$

The benchmark degree of competition in (10.18) is associated with $\mu = 1$ and $v = 0$; increased oligopolization leads to a reduction in $\mu$ (slower adjustment speeds) and a rise in $v$ (upward pressure on the markup).

Consider now the effects of increased oligopolization. The rise in $v$ implies an upward shift in the $\dot{\pi} = 0$ locus while changes in $\mu$ have no effects on the slope or position of either of the two loci. The upward shift in the $\dot{\pi} = 0$ locus entails a decline in the stationary solutions of both $a$ and $\pi$ (see Figure 10.2), and the rates of utilization and accumulation must fall too. To see this, note that by assumption $f_\pi \leq 0$, and the rise in $v$ must therefore be associated with a decline in $u$ if $f(u, \pi) + v$ is to remain equal to zero. The fall in the rate of accumulation now follows from the decline in both $u$ and $\pi$ $\left(\text{since } g = \dfrac{s(\pi)}{k} u\right)$.

Although changes in the parameter $\mu$ have no effects on the shapes and positions of the $\dot{\pi} = 0$ and $\dot{a} = 0$ loci, these changes may still be of critical importance. By assumption the pure accumulation dynamics is unstable ($H_a > 0$), and there is therefore a critical value $\bar{\mu}$ such that $tr \gtrless 0$ for $\mu \lessgtr \bar{\mu}$. It follows that a decline in competition may destabilize a previously stable equilibrium.

Overall then, assuming stability of the stationary solution, the Steindlian system (10.17)–(10.18) with the restrictions (10.19)–(10.22) implies that increased oligopolization will (i) produce a decline in the equilibrium values of utilization and the rate of accumulation, and (ii) endanger the local stability of the equilibrium. These implications are consistent with Steindl's conclusions. But somewhat surprisingly – and contrary to Steindl's analysis – increased oligopolization (an upward shift in the price Phillips curve) ultimately generates a fall in the profit share.[20] The intuition behind this result derives from the fact that the markup dynamics (10.18) defines the stationary markup (or profit share) as an increasing function of the rate of utilization, rather than as a simple parameter. An increase in oligopolization corresponds to an upward shift in this "stationary-markup function". Utilization, however, is endogenously determined, and it falls as firms begin to raise their markup. The unstable accumulation dynamics now kicks in: a fall in utilization has an adverse effect on the investment function and the fall in utilization is exacerbated. The destabilizing accumulation dynamics implies that the attempt to raise profit margins produces a large decline in utilization, so large that the markup also declines, despite the upward shift in the price Phillips curve. Of course, one could re-define increased oligopolization as a rise in the markup, rather than an upward shift in the price Phillips curve. This alternative definition evades the paradox but produces an un-Steindlian positive relation between oligopolization and growth. In any case, the paradoxical decline in the profit share following an upward shift in the price Phillips curve (the stationary-markup function) is reversed when we add reserve-army effects.

## 10.4 Adding a labor market

### *The reserve army of labor*

The dynamic systems developed so far have focused on the product market and the interaction between investment, saving, finance and pricing decisions. The neglect of the labor market is striking but not entirely un-Steindlian. Steindl (1952, p.168) for instance points out that, since it is strongly influenced by immigration, the growth of the working population is as much an effect as a cause of the trend in accumulation. The same conclusion is reached in his discussion of Marx on pp.233–234. According to this position, the growth of the labor force is endogenous and does not constrain accumulation.

It is hard to square this dismissal of any role of the labor supply with Steindl's (1979, p.12) argument that "the most striking feature of the new economic climate" is the way prolonged near-full employment "has strengthened the economic position of workers and the power of trade unions, and has led to demands for workers' participation". As a result of these demands, he argues, the attitudes of governments and big business alike have changed:

> Formerly there was a general conviction in most countries that the government would intervene to prevent a prolonged depression; this reduced uncertainty and therefore made for higher and more stable private investment. This

confidence has been shattered. Here is another reason why the function $\phi$ [the investment function] has shifted downwards.

(Steindle 1979, p.13)

Steindl's seemingly contradictory suggestions with respect to labor market conditions may be reconciled by noting that although there have been periods of low official unemployment both before the big depression and in the 1950s and 1960s, the supply of labor to the modern, capitalist part of the economy was quite elastic. Up until the 1960s most OECD countries had hidden reserves of unemployment in agriculture, in parts of the service sector and among women, and, as pointed out by Steindl, immigration also helped alleviate any shortages of labor. The hidden reserve army gradually became depleted, however, and immigration was hampered by growing political resistance. As a result, the economy became mature in Kaldor's (1966) sense of the term: its growth rate became constrained by the growth in the labor force.

We formalize this argument (which may or may not be a reasonable representation of Steindl's thinking) by including an effect of labor market conditions on the shifts in the investment function. Thus, let

$$\dot{a} = h(u(a, \pi), \pi, g(a, \pi), e); \quad h_u > 0, h_\pi \geq 0, h_g \leq 0, h_e < 0$$
$$= H(a, \pi, e), \tag{10.22}$$

where $e$ is the measure of labor market conditions. We shall refer to this variable simply as the employment rate. In any empirical application, however, the role of hidden unemployment as well as the possibility of obtaining workers through immigration must be taken into account. The equation describes how "animal spirits" suffer under full employment, leading to a gradual, downward shift in the investment function. These employment effects are likely to be non-linear: negligible at high levels of unemployment but very substantial when the economy approaches full employment. Equation (10.23) captures, we believe, Steindl's main point – a point which is closely related to Kalecki's (Kalecki 1943) insights that persistent high employment undermines "the social position of the boss" and "the self assurance and class consciousness of the working class" grows (quoted from Kalecki (1971, pp.140–141)).

The movements in the employment rate depend on changes in the labor force, output and technology. Assuming Harrod-neutral technical progress, we have

$$\dot{e} = e(\hat{u} + g - n)$$
$$= e\left[\frac{u_a(a, \pi)}{u(a, \pi)}\dot{a} + \frac{u_\pi(a, \pi)}{u(a, \pi)}\dot{\pi} + g(a, \pi) - n\right], \tag{10.23}$$

where $n$ is the growth rate of the labor force in efficiency units. The analysis could be extended to allow for induced changes in the growth of the labor supply or in the rate of technical progress. High employment and incipient labor shortages may serve as incentives for both immigration and labor saving innovation, and this possibility could be captured by assuming that $n = n(e)$, $n'(e) \geq 0.$[21] This endogenization of $n$ would leave intact the main stability result in the following two sections (that is, the result that a sufficiently strong reserve-army effect in the accumulation function ensures local stability). The endogenization complicates the analysis, however, and in the interest of expositional simplicity we focus in this chapter on the case where $n'(e) = 0$.

### Employment and accumulation dynamics

Equations (10.18), (10.22) and (10.23) and constitute a 3-D system in $a$, $\pi$, $e$. First, however, we shall consider the special case with a constant markup, that is, the case in which $\dot{\pi} \equiv 0$. We then have the following two-dimensional system

$$\dot{a} = H(a, e); H_a > 0, H_e < 0,$$

$$\dot{e} = e\left[\frac{u_a(a)}{u(a)}\dot{a} + g(a) - n\right] = F(a,e),$$

where it is assumed, as in Section 10.3, that the pure accumulation dynamics is unstable ($H_a > 0$).

At a stationary point we get

$$F_a = e\left[\frac{u_a(a)}{u(a)}H_a + g'(a)\right] > 0 \text{ since } g'(a) > 0, \frac{u_a(a)}{u(a)} > 0, H_a > 0,$$

$$F_e = e\frac{u_a(a)}{u(a)}H_e < 0.$$

Hence, evaluated at a stationary point, the Jacobian takes the following form

$$J(a,e) = \begin{pmatrix} H_a & H_e \\ e\left[\frac{u_a(a)}{u(a)}H_a + g'(a)\right] & e\frac{u_a(a)}{u(a)}H_e \end{pmatrix}$$

and

$$\det J = -eg'(a)H_e > 0,$$

$$\operatorname{tr} J = H_a + e\frac{u_a(a)}{u(a)}H_e.$$

It follows that the stationary solution represents a node or a focus. Unlike the system with markup and accumulation dynamics, saddlepoint instability can be excluded. But analogously to the case of a node/focus in Section 10.4, stability is ensured if animal spirits adjust slowly relative to the adjustment in the stabilizing variable, in this case the employment rate. A Marxian reserve-army effect, in other words, may help to stabilize the economy.

### *Employment, accumulation and markup dynamics*

Now consider the full three dimensional system consisting of (10.22) and (10.18). If $g_\pi\,(a, \pi) \geq 0$, there is (at most) one stationary solution.[22] To see this, note that stationarity requires

$$g(a, \pi) = n; \qquad g_a > 0,\, g_\pi \geq 0$$
$$G(a, \pi) = 0; \qquad G_a > 0,\, G_\pi < 0.$$

These two equations cannot have more than one solution for $a^*$ and $\pi^*$. Having found $a^*$, $\pi^*$, the equilibrium solution for the employment rate can be derived from

$$\dot{a} = H(a^*, \pi^*, e) = 0;\; H_e < 0.$$

Evaluated at a stationary point the Jacobian of the 3-D system takes the following form

$$J(a, \pi, e) = \begin{pmatrix} H_a & H_\pi & H_e \\ G_a & G_\pi & 0 \\ e\left(\dfrac{u_a}{u}H_a + \dfrac{u_\pi}{u}G_a + g_a\right) & e\left(\dfrac{u_a}{u}H_\pi + \dfrac{u_\pi}{u}G_\pi + g_\pi\right) & e\dfrac{u_a}{u}H_e \end{pmatrix}.$$

The necessary and sufficient Routh–Hurwitz conditions for local stability are that

1. $tr\, J = H_a + G_\pi + e\dfrac{u_a}{u}H_e < 0,$

2. $\det J_1 + \det J_2 + \det J_3 = eH_e\left[\dfrac{u_a}{u}G_\pi - \dfrac{u_\pi}{u}G_a - g_a\right] + H_a G_\pi - G_a H_\pi > 0,$

3. $\det J = eH_e[g_\pi G_a - g_a G_\pi] < 0,$

4. $-tr\, J[\det J_1 + \det J_2 + \det J_3] + \det J > 0.$

The second condition will be satisfied if the stabilizing effect of the reserve army is sufficiently strong (that is, for sufficiently large absolute values of $H_e$).

To see this, note that using (10.19)–(10.20) the term in square brackets can be written

$$\frac{u_a}{u}G_\pi - \frac{u_\pi}{u}G_a - g_a = \frac{u_a}{u}(1-\pi)f_\pi - g_a.$$

Since $u_a > 0, f_\pi \leq 0$ and $g_a > 0$ the right-hand side of this equation is unambiguously negative.

The third condition is satisfied if the expression in the square brackets is positive and, when combined with the signs of the other partial derivatives, our earlier condition for uniqueness ($g_\pi \geq 0$) is sufficient to ensure that this is the case. If the second and third conditions are met, finally, the first and fourth will also hold if the absolute value of $H_e$ is large. To see that the fourth condition will be met, note that $-tr\, J\, [\det(J_1) + \det(J_2) + \det(J_3)]$ is quadratic in $H_e$ while $\det J$ is linear.

It may be interesting to look briefly at the comparative statics of increasing oligopolization for the 3-D systems. Increasing oligopolization corresponds to an upward shift in the $G\,(a, \pi)$-equation that describes the mark-up dynamics. We have $G_a > 0$ and $G_\pi < 0$, and this upward shift therefore has to be offset by an increase in $\pi$ and/or a decline in $a$. Since the long-run rate of growth $g(a, \pi)$ must remain equal to $n$ and since by assumption $g_a > 0$ and $g_\pi \geq 0$, it follows that $a$ and $\pi$ cannot move in the same direction. Thus, $\pi$ must increase while the change in $a$ must be non-positive. Utilization, which is increasing in $a$ but decreasing in $\pi$, therefore must fall. The effect on employment, finally, can be found from the stationarity condition for $a$: $h(u, \pi, g, e) = 0$. Since $g = n$ is unchanged we have

$$0 = h_u\,(u_a\,da + u_\pi d\pi) + h_\pi d\pi + h_e de$$

or

$$de = \frac{[h_u(u_a da + u_\pi d\pi)] + h_\pi\,d\pi}{-h_e}.$$

The denominator of the expression on the right-hand side is positive and it follows that employment falls iff the numerator is negative. The term in square brackets is unambiguously negative and, as argued above, desired utilization is likely to be very in sensitive to changes in profitability; that is, $h_\pi\,d\pi$ will be small. Thus, although a positive employment effect cannot be ruled out, the most likely outcome is one where increasing oligopolization leads to a rise in unemployment. Intuitively, a larger reserve army is needed to boost animal spirits in order to make up for the depressing effects of lower utilization.[23] These effects, are consistent with Steindl's predictions: increased oligopolization raises the profit share but generates stagnation in the form of lower employment and capital utilization. It should be noted, perhaps, that the growth rate will also be affected if one allows for induced changes in the labor supply along the lines suggested in

Section 10.3: a decline in the employment rate leads to lower growth if $n = n\,(e)$ with $n' > 0$.

The long-term effects of a transition, finally, from a stage of large hidden unemployment (in which $h_g = 0$) to one of Kaldorian maturity may be analyzed by comparing a stationary point of the 2-D accumulation-markup dynamics (with $g > n$) to a stationary point of the 3-D system. But for the comparison to be meaningful, it must be assumed that the stationary points are stable, and the case of saddlepoint instability in the 2-D system is therefore excluded. Assuming that initially we are in the stable 2-D case, the negative effect of the employment rate on the rate of change of animal spirits as the economy reaches a mature stage can be depicted as a rightward shift of the $\dot{a} = 0$ locus in Figure 10.2. The result is a decline in both $a$ and $\pi$. The rate of utilization then must fall (or, if $f_\pi = 0$, remain unchanged).[24] Thus, the transition to a new stationary point associated with a constant employment rate implies a fall in the rate of accumulation to bring it into line with the growth of the labor force ($g = n$), and a decline in both the rate of utilization and the profit share.

## 10.5 Conclusions and extensions

We opened this chapter by comparing a standard Steindl-Kalecki model with Steindl's (1952) analysis. This comparison revealed several differences, and both the standard model and Steindl's own formalization had significant weaknesses, we argued. Steindl himself noted a puzzling and unsatisfactory aspect of his model: it generated unreasonably high values of the (locally) stable steady state solutions for utilization and the rate of growth. One contribution of this chapter is to demonstrate that weak and questionable non-linearities lie behind this problematic feature of his model. The main contribution, however, lies in the presentation and analysis of extended Steindlian models that combine unstable accumulation dynamics with the stabilizing effects of endogenous changes in the markup and the reserve army of labor.

Using a continuous time framework, we first incorporated the interaction between markup dynamics and accumulation dynamics. Steindl, more than any other contributor to the post Keynesian tradition, has emphasized the influence of competitive conditions on the sensitivity of the markup to changes in utilization, and he has consistently combined this emphasis with a keen awareness of the possibilities of Harrodian instability arising from strong, lagged effects of utilization on the rate of accumulation. In our view the dynamic interaction between accumulation and the markup therefore constitutes the core of a Steindlian model.

We formalized the interaction between markup dynamics and accumulation dynamics in the form of a 2-D system of differential equations, one for shifts in the markup and one for shifts in "animal spirits". Consistent with Steindl's vision, we find that fast adjustment of the markup may (but need not) contribute to a stabilization of the steady growth path. The model also supports Steindl's position on the stagnationist effects of increased oligopolization: an upward shift in the dynamic equation for the markup generates a decline in both utilization and growth. Paradoxically, however, in the stable case it also leads to a decline in the stationary solution for the markup.

The core model – developed in Section 10.3 – can be extended in various ways. Our extension in Section 10.4 focuses on the Marxian influence of the reserve army. There is a tension in Steindl's views on this issue. Steindl (1952) largely dismisses the idea that accumulation could be constrained by a declining reserve army. In Steindl (1979), however, his position on this issue appears to have changed since in this chapter the effect of prolonged near-full employment on accumulation plays a key role. In any case, the inclusion of a reserve army effect tends to stabilize the economy (as in Skott 1989a, b), and the effects of increasing oligopolization are quite Steindlian: increasing oligopolization has stagnationist effects in the form of a fall in both the employment rate and the rate of capital utilization. It should be noted also that in this three dimensional system, which incorporates employment dynamics as well as markup and accumulation dynamics, an upward shift of the dynamic equation for the markup raises the stationary value of the markup. Thus, the paradox that characterizes the two-dimensional system without a labor market disappears in the extended system.

Our extensions of the standard model capture, we believe, important Steindlian insights. But our models clearly have weaknesses and limitations. One set of questions concern the assumption of instantaneous output adjustment and continuous goods market equilibrium. In Flaschel et al. (2006) we therefore introduce Steindlian features into the KMG model developed by Chiarella and Flaschel (2000b). Unlike our framework in the present chapter, the KMG model includes inventories and sluggish output adjustment, but to maintain analytical tractability our KMGS(teindl) model introduces simplifications with respect to the treatment of feedback effects from the labor market. From a Steindlian perspective, moreover, the limited role played by financial factors in the present chapter may seem more questionable than the absence of inventories and gradual output adjustments. We have allowed for retained earnings to stimulate investment, and the "principle of increasing risk" – the cost and riskiness of high degrees of external finance – may provide a rationale for this aspect of the model. But with a constant retention rate, retained earnings might also appear in the investment function simply because high current profitability signals the profitability of additions to the capital stock. Furthermore, the principle of increasing risk suggests that in terms of financial constraints, the gearing ratio rather the flow of retained profits may be the more important variable. Thus, following Steindl (1952), one may extend the model by including the gearing ratio in the investment function.[25] The gearing ratio, indeed, is a key variable in Dutt's (1995) examination of the interaction between the product market and financial aspects. His analysis, which leaves out markup dynamics and labor market effects, can be seen as complementary to the one presented in this chapter.

Other prominent aspects of Steindl's verbal analysis also suggest further extension of the model. We have taken all saving rates as well as firms' financial environment as constant. These assumptions could be relaxed to allow for the presence of stock markets and capital gains as well as endogenous changes in saving behavior (Steindl 1982), the effects of institutional influences on saving (e.g. Pitelis 1997) or evolving standards of financial behavior along the lines suggested by Minsky (e.g. Steindl 1990; 1989, p.173). From an applied perspective, however, the most severe shortcomings probably arise from the neglect of policy, both fiscal and monetary, and from a closed-economy assumption that weakens the case for profit-led growth (e.g. Blecker 1989; Bhaduri and Marglin 1990b) and excludes Kaldorian processes of cumulative causation (e.g. Skott and Larudee 1998). We leave extensions in these and other directions for future research.

## Appendix I

Let

$$f(u) = \frac{mk}{s}\left(\frac{u-1}{1+su}\right); u \geq 0.$$

The function $f(u)$ is increasing and strictly concave: $f'(u) > 0, f'' < 0$. Furthermore,

$$f(u) \gtreqless 0 \quad \text{for} \quad u \gtreqless 1,$$

$$f(u) \rightarrow \frac{mk}{s}\frac{1}{s} \quad \text{for} \quad u \rightarrow \infty.$$

Hence, $u > f(u)$ both when $u$ is small and when $u$ is sufficiently large. The inequality, however, maybe reversed for intermediate values of $u$. Since $f(u) < \frac{mk}{s}u$ for all $u$, however, the parameter restriction $\frac{mk}{s} > 1$ is a necessary condition for this to happen.

## Appendix II

### *A stable case*

Assume that

- Current accumulation depends non-negatively on profitability, that the change in $a$ depends negatively on the current growth rate, and that there are no direct effects of profitability on the change in $a$; that is $hg < 0$, $h_\pi \equiv 0$ and $g_\pi \geq 0$.
- Price inflation is completely insensitive to small variations in the profit share in the neighborhood of the stationary point; that is $f_\pi \equiv 0$ in this neighborhood.
- Market conditions are competitive in the Steindlian sense that adjustments in the markup are sensitive to deviations of actual utilization from desired

utilization. Moreover, the speed of markup adjustment is fast relative to shifts in the accumulation function ($f_u \gg h_u$).

Using the first two assumptions, we get

$$\frac{d\pi}{da}\bigg|_{\dot{\pi}=0} = -\frac{G_a}{G_\pi} = \frac{u_a}{-u_\pi} > \frac{u_a + \dfrac{h_g}{h_u} g_a}{-u_\pi - \dfrac{h_g}{h_u} g_\pi} = -\frac{H_a}{H_\pi} = \frac{d\pi}{da}\bigg|_{\dot{a}=0} > 0.$$

It follows that the $\dot{\pi} = 0$ locus is steeper than the $\dot{a} = 0$ locus and, using (10.19)–(10.20), that det $J > 0$. Thus, assuming the existence of a stationary solution, the stationary point must be a node or a focus. Furthermore, the third assumption on the relative adjustment speeds of $a$ and $\pi$ ensures that the second stability condition will also be met. To see this, note that

$$tr\, J = H_a + G_\pi = h_u u_a + [h_g g_a + (1-\pi) f_u u_\pi].$$

The term in square brackets in the expression for the trace is negative while the first term is positive. Stability – quite intuitively – can be undermined if the destabilizing adjustments of investment function are fast relative to the speed of stabilizing markup adjustment

### A saddlepoint

Our second case shows that fast price adjustments will not always suffice to stabilize the system. Assume that

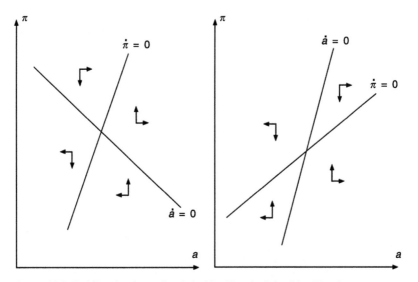

*Figure 10.3* Saddlepoint dynamics; left side: $H_\pi > 0$; right side: $H_\pi < 0$.

- there is no negative feedback from the current accumulation rate to the change in $a$ (that is, $hg = 0$); and
- the profit share exerts a positive effect on the change in $a$ and/or a direct negative effect on price inflation ($h_\pi > 0$ and/or $f_\pi < 0$).

It is readily seen that with these assumptions the determinant of the Jacobian becomes negative and the stationary point is a saddlepoint. Figure 10.3 illustrates the outcome. On the left in Figure 10.3, $H_\pi > 0$ and the $\dot{a} = 0$ locus is negatively sloped. On the right in Figure 10.3, $H_\pi < 0$, and both loci are positively sloped; the slope of the $\dot{a} = 0$ locus, however, is steeper than that of the $\dot{\pi} = 0$ locus. In Figure 10.3 the stationary point exhibits saddlepoint instability, and global analysis is needed to decide what will happen over the longer run.

# 11  Investment of firms in capital and productivity growth

## 11.1 Introduction

In the last decades an increasing part of economic literature was directed towards a new growth theory, i.e., the endogenization of technological change in a variety of ways.[1] Whereas these models usually were constructed on a neoclassical background, this chapter investigates, how endogenous technological change can be integrated into a model of temporary disequilibrium, where output and employment are constrained by demand side due to temporary wage and price stickiness and where in the medium- and long-run wages and prices then respond to the disequilibria on the markets for labor and goods as well as to cost-pressure terms. Furthermore, the capital stock adjusts in its dependence on a constant growth term by the difference between the rate of profit and the expected real long-run rate of interest.[2]

First, the model is formulated with exogenous technological change, providing the background for the subsequent analysis of the role of technical change. After the presentation of its laws of motion, the steady state and its local stability properties are considered. In a second step then, the rate of technological change is endogenized. This is done by employing two key elements of the well-known approach of Lucas (1988) on the mechanics of economic development, which connects a technology–production–function in the tradition of Uzawa (1965) and a positive externality of the technology level as in the model of Romer (1986).

In this chapter, however, the investment in R&D is not determined by utility-maximizing households as in the Lucas-model, but by a differential equation that describes the behavior of firms, which react in a specific way to the difference between their investment plans in real capital and the available workforce. The main findings are, that although there is a unique steady state, its stability may be jeopardized, if the adjustment speed concerning the evolution of (endogenously determined) R&D-investment is too high. In a special case, moreover, also the uniqueness of the steady state gets lost and hysteresis is emerging.

## 11.2 The model with exogenous technical change

The starting point of the model consists in the following determination of the temporary equilibrium of a demand-side constrained economy, where wages, prices, the capital stock and the money supply are given and output, employment as well as investment are determined on this basis:

$$Y = c(Y - \delta K - T) + [i_0 + i_1(\rho - (r^* - \pi^e))]K + \delta K + G \tag{11.1}$$

$$M^d/p = kY + (h_0 - h_1 r)W, \quad W = K \tag{11.2}$$

$$I/K = i_0 + i_1(\rho - (r^* - \pi^e)) \tag{11.3}$$

$$\rho = \frac{Y - \delta K - wL^d}{K} \tag{11.4}$$

$$G = \bar{g}K, \quad T = \bar{t}K \tag{11.5}$$

$$\hat{K} = \dot{K}/K = I/K \tag{11.6}$$

$$\hat{L} = \dot{L}/L = n \tag{11.7}$$

$$\hat{n} = \beta_n(i_0 - n - \hat{A}), \quad \beta_n > 0. \tag{11.8}$$

According to equation (11.1) output $Y$ in each period is determined by aggregate demand. The next equation describes the money market equilibrium. Equation (11.2) shows, that the real demand for money, $M^d/p$, depends with regard to its interest-rate-component on the amount of wealth, for which real capital, $K$, is taken as a proxy. According to equation (11.3) net investment $I$ per unit of capital is determined by a constant term, $i_0$ and the difference between the rate of profit, $p$, which is defined by equation (11.4), and the long-run real rate of interest, $r^* - \pi^e$, where $r^*$ depends on the short-run rate of interest, $r$, in the following way:

$$r^* = b_0 + b_1 r, \quad b_0, b_1 > 0. \tag{11.9}$$

The intuition behind this equation refers to the fact that the long-run rate of interest depends only partially on the actual short-run rate, but also on the expected future ones. Furthermore a liquidity premium is taken into account.

Equation (11.5) says that the government expenditures $G$ and taxes $T$ are linear functions of the capital stock, so that the corresponding terms in intensive form, $\bar{g}$ and $\bar{t}$, are constant over time.[3] Equation (11.6) gives the rate of growth of the capital stock in dependence on real net investment determined by (11.3).

By the next two equations (11.7) and (11.8) it is assumed, that the growth rate of the labor supply, $n$, reacts on the difference between $i_0 - \hat{A}$, and the actual value for $n$. Technically, a connection between these parameters is necessary in any way to ensure the model to have a steady state solution. Here, the trend term of investment, $i_0$, and the rate of technical progress, $\hat{A}$, are considered to be the independent variables, where $i_0$ is driven by certain "animal spirits" of the investors. The growth rate of labor supply adjusts to $i_0 - \hat{A}$ by migration. For the sake of simplicity, however, in the following an infinite speed of adjustment, $\beta_n$, will be assumed, so that $n$ equals the value of $i_0$ in any point in time.

Now the model has to be reformulated in intensive form to make it analytically tractable in the context of a growing economy. First, the temporary equilibrium in terms of $Y$ and $r$, following from equations (11.1) and (11.2), shall be considered:

$$y = \frac{i_1 b_1 (m - h_0)/h_1 + i_1 \pi^e + \delta + \bar{g} - c(\bar{t} + \delta) + i_0 + i_1(\rho - b_0)}{1 - c + i_1 k b_1 / h_1}$$

$$= \alpha_0 + \alpha_1 m + \alpha_2 \pi^e + \alpha_3 \rho, \quad \alpha_1, \alpha_2, \alpha_3 > 0, \tag{11.10}$$

$$r = \frac{(1-c)(h_0 - m) + k[i_1\pi^e + \delta + \bar{g} + i_0 + i_1(\rho - b_0) - c(\bar{t} + \delta)]}{(1-c)h_1 + k i_1 b_1}$$

$$= \beta_0 - \beta_1 m + \beta_2 \pi^e + \beta_3 \rho, \quad \beta_1, \beta_2, \beta_3 > 0, \tag{11.11}$$

with

$$y = Y/K, \quad \text{and} \quad m = M/(pK).$$

The production technology is given by a Cobb–Douglas production function of the following form:

$$Y = K^\beta (AL^d)^{1-\beta} \quad \Rightarrow \quad y = \left(\frac{AL^d}{K}\right)^{1-\beta} \tag{11.12}$$

with $A$ being the technology level and $L^d$ the labor demand by firms, which via (11.12) can now be derived from (11.10). With $e = L^d/L$ representing the employment rate this magnitude is then also a well-determined one.

After this description of the short-run the medium-run adjustment processes concerning nominal wages $w$, prices $p$, inflationary expectations $\pi^e$, and the money supply $M$, are to be determined. The growth rate of the nominal wage is assumed to react in a Phillips-curve like fashion on the difference between the actual employment rate $e$ and its "natural" level, $\bar{e}$, on a convex-combination between the actual rate of inflation $\hat{p}$ and the expected one, $\pi^e$ and the rate of technical change, $\hat{A}$:

$$\hat{w} = \beta_w(e - \bar{e}) + \kappa_w \hat{p} + (1 - \kappa_w)\pi^e + \hat{A}. \tag{11.13}$$

The price inflation reacts in a similar way on the difference between the actual utilization rate of real capital, $u$, and its natural level $\bar{u}$ as well as on wage pressure, with weight $\kappa_p$), and the inflationary climate $\pi^e$, with weight $(1 - \kappa_p)$; here, the rate of technical change $\hat{A}$ has to be subtracted, because it mitigates cost pressure from wages. So one obtains the following equation:

$$\hat{p} = \beta_p(u - \bar{u}) + \kappa_p(\hat{w} - \hat{A})(1 - \kappa_p)\pi^e. \tag{11.14}$$

The rate of capacity utilization, $u$, appearing in this equation is defined by the ratio between actual and potential output: $u := Y / Y^p$. Whereas $Y$ (or $Y/K$ respectively) is already determined by equation (11.10), the potential output $Y^p$ has still to be defined. One possibility to do this might be to take the full employment output, given by inserting the whole labor supply $L$ into the production function (11.12). But what, if in this situation the marginal product of labor $F_L(K, L)$ is lower than the real wage $\omega$, which, due to the temporarily given levels of wages and prices, is a given magnitude in each point of time? Then, obviously, there is no profit maximum for firms, so that they would not be willing to extend employment up to this point. Thus, it makes more sense to determine the potential output $Y^p$ by marginal productivity theory:

$$Y^p = F(K, L^p) \quad \text{and} \quad \omega = F_L(K, L^p) \quad \Rightarrow \quad u = \frac{Y}{Y^p} = \frac{F(K, L^d)}{F(K, L^p)}.$$

The two equations (11.13) and (11.14) can now be used to determine the dynamics of the real wage per efficiency unit, $\omega^{eff} := \dfrac{\omega}{A} = \dfrac{w}{p^A}$. First, it follows

$$\hat{p} - \pi^e = \beta_p(u - \bar{u}) + \kappa_p(\hat{w} - \pi^e - \hat{A}),$$

$$\hat{w} - \pi^e - \hat{A} = \beta_w(e - \bar{e}) + \kappa_w(\hat{p} - \pi^e).$$

With $\kappa = (1 - \kappa_p \kappa_w)$ and $\kappa \neq 0$ one gets:

$$\hat{p} - \pi^e = \kappa[\beta_p(u - \bar{u}) + \kappa_p \beta_w(e - \bar{e})], \tag{11.15}$$

$$\hat{w} - \pi^e - \hat{A} = \kappa[\kappa_w \beta_p(u - \bar{u}) + \beta_w(e - \bar{e})]. \tag{11.16}$$

Subtracting (11.15) from (11.16) then yields:

$$\hat{\omega}^{eff} = \hat{w} - \hat{p} - \hat{A} = \kappa[(1 - \kappa_p)\beta_w(e - \bar{e}) - (1 - \kappa_w)\beta_p(u - \bar{u})]. \tag{11.17}$$

As the price and wage dynamics, given by equations (11.15) and (11.16), furthermore depend on $\pi^e$, the expected rate of inflation, something has to be said about the way these expectations are formed. It is assumed that this is done by adaptive expectations, which in continuous time leads to:

$$\dot{\pi}^e = \beta_{\pi^e}(\hat{p} - \pi^e). \tag{11.18}$$

Inserting $\hat{p}$ according to (11.15) into this formula then yields:

$$\dot{\pi}^e = \beta_{\pi^e}(\hat{p} - \pi^e) = \beta_{\pi^e}\kappa[\beta_p(u - \bar{u}) + \kappa_p \beta_w(e - \bar{e})]. \tag{11.19}$$

The last item to be determined for the medium-run dynamics is the development of the money supply, which is assumed to grow at a constant rate $\mu$, i.e. $\hat{M} = \mu$.

The long-run behavior of the economy, finally, is defined by the laws of motion of the following four magnitudes:

$$\omega^{\mathit{eff}} = \frac{w}{pA}, \text{ the real wage per efficiency unit}$$

$$l^{\mathit{eff}} = \frac{AL}{K}, \text{ supply-side labor intensity in terms of efficiency units}$$

$$m = \frac{M}{pK}, \text{ the real money supply per unit of real capital}$$

$\pi^e$ the expected rate of inflation.

Whereas the first and the last one of these variables are already determined by (11.17) and (11.19), the expressions of $\hat{l}^{\mathit{eff}}$ and $\hat{m}$ still have to be determined. For $l^{\mathit{eff}}$ one gets:

$$\hat{l}^{\mathit{eff}} = \hat{A} + \hat{L} - \hat{K}$$
$$= \hat{A} + n - [i_0 + i_1(\rho - (r^* - \pi^e))] = -i_1(\rho - (r^* - \pi^e))$$

because of $n = i_0 - \hat{A}$ as has been assumed. For $\hat{m}$ one gets via (11.15) the following expression:

$$\hat{m} = \hat{M} - \hat{p} - \hat{K}$$
$$= \mu - \kappa[\beta_p(u - \bar{u}) + \kappa_p\beta_w(e - \bar{e})] - \pi^e - i_0 - i_1(\rho - (r^* - \pi^e))].$$

Taken together the following four-dimensional dynamical system results:

$$\dot{\omega}^{\mathit{eff}} = \kappa[(1 - \kappa_p)\beta_w(e - \bar{e}) - (1 - \kappa_w)\beta_p(u - \bar{u})]\omega^{\mathit{eff}} \tag{11.20}$$

$$\dot{\pi}^e = \beta_{\pi^e}\kappa[\beta_p(u - \bar{u}) + \kappa_p\beta_w(e - \bar{e})] \tag{11.21}$$

$$\dot{l}^{\mathit{eff}} = -i_1(\rho - (r^* - \pi^e))l^{\mathit{eff}} \tag{11.22}$$

$$\dot{m} = [\bar{\mu} - \kappa[\beta_p(u - \bar{u}) + \kappa_p\beta_w(e - \bar{e})] - \pi^e - i_0 - i_1(\rho - (r^* - \pi^e))]m \tag{11.23}$$

where

$$y = \alpha_0 + \alpha_1 m + \alpha_2\pi^e + \alpha_3\rho, \text{ according to (11.10)},$$

$$\left(el^{\mathit{eff}}\right)^{1-\beta} = y \Rightarrow e = \frac{y^{1/(1-\beta)}}{l^{\mathit{eff}}}, \text{ according to (11.12)},$$

$$\rho = y - \delta - \omega^{\mathit{eff}}l^{\mathit{eff}}e, \text{ according to (11.4), and}$$

$$u = y/y^p \quad \text{with} \quad y^p = (l^{peff})^{1-\beta} \text{ and}$$

$$l^{peff} \quad \text{being defined by}$$

$$l^{peff} = (1-\beta)(l^{peff})^{-\beta} = \omega^{eff}.$$

There are three main forces, that drive the dynamics of the system (11.20)–(11.23):

Keynes-effect:   $p \uparrow (m \downarrow) \Rightarrow r \uparrow \Rightarrow r^* \uparrow \Rightarrow I \downarrow \Rightarrow Y \downarrow,$
Mundell-effect:  $\pi^e \uparrow \Rightarrow (r^* - \pi^e) \downarrow \Rightarrow I \uparrow \Rightarrow Y \uparrow,$
Rose-effect:     $\omega^{eff} \uparrow \Rightarrow \rho \downarrow \Rightarrow I \downarrow \Rightarrow Y \downarrow.$

Thus, the Keynes-effect as well as the Rose-effect are stabilizing, whereas the Mundell-effect destabilizes the system. In order to ease further computations, it will now be assumed that $\kappa_p = 0$ and $\kappa_w = 1$ (and thus $\kappa = 1$), thereby removing equation (11.20) and excluding the stabilizing Rose-effect and thus making the real wage per efficiency unit a parameter of the model: $\omega^{eff} = \bar{\omega}^{eff}$. The dynamical system is then reduced to:

$$\dot{\pi}^e = \beta_{\pi^e} \beta_w (e(\pi^e, l^{eff}, m) - \bar{e})], \tag{11.24}$$

$$\dot{l}^{eff} = -i_1 (\rho - (r^* - \pi^e)) l^{eff}, \tag{11.25}$$

$$\dot{m} = [\bar{\mu} - \beta_w (e(\pi^e, l^{eff}, m) - \bar{e}) - \pi^e - i_0 - i_1 (\rho - (r^* - \pi^e))] m, \tag{11.26}$$

with the variables $e$ and $\rho$ being determined in the same way as before, i.e. by equations (11.24) and (11.24).

### Proposition 1

*There is a unique steady state of the dynamics (11.24)–(11.26) with*
*$l^{eff} \neq 0$ and $m \neq 0$. This steady state can be successively determined by*
*the following equations:*

$$e_o = \bar{e}$$

$$\pi_o^e = \bar{\mu} - i_0$$

$$y_o = \frac{\bar{g} - c\bar{t} + i_0}{1-c} + \delta$$

$$(\bar{a} l_o^{eff})^{1-\beta} = y_o \quad \Rightarrow \quad l_o^{eff} = \frac{y_o^{1/(1-\beta)}}{\bar{e}}$$

$$\rho_o = y_o - \delta - \bar{\omega}^{eff} l_o^{eff}$$

$$r_o^* = \rho_o - \pi_o^e = \rho_o + \bar{\mu} - i_0$$

$$r_o = \frac{r_o^* - b_0}{b_1}$$

$$m_o = k y_o + h_0 - h_1 r_o.$$

*Remark*

With regard to the parameters it has to be assumed that

1. $\bar{g} \geq c\bar{i}$
2. $r_o = (\rho_o + \bar{\mu} - i_0 - b_0)/b_1 > 0$
3. $m_o = k y_o + h_0 - h_1 r_o > 0.$

The first assumption implies $y_o > 0$ and ensures together with the two other assumptions, that all steady state values are economically meaningful.

**Proposition 2**

> *The steady state of the system (11.24)–(11.26) is locally asymptotically stable, if the value of the parameter $\beta_w$ is sufficiently large and the value of $\beta_{\pi^e}$ is sufficiently small in comparison to the other parameters of the model.*

This proposition is easily verified by calculating the Jacobian of the system (11.24)–(11.26) and employing the Routh–Hurwitz conditions.

## 11.3 Endogenous technological change

Based on the considerations in the previous section one can now turn to the question, how endogenous technical change can be embodied into the model and which consequences will result from it. According to Lucas (1988) technical change will be introduced by two new elements:

- a technology-production-function of the Uzawa-type;
- a positive externality of the technology level in the tradition of Romer (1986).

For this purpose the total labor demand by firms, $L^d$, is divided into two components:

- $L_1^d$ : the number of workers employed in the production of goods; and

- $L_2^d$ : the number of workers employed in the production of technical progress.

Alternatively (and more closely related to the Lucas-model) one might also think of firms leaving to their workers $(L_2^d / L^d) * 100$ percent of the whole working time to develop their knowledge, which makes them more productive thereafter. Together with the Romer-externality the production function for goods now takes on the following form:

$$Y = K^{\beta} \cdot (A \cdot L_1^d)^{1-\beta} \cdot A^{\gamma}. \tag{11.27}$$

Thus, the production function of the previous section is only modified by employing $L_1^d$ instead of $L^d$ and adding the externality $A^{\gamma}$. Dividing by $K$ and collecting terms one gets equation (11.27) in intensive form:

$$y = \frac{Y}{K} = \left( \frac{A^{\frac{1-\beta+\gamma}{1-\beta}} L^{d_1}}{K} \right)^{1-\beta} = \left( \frac{BL_1^d}{K} \right)^{1-\beta} \text{ with} \tag{11.28}$$

$$B := A^{\frac{1-\beta+\gamma}{1-\beta}} \quad \text{and thus} \quad \hat{B} = \frac{1-\beta+\gamma}{1-\beta} \hat{A}. \tag{11.29}$$

The production function of technology (or, alternatively, of human capital) on the other hand is defined by:

$$\dot{A} = \eta(\frac{L_2}{L}) \cdot A \quad \Leftrightarrow \quad \hat{A} = \eta \cdot \frac{L_2}{L}. \tag{11.30}$$

$$\tag{11.31}$$

If the partitioning of the workforce (or the working time) is now described by the variable $h$, such that

$$L_2^d = hL^d \quad \text{and thus} \quad \hat{A} = \eta h, \tag{11.32}$$

then from (11.29) one obtains

$$\hat{B} = \frac{1-\beta+\gamma}{1-\beta} \eta h. \tag{11.33}$$

With $L^d = L_1^d + L_2^d = (1-h)L^d + hL^d$ and redefining $l^{\text{eff}}$ as $\frac{BL}{K}$ while leaving $L$ and $e$ defined as before then leads to:

$$\frac{BL_1^d}{K} = \frac{B(1-h)eL}{K} = (1-h)el^{\text{eff}} \quad \Rightarrow \quad y = ((1-h)eL^{\text{eff}})^{1-\beta}. \tag{11.34}$$

Up to this point, however, the main question is still unanswered, namely how the value of $h$ is determined. While in the model of Lucas this is done by a utility maximizing procedure of the households, in the present context it is the task of the firms to decide upon the allocation of the workforce (or working time). Here it is assumed that $h$ develops according to the following differential equation:

$$\dot{h} = \beta_{h_1}(i_0 - \hat{B} - n) + \beta_{h_2}(e - \bar{e}). \tag{11.35}$$

In this equation the expression $i_0 - \hat{B}$ is interpreted as the trend growth rate of labor demand, which is viewed by firms to come about on the basis of their investment decisions and their produced productivity increases. This term is compared to the growth rate of labor supply available and the difference drives the efforts undertaken by firms to increase their productivity level. In addition to this, also the tightness of the labor market, measured by the expression $e - \bar{e}$, has for the same reason a positive influence on the decision of firms to invest into a higher productivity. Thus, firms increase their efforts in increasing the level of technology (or the human capital of their workers, respectively), if there is insufficient growth in the labor supply and a high rate of employment (so that there are only few reserves of labor that could be mobilized).

Note furthermore, that, as a consequence of the endogenization of $h$, it is now possible to assume the growth rate of the labor supply, $n$, to be exogenously fixed and thus no longer reacting to the difference between the trend term of investment and the rate of technical change.

At this stage the endogenization of technological change is complete so that one can now turn to the study of the properties of the new model. The first change in comparison with the former model with exogenous technical progress concerns the determination of the demand-constrained temporary equilibrium, represented by the rate of employment $e$. Here equation (11.34) in connection with (11.10) (which is valid here as before) yields

$$y = ((1-h)eL^{eff})^{1-\beta} = \alpha_0 + \alpha_1 m + \alpha_2 \pi^e + \alpha_3 \rho. \tag{11.36}$$

Inserting for $\rho$ its definition $y - \delta - \bar{\omega}^{eff} l^{eff} e$ then leads to

$$(1-\alpha_3)((1-h)eL^{eff})^{1-\beta} + \alpha_3(\delta + \bar{\omega}^{eff} l^{eff} e) = \alpha_0 + \alpha_1 m + \alpha_2 \pi^e$$

$$\Rightarrow e = e(\pi^e, l^{eff}, m, h), \tag{11.37}$$

so that $e$ now also depends on $h$, and that in a positive way; this fact will later be of some importance with regard to the dynamic behavior of the considered economy.

With $e$ and $\rho$ determined in the above way and $r$ and $r^*$ given by (11.11) and (11.9) respectively, one obtains the following system of differential equations, if one additionally takes into account, that the time rate of change of $l^{eff}$ is now (via (11.29)) determined by:

$$l^{eff} = \frac{BL}{K} \Rightarrow \hat{l}^{eff} = \hat{B} - \hat{L} - \hat{K} \tag{11.38}$$

$$= \frac{1-\beta+\gamma}{1-\beta}\eta h - n - [i_0 - i_1(\rho - (r* - \pi^e))].$$ (11.39)

Then one gets:

$$\dot{\pi}^e = \beta_{\pi^e}\beta_w(e(\pi^e, l^{eff}, m, h) - \bar{e})],$$ (11.40)

$$\dot{l}^{eff} = [\frac{1-\beta+\gamma}{1-\beta}\eta h + n - i_0 - i_1(\rho - (r* - \pi^e))]l^{eff},$$ (11.41)

$$\dot{m} = [\bar{\mu} - \beta_w(e(\pi^e, l^{eff}, m, h) - \bar{e}) \; -\pi^e - i_0 - i_1(\rho - (r* - \pi^e))]m,$$ (11.42)

$$\dot{h} = \beta_{h_1}(i_0 - \frac{1-\beta+\gamma}{1-\beta}\eta h - n) + \beta_{h_2}(e(\pi^e, l^{eff}, m, h) - \bar{e}).$$ (11.43)

### Proposition 3

*The (economically meaningful) steady state of (11.40)–(11.43) is again uniquely defined and determined by the following equations:*

$$e_o = \bar{e} \text{ (as before)}$$ (11.44)

$$\pi_o^e = \bar{\mu} - i_0 \text{ (as before)}$$ (11.45)

$$y_o = \frac{\bar{g} - c\bar{t} + i_0}{1-c} + \delta \text{ (as before)}$$ (11.46)

$$0 = i_0 - \hat{B} - n = i_0 - \frac{1-\beta+\gamma}{1-\beta}\eta h_o - n$$

$$\Rightarrow h_o = \frac{1-\beta+\gamma}{1-\beta}\frac{i_0-n}{\eta}$$ (11.47)

$$((1-h_o)\bar{e}l_o^{eff})^{1-\beta} = y_o \quad \Rightarrow \quad l_o^{eff} = \frac{y_o^{1/(1-\beta)}}{(1-h_o)\bar{e}}$$ (11.48)

$$\rho_o = y_o - \delta - \bar{\omega}^{eff}l_o^{eff}$$ (11.49)

$$r_o^* = \rho_o - \pi_o^e = \rho_o + \bar{\mu} - i_0$$ (11.50)

$$r_o = \frac{r_o^* - b_0}{b_1}$$ (11.51)

$$m_o = ky_o + h_0 - h_1 r_o.$$ (11.52)

Note, that via (11.47) and (11.32) the steady state rate of technical change, $(\hat{A})_o$ is now endogenously determined by

$$(\hat{A})_o = \frac{1-\beta}{1-\beta+\gamma}(i_o - n). \tag{11.53}$$

With regard to the stability properties of the steady state determined above one can state:

### Proposition 4

The system (11.40)–(11.43) will become unstable, if $\beta_{h_2}$ is sufficiently large.

This is immediately seen by the (already mentioned) positive dependence of $e$ on $h$, which leads to a positive element in the diagonal of the Jacobian, so that its trace now depends in a positive way on the value of $\beta_{h_2}$. If this value is then sufficiently high, the system will become unstable. Thus, in addition to the Mundell-effect there is now a second one, resulting from the way in which firms decide upon their R&D-investments, which is destabilizing and thus counteracts the stabilizing Keynes-effect. On the other hand, there are good reasons to presume, that the local asymptotic stability can be preserved, if the values of $\beta_{h_2}$ and $\eta$ are sufficiently low.[4] If, moreover, stability gets lost in cyclically by when $\beta_{h_2}$ is rising, then the resulting business cycles do not only concern output and employment as in the previous model, but they also feed back on the time rate of technical change.

An interesting special case is obtained if one sets $\beta_{h_1}$ equal to zero. Then the expressions for $\pi^e$ and $h$ are collinear, so that the system (11.40)–(11.43) can be reduced to three equations. As a consequence, hysteresis emerges so that the long-run center of gravity of the considered economy becomes dependent on its initial conditions.

## 11.4 Conclusions

In this chapter it has been shown, that not only neoclassical models can be augmented by an endogenization of technological change, but that the same is (of course) true for models of temporary disequilibrium, where wages and prices are adjusting sluggishly. This was done here by making use of a Uzawa-type technology production function and an externality in the production function of goods according to the approach chosen by Romer (1986). The ingredients are thus the same as in Lucas (1988). The endogenization of technical progress took place by making the corresponding allocation of labor a decision variable of the firms of the economy.

This decision about investment in R&D (or, alternatively, human capital formation) was driven by the difference between the capital stock and current productivity growth on the one hand and the growth rate of the labor supply available to firms on the other hand. If the responsiveness of investment in R&D to the rate of employment is too large, the stability of the system gets lost. Resulting business cycles will then concern not only output and employment, but also the rate of technological change. Furthermore, in the case where R&D investment depends on the employment rate solely, the steady state will be no longer unique and hysteresis is arising.

# 12 A Harrodian knife-edge theorem in the wage–price dynamics

This chapter[1] investigates a positive self-reference of the rate of inflation onto itself as it can exist in a standard IS–LM model with an appropriately formulated wage–price dynamics. The self-reference is given by a 3-D analog to the positive feedback mechanism of the Harrodian analysis of unstable steady growth. It is shown in particular that this self-reference can overturn the local asymptotic stability of such an IS–LM model by means of so-called Hopf-bifurcations if the adjustment speed of the price level becomes sufficiently large.

## 12.1 Introduction: Harrodian instability

The Harrod (1939) model of the instability of steady growth is well-known, but not often well-presented and it is completely neglected in the modern discussion on macroeconomic stability. A reason for this neglect of Harrodian ideas may be seen in Solow's (1956) influential critique of his model – which gave rise to the standard model of neoclassical growth in the sequel, and later on to the neoclassical theory of endogenous growth, see Chapter 11. Solow's critique was, however, besides the point, since he simply assumed away the Harrodian analysis of goods market dynamics by a simple return to Say's Law on the market for goods.

An ingenious simple and convincing presentation of Harrod's idea was given in Sen (1970, pp.10ff.) in a discrete time framework. It is not easy to transform his specific model into a continuous time framework. Yet, in order to give a brief introduction into Harrod's instability analysis of steady growth – which can be compared with the continuous time analysis of the wage–price dynamics of this chapter – the following modeling of it is proposed.

Let us denote by $y$ the actual output–capital ratio: $Y/K$, by $y^*$ the expected one: $Y^*/K$ and by $y^n$ the 'normal' one – planned by firms for the long run. Assume furthermore for the theory of effective demand the simplest form of it, i.e., the textbook equation $Y = I/s$, where $s$ is the marginal (= average) propensity to save. This equation implies that $g_k = I/K$, the growth rate of the capital stock, and $y = Y/K$ must both grow at the same rate

$$\hat{g}_k = \hat{I} - \hat{K} = \hat{Y} - \hat{K} = \hat{y}.$$

To build Harrod's knife-edge analysis of steady growth on this Keynesian theory of the market for goods, one has to add an appropriate accelerator mechanism to this model which we assume here to be of the form

$$\hat{g}_k = \beta_k(y^* - y''), \quad \beta_k > 0, \tag{12.1}$$

i.e., firms accelerate (decelerate) the rate of growth of their capital stock if they expect more (less) demand than they can satisfy with their normal rate of capacity utilization.

An approach to closing this multiplier–accelerator–model of economic dynamics – one, that is widely (but to some extent inappropriately) believed to be outdated – is given by assuming an adaptive formation of expectations with respect to the determination of the ratio $y^*$, here of the form:

$$\dot{y}^* = \beta_{y^*}(y - y^*), \quad \beta_{y^*} > 0. \tag{12.2}$$

Together with the above accelerator equation, which due to $g_k = \hat{y}$ can be re-written as

$$\hat{y} = \beta_k(y^* - y''),$$

this gives rise to a system of two autonomous differential equations in $y$ and $y^*$ (if $y''$ is considered as a given magnitude).

The economically meaningful steady state of this dynamics is given by

$$y_o = y_o^* = y'', \quad g_k^o = sy_o.$$

For the Jacobian at this steady state we get the expression:

$$J = \begin{pmatrix} 0 & \beta_k y'' \\ \beta_{y^*} & -\beta_{y^*} \end{pmatrix},$$

which immediately shows that the above steady state is plagued by saddlepoint instability (if viewed from the sixties) or allows for saddlepath stability (if viewed from the seventies up to the present).

However, since this is a model with adaptive expectations this last characterization is somewhat besides the point and we should therefore make use of the honored alternative of perfect foresight in the above reconsideration of the Harrod model. Yet, assuming $y = y^*$ in place of the above adaptive expectations mechanism gives rise to the single dynamic equation

$$\hat{y} = \beta_k(y - y''), \quad \beta_k > 0,$$

which instead of removing – or allowing to remove – the above cumulative instability from the model (up to its two stable arms) now in fact gives complete instability (a degenerate saddlepoint).[2]

We do not claim here that the above is more than a simple textbook demonstration of Harrod's proposition that steady growth is subject to centrifugal, and not to centripetal forces. Yet, we believe that this is a view on economic dynamics that has to be taken more seriously than it was done in the past.

Instead of developing this approach to goods market instability further, we intend to demonstrate to the reader in this chapter that there is an important wage–price module analog to Harrod's knife-edge assertion which as an economic mechanism has recently received some attention in papers addressing the issue of whether "price flexibility is bad for economic stability" – or whether it is not.[3] This further knife-edge mechanism of Keynesian dynamics will be introduced and investigated in the now following section.

## 12.2 Wage–price dynamics and the IS–LM model

The model which we shall employ to investigate the asserted analogy consists of the following standard IS–LM equations (plus a conventional production function)

$$Y = C(Y, r - \pi, m) + I(Y - \omega N - (r - \pi) \ \bar{K}) + \bar{A}, \tag{12.3}$$

$$m = M/p = l(Y, r), \tag{12.4}$$

$$Y = F(N, \ \bar{K}) = F(N), \ F' > 0, \ F'' < 0, \tag{12.5}$$

and the following dynamic equations for the wage–price module of this model:

$$\hat{\omega} = \beta_w(e-1), \omega = w/p, e = N/\bar{N}, \beta_w > 0, \tag{12.6}$$

$$\hat{\pi} = \beta_p(\omega q(N) - 1), \pi = \dot{p}/p, q(N) = 1/F'(N), \beta_p > 0, \tag{12.7}$$

$$\hat{m} = \hat{M} - \hat{p} = \bar{\mu} - \pi. \tag{12.8}$$

In the above equations and in the following we denote total derivatives by a prime, time derivatives by a dot, rates of growth by a hat and partial derivatives by lower indices – up to indices relating to the Greek letter $\beta$ which is reserved for denoting adjustment coefficients. A bar over a variable indicates that this variable is considered as exogenously given.

The IS-equation is based on a consumption function which is assumed to fulfill $C_Y \in (0, 1), C_{r-\pi} < 0$ and $C_m > 0$ and an investment function satisfying $I' > 0$. Consumption thus depends on income $Y$ in the usual way, is subject to a negative real rate of interest $r - \pi$ effect ($\pi = \dot{p}/p$ the inflation rate) and exhibits the conventional Pigou-effect. Investment behavior is of a form that is typical in particular for so-called Keynes–Wicksell models as it reacts positively with respect to an increase of the real rate of return differential $(Y - \omega N)/\bar{K} - (r - \pi)$, the capital stock $\bar{K}$ (as well as autonomous expenditures $\bar{A}$) being given magnitudes, $\omega = w/p$ the real wage. In the LM-equation we denote by the letters

$l, m$ real money balances (demanded and supplied), where demand as usually depends positively on income ($l_Y > 0$) and negatively on the nominal rate of interest $r(l_r < 0)$. Income $Y$ and interest $r$ are statically endogenous variables which instantly clear the goods- and the money market in the usual way at each moment in time.

The dynamic part of the model is based on two well-known dynamic equations and one that is less familiar. Equation (12.8) is simply a consequence of the definition of real balances $m = M/p$ and the assumption that nominal money supply grows at an exogenous rate $\bar{\mu}$. Equation (12.6) is derived from a money-wage Phillips curve of the form $\hat{w} = \beta_w(N/\bar{N} - 1) + \pi^e$, where $\bar{N}$ denotes the given labor supply, 1 stands for the natural rate of employment and $\pi^e$ for the expected rate of inflation. In order to show that the following dynamic implications do not depend on erroneous expectations we here leave aside the case of adaptive expectations and start immediately from perfect foresight ones: $\pi^e = \dot{p}/p$, which reduces the above Phillips curve to the real wage Phillips curve shown in equation (12.6).

The final equation (12.7) which relates the time rate of change of the rate of inflation to the deviation of the real wage $\omega$ from the marginal product of labor $F'(N)$ is motivated by the following discrete time approach to a theory of the rate of inflation ($h$ the period length):

$$\frac{p_{t+h} - p_t}{h} = \beta_p h\left(\frac{w\Delta N_t}{\Delta Y_t} - p_t\right) + \frac{p_t - p_{t-h}}{h}.$$

This equation states that the coming change in prices per unit of time: $(p_{t+h} - p_t)/h$ is proportional to the discrepancy between marginal nominal wage costs and actual prices plus an extra term which describes an adaptive expectation $\pi^e$ of price changes $\hat{p}$ which is based on the very recent past ($\pi_t^e = \hat{p}_{t-h}$). We thus have generalized here, on the one hand, the conventional marginal productivity rule ($\beta_p = \infty$) to the case of also finite adjustment speeds and have, on the other hand, added to it a fast adaptive expectations mechanism – which represents the inflationary climate in which the marginal productivity rule is operating – and which is close to perfect foresight if the period length $h$ is small and inflation only moderate. Dividing this equation by $p_t$ then gives rise to our equation (12.7) for $h \to 0$ (and $\Delta N \to 0$).

### Proposition 1

*The IS–LM equilibrium part of the model gives rise to the following dependence of the statically endogenous variables $Y, r$ on the dynamically endogenous ones $\omega, \pi, m$ near the steady state of (12.4)–(12.6):*

$$Y(\omega, \pi, m), \ Y_\omega < 0, \ Y_\pi > 0, \ Y_m > 0, \tag{12.9}$$

$$r(\omega, \pi, m), \ r_\omega < 0, \ r_\pi > 0, \ r_m \gtrless 0. \tag{12.10}$$

Note here that the interest rate $r$ does not play a role in the dynamics (12.6)–(12.8).

*Remark*

Due to $N = N(Y)$, $N' > 0$ and $q = q(Y)$, $q' > 0$, the restrictions on the partial derivatives in (12.9) also apply to the two (composite) functions $N(Y(.,.,.)), q(Y(.,.,.))$ and will be denoted by $N_i$, $q_i \gtrless 0$ for $i = \omega$, $\pi$, $m$ in the following. The same holds true, of course, for the composite function $e = N(Y(...))/\bar{N}$.

*Proof of Proposition 1*

Denoting aggregate demand by $D$ gives $D(Y, \omega, r - \pi, m) = Y$ for the IS–equation ($D_Y > 0$, $D_\omega < 0$, $D_{r-\pi} < 0$, $D_m > 0$). Due to $\omega = F'(N)$ at the stationary state we have $D_Y \approx 1 - C_Y$ close to this state. It is now a routine exercise to obtain from the above IS–LM equilibrium the following equations for the partial derivatives of the implicitly defined functions $Y(\omega, \pi, m)$, $r(\omega, \pi, m)$ near the stationary state:

$$\begin{pmatrix} Y_\omega & Y_\pi & Y_m \\ r_\omega & r_\pi & r_m \end{pmatrix} = \frac{1}{\Omega} \begin{pmatrix} l_r D_\omega - l_r D_{r-\pi} & l_r D_m + D_{r-\pi} \\ -l_Y D_\omega & l_Y D_{r-\pi} & l_Y D_m + (1 - D_Y) \end{pmatrix},$$

where $\Omega = (1 - D_Y)l_r + l_Y D_{r-\pi} < 0$. This implies the assertion of the proposition.

*Remark*

The result $Y_m > 0$ is due to the combined effort of the so–called Keynes-and-Pigou-effect (which act into the same direction), while $Y_\pi > 0$ has been called the Mundell-effect in the literature. $Y_\omega < 0$, finally, may be called the investment multiplier effect of real wages. We shall make use of these terms in the case of the closely related expressions $q_i$, $e_i$, $i = \omega$, $\pi$, $m$ as well.

*Proposition 2*

*The stationary state*

$$e_o = 1\,(N_o = \bar{N}), \quad \omega_o = F'(\bar{N}), \quad \pi_o = \bar{\mu}, Y_o = F(\bar{N})$$

*(plus $r_o$, $m_o$ such that IS–LM equilibrium holds for $Y_o$, $\pi_o$) of the dynamic system (12.6) – (12.8):*

$$\dot{\omega} = \beta_w (e(\omega, \pi, m) - 1)\omega, \quad \beta_w > 0, \tag{12.11}$$

$$\dot{\pi} = \beta_p (\omega q(\omega, \pi, m) - 1), \quad \beta_p > 0, \tag{12.12}$$

$$\dot{m} = (\bar{\mu} - \pi)m, \qquad\qquad (12.13)$$

is locally asymptotically stable for all

$$\beta_w < m\omega q_m/e_\pi, \quad \beta_p < \beta_w(-e_\omega)/q_\pi$$

if $q_\pi$ is sufficiently small and if $\eta = -\dfrac{\omega}{q}q_\omega > 1$ sufficiently large at the stationary state. The stationary state will be unstable if one of the first two inequalities is reversed (independently of the size of $q_\pi$ and $\eta$).

### Proof of Proposition 2

The Jacobian $J$ of the above system at the stationary state is given by

$$J = \begin{pmatrix} \beta_w e_\omega \omega & \beta_w e_\pi \omega & \beta_w e_m \omega \\ \beta_p(q + \omega q_\omega) & \beta_p \omega q_\pi & \beta_p \omega q_m \\ 0 & -m & 0 \end{pmatrix}.$$

Let us denote the characteristic polynomial of this Jacobian by

$$p(\lambda) = a_0 \lambda^3 + a_1 \lambda^2 + a_2 \lambda + a_3 \quad (a_0 = 1).$$

According to the Routh–Hurwitz criterion (see Brock and Malliaris 1989, pp.75–76) the conditions $a_1, a_2, a_3 > 0$ and $a_1 a_2 - a_3 > 0$ are necessary and sufficient for local asymptotic stability. The first three of these conditions are obtained from the above matrix $J$ in the following way ($J_i$ the principal minors of $J$):

$$a_1 = -(J_{11} + J_{22} + J_{33}) = -\beta_w e_\omega \omega - \beta_p q_\pi \omega,$$
$$a_2 = J_1 + J_2 + J_3 = -\beta_p \beta_w e_\pi + m\beta_p \omega q_m + 0,$$
$$a_3 = -|J| = m\beta_p \beta_w e_m.$$

Note that we have made use here of the proportionality of the vectors $(e_\omega, e_\pi, e_m)$ and $(q_\omega, q_\pi, q_m)$ and of elementary properties of determinants (by which such proportional row components can be removed from their calculation) as well as of $\omega q = 1$ (at the point of rest) in the calculation of the determinants leading to $a_2$, $a_3$. We thus get:

$$a_1 > 0 \Leftrightarrow \beta_p < \beta_w(-e_\omega)/q_\pi,$$
$$a_2 > 0 \Leftrightarrow \beta_w < m\omega q_m/e_\pi$$

and $a_3 > 0$ without any restriction. We note that these two restrictions are the less strict the smaller the positive Mundell-effect $e_\pi$, $q_\pi$ is, since

$$q_\pi = q'N_\pi = q'e_\pi/\bar{N} = (q'/Y')Y_\pi$$

(see the previous two remarks). Assuming this effect to be sufficiently small (close to zero) gives that $a_1 a_2$ can be approximated by

$$0 < \beta_w \beta_p m\omega^2 q_m(-e_\omega) = \beta_w \beta_p m\omega^2 q_m(-q_\omega)/q',$$

an expression which has to be larger than

$$0 < \beta_w \beta_p m e_m = \beta_w \beta_p m q_m/q'$$

in order to imply $a_1 a_2 - a_3 > 0$. This is exactly the case when

$$\omega^2(-q_\omega) = -(\omega/q)q_\omega > 1$$

holds true at the steady state. This proves the first part of the proposition. The second part follows immediately from what we have stated above for $a_2 > 0$ and $a_1 > 0$.

*Remarks*

The main result of this section is that it may not be easy to establish asymptotic stability for the stationary state of the given IS–LM model with flexible, but not infinitely flexible wages and prices and with expectations that are of the perfect foresight type: Wages and prices must react as sluggish as it is demanded by the above two inequalities, i.e., the Mundell-effect must be sufficiently small for given sizes of these adjustment speeds, and this also with respect to the elasticity term $-\frac{\omega}{q}q_\omega = F_{NN}N_\omega(q = 1/F_N)$. This term reflects the profitability effect of real wage changes on the rate of investment which must be assumed to be sufficiently larger than 1 in addition.

We, therefore, in particular have that increasing price-flexibility that can be bad for economic stability. The destabilizing role of the Mundell-effect vs. the stabilizing role of the Keynes- and Pigou-effect clearly show up in the stability conditions considered above.

Of particular importance here is the auto-feedback $J_{22} = \beta_p q_\pi \omega > 0$ which states that the trace of the Jacobian $J$ can be made as positive as desired (for any given value of $\beta_w$) as long as there is a positive Mundell-effect ($q_\pi > 0$) in the model. This Harrodian knife-edge property questions severely the usual attitude to assume that prices (but not wages) are perfectly flexible which amounts to assuming $\beta_p = \infty$. Increasing $\beta_p$ further and further incorporates ingredients of hyperinflation into the model, which provides quite a different interpretation of perfectly flexible prices than is usually put forth.

Increasing instead the parameter $\beta_w$, on the one hand, counteracts the destabilizing effect of $\beta_p$ as far as the trace of $J$ is concerned. On the other hand, this increase cannot go too far, since it then may hurt the second stability condition in the above proposition (also by means of the Mundell-effect).

## Proposition 3

Assume that the stability conditions of Proposition 2 are all fulfilled for values of $\beta_p$ that are sufficiently small.

Then there exists a uniquely determined parameter value $\beta_p^H > 0$ such that the last Routh–Hurwitz condition in the preceding proof $b(\beta_p) := a_1(\beta_p)a_2(\beta_p) - a_3(\beta_p)$ is zero for this parameter value and there exists a continuous function $\beta_p(\varepsilon)$ with $\beta_p(0) = \beta_p^H$, and for all sufficiently small values of $\varepsilon > 0$ there exists a continuous family of non-constant, periodic orbits $\omega(t, \varepsilon)$, $\pi(t, \varepsilon)$, $m(t, \varepsilon)$ for the dynamics (12.11)–(12.13), which collapse to the stationary point of this dynamics for $\varepsilon \to 0$.

To the left of the Hopf-bifurcation parameter $\beta_p^H$ the point of rest of (12.11)–(12.13) is locally asymptotically stable while it is locally unstable to its right.

## Proof of Proposition 3

Since $(a_1a_2 - a_3)/\beta_p$ is a linear function of parameter $\beta_p$ there can be at most one zero of this function. Furthermore, we know by assumption that $a_1a_2 - a_3 > 0$ must be true for $\beta_p$ sufficiently small (as well as $a_1, a_2 > 0$). But $a_1$, for example must become negative for $\beta_p$ sufficiently large, i.e., must become zero in between, which implies $b = -a_3 < 0$, at this point, i.e., there must exist a value $\beta_p^H$ at which $a_1a_2 - a_3$ is zero. This proves the first part of the proposition.

As the determinant of $J$ is always negative we get from the preceding arguments that $a_1 > 0$, $a_2 > 0$ must hold for all $\beta < \beta_p^H$ (which already proves the last statement of the proposition).

The real parts of the eigen-values of $J$ are thus all negative for such values of $\beta_p$. By Orlando's eigen-value formula

$$b = -(\lambda_1 + \lambda_2)(\lambda_2 + \lambda_3)(\lambda_1 + \lambda_3),$$

we furthermore have that the real parts of all eigen-values must be nonzero also to the right of $\beta_p^H$ and that there are two imaginary roots and one negative real one at $\beta_p = \beta_p^H$ (since $\det J < 0$ holds throughout).

According to (Lorenz 1989, 3.1.2) we thus have that the stationary state of the dynamics (12.11)–(12.13) undergoes a Hopf-bifurcation when the parameter $\beta_p$ passes through the value $\beta_p^H$. This proves the second part of the proposition.

*Remark*

This proposition shows in addition to the former (in)stability assertion that increasing price flexibility must destroy the stable adjustment pattern of prices, i.e., their reaction to price/cost–differentials, in a cyclical manner: either by repelling limit cycles which contract to the stationary state as $\beta_p^H$ is approached from below or by attracting limit cycles which come into being when $\beta_p^H$ is crossed (or in the "linear case" by crossing a center type dynamics at $\beta_p = \beta_p^H$). We stress the local character of all these statements (including the distance of $\beta_p$ from $\beta_p^H$).

## 12.3 Conclusions

We have considered in Section 12.1 a positive self-reference of the following Harrodian type ($y^* = y$):

$$I\uparrow \to Y\uparrow \to y\uparrow \to I\uparrow,$$

which was based on the interaction of the Keynesian multiplier with a simple form of an accelerator and which – due to its one-dimensional dynamics – gave immediately rise to the knife-edge property of its steady state growth solution. There have been many attempts in the literature to embed this locally explosive dynamics into a broader setup making it thereby a viable dynamics, that is one for which global stability can be proved within economically meaningful bounds. Most prominent among the various solutions to this problem is Hicks' trade cycle growth model which made use of ceilings and floors to achieve this aim.[4]

We have seen in Section 12.2 that a similar positive self-reference may exist in the interaction of the Keynesian multiplier with the price module of the economy ($\pi^e = \pi = \hat{p}$):

$$\pi\uparrow \to I\uparrow \to Y\uparrow \to \pi\uparrow.$$

This positive self-reference was, however, imbedded in a four-market model and thus gave rise to a richer dynamics then the simple Harrodian analysis of goods market dynamics. It was shown that this positive self-reference ($J_{22} > 0$) will not be harmful if prices and wages react in a sufficiently sluggish way, if in addition the Mundell-effect ($Y_\pi > 0$) is sufficiently weak in comparison to the Keynes + Pigou-effect ($Y_m > 0$) and the real wage effect ($Y_\omega < 0$). On the one hand, we therefore have for this type of a positive auto-feedback that a weakly operating Mundell-effect may still allow for asymptotic stability. On the other hand, once this stability is lost there is nothing in sight – comparable to the Hicksian ceilings and floors or the Kaldorian non-linear trade cycle mechanism – that may guarantee the global stability or viability of this inflationary dynamics.

Things may even become worse when the Harrodian type of instability is combined with this medium-run inflation-accelerating process, so that destabilizing capacity-utilization and profitability-signals ($y$ vs. $y''$ and $(Y - \omega N)/\bar{K}$ vs. $r - \pi$) may add to each other in the support of the thesis that the dynamics of capitalist economies must in general be non-steady. Such a combined knife-edge property of steady growth has, however, not been discussed in the literature so far and therefore also not the resulting question of what may be the forces which then keep such an unsteady evolution within economically meaningful bounds.

# Part IV

# Macroeconomic adjustment processes

Evidence

# 13 Estimating interacting wage–price dynamics

## 13.1 Introduction

Wage and price adjustment processes have been considered in various of the preceding chapters. We studied wage–price dynamics from a Tobinian perspective in Chapter 4 and in the preceding chapter in the context of a Harrodian type of knife-edge situation. In Chapter 7 we reconsidered the New Keynesian staggered wage and price dynamics in a continuous time framework from the viewpoint of the Rational Expectations school and the determincy analysis this solution method implies. In Chapter 9 the wage–price adjustment processes were embedded in a non-Walrasian framework and the rationing situations this approach gives rise to. In the following we will now formulate and estimate a wage–price interaction or spiral of a fairly general type which includes insider–outsider considerations as they were dicussed in Chapter 8 and which formally resembles the staggered wage and price formation rules of the New Keynesians. It does however not at all give rise to conclusions which can be related to those that arose in the context of Chapter 7 and its jump-variable solution technique.

This chapter[1] builds on and extends results obtained in Flaschel and Krolzig (2006) for a crossover type of interaction of wage and price inflation rates, or more briefly for the wage–price spiral. We now also provide evidence for the presence of Blanchard and Katz (1999) error correction terms in both the wage and the price Phillips curve for the US economy after World War II. We also add to this situation an estimated link between goods and labor markets performance in the form of an extended Okun's Law, where in addition insider–outsider aspects are distinguished and taken into account. In this way, the critical $\alpha$-condition separating normal from an adverse real wage adjustment, as implied by our interacting Phillips curves approach, is now estimated in an integrated way and not just based on the assumption of fixed proportions in production, as was the case in Flaschel and Krolzig (2006).

Up to this link between the working of the real markets, the chapter starts from the same theoretical framework and attempts to demonstrate empirically (with a new data set) that the measurement of two structural wage and price Phillips curves, one for the labor market and one for the goods market, produces theoretically and empirically much more elaborate results than the reduced-form estimate of a single Philips curve that directly relates – without satisfying much justification – price inflation to demand pressure in the labor market.

This improvement in theoretical and empirical content is obtained, since we take into account (in addition to market-specific measures of demand pressure) that cost pressure measures for workers and firms should be based on backward-looking (medium-run) averages as well as forward-looking (perfectly foreseen) price and wage inflation rates (for wage earners and firms, respectively). This crossover use of such hybrid measures for the accelerator terms in the wage and price inflation dynamics is based on work by Chiarella and Flaschel (1996, 2000), and it now also characterizes (without use of a crossover relationships) the New Keynesian approach to staggered wage and price inflation; see for example Woodford (2003), though the New Keynesian wage and price Phillips curves differ considerably in their theoretical underpinnig from the ones proposed in this chapter.

In the next section we will briefly reconsider the wage and price level based structural equations estimated in Fair (2000) and show that they may easily be turned into ordinary wage and price inflation Phillips curves when account is taken of the parameter sizes estimated by Fair (2000). We then argue that such separate wage and price inflation Phillips curves, when reformulated in sufficiently general terms with respect to demand as well as cost pressure items, can give rise to various real wage adjustment patterns, two normal or stabilizing ones and two adverse or destabilizing ones. In Section 13.3 we compare our approach to a gradual adjustment of wages and prices with the New Keynesian one of staggered wage and price setting and find significant formal similarities, yet coupled with important differences in the treatment of inflationary expectations that give rise to radically different results for the implied wage–price dynamics. In Section 13.4 reduced-form expressions and the resulting critical $\alpha$-condition for an explosive behavior of our wage–price spiral are briefly discussed. Section 13.5 then provides 3SLS estimates of our structural wage and price Phillips curves, including estimates of Okun's Law as link between goods and labor market pressure, distinguishing in addition inside employment rates from the employment rate on the external labor market. We there measure in particular, whether the critical $\alpha$-condition for an adverse real wage adjustment was fulfilled for the US economy over the period 1961:1–2004:4. In Section 13.6 we conclude and provide an outlook on possible implications of our wage–price spiral mechanism for the post-war evolution of inflation and income distribution in the US economy.

## 13.2 Structural models of the wage–price spiral

In the early 1980s, there began a movement away from the estimation of structural price and wage equations to the estimation of reduced-form price equations ... The current results (see below, the authors) call into question this practice in that considerable predictive accuracy seems to be lost when this is done.

(Fair 2000, p.69)

This observation of Fair holds especially for applied work where it appears to be quite natural to express labor market and goods market dynamics by a single Phillips curve with demand pressure based on the external labor market (the rate of employment on this market, not hours worked within the firms) and with cost pressure in the two markets represented by a single expected inflation rate. Rigid markup pricing is one possible justification for such reduced form inflation dynamics. Yet, if in fact such reduced form PC's are explicitly derived from separate wage and price equations, the very special situation underlying this reduced form approach to wage–price dynamics becomes obvious.

In order to motivate our own formulation of such wage–price dynamics, a wage–price spiral in fact, we start briefly from the two structural wage and price equations estimated in Fair (2000). His structural equations for wage and price formation are of the form

$$p_t = \beta_0 + \beta_1 p_{t-1} + \beta_2 w_t + \beta_3 pm_{t-1} + \beta_4 U_{t-1},$$

$$w_t = \gamma_0 + \gamma_1 w_{t-1} + \gamma_2 p_t + \gamma_3 p_{t-1} + \gamma_4 U_{t-1},$$

where we (as Fair) use logarithms for representing wages $w$ and prices $p$, where $pm$ denotes import price inflation and where $U$ denotes the unemployment rate in these two structural equations. The estimation of these two equations by two-stage least-squares (with time trend and a specific constraint in addition) gives in Fair's (2000) paper the result shown in Table 13.1.

The result of his estimation provides us approximately with the following two inflation relationships for the US economy, when note is taken of the fact that the obtained parameter values suggest a reformulation of Fair's wage and price level

*Table 13.1* Fair's (2000) estimated price and wage equations

$$p_t = \beta_0 + \beta_1 p_{t-1} + \beta_2 w_t + \beta_3 pm_{t-1} + \beta_4 U_{t-1} + \beta_5 t + \varepsilon_t$$

$$w_t = \gamma_0 + \gamma_1 w_{t-1} + \gamma_2 p_t + \gamma_3 p_{t-1} + \gamma_4 U_{t-1} + \gamma_5 t + \mu_t$$

| | Estimate | t-stat. | | Estimate | t-stat. |
|---|---|---|---|---|---|
| $\beta_0$ | 0.0778 | 1.65 | $\gamma_0$ | −0.0709 | −1.6 |
| $\beta_1$ | 0.9225 | 284.47 | $\gamma_1$ | 0.9887 | 109.53 |
| $\beta_2$ | 0.0200 | 2.51 | $\gamma_2$ | 0.7513 | 8.86 |
| $\beta_3$ | 0.0403 | 13.61 | $\gamma_3$ | −0.7564 | −0.28 |
| $\beta_4$ | −0.1795 | −8.51 | $\gamma_4$ | 0.000181 | 2.61 |
| $\beta_5$ | 0.00088 | 1.01 | $\gamma_5$ | −0.0104 | |
| SE | 0.00294 | | SE | 0.00817 | |

Estimation period: 1954:1–1998:1
Estimations method: 2SLS

curves towards rates of wage and price inflation. In terms of growth rates $dx = \dot{x}, ; x = w, p$ they can indeed be simplified and approximated by:

$$dp_t = 0.08 - 0.18U_{t-1},$$
$$dw_t = -0.07 + 0.75dp_t.$$

We do not think that the structure represented by these two equations is developed enough from the theoretical perspective to really represent a structural approach to the wage–price spiral in the US economy. Fair's recommendation to use two structural wage and price curves in the place of a single reduced form Phillips curve for price inflation is an appropriate one, but one should employ for each market his own measure of demand pressure and not a single one for both. Furthermore, inflationary expectations should enter the wage–price spiral in an explicit and, from today's perspective, necessarily hybrid way. We shall fulfill this latter demand by a mixture (a weighted average) of short-run perfectly foreseen inflation rates (with Neoclassical, not New Keynesian dating of expectations) and an expression for the medium-term inflationary climate into which these short-run expectations are embedded. This adds persistence to an approach which is known to be problematic when only myopic perfect foresight expectations are considered. We thus reconsider the issue of interacting wage and price dynamics from a considerably more general structural point of view, with an emphasis on measuring the parameters involved in such a wage–price spiral and not yet on predictive accuracy as in the quotation from Fair's paper we started from.

In Chiarella et al. (2000b), Fair's wage–price dynamics has been reformulated as a wage price spiral as follows:[2]

$$dw = \beta_{we}(e - \bar{e}) + \beta_{wu^w}(u^w - 1) + \kappa_w dp + (1 - \kappa_w)\pi^c, \tag{13.1}$$

$$dp = \beta_{pu}(u - \bar{u}) + \beta_{pn}(n - 1) + \kappa_p dw + (1 - \kappa_p)\pi^c. \tag{13.2}$$

These authors use two separate measures of demand pressure for wages and prices, determined in the labor and the goods market, respectively. In the above wage–price dynamics, $e - \bar{e} = \bar{U} - U, u^w - 1$ are denoting (if positive) excess labor demand on the external labor market (in terms of labor market utilization) and excess labor demand (in terms of overtime worked) within firms, and $u - \bar{u}, n - 1$ (if positive) are denoting excess demand on the market for goods in terms of utilized capacity $u$ and in terms of a desired/actual inventory ratio $n$. In the following investigation of this wage–price spiral we will set $\beta_{pn}$ equal to zero however and will thus only pay attention to capacity utilization rates $e, u$ on the labor and the goods market in their deviation from their NAIRU (non-accelerating inflation rate of unemployment) rates $\bar{e}, \bar{u}$. We will then compare the outcomes on the labor market with the results that are obtained when the rate $u^w$ is used in the place of the rate $e$, i.e., when an insider or workforce utilization view is replacing the measurement of the employment rate in terms of heads.

This formulation of wage and price Phillips curves represents in our view the minimum structure one should start from in a non-reduced-form investigation of wage and price dynamics, which should only be simplified further – for example with respect to the reduced form equations it implies – if there are definite and empirically motivated reasons to do so. Generally however all parameters of the structural wage and price Phillips curves will show up in their reduced form representations which therefore cannot be interpreted in terms of labor market phenomena or goods market characteristics alone, as in the mainstream literature and in Fair's (2000) approach.

Up to the work of Rose (1967, 1990), it remained fairly unnoticed that having specific formulations of measures of demand and cost pressure on both the labor market and the goods market must, when taken together, imply that either increasing wage or price flexibility with respect to these demand pressures must then always be destabilizing, depending on marginal propensities to consume and to invest with respect to changes in the real wage. Figure 13.1 attempts to illustrate this assertion with respect to rising wages and prices if aggregate demand is pushed into an upward direction, through increasing consumption demand caused by real wage increases (with investment demand kept constant), and falling prices and wages, caused by falling investment demand due to rising real wages (with consumption demand kept constant). In both cases we consider situations where wages are more flexible than prices and vice versa. We represent stable situations in green color and unstable ones in red color. We have – broadly speaking – normal real wage reaction patterns (leading to converging real wage adjustment and thus economic stability from this partial point of view), if investment is more responsive to real wage changes than consumption and if wages are more flexible with respect to demand pressure on their market than prices with respect to their measure of demand pressure (with additional assumptions concerning the forward looking component in the cost pressure items as will be seen later on).

In this case, aggregate demand depends negatively on the real wage and real wages tend to fall in the depression (thereby reviving economic activity via corresponding aggregate demand changes), since the numerator in real wages is reacting stronger than their denominator. The opposite occurs, of course, if it holds – in the considered aggregate demand situation – that wages are less flexible than prices with respect to demand pressure, which is not unlikely in cases of a severe depression. In such cases it would therefore be desirable to have that consumption responds stronger than investment to real wage changes, since the implied real wage increases would then revive the economy. There is a fourth case when – in the latter demand situation – wages are more flexible than prices, where again an adverse real wage adjustment would take place leading the economy via falling real wages into deeper and deeper depressions as long as this situation remains in existence.

Figure 13.1 provides a graphical illustration of these possibilities of a real wage feedback channel within the wage–price spiral. It considers only the limit cases discussed above where only one demand component is changing and only one price is flexible. It can however easily be reinterpreted in stressing the components

$$w/p \uparrow \begin{cases} \mapsto & C \uparrow \Rightarrow Y^d \uparrow \Rightarrow Y \uparrow \Rightarrow e,\, u^w \uparrow \Rightarrow w \uparrow \Rightarrow w/p \uparrow \\ \mapsto & C \uparrow \Rightarrow Y^d \uparrow \Rightarrow Y \uparrow \Rightarrow u \uparrow \quad \Rightarrow p \uparrow \Rightarrow w/p \downarrow \\ \mapsto & I \downarrow \Rightarrow Y^d \downarrow \Rightarrow Y \downarrow \Rightarrow e,\, u^w \downarrow \Rightarrow w \downarrow \Rightarrow w/p \downarrow \\ \mapsto & I \downarrow \Rightarrow Y^d \downarrow \Rightarrow Y \downarrow \Rightarrow u \downarrow \quad \Rightarrow p \downarrow \Rightarrow w/p \uparrow \end{cases}$$

*Figure 13.1* Normal vs. adverse real wage adjustments ($Y^d$ is aggregate demand and $Y$ the output level).

that are more flexible than the other ones (that are kept constant in the four possible scenarios considered in this figure). Figure 13.1, reinterpreted in this way, immediately suggest that the exact type of real wage adjustment occurring within the considered wage–price spiral can only be determined by empirical investigation and – as will be shown – will depend moreover on the short-sightedness of workers and firms with respect to the current rate of price and wage inflation, respectively.

We conclude that wage and price Phillips curves which pay sufficient attention to demand as well as cost pressure items on the market for labor as well as on the market for goods may give rise to interesting dynamic phenomena with respect to the type of real wage adjustment they imply. This definitely deserves closer inspection than was the case so far in the macrodynamic literature. The present chapter wants to discuss in this respect possible theoretical and (for the US economy after World War II) empirical outcomes, in continuation and extension of the results achieved in Flaschel and Krolzig (2006), and thus wants to provide a definite answer for a specific country over a specific time interval. In the following section we will moreover follow Chiarella et al. (2005, Ch.5) and take Blanchard and Katz (1999) error correcting real wage influences (in addition to demand pressure terms) into account in both the wage and the price Phillips curve.

The hope is that interest in further investigation of the questions raised in this chapter will be stimulated by its results on the type and form of the wage–price spiral obtained for the US economy, for other countries, for high versus low inflation regimes, for more refined measures of demand pressure, for integral and derivative besides proportional demand pressure influences and more.

## 13.3 NK Phillips curves and the wage–price spiral: a comparison

In this section we consider briefly the New Keynesian approach to macrodynamics, here already in its advanced form, where both staggered price and wage setting are assumed. We here follow Woodford (2003, p.225) in his formulation of staggered wages and prices, which there too implies a derived law of motion for real wages, but do not yet include New Keynesian IS-dynamics and the Taylor interest rate policy rule here. As in this New Keynesian formulation of the wage–price dynamics, we ignore technical change here, but will introduce labor productivity growth in our empirical investigations below. We shall only briefly look at this extended New Keynesian approach in order to compare its formulation of wage–price dynamics with ours below. It will turn out – somewhat surprisingly, but from a formal perspective solely – that their approach differs from ours only in their handling of inflationary expectations, where we use hybrid expectations formation, neoclassical dating of expectations, crossover cost-push linkages (and two measures of demand pressure, a labor market stock and a goods market flow measure in the place of a single output gap right from the start).

Woodford (2003, p.225) provides the following two loglinear equations as representation of the joint evolution of staggered wages and prices, the wage and price Phillips curves of the New Keynesian approach. In these equations we denote by $w$, $p$ the logs of wage and the price level, by $y$ the log of output (with normal output set equal to one) and by $\omega$ the log of the real wage $w/p$ (with steady state wages also set equal to one):[3]

$$dw_t \overset{NWPC}{=} \beta E_t(dw_{t+1}) + \beta_{wy} y_t - \beta_{w\omega} \omega_t,$$

$$dp_t \overset{NPPC}{=} \beta E_t(dp_{t+1}) + \beta_{py} y_t + \beta_{p\omega} \omega_t.$$

All parameters shown are assumed to be positive. Our first objective is to derive the continuous time analog of these two equations, describing the New Wage Phillips Curve and the New Price Phillips Curve, and to show how this extended model is to be solved from the New Keynesian perspective and the rational expectations methodology.

In a deterministic setting, the above translates into

$$dw_{t+1} = \frac{1}{\beta}[dw_t - \beta_{wy} y_t + \beta_{w\omega} w_t],$$

$$dp_{t+1} = \frac{1}{\beta}[dp_t - \beta_{py} y_t - \beta_{p\omega} \omega_t].$$

If we assume that the parameter $\beta$ is not only close to one, but equal to one,[4] this yields (with a reversal of all parameter signs):

$$dw_{t+1} - dw_t = -\beta_{wy} y_t + \beta_{w\omega} \omega_t,$$

$$dp_{t+1} - dp_t = -\beta_{py} y_t - \beta_{p\omega} \omega_t.$$

Denoting by $\pi^w$ the rate of wage inflation and by $\pi^p$ the rate of price inflation, these equations can be recast into continuous time:

$$\dot{\pi}^w \overset{NWPC}{=} -\beta_{wy} y + \beta_{w\omega} \omega, \tag{13.3}$$

$$\dot{\pi}^p \overset{NPPC}{=} -\beta_{py} y - \beta_{p\omega} \omega, \tag{13.4}$$

$$\dot{\omega} \overset{RWPC}{=} \pi^w - \pi^p = (\beta_{py} - \beta_{wy})y + (\beta_{p\omega} + \beta_{w\omega})\omega. \tag{13.5}$$

This reformulation of the originally given New Keynesian wage and price PCs shows that there has occurred a complete sign reversal on the right-hand side of the NWPC and the NPPC as compared to the initially given situation. This occurs in combination with the use of rates of changes of inflation rates on the left-hand sides of the NWPC and the NPPC. The continuous time equations for the NWPC and the NPPC also imply – as shown in (17.14) – a law of motion for the log of real wages, and thus a 3-D system (which is coupled with a forward-looking law of motion for (the log of) output and a Taylor interest rate policy rule in the New Keynesian approach).

There are a variety of critical arguments raised in the literature against the New Phillips Curves of the (baseline) model of New Keynesian macrodynamics, see in particular Mankiw (2001) and recently Eller and Gordon (2003) for particular strong statements on the empirical irrelevance of such PCs. These and other criticisms also apply to the above extended wage and price dynamics. In view of these and other critiques, as well as in view of the approach established in Chiarella and Flaschel (2000b) and by further work along these lines, see in particular Chiarella et al. (2005), we propose the following modifications to the above New Keynesian wage–price dynamics, which will remove the questionable feature of a sign reversal in the role of output and wage gaps, caused by the fact that future values of the considered state variables are used on the right hand side of their determining equations, implying that the time rates of change of these variables depend on output and wage gaps with a reversed sign in front on them. These sign reversals are at the root of the problem when the empirical relevance of such NPCs is investigated.

We tackle this issue by using the following expectations augmented wage and price Phillips curves, which provide a wage–price spiral in the sense of the preceding section that (from a formal perspective) is in close correspondence to the New Keynesian approach. The letter "M = Mature" in front of these wage PC and price PC denotes their traditional orientation, however certainly in a matured form from the perspective of macroeconomic theorizing.[5]

$$dw_{t+1} \overset{MWPC}{=} \kappa_w dp_{t+1} + (1 - \kappa_w)\pi_t^c + \beta_{we}(e - \bar{e}) - \beta_{w\omega}\omega_t,$$

$$dp_{t+1} \overset{MPPC}{=} \kappa_p dw_{t+1} + (1 - \kappa_p)\pi_t^c + \beta_{pu}(u - \bar{u}) + \beta_{p\omega}\omega t.$$

We have modified the New Keynesian approach to wage and price dynamics here with respect to the terms concerning inflationary expectations, in order to indeed obtain a wage–price spiral and not just wage and price dynamics. We first assume that expectation formation is of a crossover type, with perfectly foreseen price inflation in the wage PC and perfectly foreseen wage inflation in the price PC. Furthermore, we use a neoclassical dating in the considered PCs, which means that – as in Lucas supply curves – we have the same dating for the expected and the actual wage and price inflation rates on both sides of the PCs. Finally, following Chiarella and Flaschel (2000), we assume expectation formation to be of a hybrid type, with a certain weight given to current (perfectly foreseen) inflation rates ($\kappa_w$, $\kappa_p$) and the counterweight attached to a expression which we call the inflationary climate $\pi^c$ that is surrounding the currently evolving wage–price spiral. We thus assume that workers as well as firms pay some attention to whether the current situation is embedded in a high or low inflation regime.

These relatively straightforward modifications of the expectational part of the New Keynesian approach to expectations formation will imply radically different solutions and stability features for this matured Keynesian approach to wage and price dynamics. There is, in particular, no need to single out the steady state as the only relevant situation for economic analysis in the deterministic setup here considered (when goods market dynamics and interest rates rules are added to the model and when note is taken of the fact that all variables are forward-looking in the considered New Keynesian framework). Concerning microfoundations for the assumed wage–price spiral we note here that the wage PC can be microfounded as in Blanchard and Katz (1999), using wage curves from standard labor market theories, if hybrid expectations formation is added to the Blanchard and Katz approach. We thus obtain from Blanchard and Katz (1999) in particular a foundation for the fact that it is indeed the log of the real wage or the wage share that should appear on the right-hand side of the wage PC (due to their theoretical starting point, given by an expected real wage curve). We will call the $\omega$ expressions in the MWPC (and the MPPC) Blanchard and Katz error corrections terms in the following. Concerning the price PC a similar procedure can be applied, based on desired markups of firms and implied expected real wages (now with the rate of capacity utilization gap $u - \bar{u}$ in the place of the employment rate gap).[6] Along these lines, we obtain an economic motivation for including the log of real wages with a negative sign into the MWPC and with a positive sign into the MPPC, without any need for loglinear approximations. We furthermore use the employment gap $e - \bar{e}$ (a stock measure) and the capacity utilization gap $u - \bar{u}$ (a flow measure) in these two PCs, respectively, in the place of a single measure (the log of the output gap, $y$), in order to distinguish between the demand forces that drive wages and those that drive prices.

In continuous time the two Phillips curves (13.6), (13.6) read (with $d\omega = dw - dp$):

$$dw \overset{MWPC}{=} \kappa_w dp + (1 - \kappa_w)\pi^c + \beta_{we}(e - \bar{e}) - \beta_{w\omega}\omega, \qquad (13.6)$$

$$dp \overset{MPPC}{=} \kappa_p dw + (1 - \kappa_p)\pi^c + \beta_{pu}(u - \bar{u}) + \beta_{p\omega}\omega. \qquad (13.7)$$

This is the model of the wage–price spiral that we will investigate from the analytical perspective in the next section and from the empirical perspective in the section thereafter.

We conclude that this model of a wage–price spiral is an interesting alternative to the – theoretically rarely investigated and empirically questionable – New Keynesian form of wage–price dynamics. This wage–price spiral, when implanted into a somewhat conventional Keynesian macrodynamical model, will produce stability results as they are expected from a Keynesian theory of the business cycle, with much closer resemblance to what is stated in Keynes (1936) "Notes on the trade cycle" than is the case for the New Keynesian theory of business fluctuations (which – when there are cycles at all – is entirely based on the Frisch paradigm, see Chen et al. (2006) for details).

In the present chapter, however, we will study the wage–price spiral in its own right and will do so primarily from an empirical perspective. In distinction to the results obtained in Flaschel and Krolzing (2006) we will find here that the above Blanchard and Katz (1999) error correction terms should be included into the working of the wage–price spiral also in the case of the US economy and that furthermore attention must be paid to the empirical link between labor and goods market utilization rates as it is normally discussed under the heading of "Okun's Law". This law should in a generalized form consider the link leading from firms' capacity utilization rates to utilization rates of the employed labor force and from there to the (un-)employment rate on the external labor market. Taking this two-stage link into account is generally needed in order to find out whether real wage dynamics has been normal (stable) or adverse (unstable) on an average in the US economy after World War II.

## 13.4 Real wage dynamics: the critical stability condition

We now derive reduced form expressions from the wage and price PCs of Section 13.2 (augmented by the error correction terms of Section 13.3), one for the real part of the overall dynamics (for the real wage) and one for the nominal part of the dynamics (for price inflation), where both of these reduced form dynamics are now driven by mixtures of excess demand expressions on the market for goods and for labor (and within firms) plus real wage error correction, and – in the case of the price inflation rate – in addition by the inflationary climate (accelerator) term with a unity coefficient in front of it.

Note in this respect first that the wage and price Phillips curves of the preceding sections are of the general form

$$dw = \beta_{w's}(\cdot) + \kappa_w dp + (1 - \kappa_w)\pi^c,$$
$$dp = \beta_{p's}(\cdot) + \kappa_p dw + (1 - \kappa_p)\pi^c,$$

where demand pressure and error correction expressions $\beta_{w's}, \beta_{p's}$ for the labor and the goods market may be formulated as advanced or numerous as possible and sensible. Appropriately reordered, these equations are just two linear equations in the two unknowns $dw - \pi^c$, $dp - \pi^c$, the deviations of wage and price inflation from the inflationary climate currently prevailing. They can be uniquely solved for $dw - \pi^c$, $dp - \pi^c$, when the weights applied to current inflation rates, $\kappa_w$, $\kappa_p \in [0, 1]$ fulfill $\kappa_w \kappa_p < 1$, then giving rise to the following reduced-form expressions for wage and price inflation rates, detrended by our concept of the inflationary climate into which current inflation is embedded:

$$dw - \pi^c = \frac{1}{1-\kappa_w \kappa_p}[\beta_{w's}(\cdot)+\kappa_w \beta_{p's}(\cdot)], \qquad (13.8)$$

$$dp - \pi^c = \frac{1}{1-\kappa_w \kappa_p}[\beta_{p's}(\cdot)+\kappa_p \beta_{w's}(\cdot)]. \qquad (13.9)$$

Note that all demand pressure variables are acting positively on the deviation of nominal wage and price inflation rates from the inflationary climate variable $\pi^c$. Integrating across markets for example the two PCs approach (13.1), (13.2) thus implies that two qualitatively different measures for demand pressure in the markets for labor as well as for goods have to be used both for money wage and price inflation for describing their deviation from the prevailing inflation climate, formally seen equivalent to a standard expectations augmented PC of the literature, see Laxton et al. (2000) for a typical example (with only one measure of demand pressure, the one on the labor market). Furthermore two different types of NAIRUs (one on the labor and one on the goods market) are here present in the integrated nominal wage and price PC which in general cannot be identified with each other (without knowledge of their link, i.e., Okun's Law).

As a special case of the general reduced form (13.6) and (13.7) we obtain in the light of the preceding section and its representation of a wage–price spiral (13.6), (13.7) the following detailed equations for real wage growth and price inflation dynamics. Note that these two equations for the growth rate of real wages $\omega = w - p$ and price inflation $dp$ are equivalent to the two structural equations from a mathematical perspective.

$$d\omega = \frac{1}{1-\kappa_w \kappa_p}[(1-\kappa_p)(\beta_{we}(e-\bar{e})-\beta_{w\omega}\omega), -(1-\kappa_w)(\beta_{pu}(u-\bar{u})+\beta_{p\omega}\omega)],$$

$$dp = \frac{1}{1-\kappa_w \kappa_p}[\beta_{pu}(u-\bar{u})+-\beta_{p\omega}\omega+\kappa_p(\beta_{we}(e-\bar{e})-\beta_{w\omega}\omega)]+\pi^c.$$

On the basis of the law of motion for the real wage $\omega = w - p$ we get as critical condition for the establishment of a positive dependence of the growth rate of real wages on economic activity the following term:

$$\alpha = (1-\kappa_p)\beta_{we} - (1-\kappa_w)\beta_{pu} \begin{Bmatrix} < \\ > \end{Bmatrix} 0 \Leftrightarrow \begin{Bmatrix} \text{normal} \\ \text{adverse} \end{Bmatrix} \text{RE,}$$

the critical α condition for the occurrence of *normal (respectively: adverse) real wage effects*, if we assume that the rate of employment $e$ and the rate of capacity utilization $u$ are related to each other by an elasticity coefficient of unity (which they are not in reality). Following Okun (1970) one might however argue that the relationship between these two rates is of the kind:

$$\frac{e}{\bar{e}} = \frac{u^{b}}{\bar{u}} \quad \text{or} \quad \ln e = b \ln u + const, \quad \text{i.e.,} \quad d\ln e = bd\ln u$$

with $b = \frac{1}{3}$ according to Okun's own estimates. In this case we have to use

$$\alpha = (1 - \kappa_{p})\beta_{we}b\bar{u}/\bar{e} - (1 - \kappa_{w})\beta_{pu}$$

as term in the above critical α-condition in order to distinguish normal from adverse real wage adjustment patterns, see our estimates in the next section.

In the next section we shall reformulate this one step Okun link between goods and labor markets as a two stage procedure, leading from changes in the capacity utilization rate $u$ of firms to the utilization rate of their labor force $u^{w}$ and from there to the employment rate $e$ on the labor market (i.e., from overtime work to new employees in the place of further increases in overtime work).[7] We shall also allow for the possibility that insiders (the workforce of firms and their utilization rate $u^{w}$) determine the measure of demand pressure that drives wage inflation and not so much the outside employment rate, which there provides a second model of the working of the wage–price spiral (where of course only the first stage of Okun's law is needed in order to close the model as far as supply side aspects are concerned).

If economic activity depends positively on the real wage, we thus get a positive feedback of the real wage on its rate of growth if $α > 0$ holds true (and a negative one, i.e., a partially stabilizing one, if activity depends negatively on the real wage). In the latter case, the situation $α < 0$ will however again imply a destabilizing effect of real wages on their rate of growth, while the case $α > 0$ is now coupled with a stabilizing feedback chain.[8] The result of these considerations can be represented as shown in Table 13.2

In the Table 13.2 we denote by wage-led (profit-led) the situation where aggregate demand depends positively (negatively) on the real wage and by labor-market-led (goods market led) the case $α > 0$ ($α < 0$). The important question now

*Table 13.2* The four baseline scenarios of real wage adjustments

|  | *Wage-led goods demand* | *Profit-led goods demand* |
| --- | --- | --- |
| Labor-market-led real wage adjustment | Adverse = divergent | Normal = convergent |
| Goods market led real wage adjustment | Normal = convergent | Adverse = divergent |

is which case in Table 13.2 applies to the US economy after World War II, a question that we will approach in the next section, together with the topic of whether wage inflation is primarily due to demand pressure on the external labor market or demand pressure within firms, as measured by the utilization rate of the workforce currently employed by them.

## 13.5 Estimating the wage–price spiral for the US economy

So far we have argued from the theoretical perspective that the PC approach to describe labor and goods market behavior is better modeled as a 2-D dynamic system instead of a single labor market oriented PC (or goods market PC as in the baseline New Keynesian approach). In this section we are now going to provide empirical answers to the issues raised in the last two sections, i.e.:

- Do the two PCs as described in (13.1) and (13.2) provide a suitable model structure to capture the dynamics of the wage–price spiral implied by the empirical data?
- What is an appropriate empirical specification of the demand pressure terms in the two PCs including the quantity link between goods and labor markets (Okun's Law)?
- How can we evaluate diverse specifications of the PCs and the resulting types of a wage–price spiral (outsider vs. insider formulations)?

In the following section we will give empirical answers to the above questions, while an econometric analysis of a more general model is provided and compared in the appendix to this chapter. Note with respect to the following that all variables in the displayed formula are expressed in logarithms now.

### *Data description*

The empirical data for the relevant variables discussed above are taken from Economic Data – FRED® at http://research.stlouisfed.org/fred2/. The data shown below are quarterly, seasonally adjusted, annualized where necessary and are all available from 1947:1 to 2004:4. Up to the rate of unemployment they represent the business sector of the US economy. We will make use in our estimations below of the range 1961:1 to 2004:4 solely, i.e., roughly speaking of the last five business cycles that characterized the evolution of the US economy. We thus neglect the evolution following World War II to a larger degree (starting with the time when John F. Kennedy came into office and with the subsequent adoption of Keynesian economic policies).

Note that the time series of the variables employed in our model can be and have all been constructed from these basic time series.[9] We now use as inflationary climate expression $\pi^c$ a moving average of price inflation over the past 12 quarters with linearly declining weights (as an especially simple measure of this inflationary climate expression). Note that we are making use of the variable $z$, the log of labor

*Table 13.3* Raw data used for empirical investigation of the model

| Variable | Transformation | Mnemonic | Description of the untransformed series |
|---|---|---|---|
| $e$ | log(1-UNRATE/100) | UNRATE | Unemployment rate (%) |
| $u^w$ | log(HOABS/ HP(HOABS)) | HOABS | Hours of all persons, business sector: index 1992 = 100, $e_h$: ratio to the long-run trend calculated by HP-filtering |
| $u$ | log(GDPC1/GDPPOT) | GDPC1, GDPPOT | GDPC1: Real gross domestic product of billions of chained 2000 dollars, GDPPOT: real potential gross domestic product of billions of chained 2000 dollars, u: capacity utilization: business sector (%) |
| $w$ | log(HCOMPBS) | HCOMPBS | Business sector: compensation per hour, index 1992 = 100 |
| $p$ | log(IPDBS) | IPDBS | Business sector: implicit price deflator, index 1992 = 100 |
| $z$ | log(OPHPBS) | OPHPBS | Business sector: output per hour of all persons, index 1992 = 100 |
| $v$ | $\log\left(\dfrac{HCOMPBS}{IPDBS*OPHPBS}\right)$ | | Wage share centered at 60% |

productivity, its rate of growth ($dz$) and the variable $v = w - p - z$, the log of the wage share or real unit wage costs in addition to the variables employed in the preceding sections, since this is needed from the empirical perspective, but was ignored in the theoretical comparison with the New Keynesian wage and price dynamics considered in Section 13.3.

The Blanchard and Katz (1999) error correction terms are thus now represented as in their paper by the log of the wage share and the growth rate of labor productivity is now added with a positive (negative) parameter value to the

*Table 13.4* Summary of DF test results

| Variable | Sample | Critical value | Test statistic |
|---|---|---|---|
| $dw$ | 1947:02 TO 2004:04 | −3.41 | −4.75 |
| $dp$ | 1947:02 TO 2004:04 | −3.41 | −4.14 |
| $e$ | 1947:02 TO 2004:04 | −3.41 | −3.69 |
| $u^w$ | 1947:02 TO 2004:04 | −3.41 | −6.80 |
| $u$ | 1947:02 TO 2000:04 | −3.41 | −4.90 |
| $dz$ | 1947:02 TO 2004:04 | −3.41 | −9.58 |

structural wage (price) Phillips curve. We note that the approach of Blanchard and Katz suggests that the parameters in front of $v$ and $dz$ are of the same size, but of opposite sign in the wage Phillips curve and considerably less than one (if not zero as they claim it to hold for the US economy). A similar observation holds for the price PC with opposite signs, see Flaschel and Krolzig (2006) in this regard.

Before we start with our empirical investigation, we examine the stationarity of the relevant time series. The shown graphs of the series for wage and price inflation, capacity utilization rates and labor productivity growth suggest the stationarity of the time series (as expected). In addition we carry out the augmented DF unit root test for each series. The test results are reported in Table 13.4. The unit root tests confirms our expectation.

## *Estimation results*

When one estimates the model of this chapter in its most general form, with both rates of employment, $e$, $u^w$ in the money–wage Phillips curve, and with an Okun's Law for employment inside the firm sector, $u^w$, as a function of $u$, primarily representing the production technology of the economy, supplemented by an Okun's Law for $e$ as a function of $u^w$, representing the employment policy of firms, and when one finally allows that the weights concerning actual inflation and the inflationary climate need not sum to one, one gets in the case of a three-stage least-square estimate all parameter signs as suggested by theory, though not always with a convincing t-statistics in particular. Removing the insignificant variables from the right-hand side of our structural equations then provides us with the following two alterative approaches, one with the insiders' employment rate solely and one with the employment rate on the labor market solely, which as we shall see will both perform quite well as competing approaches to labor market phenomena. We thus shall test below the following two specific wage–price spiral models of our general approach to supply side macrodynamics.

Model I (outsider approach)

$$dw_t = a_1 dp_t + a_2 \pi_t^c + a_3 e_{t-1} - a_4 v_{t-1} + a_5 dz_t + a_6 + \varepsilon_{1t},\qquad(13.10)$$

$$dp_t = b_1 dw_t + b_2 \pi_t^c + b_3 u_t + b_4 v_{t-1} - b_5 dz_t + b_6 + b_7 d74 + \varepsilon_{2t},\qquad(13.11)$$

$$du_t^w = c_1 du_t + c_2 du_{t-1} + c_3 du_{t-2} + \varepsilon_{3t},\qquad(13.12)$$

$$de_t = d_1 du_t^w + d_2 du_{t-1}^w + \varepsilon_{4t}.\qquad(13.13)$$

Model I makes use of the outside employment rate solely in the money–wage PC and summarizes the variables that are then involved in a complete measurement of the resulting wage price spiral (with all parameters of the model collected in a single constant parameter in the equations to be estimated). It now exhibits the influence of the growth rate of labor productivity in addition to what was formulated in Sections 13.2 and 13.3. Note that Blanchard and Katz (1999) show for their microfounded money–wage PC that the parameters in front of $v, z$ should be equal in size, but opposite in sign (which they approximately are in our subsequent estimates). Note also that we make use the current utilization rate in the place of the lagged one in the price inflation equation. Okun's Law is formulated in two steps here, leading from capacity utilization to workforce utilization and from there to the outside employment rate. Here, the lag structure shown above performed best in the estimates that were considered. This shows that a distributed lags of past growth rates of utilization rates explains growth in workforce participation and labor-force utilization better than just a single term on the right-hand side of these equations. The symbol $d74$ denotes a dummy variable to take account of the influence of the first oil crisis in 1974 on the price level.

Model II (insider approach)

$$dw_t = a_1 dp_t + a_2 \pi_t^c + a_3 u_{t-1}^w - a_4 v_{t-1} + a_5 dz_t + a_6 + \varepsilon_{1t}, \tag{13.14}$$

$$dp_t = b_1 dw_t + b_2 \pi_t^c + b_3 u_t + b_4 v_{t-1} - b_5 dz_t + b_6 + b_7 d74 + \varepsilon_{2t}, \tag{13.15}$$

$$du_t^w = c_1 du_t + c_2 du_{t-1} + c_3 du_{t-2} + \varepsilon_{3t}. \tag{13.16}$$

In the second formulation of the model to be estimated, where insiders (the utilization of the workforce employed by firms) are the ones that represent demand pressure in the money–wage PC, we just replace the variable $e$ by $u^w$ and can of course then suppress the second stage in the formulation of Okun's Law. The three-stage least-square estimates of these two possible theoretical approaches to the labor market and to the wage–price spiral are shown in the tables below.

Unrestricted estimation shows that the estimated coefficients $a_1$ and $a_2$, and $b_1$ and $b_2$ sum approximately to unit respectively, which confirms our general formulation of the price and wage Phillips curves in the theoretical part of this chapter. Blanchard and Katz (1999) furthermore have shown with respect to their augmented wage PC (see their equ. 6), that the coefficient in front of labor productivity should be equal in size (but opposite in sign) to the one in front of the wage share, which is approximately true in our estimated wage PC, and thus fairly different from unity (as it may be suggested by standard steady state calculations in standard macrodynamic models; a similar argument applies to the parameter in front of labor productivity growth in the price PC).

In sum, the estimated parameter values suggest for the critical $\alpha$-condition derived in Section 13.4 the approximate value $\alpha = -.005$ if only the unlagged terms of our formulation of Okun's Law are taken into account. Yet, this result indicates that real wage adjustments to activity changes may be uncertain in sign, in particular if the lagged terms in Okun's Law are also taken into account. The

*Table 13.5* Three-stage least-square estimates with outsider employment rate *e* solely and two-step formulation of Okun's Law

| Wage PC: dependent variable *dw* | | | Price PC: dependent variable *dp* | | |
|---|---|---|---|---|---|
| Variable | Estimate | T-values | Variable | Estimate | T-values |
| *dp* | 0.51 | 2.8 | *dw* | 0.27 | 6.9 |
| $\pi^c$ | 0.49 | – | $\pi^c$ | 0.73 | – |
| *e* | 0.63 | 4.8 | *u* | 0.21 | 3.2 |
| *v* | –0.12 | –6.7 | *v* | 0.16 | 3.2 |
| *dz* | 0.14 | 2.88 | *dz* | –0.12 | –3.5 |
| | | | *d74* | –0.04 | 4.9 |
| | | | *const.* | 0.07 | 3.0 |
| $R^2$ | 0.49 | | | | |
| $\bar{R}^2$ | 0.48 | | $R^2$ | 0.78 | |
| RSS | 0.02 | | $\bar{R}^2$ | 0.77 | |
| DW | 1.97 | | RSS | 0.01 | |
| | | | DW | 1.58 | |

| Okun's Law: dependent variables $u^w$, *e* | | |
|---|---|---|
| Variable | Estimate | T-values |
| *u*(0) | 0.50 | 11.2 |
| *u*(–1) | 0.23 | 5.2 |
| *u*(–2) | 0.13 | 3.0 |
| $u^w$(0) | 0.39 | 16.1 |
| $u^w$(–1) | 0.09 | 4.0 |
| $R^2$ | 0.91, 0.98 | |
| $\bar{R}^2$ | 0.91, 0.98 | |
| RSS | 0.01, 0.008 | |
| DW | 1.76, 1.86 | |

transmission of business fluctuations into real wage changes may therefore here be characterized as being weak and uncertain in sign, and may therefore change sign in particular if certain subperiods of the here considered time interval are to be investigated. If even $\kappa_w = 1$ is assumed as restriction, we must of course have a positive value for α in the critical condition that translates changes in economic activity into real wage growth. Real wages are then definitely moving procyclically, though lagging behind economic activity with a quarter phase displacement.

Table 13.6 presents the estimation results of Model II. They are the same as the ones shown in Table 13.5 as far as parameter signs are concerned, also with respect to the Blanchard and Katz error correction coefficients. Parameter sizes are however somewhat different, in particular as far as the parameter $\kappa_w$ in front of $dp$ in the WPC is concerned which is now fairly close to unity, indicating that the inflation climate is of not much importance in the formation of wage inflation. Demand pressures in the two PCs are now less important, while error correction is now working with more strength. However, wages are still more flexible than prices with respect to their measures of demand pressure and workers remain more short-sighted than firms concerning medium-run inflation dynamics. Again the parameters for error correction and labor productivity are by and large equal in size, but opposite in sign. And with respect to the critical parameter $\alpha$ we now approximately get the value 0.14, again by only employing the unlagged term in the estimated Okun's Law and thus now a positive value that can be considered a lower bound for the implied adverse working of the wage price spiral.

*Table 13.6* Three-stage least-square estimates with insider employment rate $u^w$ solely and one-step formulation of Okun's Law

| Wage PC: dependent variable $dw$ | | | Price PC: dependent variable $dp$ | | |
|---|---|---|---|---|---|
| *Variable* | *Estimate* | *T-values* | *Variable* | *Estimate* | *T-values* |
| $dp$ | 0.86 | 4.1 | $dw$ | 0.35 | – |
| $\pi^c$ | 0.14 | – | $\pi^c$ | 0.65 | 6.4 |
| $u^w$ | 0.29 | 2.0 | $u$ | 0.18 | 2.9 |
| $v$ | −0.23 | −2.6 | $v$ | 0.17 | 3.4 |
| $dz$ | 0.24 | 4.6 | $dz$ | −0.13 | −4.1 |
| *const.* | −0.1 | −2.2 | $d74$ | 0.04 | 4.4 |
| | | | *const.* | 0.08 | 3.2 |
| $R^2$ | 0.44 | | $R^2$ | 0.77 | |
| $\bar{R}^2$ | 0.43 | | $\bar{R}^2$ | 0.76 | |
| $RSS$ | 0.02 | | $RSS$ | 0.01 | |
| $DW$ | 1.84 | | $DW$ | 1.62 | |

| Okun's Law: dependent variables $u^w$ | | |
|---|---|---|
| *Variable* | *Estimate* | *T-values* |
| $u(0)$ | 0.48 | 10.5 |
| $u(-1)$ | 0.23 | 5.1 |
| $u(-2)$ | 0.10 | 2.3 |
| $R^2$ | 0.91 | |
| $\bar{R}^2$ | 0.91 | |
| $RSS$ | 0.01 | |
| $DW$ | 1.74 | |

Summing up, Table 13.5 claims that conditions on the external labor market are the important ones for the working of the US wage–price spiral, while Table 13.6 states the same for the inside employment of the workforce of firms, though the parameter in front of inside demand pressure in the wage PC is smaller than the corresponding one for the outside demand pressure term. When one uses the parameter restrictions shown above, but integrates again both measures of demand pressure into the considered wage PC, it is however again suggested that outside demand pressure is the significant (dominant) one.

However, we admit here that this point deserves closer inspection in future research, also from the theoretical point of view. Be that as it may, only estimate II shows that real wage dynamics are labor-market led and will thus imply instability of real wage adjustment in situations where aggregate goods demand is wage-led and thus increasing with economic activity. The other estimate (Model I) suggests in addition that real wage growth is not strongly driven by economic activity levels on an average and thus indicates that unstable real wage adjustment may be possible, but will be small in degree.

## 13.6 Conclusions

We have investigated in this chapter structural wage and price Phillips curves from the theoretical and the empirical point of view. From the theoretical perspective we found that their specification is generally much too simple in the literature in order to allow a thorough discussion of the wage–price spiral mechanism and its implications. There are in this context two fundamentally different measures of demand pressure to be distinguished carefully, one on the labor market (a stock measure) and one on the market for goods (a flow measure), that are to be employed to the issues of wage inflation and price inflation separately (related to each other via an intermediate flow measure, the utilization rate of the workforce of firms). These measures may appear as determinants of wage and price inflation in principle in proportional, derivative or integral form, and may be very different for certain countries and for certain times. Specifying PCs in this general format indeed allows a comparative evaluation of approaches that favor the wage level curve or the change in the wage inflation rate over the usual specification of the left-hand side of the money–wage Phillips curve.

With regard to cost pressure items we did choose a specific, though also quite general format. In view of the literature on rational – and nowadays on forward- and backward-looking expectations, we assumed as cost pressure items a weighted average of the current perfectly foreseen cost pressure items (price inflation in the case of workers and wage inflation in the case of firms) and an inflationary climate item that characterizes, for example, the last twelve quarters of the working of the economy on an average. We insist on myopic perfect foresight in this hybrid format in order to show that the purely forward-looking rational expectations methodology need not be the implication of a myopic perfect foresight assumption and, moreover, that there can be enough inertia in the wage–price spiral despite the non-existence of systematic errors in the prediction of current wage and price inflation – as it is suggested by empirical observations.

From the empirical perspective we found indications that separately specified and estimated wage and price PCs perform statistically quite well compared to the commonly employed reduced types of single price inflation Phillips curve. These two curves – here still of the proportional control type with respect to demand pressure items – moreover imply a simple, yet very important real feedback chain (the real wage channel), that appears to be slightly destabilizing in periods where economic activity is positively dependent on the real wage. This feedback channel can be usefully compared to another related feedback chain, the real rate of interest channel of old and new Keynesian approaches to economic dynamics, and is indeed even richer in its stability implications than the real rate of interest channel (which concerns the interaction of the Keynes-effect or a Taylor interest rate rule with the destabilizing Mundell effect). Should such a mechanism really exist in some countries at some time, it must be taken into account in the conduct of monetary (and fiscal) policy. Our findings here are that demand pressure matters in specific ways both in the labor and the goods market and thereby establishes a link – via Okun's Law – between the current level of real wages and its rate of change to be paid attention to in the conduct of economic policy.

## Appendix: econometric analysis of the models

The theoretically motivated formulation of the structural Model I (and Model II) implies a number of economic hypotheses. The empirical evidence of these economic hypotheses can be verified, if the statistical implication of these hypotheses on the data generating process can be confirmed by the observed data.

Beside the general assumption on the stationarity of the relevant variables,[10] the structural models imply the exogeneity of variables $u_t$, $z_t$, $e_t$ and $u_t^w$ for the two Phillips curves, the validity of the unconstrained reduced form and validity of the over identification of the structural form. Spanos (1990) calls this the statistical adequacy of the structural model. In the following we are going to investigate the statistical adequacy of the two structural models by testing the exogeneity, the validity of the reduced form and the overidentification restriction.

Since all these hypotheses can be formulated sequentially as restrictions on the parameters of a general VAR model, we will test them sequentially step by step. Because $v$ is not an independent variable, it is not explicitly included in the VAR model. The general VAR model consists of six endogenous variables: $dw$, $dp$, $e$, $u^w$, $u$ and $z$ and one exogenous dummy variable $d74$ that is used to take into account of the impact of the oil crisis in 1974.

$$
\begin{pmatrix} dw_t \\ dp_t \\ e_t \\ u_t^w \\ u_t \\ z_t \end{pmatrix} = \begin{pmatrix} c_1 \\ c_2 \\ c_3 \\ c_4 \\ c_5 \\ c_6 \end{pmatrix} + \begin{pmatrix} b_1 \\ b_2 \\ b_3 \\ b_4 \\ b_5 \\ b_6 \end{pmatrix} d74 +
$$

$$
\sum_{k=1}^{P} \begin{pmatrix} a_{11k} & a_{12k} & a_{13k} & a_{14k} & a_{15k} & a_{16k} \\ a_{21k} & a_{22k} & a_{23k} & a_{24k} & a_{25k} & a_{26k} \\ a_{31k} & a_{32k} & a_{33k} & a_{34k} & a_{35k} & a_{36k} \\ a_{41k} & a_{42k} & a_{43k} & a_{44k} & a_{45k} & a_{46k} \\ a_{51k} & a_{52k} & a_{53k} & a_{54k} & a_{55k} & a_{56k} \\ a_{51k} & a_{52k} & a_{53k} & a_{54k} & a_{55k} & a_{66k} \end{pmatrix} \begin{pmatrix} dw_{t-k} \\ dp_{t-k} \\ e_{t-k} \\ u_{t-k}^w \\ u_{t-k} \\ z_{t-k} \end{pmatrix} + \begin{pmatrix} \epsilon_{1t} \\ \epsilon_{2t} \\ \epsilon_{3t} \\ \epsilon_{4t} \\ \epsilon_{5t} \\ \epsilon_{6t} \end{pmatrix}.
$$

The sequential likelihood ratio tests suggests a lag length of 10 quarters, while the AIC information criterion suggests a lag length of 20 quarters. We choose the lag length to be 12 quarters that corresponds to three years, i.e. $P = 12$, and we denote the implied VAR model by VAR(12). Because our structural models are nested in the conditional process of VAR(12), we test the strong exogeneity[11] of $u_t$, $z_t$, $e_t$ and $u_t^w$ for the Phillips curves, i.e., we need to test the weak exogeneity and the non-Granger causality of $dw_t$ and $dp_t$ for $u_t$, $z_t$, $e_t$ and $u_t^w$. Because in an unconstrained conditional VAR the weak exogeneity is guaranteed by construction, we need only to test the Granger causality, i.e. we need to test $H : a_{i,j,k} = 0$, $i = 3$, $4, 5, 6; j = 1, 2; k = 1, .., 12$. The test result is as follows:

Chi-squared(96) = 119.65 with significance level 0.051.

Next we test whether the unconstrained reduced form is a valid presentation of the unconstrained conditional VAR model. It is to note that although the variables $v_{t-1}$ and $\pi_t$ do not appear explicitly in the VAR model, they are however linear combinations of lagged $dw_t$, $dp_t$ and $z_t$ terms, therefore the unconstrained reduced form is nested in the conditional VAR model. Obviously Model I is nested in the factorization of the unconstrained VAR(12) into $VAR(dw_t, dp_t | e_t, u_t^w, u_t, dz_t, \Omega_{t-1})$, $VAR(e_t | u_t^w, u_t, dz_t, \Omega_{t-1})$, and $VAR(u_t^w | u_t, dz_t, \Omega_{t-1})$.[12]
The conditional VAR model can be written as follows:

$$
\begin{pmatrix} dw_t \\ dp_t \end{pmatrix} = \begin{pmatrix} c_1^* \\ c_2^* \end{pmatrix} + \begin{pmatrix} b_1^* \\ b_2^* \end{pmatrix} d74 + \begin{pmatrix} b_{13} & b_{14} & b_{15} & b_{16} \\ b_{23} & b_{24} & b_{25} & b_{26} \end{pmatrix} \begin{pmatrix} e_t \\ u_t^w \\ u_t \\ z_t \end{pmatrix}
$$

(13.17)

$$+\sum_{k=1}^{P}\begin{pmatrix} a_{11k}^* & a_{12k}^* & a_{13k}^* & a_{14k}^* & a_{15k}^* & a_{16k}^* \\ a_{21k}^* & a_{22k}^* & a_{23k}^* & a_{24k}^* & a_{25k}^* & a_{26k}^* \end{pmatrix}\begin{pmatrix} dw_{t-k} \\ dp_{t-k} \\ e_{t-k} \\ u_{t-k}^w \\ u_{t-k} \\ z_{t-k} \end{pmatrix}+\begin{pmatrix} \epsilon_{1t}^* \\ \epsilon_{2t}^* \end{pmatrix}$$

$$\begin{pmatrix} e_t \\ u_t^w \end{pmatrix}=\begin{pmatrix} c_3 \\ c_4 \end{pmatrix}+\begin{pmatrix} b_3 \\ b_4 \end{pmatrix}d74+\sum_{k=1}^{P}\begin{pmatrix} a_{33k} & a_{34k} & a_{35k} & a_{36k} \\ a_{43k} & a_{44k} & a_{45k} & a_{46k} \end{pmatrix}\begin{pmatrix} e_{t-k} \\ u_{t-k}^w \\ u_{t-k} \\ z_{t-k} \end{pmatrix}+\begin{pmatrix} \epsilon_{3t} \\ \epsilon_{4t} \end{pmatrix}.$$

$$(13.18)$$

In (13.18) we have used the non-Granger-causality result. When we rewrite the first difference variables as differences of the level variables, the unconstrained reduced form of structural Model I can be written as follows:

Model I (reduced form)

$$dw_t = c_{11}+c_{12}\pi_t^c+c_{13}e_{t-1}+c_{14}v_{t-1}+c_{15}dz_t+c_{16}u_t+c_{17}u_{t-1}$$
$$+c_{18}u_{t-2}+c_{19}u_{t-3}+c_{1,10}u_{t-1}^w+c_{1,11}u_{t-2}^w+c_{1,12}u_{t-3}^w+\epsilon_{1t},$$

$$dp_t = c_{21}+c_{22}\pi_t^c+c_{23}e_{t-1}+c_{24}v_{t-1}+c_{25}dz_t+c_{26}u_t+c_{27}u_{t-1}$$
$$+c_{28}u_{t-2}+c_{29}u_{t-3}+c_{2,10}u_{t-1}^w+c_{2,11}u_{t-2}^w+c_{2,12}u_{t-3}^w+\epsilon_{2t},$$

$$u_t^w = c_{31}+c_{32}e_{t-1}+c_{33}v_{t-1}+c_{34}dz_t+c_{35}u_t+c_{36}u_{t-1}$$
$$+c_{37}u_{t-2}+c_{38}du_{t-3}+c_{3,9}u_{t-1}^w+c_{3,10}u_{t-2}^w+c_{3,11}u_{t-3}^w+\epsilon_{3t},$$

$$e_t = c_{41}+c_{42}e_{t-1}+c_{43}v_{t-1}+c_{44}dz_t+c_{45}u_t+c_{46}u_{t-1}$$
$$+c_{47}u_{t-2}+c_{48}du_{t-3}+c_{49}u_{t-1}^w+c_{4,10}u_{t-2}^w+c_{4,11}u_{t-3}^w+\epsilon_{4t}. \qquad (13.19)$$

This reduced form of Model I is nested in the conditional VAR model (13.17) and (13.18), because $\pi^c$ and $v_{t-1}$ are approximately linear combinations of the lagged $dw_t$, $dp_t$ and $dz_t$. Hence likelihood ratio test can be applied to test the validity of the unconstrained reduced form (13.19).

Chi-squared(214) = 239.268 with significance level 0.11.

Therefore the unconstrained reduced form encompasses the conditional VAR(12). Next we test the overidentification restrictions implied by the structural models. We compare here the likelihood of the unconstrained reduced form and that of the derived reduced form. Because the dependent variables $de_t$ and $du_t^w$ in the structural form of Model I can be reformulated as linear restrictions on the parameter of the reduced form:

$$c_{31} = c_{32} = c_{33} = c_{34} = c_{39} = 0$$

$$c_{39} = 1$$

$$c_{35} + c_{36} + c_{37} + c_{38} = 1$$

$$c_{41} = c_{43} = c_{44} + c_{45} = c_{46} = c_{47} = c_{48} = 0$$

$$c_{42} = 1$$

$$c_{4,9} + c_{4,10} + c_{4,11} = 1,$$

we can apply to test these restrictions implied by the structural form. The test result reject this set of restrictions. We proceed then to test the less restrictive exclusion restrictions:

$$c_{31} = c_{32} = c_{33} = 0$$

$$c_{41} = c_{43} = c_{44} = c_{45} = c_{46} = c_{47} = c_{48} = 0.$$

Together with the 11 restrictions on the first two PC equations we test 21 linear and nonlinear restrictions on the unconstrained reduced form. We compare the likelihood ratio between the reduced form and the derived reduced form. The test result is:

Chi-squared(21) = 26.940 with significance level 0.32.

Further we test the constraints on the structural form is:

$$a_1 + a_2 = 1$$

$$b_1 + b_1 = 1$$

$$c_{35} + c_{36} + c_{37} + c_{38} = 1$$

$$c_{42} = 1$$

and get in this case:

Chi-squared(4) = 3.1 with significance level 0.54.

We conclude that Model I provides, generally speaking, an adequate description of the empirical data, i.e. most economic/statistical hypotheses embedded in model I can be accepted from this point of view. Yet, this appendix suggests that the specification of Okun's Law deserves further reflection both from the theoretical and the empirical point of view so that its structural form can really be supported by the data (see Flaschel, Franke and Semmler (2007) for a refined formulation of this link between goods and labor markets).

Similarly we can do this analysis for Model II, the insider approach. Statistically, the main difference between Model I and Model II is that the variable $e_t$ is not considered in Model II. Therefore the resulting unconditional VAR(12) model contains only five variables. We view the two Phillips curves as nested in the conditional VAR(12) model with the five variables $(dw_t, dp_t, u_t^w, u_t, dz_t)$. The Granger causality test of $(dw_t, dp_t)$ for the remaining three variables $(u_t^w, u_t, dz_t)$ gives the following results:

Chi-squared(72) = 87.045 with significance level 0.11.

We have again factorized the unconditional $VAR(dw_t, dp_t, u_t^w, u_t, dz_t | \Omega_{t-1})$ into $(dw_t, dp_t, | u_t^w, u_t, dz_t, \Omega_{t-1})$, and $VAR(u_t^w | u_t, dz_t, \Omega_{t-1})$.[13] The corresponding unconstrained reduced form of Model II is nested in the conditional VARs.

Model II (reduced form)

$$dw_t = c_{11} + c_{12}\pi_t^c + c_{13}v_{t-1} + c_{14}dz_t + c_{15}u_t + c_{16}u_{t-1}$$
$$c_{17}u_{t-2} + c_{18}u_{t-3} + c_{19}u_{t-1}^w + c_{1,10}u_{t-2}^w + \in_{1t},$$
$$dp_t = c_{21} + c_{22}\pi_t^c + c_{23}v_{t-1} + c_{24}dz_t + c_{25}u_t + c_{26}u_{t-1}$$
$$c_{27}u_{t-2} + c_{28}u_{t-3} + c_{29}u_{t-1}^w + c_{2,10}u_{t-2}^w + \in_{1t},$$
$$du_t^w = c_{31} + c_{32}v_{t-1} + c_{33}dz_t + c_{34}u_t + c_{35}u_{t-1} +$$
$$c_{36}u_{t-2} + c_{37}u_{t-3} + c_{38}u_{t-1}^w + c_{39}u_{t-2}^w + \in_{1t}.$$

We can run likelihood ratio test to check the statistical adequacy of the unconstrained reduced form. The test result is:

Chi-squared(127) = 148.054 with significance level 0.10.

Then we test the overidentification restrictions implied by the structural form. The result of the likelihood ratio test of the overidentification restrictions on the unconstrained reduced form is:

Chi-squared(20)= 34.908 with significance level 0.02.

The test of the restrictions on the structural form is:

Chi-squared(3) = 7.460 with significance level 0.058.

This result shows that (at a significance level of 0.01) the economic/statistical hypotheses implied in Model II are not rejected by the observed data.

# 14 ES calibration of wage and price Phillips curves

## 14.1 Introduction

In this chapter,[1] we investigate the wage and price Phillips curves – the focal point of this part of the book – from an empirical perspective that combines calibration with other estimation procedures. The approach is therefore called an Estimation Supported (ES) calibration. The chapter supplements various empirical analyses of the wage–price spiral we have undertaken in the past (see, for example, Chen et al. (2006); Chen and Flaschel (2006)), which on the theoretical side are based on the model and the submodules developed, in particular, in Chiarella et al. (2005) and Asada et al. (2006). Our treatment will shed light on the various estimates of the model of the wage–price spiral that we are advocating from quite a different and new angle. Another issue will be the question of the detrending of the time series we have used so far.[2]

## 14.2 Wage Phillips curve

Our empirical analysis starts out from a straightforward estimation of the following wage PC.[3] As demand pressure terms it includes the employment rate $e$ on the external labor market and the utilization rate $u^w$ of the workers within the firms. In addition to the growth rate of labor productivity $z$ and to the wage share $v$ as an error correction term of Blanchard–Katz type, price inflation $\hat{p}$ and the inflation climate $\pi^c$ serve as cost-pressure terms (cf. the preceding chapter for more details). The parameter estimates are comparable to those obtained in Chen and Flaschel (2006) (again, see also Chapter 13), although the present specification of the wage PC is somewhat different in that now insider and outsider effects enter it simultaneously, while in Chapter 13 they were treated separately. As will be seen shortly, the estimation with the outsider effects is otherwise fairly similar to the one where only insiders were considered (in this respect, it may be noted that the quarterly data are now annualized). In detail, an unconstrained OLS regression on the (undetrended) variables listed above yields the following result:

$$\hat{w} = c_{11}\hat{p} + c_{12}\pi^c + c_{13}e_{-1} + c_{14}u^w_{-1} + c_{15}\ln v_{-1} + c_{16}\hat{z} + c_{17}$$

$$= 0.39\hat{p} + 0.55\pi^c + 0.44e_{-1} + 0.28u^w_{-1} - 0.15\ln v_{-1} + 0.24\hat{z} - 0.75. \qquad (14.1)$$

The structural equation behind this formulation is given by

$$\hat{w} = \kappa_{wz}\hat{z} + (1-\kappa_{wz})g_z + \kappa_{wp}\hat{p} + (1-\kappa_{wp})\pi^c$$
$$+ \beta_{we}(e_{-1} - e^o) + \beta_{we}^h(u_{-1}^w - u^{wo}) - \beta_{wv}(\ln v_{-1} - \ln v^o) \qquad (14.2)$$
$$= \kappa_{wp}\hat{p} + (1-\kappa_{wp})\pi^c + \beta_{we}e_{-1} + \beta_{we}^h u_{-1}^w - \beta_{wv}\ln v_{-1} + \kappa_{wz}\hat{z}$$
$$+ (1-\kappa_{wz})g_z - \beta_{we}e^o - \beta_{we}^h u^{wo} + \beta_{wv}\ln v^o,$$

which is the type of wage PC that has already been considered in detail in Chiarella et al. (2005).

As estimated structural coefficients one then obtains from the above OLS estimate the following ones:

$$\kappa_{wz} = c_{16} = 0.24$$

$$\kappa_{wp} = c_{11} = 0.39 \qquad \text{with } 1-\kappa_{wp} \approx 0.55 = c_{12}$$

$$\beta_{we} = c_{13} = 0.44$$

$$\beta_{we}^h = c_{14} = 0.28 \qquad \text{and } \beta_{we} + \beta_{we}^h = 0.72$$

$$\beta_{wv} - c_{15} = 0.15.$$

In order to check the constant we set (free-hand) the following parameter values: $g_z = 0.02$, $e^o = u^{wo} = 1$, $v^o = 0.70$. From this we get for the constant in (14.2):

$$c_{17} = -0.75 \approx -0.76 = g_z - 0.44e^o - 0.28u^{wo} + 0.15\ln v^o. \qquad (14.3)$$

We observe that all coefficients are economically meaningful (correct sign and within reasonable range), $c_{11}$ and $c_{12}$ nearly sum up to unity (which could be subsequently imposed), and the estimated constant is compatible with the steady state values of the state variables.

## 14.3 Price Phillips curve

We now turn to the price Phillips, which apart from its specific demand pressure term is similarly specified to the wage Phillips curve. This price PC employs as demand pressure term the rate of capacity utilization $u$ of the capital stock of firms, besides the cost-pressure terms: wage inflation $\hat{w}$ and the inflationary climate $\pi^c$, and again a Blanchard–Katz error correction term together with the growth rate of labor productivity $z$. The parameter estimates from an unconstrained OLS are close to those obtained in Chen and Flaschel (2006); see also Chapter 13. They read:

$$\hat{p} = c_{21}\hat{w} + c_{22}\pi^c + c_{23}u_{-1} + c_{24}\ln v_{-1} + c_{25}\hat{z} + c_{26} \qquad (14.4)$$
$$= 0.15\hat{w} + 0.83\pi^c + 0.23u_{-1} + 0.13\ln v_{-1} - 0.12\hat{z} - 0.16.$$

Corresponding to it is the following structural price PC from Chiarella et al. (2005):

$$\hat{p}_t = \kappa_p \{\hat{w} - [\kappa_{wz}\hat{z} + (1-\kappa_{wz})g_z]\} + (1-\kappa_p)\pi^c$$
$$+ \beta_{pu}(u_{-1} - u^o) + \beta_{pv}(\ln v_{-1} - \ln v^o)$$
$$= \kappa_p \hat{w} + (1-\kappa_p)\pi^c + \beta_{pu}u_{-1} + \beta_{pv}\ln v_{-1} - \kappa_p \kappa_{wz}\hat{z} \qquad (14.5)$$
$$-\kappa_p(1-\kappa_{wz})g_z - \beta_{pu}u^o - \beta_{pv}\ln v^o.$$

In this way, we obtain as structural coefficients:

$$\kappa_{wz} = c_{16} = 0.24 \qquad \text{see the WPC}$$

$$\kappa_p = c_{21} = 0.15 \qquad \text{and now } 1-\kappa_p \approx 0.83 = c_{22}$$

$$\beta_{pu} = c_{23} = 0.23$$

$$\beta_{pv} = c_{24} = 0.13.$$

Checking the constant in the same way as in the case of the WPC gives

$$c_{26} = -0.16 \approx -0.19 = -0.15 \cdot 0.76g_z - 0.23u^o - 0.13\ln v^o, \qquad (14.6)$$

whereas for the coefficient on $\hat{z}$ in the PPC we observe,

$$\kappa_{wz} = -c_{25}/\kappa_p = 0.12/0.15 = 0.80 \neq 0.24 = \kappa_{wz}, \text{ in the WPC.} \qquad (14.7)$$

Again, all coefficients are meaningful (correct sign and within reasonable range), the coefficients $c_{21}$ and $c_{22}$ nearly sum up to unity (which could be subsequently imposed), and the estimated constant is compatible with the steady state values. However, the estimated coefficients on $\hat{z}$ in the unconstrained equations (14.2) and (14.5) are not compatible with the structural requirements across the two Phillips curves (14.2) and (14.5).

## 14.4 WPC: comparing results from detrended and undetrended data

In the following, the detrended data (by HP 1600) from Chiarella et al. (2005) are used, with sample period 1961:1 to 2003:1. With respect to a dynamic variable $x$ let the symbol $x^o$, in a theoretical context, denote the (constant) steady state value of $x$; and its (HP 1600) trend in a context with empirical data. Furthermore, to avoid notational confusion, write $x^{dv}$ for $x - x^o$ (but $v^{dv} := (v - v^o)/v^o$). Besides, the inflation climate $\pi_{dv}^c$ is pi12, here directly computed from detrended inflation $\hat{p}^{dv}$.

Following Section 14.1, we begin with an estimation that does not constrain the coefficient on the inflation climate. The results reported in the second column of

Table 14.1 can be directly compared with equations (14.2) (noting that ln $v_{-1}$ − ln $v^o$ approximates $v_{-1}^{dv}$). To put the standard error of the regression (SER) in perspective, we mention that the standard deviation of the dependent variable $\hat{w}^{dv}$ itself is 2.10 percent. Thus, the $R^2$ of this estimation is (as low as) 0.36.

• The crucial difference from (14.2) is that here the inflation climate has no significant influence on wage inflation. This equally holds true for slightly different specifications of the regression.

The other coefficients of the regression, however, remain significant and economically meaningful.

Table 14.1[4] shows that the employment rate better enters with the one-quarter lag. The effects of utilization are similar to those from the employment rate, their fits are slightly worse. Including lagged as well as unlagged employment results in a considerable improvement of the fit.[5] However, the negative coefficient on the inflation climate (which is almost significant) and the negative impact on the wage of contemporaneous employment, or its rate of change $e^{dv} - e_{-1}^{dv}$, for that matter, would be rejected on theoretical grounds.

What results do we get if we impose the constraint that the coefficients on $\hat{p}^{dv}$ and $\pi_{dv}^c$ sum up to unity? To this end, subtract $\hat{w}^o$ on both sides of equation (14.2) and use that theoretically $\hat{w}^o = \hat{p}^o + \hat{z}^o = \pi^{co} + g_z$. The equation can then equivalently be rewritten as

$$\hat{w} - \hat{w}^o = \kappa_{wz}(\hat{z} - g_z) + \kappa_{wp}(\hat{p} - \hat{p}^o) + (1 - \kappa_{wp})(\pi^c - \pi^{co})$$
$$+ \beta_{we}(e_{-1} - e^o) - \beta_{wv}(v_{-1} - v^o)/v^o. \tag{14.8}$$

*Table 14.1* Regressions of wage inflation (detrended data, 1961:1 to 2003:1)

| Regressors | | Dependent variable: $\hat{w}^{dv} = \hat{w} - \hat{w}^o$ | | | | |
|---|---|---|---|---|---|---|
| $\hat{z}^{dv}$ | : | 0.375 | 0.348 | 0.393 | 0.396 | 0.320 |
| $\hat{p}^{dv}$ | : | 0.524 | 0.593 | 0.624 | 0.530 | 0.617 |
| $\pi_{dv}^c$ | : | 0.013 | 0.039 | −0.338 | 0.093 | 0.188 |
| $e^{dv}$ | : | − − | 0.202 | −0.812 | − − | − − |
| $e_{-1}^{dv}$ | : | 0.346 | − − | 1.086 | − − | − − |
| $u^{dv}$ | : | − − | − − | − − | − − | 0.148 |
| $u_{-1}^{dv}$ | : | − − | − − | − − | 0.297 | − − |
| $v_{-1}^{dv}$ | : | −0.385 | −0.325 | −0.635 | −0.264 | −0.281 |
| SER | : | 1.698 | 1.765 | 1.618 | 1.719 | 1.777 |
| SSR | : | 472.7 | | 426.9 | | |
| AIC | : | 663.4 | | 648.2 | | |
| BIC | : | 679.1 | | 667.0 | | |

For the estimation, subtract $\pi_{dv}^c = \pi^c - \pi^{co}$ from both sides of (14.8), which yields

$$\hat{w}^{dv} - \pi_{dv}^c = \kappa_{wz}\hat{z}^{dv} + \kappa_{wp}(\hat{p}^{dv} - \pi_{dv}^c) + \beta_{we}e_{-1}^{dv} - \beta_{wv}v_{-1}^{dv}. \tag{14.9}$$

The main results are reported in Table 14.2. It is clear that the constraint worsens the fits vis-à-vis Table 14.1 (the $R^2$ in the second column is now 0.35). On the other hand, all coefficients are significant: actually, they do not change very much and so remain meaningful (except for the fourth column, which again buys the better fit at the price of theoretical significance). This is not very surprising, since most of the time the series $\hat{w}^{dv}$ and $\hat{w}^{dv} - \pi_{dv}^c$ on the one hand, and $\hat{p}^{dv}$ and $\hat{p}^{dv} - \pi_{dv}^c$ on the other hand, do not differ very much from each other: their correlation coefficients are as high as 0.92 and 0.86, respectively.

- At least with the 12-quarter horizon, the inflation climate is no more than an alibi for a theoretical formulation; its contribution as a time series to the determination of the numerical parameters in (14.9) is largely negligible. So far, the "climate" variable is therefore not convincing at a theoretical level, either!
- That is, $\pi_t^c$ is undistinguishable from a constant reference rate of inflation.

These critical remarks notwithstanding, the following coefficients can provide a basis for further investigations with the detrended data:

$$\kappa_{wz} = 0.39$$
$$\kappa_{wp} = 0.58$$
$$\beta_{we} = 0.33$$
$$\beta_{wv} = 0.53.$$

The coefficients maintain the qualitative features of the estimates with un-detrended data in Section 14.1. However, the influence of employment on the wage changes appears to be weaker, while the (negative) influence of the wage share is stronger.

The present approach with the inflation climate cannot discriminate against the competitive alternative of an accelerationist Phillips curve (augmented with the wage share), i.e., the empirical support for $\pi_t^c$ as a theoretical concept on its own is not really strong. Such a discrimination is, however, theoretically desirable, since accelerationist Phillips curves tend to exhibit too much inflation persistence: convergence in the impulse-response functions back to the steady state values take too much time, or in a model context the central bank is required to take excessively strong policy measures to speed up these adjustments or contain inflation rates within reasonable bounds.

*Table 14.2* Regressions of $\hat{w}^{dv} - \pi_{dv}^c$ (detrended data, 1961:1 to 2003:1)

| Regressors | | | | | | 61:1–80:1 | 80:1–03:1 |
|---|---|---|---|---|---|---|---|
| $\hat{z}^{dv}$ | : | 0.385 | 0.359 | 0.401 | 0.313 | | 0.492 |
| $\hat{p}^{dv} - \pi_{dv}^c$ | : | 0.577 | 0.621 | 0.663 | 0.492 | | 0.629 |
| $e^{dv}$ | : | $--$ | 0.211 | $-0.400$ | $--$ | | $--$ |
| $e_{-1}^{dv}$ | : | 0.327 | $--$ | 0.812 | 0.406 | | 0.226 |
| $v_{-1}^{dv}$ | : | $-0.534$ | $-0.440$ | $-0.753$ | $-0.567$ | | $-0.527$ |
| SER | : | 1.730 | 1.782 | 1.694 | 1.430 | | 1.923 |
| SSR | : | 493.6 | | 470.7 | | | |
| AIC | : | 668.8 | | 662.7 | | | |
| BIC | : | 681.3 | | 678.4 | | | |

## 14.5 PPC: comparing results from detrended and undetrended data

Similar to the derivation of (14.8), the structural price Phillips curve equation (14.5) can be reformulated as

$$\hat{p} - \hat{p}^o = \kappa_p [(\hat{w} - \hat{w}^o) - \kappa_{wz} (\hat{z} - g_z)] + (1 - \kappa_p)(\pi^c - \pi^{co})$$
$$+ \, \beta_{pu} (u_{-1} - 1) + \beta_{pv} (v_{-1} - v^o)/v^o. \qquad (14.10)$$

The coefficient $\kappa_{wz}$ has here to be identical with the one in the wage Philips curve. From there we adopt $\kappa_{wz} = 0.3846$, according to the second column in Table 14.2. Analogously to equation (14.9), the regression equation thus is

$$\hat{p}^{dv} - \pi_{dv}^c = \kappa_p (\hat{w}^{dv} - \pi_{dv}^c - \kappa_{wz} \hat{z}^{dv}) + \beta_{pu} u_{-1}^{dv} + \beta_{pv} v_{-1}^{dv}. \qquad (14.11)$$

If the constraint on $\kappa_{wz}$ is dropped and $\tilde{\kappa}_{wz}$ is free to assume any value, the regression reads

$$\hat{p}^{dv} - \pi_{dv}^c = \kappa_p (\hat{w}^{dv} - \pi_{dv}^c) - \kappa_p \tilde{\kappa}_{wz} \hat{z}^{dv} + \beta_{pu} u_{-1}^{dv} + \beta_{pv} v_{-1}^{dv}. \qquad (14.12)$$

In the estimation, $\tilde{\kappa}_{wz}$ derives from dividing the estimated coefficient on $\hat{z}^{dv}$ by the estimated $\kappa_p$. Considering also lagged and unlagged utilization and wage shares in (14.11), Table 14.3 is obtained. The best fits, however, result if these variables are lagged (in particular, the wage share).

It is obvious that the unconstrained version (14.12) yields a better fit. However, the difference in the standard error of the regression is not very large, even though

*Table 14.3* Regressions of price inflation (detrended data, 1961:1 to 2003:1)

| Regressors | | Dependent variable: $\hat{p}^{dv} - \pi_{dv}^c$ | | | | |
|---|---|---|---|---|---|---|
| $\hat{z}^{dv}$ | : | −0.168 | −− | −− | −− | −− |
| $\tilde{\kappa}_{wz}$ | : | 0.778 | −− | −− | −− | −− |
| $\hat{w}^{dv} - \pi_{dv}^c$ | : | 0.216 | −− | −− | −− | −− |
| $\hat{w}^{dv} - \pi_{dv}^c - 0.3846\,\hat{z}^{dv}$ | : | −− | 0.220 | 0.266 | 0.168 | 0.187 |
| $u^{dv}$ | : | −− | −− | 0.209 | −− | 0.188 |
| $u_{-1}^{dv}$ | : | 0.188 | 0.237 | −− | 0.210 | −− |
| $v^{dv}$ | : | −− | −− | −− | 0.245 | 0.356 |
| $v_{-1}^{dv}$ | : | 0.476 | 0.473 | 0.537 | −− | −− |
| SER | : | 1.091 | 1.107 | 1.122 | 1.188 | 1.200 |

the implied $\tilde{\kappa}_{wz} = 0.778$ is much larger than the estimate from the wage Phillips curve, $\kappa_{wz} = 0.385$.

Regarding the price Phillips curve, we may therefore, on the whole, settle down on the following numerical parameters:

$$\kappa_{wz} = 0.39$$

$$\kappa_p = 0.22$$

$$\beta_{pu} = 0.23$$

$$\beta_{pv} = 0.47$$

which in particular show that demand pressure matters on the market for goods, that firms are not very myopic in their reaction to cost pressure, and income distribution (or unit labor cost) is of significant importance in the study of the causes that drive price inflation.

## 14.6 ES-calibration of the WPC

### *The VAR background*

We proceed to an atheoretical description of the wage inflation process and an identification of the main exogenous forces impacting on it. A convenient, powerful and reliable tool in this respect are vector autoregressions (VARs). That is, as our present interest is limited to the wage Phillips curve alone, we are here only dealing with such a regression equation for wage inflation.

Conceptually in our modeling framework, wage inflation is determined by price inflation, the inflation climate, productivity growth, employment and the wage share. While the theoretical model confines itself either to the contemporaneous or to one lagged value of each of these variables, an atheoretical approach can include several lags of them, including wage inflation itself.

Doing this it has, however, to be taken into account that the variables are not all independent of each other. First, this is obvious for the inflation climate $\pi_t^c$. Since it is defined as a weighted average of the past twelve rates of price inflation, $\pi_t^c$ should be excluded from the list of regressors. Second, the wage share $v$ is composed of the wage rate $w$, the price level $p$ and labor productivity $z$ (i.e., $v = w/pz$). In continuous time, the growth rates of these variables are related by the identity $\hat{v} = \hat{w} - \hat{p} - \hat{z}$. A firm relationship between them is preserved in discrete time and if the variables are detrended, an estimation yields

$$v^{dv} = v_{-1}^{dv} + 0.23\, \hat{w}^{dv} - 0.23\, \hat{p}^{dv} - 0.24\, \hat{z}^{dv} \tag{14.13}$$

with an almost perfect "fit" of $R^2 = 0.987$. Hence, with several lags in the regression of $\hat{w}$, the wage share should not be employed as a regressor, either.

On the whole, we consider eight lags of wage inflation, price inflation, the productivity growth rate, and the employment rate. In addition, the fit is significantly improved by including the contemporaneous values of these variables (except $\hat{w}$, of course).[6] It being understood that from now on all variables are detrended, so that the superscript "*dev*" can be henceforth omitted, our atheoretical regression for wage inflation reads

$$
\begin{aligned}
\hat{w}_t^{em} = {}& \mu_{wp,0}\, \hat{p}_t^{em} + \mu_{wz,0}\, \hat{z}_t^{em} + \mu_{we,0}\, e_t^{em} \\
& + \sum_{k=1}^{8} \left[ \mu_{ww,k}\, \hat{w}_{t-k}^{em} + \mu_{wp,k}\, \hat{p}_{t-k}^{em} + \mu_{wz,k}\, \hat{z}_{t-k}^{em} + \mu_{we,k}\, e_{t-k}^{em} \right] + \eta_{w,t}. \quad (14.14)
\end{aligned}
$$

Despite the many lags in the regression equation, the resulting fit is not very close. While $\hat{w}_t$ has a standard deviation of 2.096 percentage points, the standard error of the regression is still 1.600 percentage points (to which corresponds $R^2 = 0.536$; estimation by OLS).[7]

Nevertheless, the explanatory variables and their lags describe, in a convenient and atheoretical form, the data generation process for wage inflation, as far as the variables of our modeling framework are contributing to it. What remains are the exogenous influences, which are summarized in the estimated residuals $\eta_{w,t} = \eta_{w,t}^{est}$. These terms are also often called "innovations", and the calibration procedure below will not venture into neglecting them. The extent to which already these outside forces, which have just been seen to be considerable, determine the actual time path of wage inflation is illustrated in Figure 14.1, which plots $\eta_{w,t}^{est}$ together with $\hat{w}_t^{em}$.

The theoretical determination of the rate of wage inflation is given by equation (14.8). Since presently all variables except wage inflation are re-garded as predetermined, we substitute the actual values for them in (14.8). The remaining influences are represented by a term $\varepsilon_{w,t}$. They are not explained within our framework, even if it is later fully specified, and are generally treated

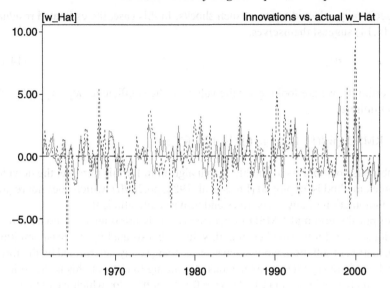

*Figure 14.1* Estimated innovations in "VAR(8)", equation (14.14)
and actual wage inflation (bold and dotted line respectively).

as exogenous shocks to the wage rate. For the present purpose, equation (14.8)
thus becomes

$$\pi_t^c = \sum_{k=1}^{12} \mu_{\pi^c \pi^c, k} \hat{p}_{t+1-k}^{em} \quad \text{(linearly decreasing weights } \mu_{\pi^c \pi^c, k}\text{),} \qquad (14.15)$$

$$\hat{w}_t = \kappa_{wz} \hat{z}_t^{em} + \kappa_{wp} \hat{p}_t^{em} + (1 - \kappa_{wp}) \pi_t^c + \beta_{we} e_{t-1}^{em} - \beta_{wv} v_{t-1}^{em}. \qquad (14.16)$$

The calibration idea is to simulate equations (14.15), (14.16), and, given a shocks
series $\varepsilon_{w,t}$ added to equation (14.16), find numerical values for the four parameters
$\kappa_{wz}, \kappa_{wp}, \beta_{we}, \beta_{wv}$ such that the thus generated time path of $\hat{w}_t$ comes close to the
actual inflation series $\hat{w}_t^{em}$. The distance between the two series is measured by the
root mean squared deviation (RMSD). It measures the approximation error, which
is the extent to which the parsimonious and purposeful theoretical wage Phillips
curve (14.16) fails to reproduce the dynamics of the atheoretical, but "complete",
description of the data generation process (14.14).

### Experiment 1: actual shocks to wage inflation

It follows from what has just been said that the two rules (14.14) and (14.16)
determining wage inflation are viewed as being on the same footing. The shocks
$\varepsilon_{w,t}$ to wage inflation in the structural Phillips curve (14.16) are, therefore,
interpreted as corresponding to the innovations $\eta_{w,t}$ in the atheoretical regression
equation (14.14).[8] To calibrate the structural coefficients in (14.16), we begin with

a specifically selected series of such shocks. In this case, the estimated residuals in (14.14) suggest themselves,

$$\varepsilon_{w,t} = \eta_{w,t}^{est}. \tag{14.17}$$

Accordingly, we are looking for the values of the coefficients $\kappa_{wz}, \kappa_{wp}, \beta_{we}, \beta_{wv}$ that minimize

$$\text{RMSD } \{\hat{w}_t [(14.15), (14.16), (14.17)], \hat{w}_t^{em} \},$$

in obvious notation. As a suitable search algorithm for this purpose, the downhill simplex method is employed (Press et al. 1986, pp.289ff), which does not require the computation of any derivatives and proves quite efficient.

To put the minimal RMSD in perspective, it is informative to relate it to an obvious lower limit. This benchmark value is constituted by the least ambitious explanation of inflation, which views $\hat{w}_t$ as being solely determined by the forces which are here regarded as exogenous. According to (14.17), this is the series of the estimated residuals in (14.14), $\hat{w}_t = 0 + \varepsilon_{w,t} = \eta_{w,t}^{est}$, for which we obtain

$$\text{RMSD}_o := \text{RMSD } \{\eta_{w,t}^{est}, \hat{w}_t^{em} \} = 1.5296.$$

Of course, we expect to find coefficients in (14.16) that do better than that, i.e., coefficients that are able to produce a series $\hat{w}_t$ with RMSD $\{\hat{w}_t, \hat{w}_t^{em} \} < \text{RMSD}_o$. To evaluate the extent to which a series $\hat{w}_t$ improves its RMSD upon $\text{RMSD}_o$, it is convenient to define the following statistic $\phi$,

$$\phi = \phi(\hat{w}_t, \hat{w}_t^{em}) := \frac{\text{RMSD}_o - \text{RMSD } \{\hat{w}_t, \hat{w}_t^{em} \}}{\text{RMSD}_o}. \tag{14.18}$$

Obviously, a perfect fit would be achieved by computing $\hat{w}_t$ directly from (14.14) with the estimated $\mu$s and the estimated innovations; RMSD $= 0$ then and $\phi = 1$ attains its maximal value. On the other hand, any improvement upon $\text{RMSD}_o$ gives at least a positive value of $\phi$.

It may be noted that an alternative RMSD minimization, which discards the shocks from (14.17) and instead employs the estimated residuals from the structural regression reported in the second column of Table 14.2, would yield just these estimated coefficients, with RMSD $= 0.$[9] Denoting these residuals temporarily as $\eta_{w,t}^{reg}$, it is easily seen that our RMSD minimization on the basis of (14.17) would yield similar coefficients if the innovation series $\eta_{w,t}^{est}$ does not differ too much from the residuals $\eta_{w,t}^{reg}$. Actually, the two series are correlated with a coefficient 0.79, so that this "not too much" may still be in effect. The precise results of fitting $\hat{w}_t$ [(14.15), (14.16), (14.17)] to actual wage inflation $\hat{w}_t^{em}$ are given in Table 14.4.

The second column of the table reproduces the benchmark $\text{RMSD}_o$ from above. The rest of the table shows that the RMSD implied by the estimated

*Table 14.4* RMSD of wage inflation from (14.15), (14.16) and under actual shocks (14.17)

| | | | Coefficients | |
|---|---|---|---|---|
| | | $\eta_{w,t}^{est}$ | Estimated | Calibrated |
| $\kappa_{wz}$ | : | $--$ | 0.385 | 0.368 |
| $\kappa_{wp}$ | : | $--$ | 0.577 | 0.530 |
| $\beta_{we}$ | : | $--$ | 0.327 | 0.325 |
| $\beta_{wv}$ | : | $--$ | 0.534 | 0.342 |
| RMSD | : | 1.5296 | 1.0459 | 1.0275 |
| $\phi$ | : | 0.0000 | 0.3162 | 0.3282 |

structural coefficients from Table 14.2 is already close to the lowest RMSD that could be possibly achieved. Correspondingly, the optimal coefficients in the last column of Table 14.4 do not deviate very much from the estimated values; the only exception being the coefficient $\beta_{wv}$ on the wage share, which comes out considerably smaller.

The $\phi$-statistic indicates that the fit of the optimal inflation series to $\hat{w}_t^{em}$ is by no means perfect. The improvement upon the mere estimated innovations $\eta_{w,t}^{est}$ is no better than roughly one third. In this sense, the approximation of the theoretical wage Phillips curve to the VAR-like description of wage inflation is rather limited. The shortcomings in the time series itself can be seen in Figure 14.2. The additional information is helpful since, on the whole, the gaps between $\hat{w}_t$ and $\hat{w}_t^{em}$ look less unsatisfactory to the eye than the value $\phi$ suggests. Also, a comparison with the estimated innovations in Figure 14.1 shows that equation (14.16) and the optimal structural parameters do indeed contribute to a noticeable improvement in the fit.

### *Experiment 2: a bootstrap procedure*

It has been made clear enough that our procedure to obtain numerical values for the parameters in the wage Phillips curve is a combination of estimation and calibration. Because of the iterated simulations of this small structural model in search for the RMSD minimizing coefficients, it is appropriate to emphasize the calibration element. For lack of a better expression, the optimal coefficients may nevertheless be occasionally called the "estimates" of the Phillips curve.[10]

Such as estimates in econometric applications are susceptible to randomness and there exist methods to assess the reliability of the coefficients obtained from a specific sample, it is now time to ask how much we can trust in our estimate, i.e., in the coefficients given in Table 14.4. To shape this discussion, we proceed as if equation (14.14) were an accurate, though atheoretical, representation of the dynamic process generating wage inflation. Although the structural wage Phillips curve is meant to be a succinct theoretical description, the concrete coefficients minimizing RMSD will to some degree still depend on the specific random forces

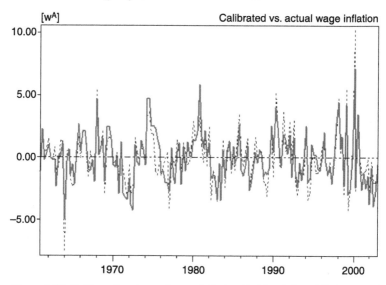

*Figure 14.2* Calibrated and actual wage inflation (bold and dotted line, respectively).

from (14.17) that were estimated to be at work in the sample period. If we imagine that the same deterministic data generation process of equation (14.14) (over another period or in a different country, say) had been affected by different exogenous forces, the estimates of $\kappa_{wz}, \kappa_{wp}, \beta_{we}, \beta_{wv}$ would have somewhat departed from the present result.

In order to interpret the estimates of Table 14.4 in this perspective, we generate artificial data. We want to know, at least approximately, how the estimates are distributed if assumption (14.17) is dropped and, instead of the estimated innovations $\eta_{w,t}^{est}$ from (14.14), the Phillips curve is subjected to alternative sequences of the shocks $\varepsilon_{w,t}$. To this end we have to make an assumption about the probability distribution of these shocks, which will certainly be based on the properties of the estimated innovations. It is helpful in this respect that the latter show no sign of serial correlation or heteroskedasticity, so the shocks can be safely assumed to be i.i.d..

The true distribution of the innovations $\eta_{w,t}$ in (14.14) is, of course, unknown. We can, however, make use of the fact that the empirical distribution function of these residuals is a consistent estimator of the unknown distribution. This allows us to draw the random shocks to wage inflation from the empirical distribution of the innovations (Davidson and MacKinnon 2004, p.161): at each $t$ the shock $\varepsilon_{w,t}$ is assigned the value of one of the estimated innovations, with equal probability. It is understood that an innovation that has been pulled out of the "hat" into which metaphorically speaking all innovations are thrown, is subsequently replaced. $U$ indicating the uniform distribution, and the time index $t$ ranging from 1961:1, which is identified with $t = 1$, to 2003:1, which is identified with $t = T = 169$, this probability distribution of the shocks can be briefly denoted by

$$\varepsilon_{w,t} \sim U[\eta_{w,1}^{est}, \eta_{w,2}^{est}, \ldots, \eta_{w,T}^{est}], \quad t = 1, \ldots, T.$$

Before this idea is carried out, one subtlety has still to be taken into account. While the distribution $U$ has variance $(1/T) \sum_t (\eta_{w,t}^{est})^2$, the unbiased estimate of the variance of the residuals in (14.14) with its $3 + 4 \times 8 = 35$ regressors is $[1/(T-35)] \sum_t (\eta_{w,t}^{est})^2$ (Davidson and MacKinnon 2004, p.110). To correct for the downward bias, the distribution of the $\varepsilon_{w,t}$ should therefore be rescaled (p.163). Accordingly, we assume that the shocks to the wage Phillips curve are distributed as

$$\varepsilon_{w,t} \sim [\frac{T}{T-35}]^{1/2} U[\eta_{w,1}^{est}, \eta_{w,2}^{est}, \ldots \eta_{w,T}^{est}], t = 1, \ldots T = 169. \tag{14.19}$$

The kind of resampling here described is called bootstrapping, though in econometrics these errors are usually directly plugged in a regression equation (pp.159ff). A set $\varepsilon_{w,t}$ for $t = 1, \ldots, T$ obtained from (14.19) is correspondingly called a bootstrap sample.

If equations (14.15), (14.16) are combined with a sequence of random shocks from (14.19), then also the inflation series to which the outcome of the wage Phillips curve is to be fitted has to be modified. It can no longer be actual wage inflation that serves this purpose, but from the pivotal role stated for the deterministic part of the VAR-like equation (14.14) determining wage inflation, it follows that now the estimated innovations in this equation have to be replaced with the same shocks. In addition, since (14.14) is currently read as a data generation process, $\hat{w}_t$ is to be treated as an endogenous variable, which means that on the right-hand side of (14.14) the previously computed wage inflation rates substitute for the actual rates $\hat{w}_{t-k}^{em}$. We characterize this reference series by an asterisk symbol. Hence, given a bootstrap sample $b = \{\varepsilon_{w,t}\}_{t=1}^{T}$ and the estimated $\mu$-coefficients from (14.14), the wage inflation series $\hat{w}_t^*$ system (14.15), (14.16), (14.19) is to fit to has to be simulated as

$$\hat{w}_t^* = \mu_{wp,0} \hat{p}_t^{em} + \mu_{wz,0} \hat{z}_t^{em} + \mu_{we,0} e_t^{em}$$

$$+ \sum_{k=1}^{8} [\mu_{ww,k} \hat{w}_{t-k}^* + \mu_{wp,k} \hat{p}_{t-k}^{em} + \mu_{wz,k} \hat{z}_{t-k}^{em} + \mu_{we,k} e_{t-k}^{em}] + \varepsilon_{w,t} \tag{14.20}$$

(for $t = -7, \ldots, 0$ the variables on the right-hand side are initialized with their historical values). Of course, different bootstrap samples $b$ give rise to different reference series $\hat{w}_t^* = w_{t,b}^*$. Denoting likewise by $\hat{w}_{t,b}$ the inflation series generated by (14.15), (14.16) together with (14.19) on the basis of a bootstrap sample $b$, for each such sample $b$ numerical values for $\kappa_{wz}, \kappa_{wp}, \beta_{we}, \beta_{wv}$ have to be found that minimize RMSD $(\hat{w}_{t,b}, \hat{w}_{t,b}^*)$.

In this way 5000 bootstrap samples (14.19) are drawn, which proves to be more than sufficient. Computing the time path of wage inflation from the structural

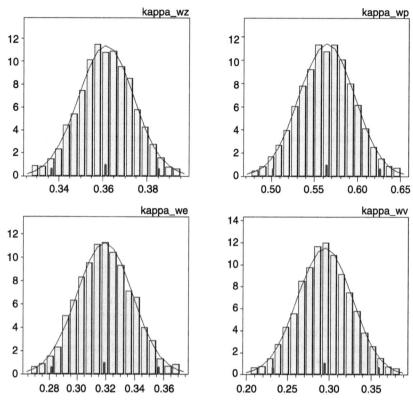

*Figure 14.3* Frequency distributions of the RMSD-minimizing coefficients from 5000 bootstrap samples.

Phillips curve and minimizing RMSD for each sample, we obtain the frequency distributions of the four parameters that are shown in Figure 14.3.[11] The solid line in each panel fits in the density function of the normal distribution with the same mean and standard deviation. Formal tests confirm the visual impression that all four samples of the optimal coefficients can be considered to be normally distributed.[12]

The precise statistics of the frequency distributions are given in Table 14.5, where for comparison the calibrated coefficients from Table 14.4 are reproduced. Besides the mean values and the standard deviations, the table also reports the 2.5 percent and 97.5 percent quantiles.[13] The interval constituted by the quantiles is somewhat akin to a confidence interval in econometric theory. To avoid confusion, however, this expression may here be better avoided. So we say that the bootstrap experiments provide us, for each of the structural coefficients, with an interval of numerical values that can be regarded as *feasible*.

Since the present bootstrap procedure is set out to answer a different question from the fits of ordinary regressions of the wage inflation rates, it should not be surprising that the width of these feasibility intervals does

*Table 14.5* RMSD-minimizing coefficients from 5000 bootstrap samples

| | | Shocks $\eta_{w,t}^{est}$ | Bootstrap Mean | Lower 2.5% | Upper 2.5% | Std.dev. | Reg. Est. |
|---|---|---|---|---|---|---|---|
| $K_{wz}$ | : | 0.368 | 0.361 | 0.337 | 0.385 | 0.012 | 0.385 |
| $K_{wp}$ | : | 0.530 | 0.564 | 0.502 | 0.626 | 0.032 | 0.577 |
| $\beta_{we}$ | : | 0.325 | 0.319 | 0.282 | 0.357 | 0.019 | 0.327 |
| $\beta_{wv}$ | : | 0.342 | 0.295 | 0.232 | 0.359 | 0.032 | 0.524 |
| $\phi$ | : | 0.328 | 0.317 | 0.282 | 0.352 | 0.018 | 0.316 |

not conform to the width of the confidence intervals that are associated with the estimated coefficients in the second column of Table 14.2. In fact, since the problem we pose is more refined than a regression equation, the feasibility intervals are considerably narrower than the confidence intervals (the standard errors for the regression estimates of $K_{wz}$, $K_{wp}$, $\beta_{we}$, $\beta_{wv}$ were, in that order, 0.051, 0.113, 0.079, and 0.131).

The last column in the table shows that the estimation and calibration results do not contradict each other, as the 95 percent-confidence intervals of the estimated coefficients and the feasibility intervals of our calibrated coefficients overlap. This also holds for the wage share coefficient $\beta_{wv}$, whose estimated value with 0.534 appears, at first sight, to be appreciably higher than the average bootstrap value of 0.295.

It may also be noted that the variations in the "goodness-of-fit", as we have measured it in (14.18) by the number $\phi$, are quite limited.[14] Hence, the feasibility intervals given in Table 14.5 can be regarded as the upshot of our calibration of the structural wage Phillips curve in a single equation context. Accepting the stage as we have set it, the main merits of the calibration approach lie in the clues that it gives us to limit the regions from which the structural parameters can be reasonably taken when later we are working with the wage Phillips curve in a more encompassing modeling framework.

## 14.7 ES-calibration of the PPC

The calibration of the price Phillips curve (14.10) can be carried out completely analogous to the wage Phillips curve; so the description can be rather brief. The counterpart of the atheoretical equation for wage inflation (14.14) is the regression approach

$$\hat{p}_t^{em} = \mu_{pw,0}\,\hat{w}_t^{em} + \mu_{pz,0}\,\hat{z}_t^{em} + \mu_{pu,0}\,u_t^{em}$$

$$= \sum_{k=1}^{8}\left[\mu_{pw,k}\hat{w}_{t-k}^{em} + \mu_{pp,k}\hat{p}_{t-k}^{em} + \mu_{pz,k}\hat{z}_{t-k}^{em} + \mu_{pu,k}u_{t-k}^{em}\right] + \eta_{p,t}. \qquad (14.21)$$

When simulating the structural price Phillips curve, contemporaneous price inflation is no longer included in the moving average of the inflation climate. The counterpart of (14.15), (14.16) thus reads

$$\pi_t^c = \sum_{k=1}^{12} \mu_{\pi^c \pi^c, k} \hat{p}_{t-k} \quad \text{(linearly decreasing weights } \mu_{\pi^c \pi^c, k}), \qquad (14.22)$$

$$\hat{p}_t = \kappa_p [\hat{w}_t^{em} - \kappa_{wz} \hat{z}_t^{em}] + (1 - \kappa_p)\pi_t^c + \beta_{pu} u_{t-1}^{em} + \beta_{pv} v_{t-1}^{em} + \varepsilon_{p,t}. \qquad (14.23)$$

Observe that the past inflation rates in the inflation climate are not the actual rates but are computed, at earlier points in time, within in this small model. This makes the determination of $\hat{p}_t$ in (14.23) "more endogenous". If for forecasting purposes the random terms $\varepsilon_{p,t}$ were neglected, then, in the wording of an econometrics software package, equation (14.23) would constitute a "dynamic forecast" of price inflation, as opposed to the predictions of a "static forecast" from an ordinary regression equation.

As in the estimation in Table 14.3, third column, the coefficient on the productivity growth rate, $\kappa_{wz}$, is not treated as a free parameter. We rather invoke the calibration of the wage Phillips curve and adopt the mean value of the bootstrap experiments, which is $\kappa_{wz} = 0.361$ (see Table 14.5). Beginning again with the estimated innovations in the VAR-like equation,

$$\varepsilon_{p,t} = \eta_{p,t}^{est} \qquad (14.24)$$

we are therefore first looking for the values of the three parameters $\kappa_p, \beta_{pu}, \beta_{pv}$ that minimize

$$\text{RMSD } \{\hat{p}_t[(14.22), (14.23), (14.24)], \hat{p}_t^{em}\}.$$

Table 14.6 reports the coefficients thus obtained and contrasts them with the

*Table 14.6* RMSD of price inflation from (14.22), (14.23) and under actual shocks (14.24)

|  | | $\eta_{p,t}^{est}$ | Coefficients | |
|---|---|---|---|---|
|  | | | Estimated | Calibrated |
| $\kappa_{wz}$ | : | $--$ | 0.361 | 0.361 |
| $\kappa_p$ | : | $--$ | 0.222 | 0.337 |
| $\beta_{pu}$ | : | $--$ | 0.237 | 0.190 |
| $\beta_{pv}$ | : | $--$ | 0.473 | 0.332 |
| RMSD | : | 1.2722 | 0.8498 | 0.8032 |
| $\phi$ | : | 0.0000 | 0.3320 | 0.3687 |

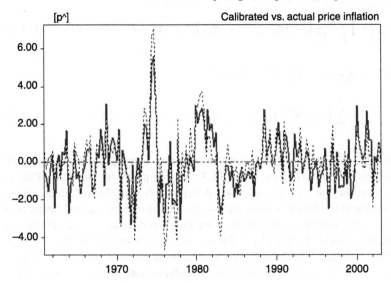

*Figure 14.4* Calibrated and actual price inflation (bold and dotted line, respectively).

parameters from the regression estimation. Similar to Table 14.4 for the wage Phillips curve, the numerical parameter values are not dramatically different across the two approaches.

The "goodness-of-fit" is illustrated in Figure 14.4 by juxtaposing the optimal model-generated price inflation series with actual price inflation. We note in this respect that actual price inflation is less(!) variable than wage inflation (see Figure 14.2, taking the scaling of its vertical axis into account; concretely, the standard deviation of $\hat{p}_t^{em}$ is 1.65 percentage points, as compared to 2.10 percentage points for $\hat{w}_t^{em}$). Not surprisingly, the atheoretical regression of $\hat{p}_t^{em}$ in (14.21) exhibits a lower standard error (SER = 1.17) than regression (14.14) for $\hat{w}_t^{em}$ (where SER = 1.60). This is reflected in a lower RMSD of the estimated innovations $\eta_{p,t}^{est}$ from actual price inflation; i.e., $\text{RMSD}_o = 1.27$ for price inflation versus $\text{RMSD}_o = 1.53$ for wage inflation (cf. Table 14.4).

On the other hand, the reduction of RMSD by the optimal coefficients in the theoretical wage and price Phillips curves is, in absolute terms, greater for wage inflation than for price inflation ($\text{RMSD}_o - \text{RMSD} = 0.502$ in Table 14.4 for $\hat{w}_t^{em}$ versus 0.469 in Table 14.6). It is only the smaller denominator $\text{RMSD}_o$ in the $\phi$-statistic (14.8) that lets the fitting of $\hat{p}_t$ to $\hat{p}_t^{em}$ appear more successful than the fitting of $\hat{w}_t$ to $\hat{w}_t^{em}$. On balance, it could be said that the goodness-of-fit is of a similar order of magnitude for calibrating the wage and the price Phillips curve (under the estimated innovation (14.17) and (14.24), respectively).

We can thus turn to the core of our calibration analysis, which are the bootstrap experiments. The counterpart of equations (14.19) and (14.21) for the distribution of the random shocks to price inflation, and the determination of the reference inflation series $\hat{p}_t^*$ to which the model-generated inflation rates are to fit to, are given by

$$\varepsilon_{p,t} ~ [\frac{T}{T-35}]^{1/2} U[\eta_{p,1}^{est}, \eta_{p,2}^{est}, \dots, \eta_{p,T}^{est}], \quad t = 1, \dots, T = 169, \tag{14.25}$$

$$\hat{p}_t^* = \mu_{pw,0} \hat{w}_t^{em} + \mu_{pz,0} \hat{z}_t^{em} + \mu_{pu,0} u_t^{em}$$

$$+ \sum_{k=1}^{8} [\mu_{pw,k} \hat{w}_{t-k}^{em} + \mu_{pp,k} \hat{p}_{t-k}^* + \mu_{pz,k} \hat{z}_{t-k}^{em} + \mu_{pu,k} u_{t-k}^{em}] + \eta_{p,t}. \tag{14.26}$$

The results of a Monte Carlo simulation comprising again 5000 bootstrap samples are summarized in Table 14.7. As compared to the wage Phillips curve, there is one first conspicuous difference from Table 14.5: the strong deterioration in the fitting statistic $\phi$ as we go over from the estimated innovations (here $\varepsilon_{p,t} = \eta_{p,t}^{est}$) in the computation of the inflation rates to, instead, employing the random shocks from (14.25) (which was equation (14.19) for the wage inflation bootstrap). The deterioration is actually so pronounced that the original value $\phi = 0.369$ is not even in the feasibility interval established by the bootstrap procedure.

An immediate reason that may come to one's mind to explain this phenomenon is the higher noise level in the bootstrap samples $\varepsilon_{p,t}$, which is due to the rescaling of the innovations in (14.25). However, why did the same phenomenon not occur in the calibration of wage inflation? Also, repeating all 5000 bootstrap samples without rescaling (i.e., by replacing the factor $(T/(T-35))^{1/2}$ in (14.25) with unity), we found only slightly better fits, $\phi$ just rising from 0.270 to 0.283.

Hence, the estimated innovations are a very special sequence indeed. It seems that by and large this concerns the sequence as a whole (despite the non-existence of serial correlation). We infer this conjecture from adopting $\varepsilon_{p,t} = \eta_{p,t}^{est}$ in the simulations and substituting the random draws from (14.25) for these values over only some relatively short subperiod, which extends over $\tau = 5, 10, 20, 50$ quarters. In all our explorations, $\phi$ was thus reduced from its upper limit $\phi = 0.369$, but only to a limited degree. With $\tau \leq 20$ (or $\tau = 50$), we detected no case where the mean value of $\phi$ had fallen below 0.320 (below 0.310).[15]

*Table 14.7* RMSD-minimizing coefficients of PPC from 5000 bootstrap samples (imposing $\kappa_{wz} = 0.361$)

| Shocks | Bootstrap | | | | | Reg. |
|---|---|---|---|---|---|---|
| | $\eta_{p,t}^{est}$ | Mean | Lower 2.5% | Upper 2.5% | Std. dev. | Est. |
| $\kappa_p$ : | 0.337 | 0.423 | 0.358 | 0.489 | 0.034 | 0.222 |
| $\beta_{pu}$ : | 0.190 | 0.127 | 0.070 | 0.187 | 0.030 | 0.237 |
| $\beta_{pv}$ : | 0.332 | 0.271 | 0.167 | 0.374 | 0.053 | 0.473 |
| $\phi$ : | 0.369 | 0.270 | 0.208 | 0.331 | 0.031 | 0.332 |

Regarding the structural coefficients in the price Phillips curve, the weight $\kappa_p$ on contemporaneous wage inflation is considerably higher in the bootstrap samples, while the responsiveness to both utilization and the wage share ($\beta_{pu}$ and $\beta_{pu}$) is lower. The original "estimates" $\kappa_p = 0.337$ and $\beta_{pu} = 0.190$ even fail to be contained in the bootstrap's feasibility intervals.

All the more important is the observation in Tables 14.7 that the regression estimates of these coefficients are in all three cases outside their feasibility intervals. In this respect it has to be concluded that in contrast to the wage Phillips curve above, for the price Phillips curve the results from the ordinary regression estimation and from our calibration approach are not compatible.

## 14.8 Conclusions

We have discussed in this chapter the problem of how to obtain numerical parameters for two already fairly elaborated wage and price Phillips curves. To this end, we proposed a combination of calibration and estimation methods, where the focus was now on detrended inflation series. The overall outcome was quite satisfactory (though perhaps not the fitting itself) and made good economic sense. Our procedure may therefore be of a wider methodological interest. In finer detail, however, we also revealed a certain incompatibility of the results from the estimation supported calibration and an ordinary regression equation. This is an interesting finding since a deeper analysis might give us some clues about the circumstances under which one approach could or should be preferred over the other.

More generally, there are two other issues that we think are necessary to pursue. The first one is the specification of the inflation climate, which was basically *ad hoc* and should be tested against more convincing alternatives.[16] It is, secondly, important to check all of the results against the results from the two subsamples of the so-called Great Inflation and Great Moderation. One reason of concern is here the fact that the two periods are characterized by quite different profiles of the lagged auto- and cross-covariances of the variables in the output–inflation nexus.

A third issue is completely new and conceptually more fundamental. It will be shown in Chapter 16 that from a theoretical as well as empirical point of view there are good reasons to expect a long-phased cycle in the data on income distribution and, thus, in the evolution of wage and price inflation together with labor productivity over time. Such a phenomenon is now fairly visible even without econometric techniques, in that after WWII there is first an episode of prosperity and later a stagnant phase, at least as far as employment is concerned. At a theoretical level a distinction may therefore be drawn between a business cycle frequency and a long-phased cycle of, say, about 50 years. Behind the latter there are (reminiscent of the Kaldorian stylized facts) secular movements of labor productivity and capital intensity, while such movements seem largely absent in the rate of profit and the output–capital ratio.

In this perspective, it is a somewhat problematic use of scientific language to assign all lower frequencies than the business cycle to the "trend". If in addition to the business cycle there is indeed a longer cycle in the inflation dynamics, then the usual detrending procedures would possibly remove too much that might be of relevance for the wage and price adjustments and perhaps also for the inflation climate in which the business cycle is operating. Other and more advanced filtering methods in the analysis of (multiple) time series are therefore worth trying, where in the first instance we are thinking of the work in Kauermann et al. (2011) and Flaschel et al. (2011)

From the viewpoint of theory it is definitely preferable in comparison to the conventional ways of speaking about the trend. Secular trends correspond to steady state solutions of a model (Kaldor's stylized facts), the separation/ estimation of the long-phased cycle corresponds to the dynamical theories which focus on income distribution and growth and the business cycle to what we have described as Keynes' trade cycle analysis in the general introduction of this book (where time-varying parameters become an essential aspect and thus sooner or later a methodological must).

# 15 Testing non-linear wage and price Phillips curves for the USA

## 15.1 Introduction

Since the 1980s it has become customary to formulate and estimate labor and goods market dynamics by a single reduced-form Phillips curve (PC), relating price inflation directly to excess demand on the market for labor. Yet, as Fair has stated recently this might be regrettable, since it – in his view – implies a considerable loss of predictive accuracy (see Fair 2000, p. 69). Phillips (1958) already had strongly emphasized that two markets are involved in the unemployment-inflation trade-off. He viewed the relationship between unemployment (demand pressure) and wage change as a non-linear one and stressed that product market prices (cost pressure) do effect the unemployment–wage relationship in certain time periods of his estimates. Although he did not estimate wage and price Phillips curves (WPC, PPC) separately he pointed out that those two are interacting. Fair (2000) then indeed employs and estimates two PCs, in fact for wage and price levels in the place of wage and price inflation rates, instead of only the conventional single price–inflation unemployment trade-off relationships. He finds that demand pressure (measured by the employment gap) matters in the market for goods, but not in the market for labor, where money wages are following the evolution of the price level more or less passively.

In Chen and Flaschel (2005) it has been shown that Fair's level estimates can however – based on the estimated sizes of the parameters of his two structural equations – be translated back into wage and price inflation rates, that one should use the employment gap only in the WPC and the capacity utilization rate in the PPC and that hybrid expectations formation should be allowed for in the cost pressure items of these two PCs in order to include both forward as well as backward-looking behavior, i.e. in our case, myopic perfect foresight coupled with a slowly evolving measure of the inflationary climate surrounding these short-run error free expectations. Extending the two structural PCs of Fair in this way will allow us in the present chapter[1] to further improve Fair's estimates significantly, giving rise to a real wage feedback channel in addition, and furthermore to consider again the old and new question of how much non-linearity is present, here in both wage and price Phillips curves. If one follows this approach, one thus should formulate and estimate separate wage and price PCs, where both demand and cost pressures, originating in the labor and the goods markets, should then appear in their reduced form expressions. This is in particular needed if the two measures of demand pressure in these two markets, excess labor on the external labor market and excess capacity within firms, do not move in line with each other.

New Keynesian approaches generally also only employ one Phillips curve in theory and in practice, a structural PPC based on the assumption of labor market equilibrium. Yet, their approach to staggered price setting with purely forward-looking expectations has been heavily criticized on empirical grounds, see in particular Mankiw (2001), Eller and Gordon (2003). As in our above approach they therefore now generally also use some backward-looking behavior in their estimation of their PPC. Furthermore, they also allow to some extent, primarily in empirically oriented work, for both staggered wage and price setting and thus for structural wage and price PC's (see Woodford (2003) for their formulation) as in our following approach to the wage–price dynamics. Yet, it is a unique feature of our approach to a gradual wage and price adjustment dynamics that a real wage channel will be established by it that can be stabilizing or destabilizing as we shall show in this chapter.

One argument that allows for such conclusions is generally discussed under the heading of wage-led or profit-led goods market behavior in the Post-Keynesian literature, see Barbosa-Filho and Taylor (2006) for example. In the body of the present chapter we will assume, in line with what is generally assumed in the Post-Keynesian literature, but not always in the literature on procyclical real wages,[2] that goods market dynamics are indeed wage-led, meaning that aggregate demand and the output of firms thus depend positively on the real wage. Together with our empirical findings on the two PCs of this chapter, which in particular imply that the adjustment speed of wage inflation with respect to the employment gap is higher than the one of price inflation with respect to the capacity utilization gap (and workers more short-sighted with respect to cost pressure than firms), this gives that the real wage growth will depend positively on the level of real wages (for wage-led periods) and will thus be of a destabilizing kind (cumulative in nature) from this partial perspective.[3]

Taken together, the findings of this chapter can therefore usefully contrasted with achievements in the RBC, the New-Keynesian and the Post-Keynesian literature and it introduces into such discussions that real wage dynamic depends positively on the level of economic activity (measured by capacity utilizations rates of both labor and capital) and thus positively on their own level in a wage-led regime as it may have been the case for certain periods in the US economy after World War II. Our modeling approach of the wage–price dynamics is definitely close in structure (but not in implications) to the New Keynesian one, see Taylor (1999) and Woodford (2003) for the latter approach and Flaschel and Schlicht (2005) for a comparison between our gradual and their staggered wage adjustment. By contrast, our formulation of the wage and price dynamics substantially differs from the RBC-modeling of such a module, see King and Rebelo (2003) for a detailed discussion of this latter type of theory.

Following up the above considerations concerning two Phillips curves we will estimate linear as well as non-linear relationships. In contrast to Phillips (1954) who presumed a parametric form for the non-linear estimation, we will apply nonparametric estimation techniques to capture non-linearities. To test for non-linearities appears to be useful, since recent theoretical and empirical studies seem to indicate that wage Phillips curves are different for high and low unemployment rates. The studies by Stiglitz (1997) and Eisner (1997) suggest that inflation rates do not increase proportionally with lower unemployment and higher capacity utilization. Moreover, another non-linearity has been stated with respect to periods of high and low inflation rates (see Akerlof (2002) and Fehr and Tyran (2001)). Akerlof, for example argues, that at

> a very low inflation, a significant number of workers do not consider inflation sufficiently salient to be factored into their discussions. However, as inflation increases, the losses from ignoring it also rise, and therefore an increasing number of firms and workers take it into account in bargaining.
>
> (Akerlof 2002, p.421)

Moreover, numerous empirical studies have documented downward stickiness of wages (see Fehr and Tyran 2001) as Keynes originally had conjectured. This literature then implies that there is indeed a long-run trade-off between output and inflation and monetary policy matters (see also Mankiw and Reis 2002). In order to evaluate the above statements correctly one needs separate wage and price Phillips curves. Another crucial point is the fact that the NAIRU itself, used to define an employment gap, may move over time (one may need to allow for a time varying NAIRU, see Gordon (1997) and Eller and Gordon (2003)), an issue which however will not be investigated in the present chapter, see Semmler and Zhang (2006, Ch.3) on this matter.

The remainder of the chapter is organized as follows. In Section 15.2 we will extend Fair's WPC and PPC equations to two general structural linear wage and price Phillips curves. We compare these equations with various special types used in the literature. We argue that such separate wage and price inflation Phillips curves can give rise to various real wage adjustment patterns, two normal or stabilizing ones and two adverse or destabilizing ones. In Section 15.3 we provide single equation OLS estimates for these various expressions in order to determine on this basis in particular whether a certain critical condition for real wage instability was fulfilled for the US economy over the period after World War II. In Section 15.4 we explore non-linearities in those two Phillips curves on the structural level and will find that these curves may indeed be somewhat non-linear with respect to specific explaining variables in the US.[4] Section 15.5 presents some extensions pertaining to system estimates and Section 15.6 concludes the chapter.

## 15.2 Wage and price Phillips curves

The stated observation by Fair (2000) that in the last two decades the work on the Phillips curve has moved away from wage and price Phillips curves to the estimation of reduced form price equations is certainly true for applied work. There it appears to be quite common to express labor market and goods market dynamics by a single Phillips curve with demand pressure based on the external labor market and with cost pressure in the two markets represented by a single expected rate of inflation (with markup pricing as a possible justification for such reduced form inflation dynamics, see Blanchard and Katz (1999), for example). It seems, however, also to hold for theoretical work, in particular on the New Keynesian Phillips curve,[5] where beside the IS equation and a Taylor policy rule only a single inflation equation, for price inflation, is included in the core macrodynamic equations.[6]

In order to derive our own 2-D formulation of the wage–price spiral[7] we start from the two structural wage and price equations in level form provided and estimated in Fair (2000), see his p.68. His estimations, when rewritten in terms of growth rates, are basically of the form that the inflation rate predicts the wage inflation rate and that the unemployment rate as well as the wage inflation rate predicts well the price inflation rate. Yet such a structure of the two equations is not sufficient, from the theoretical perspective, to really represent a structural approach to the wage–price spiral. It represents an interesting special hypothesis on the working of this spiral, which states that wages follow prices more or less passively and that demand pressure (measured by the unemployment rate) matters in the market for goods, but not in the market for labor. More generally, one can reformulate wage–price dynamics as follows.[8]

$$Dw = \beta_{w_1}(e^l - \bar{e}^l) + \beta_{w_2}(e^w - 1) + \kappa_w Dp + (1 - \kappa_w)Dp^c, \tag{15.1}$$

$$Dp = \beta_{p_1}(e^c - \bar{e}^c) - \beta_{p_2}(e^n - 1) + \kappa_p Dw + (1 - \kappa_p)Dp^c, \tag{15.2}$$

where $Dw$ and $Dp$ stand for wage and price inflation (the time derivative of the log of wages and prices). We use two measures of demand pressure both in the labor and the goods market, $e^l - \bar{e}^l$, $e^w - 1$ denoting excess labor demand on the external labor market and (in terms of overtime worked) within firms, and $e^c - \bar{e}^c$, $e^n - 1$ denoting excess demand on the market for goods in terms of capacity and inventory use. As variables for expected cost pressures in the wage and the price Phillips curves we use a weighted average of perfectly foreseen price and wage inflation rates (representing temporary effects), respectively, and an inflationary climate expression $Dp^c$ (meant to represent permanent effects and inflation inertia) which in our estimates is provided by a 12 quarter moving average,[9] see Appendix II. As concerns the NAIRU $U^l = 1 - \bar{e}^l$, we may allow, as Tobin (1998) suggest, that the NAIRU shifts over time as the relationship of unemployment, vacancies and wages varies and as the dispersion of excess demands and supplies across markets change over time.[10] But we may presume that $\bar{e}^l$, as well as $\bar{e}^c$, are fixed for certain time periods. We point out that we prefer to write in this section the various measures of demand pressure in terms of employment ($e^l$) and not in terms of unemployment ($U^l = 1 - e^l$), since rates of employment are more flexible in their treatment with respect to growth rate concepts and the integration of alternative measures of demand pressure. We shall return to straightforward reformulations in terms of rates of unemployment in the empirical part of the chapter in order to be closer to common econometric practice.

In the following we will set $\beta_{w_2}, \beta_{p_2}$ equal to zero and will thus only pay attention to employment and capacity utilization rates $e^l$, $e^c$ in their deviation from the NAIRU type rates at $\bar{e}^l$, $\bar{e}^c$. This simplification of wage and price Phillips curves, in our view, represents the minimum structure one should start from. It should be simplified further only if there are definite and empirically motivated reasons to do so.

In macrotheoretic models the above type of wage and price PCs (disregarding our inflationary climate expression $Dp^c$ however) have played a significant role in the rationing approaches of the 1970s and 1980s. Yet, with some exceptions it was fairly unnoticed in theory that having specific formulations of demand and cost pressure on both the labor market and goods market would imply that either wage or price flexibility must always be destabilizing, depending on marginal propensities to consume and to invest with respect to changes in the real wage. In Section 15.3 we will come back to this issue. Stressing the use of separate Phillips curves for wage and price dynamics one can find in the literature on the Phillips curve even more general forms than represented in our equations (15.1)–(15.2). In order to show this, the re-reading of the articles by Phillips is of great help. Phillips (1954) investigated three possible types of fiscal policies, proportional, derivative and integral feedback policy rules, which change for example government expenditures, broadly speaking, in proportion to output gaps, in proportion to their time rate of change and in proportion to the accumulated differences of such gaps, of course with a negative feedback sign in order to counteract less than normal situations in particular. Similarly, inflation rates may be driven by factor utilization gaps, or, in the case of wage inflation specifically, by deviations of the rate of employment from its NAIRU level, but also by the rate of change of the employment rate or the accumulated differences (where positive and negative signs may occur) of the deviation of unemployment rates from normal levels, here again considered in continuous time. Some of those feedback effects can also be found in Phillips (1958).

Though not framed in the same language, all three possibilities are in fact also to be found in early and recent investigations of PC approaches. The proportional control can be found in the standard approaches to the Phillips curve. The derivative control often takes the form of the so-called Phillips loops, see Blanchflower and Oswald (1994) for a revival of this approach, where – when derivative expressions are integrated – the level of wages or of the wage share, and not its growth rate, is related to the rate of unemployment. The integral control can be found in Stock and Watson (1999) where it is claimed that the rate of unemployment is not in fact determining the rate of inflation itself, but rather its time rate of change which – when integrated again – leads us to an integral control mechanism. Marrying Phillips (1954) with Phillips (1958) with respect to a treatment of wage and price inflation thus provides a fairly general framework on the basis of which the various findings in the literature on "the" Phillips curve can be evaluated and investigated in a unified way.

Including the above feedback effects into a more general formulation of wage and price PCs yet, leaving aside here the issue for the cost-pressure terms which in principle could be treated similarly, the wage and price PC's extended in this way may then read:

$$Dw = \beta_{w_1}(e^l - \bar{e}^l) + \beta_{w_2}\frac{\dot{e}^l}{e^l} + \beta_{w_3}\int(e^l - \bar{e}^l)dt + \kappa_w Dp + (1-\kappa_w)Dp^c, \quad (15.3)$$

$$Dp = \beta_{p_1}(e^c - \bar{e}^c) + \beta_{p_2}\frac{\dot{e}^c}{e^c} + \beta_{p_3}\int(e^c - \bar{e}^c)dt + \kappa_p Dw + (1-\kappa_p)Dp^c. \quad (15.4)$$

Both the wage and the price Phillips curve are characterized by three measures of demand pressure on their respective market, all working in the traditional way also on the reduced form level (compared to the New Keynesian staggered wage and price PCs where – due to the specific type of forward-looking behavior of workers and firms – a sign reversal is implied when the reduced form of these PCs are calculated, see Chiarella et al. (2005, Ch.1) for details). In the above wage and price PCs we include again appropriate cost pressure terms, as weighted averages based on currently established price and wage inflation rates and the inflationary climate $Dp^c$ in which the economy is operating. Note finally that this approach guarantees that these equations – in contrast to the ones employed by Fair (2000) – are model consistent in the sense that they are compatible with balanced growth.

We observe that our wage and price Phillips curves are of the general form

$$Dw = \beta_{w's}(\cdot) + \kappa_w Dp + (1-\kappa_w)Dp^c,$$

$$Dp = \beta_{p's}(\cdot) + \kappa_p Dw + (1-\kappa_p)Dp^c$$

and thus represent, when appropriately reordered, two linear equations in the unknowns $Dw - Dp^c, Dp - Dp^c$ that can be uniquely solved for $Dw - Dp^c, Dp - Dp^c$, when $\kappa_w, \kappa_p \in [0,1]$ fulfill $\kappa_w\kappa_p < 1$, giving rise then to the following reduced form expressions:

$$Dw - Dp^c = \frac{1}{1-\kappa_w\kappa_p}[\beta_{w's}(\cdot) + \kappa_w\beta_{p's}(\cdot)],$$

$$Dp - Dp^c = \frac{1}{1-\kappa_w\kappa_p}[\beta_{p's}(\cdot) + \kappa_p\beta_{w's}(\cdot)],$$

$$D\omega = \frac{1}{1-\kappa_w\kappa_p}[(1-\kappa_p)\beta_{w's}(\cdot) - (1-\kappa_p)\beta_{p's}(\cdot)],$$

with all demand pressure variables impacting positively the deviation of wage as well as price inflation from the inflationary climate variable $Dp^c$ and with real wage growth being independent of this climate expression (since $\omega = w - p$).

In view of equations (15.3) and (15.4), we can now briefly comment on applied approaches to PC measurements. Fair (2000), as already shown, provides one of the rare studies which starts from the two PCs, though he makes use of $\beta_{p_1} \neq 0$ solely as far as demand pressure variables are concerned. In his view the price Phillips curve is therefore the important one. Laxton et al. (1998) use for the Multimod Mark III model of the IMF an integrated, or hybrid, PC of the conventional type with only $\beta_{w_1} \neq 0$, and thus the most basic type of PC approach, but stress instead the strict convexity of this curve and the dynamic NAIRU considerations this may give rise to. In their view, therefore, the wage Phillips curve, with proportional term only, is the important one. As already noted, Stock and Watson (1999) find evidence for a Phillips curve of the type $\dot{\pi} = \beta_{w_3}(e^l - \bar{e}^l)$, $\pi = Dp$, which – by the choice of notation here used – indicates that this view is in fact based on an integral control in the money-wage Phillips curve (solely) and possibly also on a specific, implicit treatment of inflationary expectations in addition. Roberts (1997) derives a conventional expectations-augmented price Phillips curve from regional wage curves as in Blanchflower and Oswald (1994) and thus argues that proportional control is the relevant one on the aggregate level even if derivative control applies to the regional level.

At least the possibility for proportional, derivative and integral control is thus taken into account by this literature, though not reflected and compared in these terms. Overall, we can see from our brief discussion that a variety of views have been developed originating in Phillips (1954, 1958) seminal work. In the present chapter we therefore will use proportional control solely in the estimation of our two structural wage and price Phillips curves. It must be noted nevertheless that the discussion on Phillips curves is still an unsettled one, in particular with respect to the empirical significance of all those terms in the equations (15.1)–(15.2), (15.3)–(15.4). Indeed, not all of the expressions shown in equations (15.1)–(15.2), (15.3)–(15.4) will generally be relevant from the empirical point of view, at all times and in all countries. But this should be the outcome of a systematic investigation and not the result of more or less isolated perspectives. It therefore appears that the analysis and investigation of those curves need to be approached from the extended perspective we have described above.

Furthermore we want to note that also the theory of inflationary expectations may be developed further along the lines suggested by our analysis of Phillips curves. In this respect recall first that we have myopic perfect foresight in our wage–price dynamics of price and wage inflation respectively, but have also assumed that these rates of inflation enter wage and price formation processes only with a weight $\kappa_w, \kappa_p < 1$, respectively. In addition we have employed a uniform measure of average inflation, viewed to characterize the medium-run, which enters these processes with weight $1 - \kappa_w, 1 - \kappa_p$, respectively. We have thus, as recently also presumed in the hybrid New Keynesian Phillips curve, a weighted average of forward and backward looking expectation dynamics.[11] We are inclined to assume that the expectation of medium-run inflation cannot be perfect (is not a matter of removing small errors from current inflationary expectations), but that it is based on some time series method, simple adaptive expectations schemes, or, humped shaped weighting schemes of past observation expressing some price inertia. There is thus considerable scope to extend the discussion on the expectational terms in the Phillips curves which, however, is left here for future investigations.[12] The remainder of the chapter will now present some empirical results on proportional control version of the linear approach to WPC's and PC's and then explore non-linearities in these structural PC relationships.

## 15.3 OLS estimates

In this section, we provide some single equation OLS estimates for the structural form of our wage and the price Phillips curves on the basis of the linear curves as above discussed. We will explore the question of their non-linearity in the next section. Besides current price inflation $Dp$, we make use of the inflationary climate expression $Dp12 = Dp^c$, here simply based on the arithmetic mean over the past 12 quarters. We use the US data as described in Appendix II, for the range 1950:2 to 1999:4. On this data basis we estimate the two linear curves[13]

$$Dw = a_o - a_1 U^l_{-1} + a_2 Dp + a_3 Dp12 + a_4 dyn, \tag{15.5}$$

$$Dp = b_o - b_1 U^c_{-1} + b_2 Dw + b_3 Dp12 + b_4 dyn, \tag{15.6}$$

where $U^l = 1 - e^l, U^c = 1 - e^c$ with $e^l, e^c$ are the rates of utilization of the stock of labor and the capital stock and $dyn$ representing the growth rate of labor productivity. Note that these two Phillips curves focus on the proportional influence of demand pressure terms and neglect derivative and integral terms which have been found to be of little significance in Flaschel et al. (2005), see also Flaschel and Krolzig (2006) in this regard. Note again that $w$, $p$ represent logarithms, i.e., their first differences $Dw$, $Dp$ is the current rate of wage and price inflation. Besides model-consistent short-term expectations, we use now $Dp12$ to denote now specifically the moving average of price inflation over the past 12 quarters (as a simple measure of the employed inflationary climate expression), and denote by subscript $-1$ a time lag of one quarter. Finally, for notational simplicity we have carried out a slight change in notation by using for estimation purposes coefficients $a$ and $b$ in (15.5) and (15.6) instead of the $\beta$'s and $\kappa$'s of the theoretical model. Together with the nonparametric approach in the next section this avoids double indexing and makes the model more readable from the empirical point of view, as now $a$-coefficients relate to the wage Phillips curve while $b$-coefficients occur in the price Phillips curve. The connection to the previous section is obvious. For instance $-a_1$ is a proxy for $\beta_{w_1}$ or $b_2$ mirrors $\kappa_p$ in (15.4).

Equations (15.5) and (15.6) are estimated in three different forms:

$$Dw = a_o - a_1 U^l_{-1} + a_2 Dp + a_3 Dp12 + a_4 dyn,$$

$$Dw - Dp12 = a_o - a_1 U^l_{-1} + a_2 (Dp - Dp12) + a_4 dyn,$$

$$Dw - Dp12 = a_o - a_1 U^l_{-1} + a_2 (Dw - Dp12)_{-1} + a_3 (Dw - Dp12)_{-2}) + a_4 dyn.$$

The first equation has already been discussed in Section 15.2. The second considers wage and price inflation in terms of their deviation from the inflationary climate $Dp12$ lagged by one period with respect to current price inflation. This form of the equation imposes the restriction $a_3 = 1 - a_2$ on the first equation, and thus assumes a coefficient of unity with respect to total cost pressure in the wage inflation Phillips curve. The third equation finally can be considered as an approximation to the reduced form equation

$$Dw - Dp12 = a_o - a_1 U_{-1}^l - a_2 U_{-1}^c$$

considered in Section 15.2. Empirically this equation does not produce good estimates, at least in the case of price inflation. In this latter equation we have therefore replaced the indirect cost pressure $a_2 U_{-1}^c$ term by lagged direct expressions for cost pressure in the money-wage PC in order to produce estimates that can reasonably be compared to the other ones. The estimation results for the three forms of the wage PC are provided in Table 15.1. Data sources for the estimation are reported in Appendix II.

*Table 15.1* Estimates for wage PC

| Dependent variable: $Dw$ | | | Dependent variable: $Dw - Dp12$ | | |
|---|---|---|---|---|---|
| Variable | Estimate | T-values | Variable | Estimate | T-values |
| Constant | 0.0131 | 9.8395 | Constant | 0.0130 | 9.8394 |
| $U_{-1}^l$ | −0.1720 | −6.2885 | $U_{-1}^l$ | −0.1621 | −7.1940 |
| $Dp$ | 0.4464 | 6.0274 | $Dp - Dp12$ | 0.4448 | 6.0386 |
| $Dp12$ | 0.6056 | 5.6103 | dyn | 0.1624 | 4.2218 |
| dyn | 0.1676 | 4.2577 | – | | |
| $R^2$ | 0.5165 | | $R^2$ | 0.4084 | |
| $\bar{R}^2$ | 0.5099 | | $\bar{R}^2$ | 0.3995 | |
| RSS | 0.0047 | | RSS | 0.0047 | |
| DW | 2.0058 | | DW | 2.0026 | |

| Dependent Variable: $Dw - Dp12$ | | |
|---|---|---|
| Variable | Estimate | T-values |
| Constant | 0.0125 | 7.7373 |
| $U_{-1}^l$ | −0.1660 | −6.4120 |
| $(Dw - Dp12)_{-1}$ | 0.2196 | 3.2964 |
| dyn | 0.1202 | 3.0484 |
| $R^2$ | 0.3474 | |
| $\bar{R}^2$ | 0.3376 | |
| RSS | 0.0048 | |
| DW | 2.0092 | |

All three estimates shown in Table 15.1 provide for the speed with which wages adjust to demand pressure $\beta_w$ approximately the value 0.16, for quarterly data. Estimates for $a_3$ corresponding to the term $\kappa_w$ in (15.3) represent the short-sightedness of wage earners with respect to their cost-pressure variable, price inflation, where a value of approximately 0.44 results. Wage adjustment with respect to demand pressure in the labor market is thus fairly high (in particular in comparison to the respective price inflation adjustment term, see Table 15.2) and wage earners are fairly short-sighted, giving nearly ½ as weight to the present evolution of price inflation. The growth rate of labor productivity however does not play a significant role in the evolution of wage inflation (where from a theoretical and steady state perspective it should have the weight 1 in the place of approximately 0.15). Comparing these results with the ones for the PPC in Table 15.2 we thus find that demand pressure matters more on the labor market than on the goods market (contrary to what has been found out by Fair) and now in

*Table 15.2* Estimates for price PC

| Dependent variable: $Dp$ | | | Dependent variable: $Dp - Dp12$ | | |
|---|---|---|---|---|---|
| *Variable* | *Estimate* | *T-values* | *Variable* | *Estimate* | *T-values* |
| Constant | 0.0033 | 2.2133 | Constant | 0.0033 | 2.2198 |
| $U^c_{-1}$ | −0.0226 | −2.8190 | $U^c_{-1}$ | −0.0229 | −2.9968 |
| $Dw$ | 0.3141 | 5.7673 | $Dw - Dp12$ | 0.3149 | 5.8444 |
| $Dp12$ | 0.6788 | 8.9434 | $dyn$ | −0.1110 | −3.2070 |
| $dyn$ | −0.1117 | −3.1725 | – | | |
| $R^2$ | 0.6108 | | $R^2$ | 0.3083 | |
| $\bar{R}^2$ | 0.6030 | | $\bar{R}^2$ | 0.2980 | |
| $RSS$ | 0.0041 | | $RSS$ | 0.0040 | |
| $DW$ | 1.6382 | | $DW$ | 1.6404 | |

| Dependent variable: $Dp - Dp12$ | | |
|---|---|---|
| *Variable* | *Estimate* | *T-values* |
| Constant | 0.0043 | 3.4101 |
| $U^c_{-1}$ | −0.0213 | −3.0764 |
| $(Dp - Dp12)_{-1}$ | 0.3532 | 5.3405 |
| $(Dp - Dp12)_{-2}$ | 0.1592 | 2.4517 |
| $dyn$ | −0.0874 | −2.7907 |
| $R^2$ | 0.3909 | |
| $\bar{R}^2$ | 0.3786 | |
| $RSS$ | 0.0038 | |
| $DW$ | 2.0989 | |

addition that firms are less short-sighted with respect to current inflation and its surrounding climate than are workers. The consequence of these results will be – as shown below – that real wages will increase with economic activity, though not instantaneously but with a time delay.

An approximate expression for NAIRU rate $\bar{U}^l$ in the labor market can be obtained from the expression $-a_0/a_1$ given by $0.0132/0.1720 = 0.0767$. We thus in sum get – in contrast to what is obtained in Fair (2000) for the money–wage PC – that demand pressure (on the labor market) matters and that wage earners do not only use present or recent information in order to formulate their wage claims, but in fact also rely on the inflationary climate into which current goods price inflation is embedded, at least to a certain degree. There is thus considerable persistence of wage inflation with respect to price inflation in the wage PC (and even more in the price PC).

We in sum get that wages are more flexible than prices with respect to demand pressure on their respective markets (even if the higher volatility of capacity utilization compared to the employment rate is taken into account, see the plots top left in Figures 15.1 and 15.2) and that wage earners are more short-sighted than firms with respect to the cost-pressure items these two sectors in the economy are subject to. For the NAIRU rate of capacity utilization on the market for goods we finally get, formally as in the case of wage inflation, now the value $\bar{U}^c = 0.147$. Flaschel and Krolzig (2006) have also estimated the wage and price Phillips curves of this section, with by and large similar results and with the additional result that Blanchard and Katz (1999) error correction terms are not significant in the wage–price spiral of the US economy.[14] They used as lag structure in the estimation of an extended model of the wage–price spiral of this chapter a length of five lags on the right-hand side in both the wage and price PC. They then obtained as specific result by the PcGets optimization routine that primarily only proportional terms with respect to demand pressure on the market for labor and for goods remained in operation as determinants of wage as well as price inflation (while cost pressure exhibits of course also some integral control due to the inflationary climate expression used). We also note here that three-stage least squares simultaneous equations estimates of the wage and price PC do not significantly alter the result we obtained above in the case of OLS, see the concluding section for such a system approach which also includes Okun's Law and a dynamic IS-curve in order to get a more complete picture of the real wage feedback structure considered in this chapter. Yet, since a simultaneous equations approach is not yet available in the case of non-parametric estimation procedures, we have used here simple OLS estimation in order to be directly comparable to the estimates that are provided in the next section of the chapter.

The results here obtained imply as in earlier work an adverse type of real wage effect if it is assumed[15] that consumption is more responsive to real wage changes than investment (which appears likely to be the case with respect to temporary as opposed to permanent real wage changes, in particular in periods of high economic activity). In such a case economic activity would depend positively on the real wage whose dynamics are described according to Section 15.2 by:[16]

$$Dω = \frac{(1-κ_p)β_{w_1}(\bar{U}^l - U^l(ω)) - (1-κ_w)β_{p_1}(\bar{U}^c - U^c(ω))}{1-κ_wκ_p}, \quad U^{l\prime}, U^{c\prime} < 0$$

as can easily be shown by means of the reduced form expressions for wage and price inflation of the preceding section.

On the basis of the obtained reduced form law of motion for the real wage $ω = w - p$ one gets as critical $α$-condition for the establishment of a positive dependence of the growth rate of real wages on their current level (under the conventional Post-Keynesian assumption of aggregate demand that is wage-led, i.e., with $e^l = 1 - U^l, e^c = 1 - U^c$ strictly increasing in $ω$) the following term:

$$α = (1-κ_p)β_{w_1}/\bar{y} - (1-κ_w)β_{p_1}/y^p \begin{Bmatrix}<\\>\end{Bmatrix} 0 \Leftrightarrow \begin{Bmatrix}\text{normal}\\\text{adverse}\end{Bmatrix} \text{RE.}$$

The above is the critical $α$-condition for the occurrence of normal or adverse real wage or Rose effects,[17] in such wage-led regimes.[18] This critical $α$-condition applies to the estimation results as reported in Tables 15.1 and 15.2. In all estimates provided in Tables 15.1 and 15.2 this critical condition is always positive in sign. Thus, real wage adjustment is of an adverse type in the US economy in the case where its economic activity depends positively on the real wage. This would imply then that there is a mechanism at work that can explain the occurrence of destabilizing or cumulative wage–price spirals as they where observed in the 1960s and 1970s during the prosperity phase after World War II. Periods of low inflation as they are now discussed in the literature may be different however in this regard, see also the concluding section. This is a topic that should be addressed more extensively in future research, by extending the results on non-linearity we obtain in the next section of this chapter, which still to some extent support the views of the present section even for low inflation regimes, at least as far as the US economy was concerned. We will come back to the issue of whether the US economy was on average wage-led or profit-led in the final section of this chapter where we provide further evidence for our above finding $α > 0$ in the working of the wage–price spiral for the US economy on an average.

## 15.4 Exploring non-linearities

Next, we will explore non-linearities in the two Phillips curves. Following Phillips (1958) in exploring non-linearities in some key relationships, we here replace all relationships by unspecified functional forms. For wage Phillips curve (15.5) this means we let $U^l_{-1}$ enter the curve as function $a_1(U^l_{-1})$ say, where $a_1(.)$ is supposed to be estimated from the data. In the same fashion we allow the other quantities in (15.5) to have a non-linear effect so that (15.5) is replaced by the general form

$$Dw = a_0 + a_1(U^l_{-1}) + a_2(Dp) + a_3(Dp12) + a_4(dyn).$$ (15.7)

For the different functions we assume sufficient smoothness, i.e. we postulate that they are two times continuously differentiable but otherwise unspecified. Accordingly, the price Phillips curve is generalized to

$$Dp = b_0 + b_1(U^c_{-1}) + b_2(Dw) + b_3(Dp12) + b_4(dyn).$$ (15.8)

To keep the notation simple we subsequently also write $a(U^l)$ for $a_1(U^l)$ and likewise for the other functions. Let us explain the generalization (15.7) and (15.8) in more depth. First, if we assume that all functions in (15.7) and (15.8) are linear, that is $a_1(U^l_{-1}) = a_1 U^l_{-1}$, we obtain the Phillips curves. Hence, the Phillips curves (15.5) and (15.6) (15.7) and (15.8) are natural and general extensions of (15.5) and (15.6). Secondly, it becomes obvious that further constraints are necessary to make the functions in (15.7) and (15.8) identifiable. Note that for instance adding a constant to one of the functions $a$ (.) and subtracting it from $a_0$ gives another solution to (15.7). We therefore impose the constraint that the functions are centered around zero. For $a_1(U^l)$ this means for instance $a_1(U^l) - a_1(\bar{U}^l) = 0$, where $a_1(\bar{U}^l) = \sum_{i=1}^n a_1(U^l_i)/n$. Note that we have used similar constraints in the linear Phillips curves (15.5) and (15.6) by putting $\beta_w \bar{U}^l$ in the intercept $a_0$.

As previously mentioned, Phillips (1958) in his original article already considered non-linear functions. Unlike his approach however our functions are nonparametric, that is no parametric functional form is imposed. The idea behind (15.7) and (15.8) is to let the data decide upon the structure and form of the functions. This can be done by what is called nonparametric regression. Estimation of nonparametric models like (15.7) and (15.8) has been a major field of research in statistics over the last two decades with an initial milestone set by Hastie and Tibshirani (1990). An up to date demonstration of the state of the art including most recent references is found in Ruppert et al. (2003). We provide a short sketch in Appendix I. The technique is numerically easily applicable and part of modern statistical software packages like S-PLUS (http://www.insightful.com) or R (http://www.r-project.org), see also Venables and Ripley (1999).

Nonparametric, smooth regression is carried out using a smoothing parameters steering the amount of smoothing. If the smoothing parameter is set large, in the extreme case to infinity, the resulting fitting step breaks down to simple parametric fitting and the parametric models (15.5) and (15.6) arise. In contrast, if the smoothing parameters are set to small values, estimates will be highly structured and highly variable therefore. It is therefore necessary to choose a smoothing parameter which provides a good balance between flexibility and variability. This can be done data driven, so that nonparametric estimation not only allows to estimate functional relationships without stringent parametric assumptions, it also provides an estimate for the functional complexity of the model. This means that the functional form and complexity can be chosen data driven. A conventional tool for this is cross validation or the Akaike criterion (see Akaike 1973). The latter has the form

$$AIC(\lambda) = \log \left\{ \sum_{i=1}^{n} (Dw_i - \widehat{Dw_i})^2 \right\} + 2df(\lambda)/n \qquad (15.9)$$

where $\widehat{Dw_i}$ are the fitted values.

The first component (15.9) measures the goodness of fit as sum of squared residuals while $df(\lambda)$ is a measure for the degree of complexity of the fitted model. The parameter $\lambda$ is thereby the tuning parameter steering the smoothness of the fitted functions. The Akaike criterion itself works as follows. Setting $\lambda$ to zero leads to complex functions and hence small residuals $Dw_i - \widehat{Dw_i}$. Consequently the first component in (15.9) is small while the latter is large. Vice versa if $\lambda$ is large, the sum of squared residuals will increase while the complexity $df(\lambda)$ is small, in the extreme case $df(\lambda \to \infty) = 1$. An optimal smoothing parameter now balances out these two extremes and selects the minimum of $AIC(\lambda)$. The resulting fits are shown for wage and price Phillips curves in Figures 15.1 and 15.2, respectively. The solid curves show the nonparametric fitted functions with complexity degree chosen by the data. The degree is thereby stated on the $y$ axes of the plots. For instance $a(U_{-1}^l, 5.25)$ is a function of complexity degree 5.25 while $a(Dyn, 1.03)$ has complexity 1.03 which is about linear line as can be seen from the bottom right plot of Figure 15.1. The dashed lines above and below the smooth curves indicate pointwise confidence intervals while the dotted line shows simple OLS estimates in the linear model that is function $a_1(U_1^l) \equiv a_1(U_{-1}^l - \bar{U}_{-1}^l)$ as fitted in Section 15.3. The parameter estimates for the latter are listed in Table 15.2. The ticks in the bottom of the graphs indicate the observed values for the explanatory variables.

Before interpreting the curves in more depth we want to explore the reliability of the fits, in particular the chosen complexity of the functions. To do so we run a bootstrap/Jackknife simulation. We refit the model using 85 percent of the observation by omitting randomly 15 percent of the observations. This is repeated 200 times and the estimated degrees of complexity are recorded. These are shown in Figure 15.3 and Figure 15.4, respectively. The two main features that can be observed are the following. For the wage Phillips curve there is indication of a hyper-linear structure for unemployment rate $U_{-1}^l$ while the remaining components $Dp$, $Dp12$ and $Dyn$ follow a linear structure.

The Phillips curve for the inflation rate also shows some evidence for a non-linear relation for $U_{-1}^c$, $Dw$ and $Dp12$. The non-linearity of the price change with respect to $U_{-1}^c$ in Figure 15.2 confirms the position taken by Stiglitz (1997) and Eisner (1997) who have viewed the Phillips curve as concave with respect to the output gap. As to $U_{-1}^c$, we can observe in Figure 15.2 that an increase in capacity utilization increases prices less than proportional.

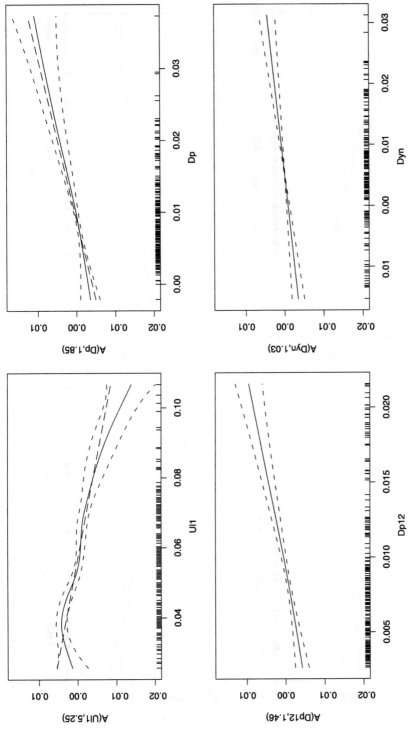

*Figure 15.1* Nonparametric estimates for the wage PC.

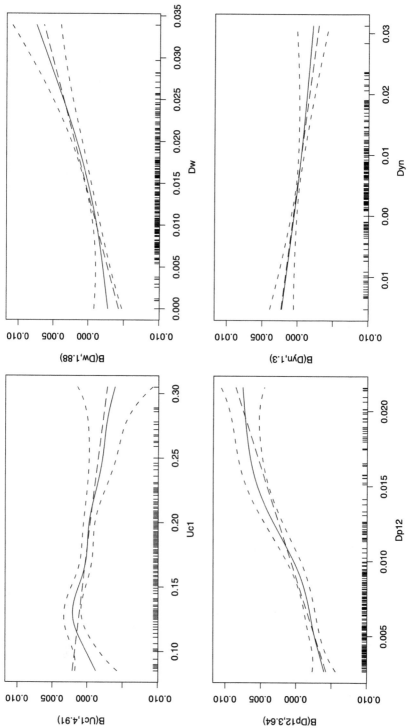

*Figure 15.2* Nonparametric estimates for the price PC.

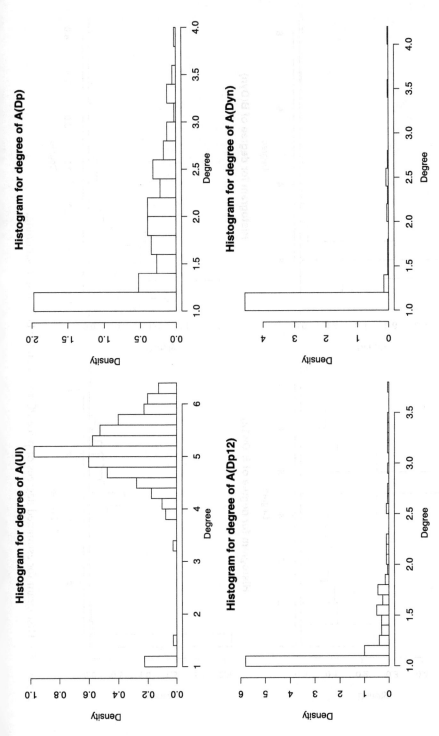

*Figure 15.3* Histogram for estimated degrees of wage PC based on the bootstrap resampling.

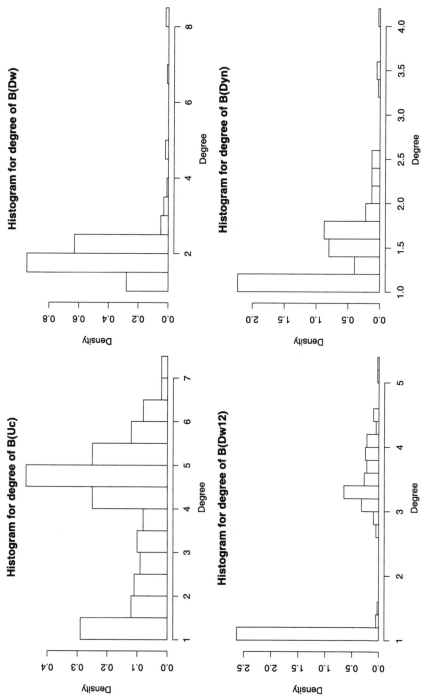

*Figure 15.4* Histogram for estimated degrees of price PC based on the bootstrap resampling.

On the other hand the shape of the relationship of $Dp12$, our expression for inflation expectations, in Figure 15.2, does indicate only a slight non-linearity for the price Phillips curve, a non-linearity that Akerlof (2002) referred to as "information stickiness" (see also Mankiw and Reis 2002). As can be seen nominal wages (and inflation rates) react to anticipated variables only slightly more if the variable is high as compared to being low, see Figure 15.2.

In sum, the functional form of $a(U^l_{-1})$ as well as $b(U^c_{-1})$ shows a convex structure with a negative slope for small values of $U^l_{-1}$ and $U^c_{-1}$, respectively. This means that with increasing capacity utilization prices do not rise unboundedly but inflation rates may become flat or even decline. On the other hand inflation rates, of course, will fall with very low capacity utilization.

Overall, the non-linear estimates roughly confirm our linear wage and price Phillips curves which are represented by the dotted lines in Figures 15.1 and 15.2. In addition, as our comparison of linear and non-linear Phillips curves show, for some relationships non-linearities are important, for others not. In particular the non-linearity in the relationship between wage change (price change) and unemployment (capacity utilization) is an important result.

We conclude from the above that non-linearities in the wage–price spiral are of some importance in the US economy, but are not at all comparable in kind to the ones found to exist in Hoogenveen and Kuipers (2000) for six European countries in the case of the WPC, see also Laxton et al. (2000) on this matter. The implications of the critical condition considered in the preceding section thus do not seem to depend very much on the specific inflationary regime the economy may be in for some time.

## 15.5 Some extensions

The question might be raised of how our estimates perform when simultaneity issues are taken into account, when note is taken of the fact that the rate of employment and the rate of capacity utilization are related by an estimate of Okun's Law, when Blanchard and Katz's (1999) error correction terms are taken into account and what happens when a more complete model is used to study the real wage channel that is created by the wage–price spiral of this chapter. As in Blanchard and Katz (1999) we could not find evidence for wage share error correction terms in both the wage and the price Phillips curve, but could obtain statistically significant system estimates for our wage–price spiral mechanism that were in all respects close to the OLS estimates of Section 15.3 of the chapter. We do not report these estimates here, but extend them here immediately towards an inclusion of Okun's Law in the following growth rate form

$$D\ln e^l = bD\ln e^c, \quad b > 0 \quad [i.e., \ln e^l = const + \ln e^c]$$

and a dynamic multiplier equation of the following type:

$$\ln e^c = c_1 \ln e^c_{-1} + c_2(r_{-1} - Dp) + c_3 \ln v_{-1} + c_4 + c_5 D75 \qquad (15.10)$$

where $e^c$ is the rate of capacity utilization, $r_{-1} - Dp$ last quarter's real rate of interest, $v_{-1}$ last quarter's wage share and $D75$ (and also $D74$ below) a dummy variable. This goods market adjustment equation represents a reduced form equation that reflects consumption and investment behavior in aggregate form only, where we therefore cannot determine the sign of the parameter $c_3$ on purely theoretical grounds. The sign of $c_2$ should of course be negative, while the assumption that the marginal propensity to spend is less than one is reflected by assuming $c_1 \in (0, 1)$. We will find below that the wage share has a significant influence on this dynamic multiplier process though it does not appear as error correction mechanism in the two equations that describe the wage–price spiral itself.

We have already excluded from the following summary of the system estimate of our extended model of the wage–price spiral the insignificant parameters in the displayed quantitative representation of the model and also the stochastic terms. By putting furthermore the NAIRU expressions and all other expressions that are here still assumed as constant into overall constant terms, we finally obtain the following (approximate) three-stage least squares estimation result (with $t$-statistics in parenthesis, $e^l = 1 - U^l, e^c = 1 - U^c$):[19]

We obtain from this estimate evidence that the dynamic multiplier is – as is usually assumed – stabilizing (from its partial perspective) and that economic activity depends – again, as it is usually assumed – negatively on the evolution of the real rate of interest. New in this estimate is the result of a strong negative dependence of the change of capacity utilization on the wage share (or real unit wage costs) which – in contrast to our earlier assumption a positive level relationship between economic activity and real wages – implies that the US economy was on an average profit-led in the considered time period (with a certain delay however). Combined with our finding: $\alpha > 0$ for the critical condition introduced in Section 15.3, i.e., combined with a positive dependence of real wage growth on economic activity we thus would here get as result for the US economy that real wage growth by and large depended negatively on the level of real wages, which thus now provides a stabilizing check to for example positive real wage

*Table 15.3* The wage–price spiral, Okun's Law and goods market dynamics: a system estimate

$$Dw = \begin{array}{ccccc} 0.10\ln e^l_{-1} & +0.80Dp & +0.20Dp12 & -0.12 \\ (-3.67) & (6.00) & (--) & (5.23) \end{array}$$

$$Dp = \begin{array}{ccccc} 0.02\ln e^c_{-1} & +0.44Dw & +0.56Dp12 & -.003 & -.008D74 \\ (-3.28) & (5.19) & (--) & (1.91) & (4.59) \end{array}$$

$$D\ln e^l = \begin{array}{c} 0.16D\ln e^c \\ (17.56) \end{array}$$

$$\ln e^c = \begin{array}{ccccc} 0.84\ln e^c_{-1} & -1.05(r_{-1} - Dp) & -0.82\ln v_{-1} & -0.03 & -0.10D75 \\ (31.24) & (-4.29) & (-6.50) & (-4.80) & (-6.23) \end{array}$$

shocks – due to the declining economic activity that is accompanying such real wage increases. This is an important, and for the authors of this chapter unexpected, result on the real wage channel in the US economy. Yet, the presence of the real rate of interest in this estimate indicates that a more complete macroeconomic framework must still be chosen in order to investigate such questions in more depth. We also stress here again that the distinction between consumption and investment effects of real wage increases is still missing here which might alter the situation again.

We have already stated that the system estimate of the wage–price spiral itself is very close to the OLS estimate of the laws of motion for wages and prices. Yet, with Okun's Law (and the dynamic multiplier story) included into these system estimates we are getting parameter estimates that are no longer very close to the OLS estimates of the main part of this chapter as a comparison of the above parameter estimates with those of Section 15.3 (as far as the first two equations are concerned) immediately shows.[20] When Okun's Law is used in the above form in the place of a fixed proportions technology moreover, the critical conditions for a normal or adverse dependence of the growth rate of real wages on their level reads – now in the case of a profit-led regime as it was estimated above:

$$\alpha = (1-\kappa_p)\beta_{w_1} b - (1-\kappa_w)\beta_{p_1} \begin{Bmatrix} < \\ > \end{Bmatrix} 0 \Leftrightarrow \begin{Bmatrix} \text{adverse} \\ \text{normal} \end{Bmatrix} \text{RE.}$$

Inserting the estimated parameter values then gives approximately $\alpha = 0.009 - 0.004 = 0.005$ and thus a very weak, but still positive influence of activity changes on real wage growth. Though there is a strong effect of real wage changes on activity changes on the market for goods the overall result is in this case that the real wage feedback channel is only in a very weak sense a stabilizing one, leading from real wage increases to activity decreases and from there to decreases in the growth rate of real wages. The results of the main part of the chapter are therefore weakened in this extended version of the model (due to the low value that now relates percentage capacity utilization changes with percentage changes in the rate of employment) and the assumption of a wage-led economy is here changed into the opposite assumption (supported by the above estimate) that at least the US economy was profit-led on an average after World War II. The above results of the system estimates thus imply the need for further research which is however beyond the scope of the present chapter.

Yet, roughly speaking, we may however state that we have investigated in this chapter a relationship of the type $D\omega = f(e,u)$ with $f_1 > 0, f_2 < 0$ and found that the signs of the partial derivatives are confirmed by all of our estimates. Moreover, the first partial derivative seems to dominate to a certain degree the second one if a link between these two utilization rates is added to the model. This dominance may be a weak one, and may thus explain to a certain degree why real wages are much less volatile than the business cycle itself as stated as an empirical fact in Rotemberg and Woodford (2003). The next step of the investigation should then be whether we have a further, goods market oriented relationship of the wage-led type $u(\omega), u' > 0$ or of the profit-led type $\hat{u}(\omega), \hat{u}' < 0$, i.e., whether our estimated wage–price module gives rise to (unstable!) Post-Keynesian macrodynamics or a stable dynamics of the Goodwin (1967) growth cycle type. As stated this must however be left for future research, see Chen et al. (2006) for first steps into such a direction.

## 15.6 Conclusions

We have investigated in this chapter structural wage and price equations from the theoretical and the empirical point of view. From the theoretical perspective we found that their specification is generally much too simple or specific in order to allow a thorough discussion and evaluation of the various approaches and statements in the literature. There are indeed various measures of demand pressure to be employed in this context and these measures may appear as Phillips (1954) suggests in proportional, derivative or integral form in certain countries and at certain times. Specifying PCs in this general format does indeed allow for a better comparative evaluation of the approaches in the literature, an improved predictive accuracy and for a better understanding of the role of labor and product market distinctions in macrodynamics. The general form for wage–price dynamics offered in Section 15.2 therefore should indeed be used in order to move on to what specific forms of wage and price PCs may hold in certain countries in certain periods. In this chapter we have, following Flaschel et al. (2005), used a proportional approach to demand pressure variables in our estimations throughout, but have used market specific characteristics in the specification of both the labor market oriented WPC and the goods market oriented PPC.

With regard to cost pressure variables we also did choose a specific, though fairly general format. In view of the literature on rational – and nowadays on both forward and backward looking – expectations, we assumed as cost pressure variable a weighted average of the currently perfectly foreseen cost pressure (price inflation in the case of workers and wage inflation in the case of firms) and an inflationary climate expression that was given as a moving average over the past last twelve quarters in the empirical estimates. This allowed us to obtain – despite forward looking variables in both the wage and the price PC – enough inertia in the wage–price spiral as it is suggested by empirical observations. From the empirical perspective we found indications that separately specified and estimated linear as well as non-linear wage and price PCs perform very well compared to the commonly employed reduced types of single Phillips curve often characterized by the special assumptions $\beta_p = 0$, $\kappa_p = 1$ which are not supported by our empirical findings.

Our linear and non-linear estimates of the two Phillips curves in the main part of the chapter in principle imply an important real wage feedback chain that will only be destabilizing in periods where economic activity is positively dependent on the real wage. In terms of slopes the non-linear estimation roughly confirmed our linear estimates. Should such slopes really exist in some countries at some time, it should therefore be taken account of in the formulation of monetary (and fiscal) policy, in particular in recent formulations of so-called Taylor or interest rate policy rules, at least in periods where demand is definitely wage-led. Demand pressure matters both in the labor and the goods market and establishes a link between the current level of real wages and its rate of change that must be paid attention to in the conduct of monetary policy.

In terms of macrodynamics, the standard type of Taylor rule may perform well in the case of adverse real interest rate adjustments (based on the destabilizing Mundell-effect in comparison to the then simplified stabilizing Keynes-effect), but its inflation targeting may be quite impotent if an accelerating wage–price spiral becomes indeed established, by either prices becoming more flexible than wages or by consumption becoming more responsive to real wage changes than investment. In such a situation a wage gap expression should therefore enter the formulation of Taylor rules which when sufficiently strong in its operation may indeed tame the instability of this type of wage–price spirals, see also Flashchel and Krolzig (2006) in this regard. The analysis of this chapter therefore suggests a redesign of interest rate policy rules at least in certain episodes of wage–price interactions as maybe was the case in the late 1960s and 1970s.

Finally we want to note that the detected non-linear relationship, in particular, between the unemployment rate and wage change and capacity utilization and price change is an important one as Stiglitz (1997) and Eisner (1997) have predicted. On the other hand, we find less evidence of significant non-linearities for our expression for price (and wage) expectations. This predicts, for example, that at low inflation rates, a wage stickiness with respect to inflation expectation would be observable as suggested by Akerlof (2002) and others (see Mankiw and Reis 2002). Although there is an overall wage and price stickiness, as the above literature argues, there is not an explicit "expectation stickiness" observable in our estimates. This may not reject the hypothesis of "expectation stickiness" at low inflation rates as stated for example, by Akerlof (2002), since the hypothesis might hold with other measures of price expectations and it might also hold for the reduced form of the Phillips curve, as referred to in the statement by Akerlof (2002), which we have not tested here.

## Appendix I: sketch of nonparametric estimation

The subsequent algorithm is based on Wood (2000) and implemented in the public domain software *R* (see Ihaka and Gentleman 1996). The program and more information about it can be downloaded from http://www.r-project.org/. We exemplify the fit with the simplified model

$$Dw = \beta_0 + A(U^l).$$

Let $Dw_i$ and $U_i^l$ be the observed values for $i = 1,\ldots,n$ following the model

$$Dw_i = \beta_0 + A(U_i^l) + \varepsilon_i.$$

with $\varepsilon_i$ as residual. For fitting we replace $A(U^l)$ by the parametric form

$$A(U^l) = a_1 U^l + Z(U^l)c \qquad (15.11)$$

where $Z(U^l)$ is a high dimensional basis in $U^l$, for instance a cubic spline basis. Conventionally $Z(U^l)$ is 10 to 40 dimensional. That is, if a larger basis is in use this is reduced to a smaller basis using only those basis functions corresponding to the largest eigen-values of $Z^T(U^l)Z(U^l)$, see Wood (2000) for more details. In principle with replacement (15.11) one ends up with a parametric model. However, fitting the model in a standard OLS fashion is unsatisfactory due to the large dimensionality of $Z(U^l)$ which will lead to highly variable estimates. This can be avoided by imposing an additional penalty term on $c$, shrinking its values to zero. To be more specific, we obtain an estimate by maximizing the penalized OLS criterion

$$\sum_{i=1}^{n} \{Dw_i - a_1 U_i^l - 2(U_i^l)c + \lambda c^T P c$$

with $\lambda$ called the smoothing or penalty parameter and $c^T P c$ as penalty. Matrix $P$ is thereby chosen in accordance to the basis, but for simplicity one can assume $P$ to be the identity matrix (see Ruppert et al. (2003), for more details). It is easy to see that choosing $\lambda = 0$ yields an unpenalized OLS fit, while $\lambda \to \infty$ implies $c = 0$ so that a simple linear fit results, since coefficient $a_1$ is unpenalized. Hence, $\lambda$ steers the amount of smoothness of the function with a simple linear fit on the one side and a high dimensional parametric fit on the other side. The fitted function itself can be written as $\hat{A}(U^l) = H(\lambda)Dw$ where $Dw = (Dw_1,\ldots,Dw_n)$ here is the vector of observed values and likewise definition for $U^l$. The matrix $H(\lambda)$ results thereby as

$$H(\lambda) = \begin{pmatrix} U^l \\ Z(U^l) \end{pmatrix} \left( \begin{pmatrix} U^l \\ Z(U^l) \end{pmatrix}^T \begin{pmatrix} U^l \\ Z(U^l) \end{pmatrix} + \lambda \begin{pmatrix} 0 & 0 \\ 0 & P \end{pmatrix} \right)^{-1} \begin{pmatrix} U^l \\ Z(U^l) \end{pmatrix}^T.$$

The degree of complexity of the function is now defined as the trace of $H(\lambda)$. Note that as special case we get trace of $H(\infty)$ equals 1 while trace of $H(0)$ is $p+1$ with p as dimension of $Z(U^l)$. The degree can now be estimated from the data by minimizing a cross validation or the Akaike criterion (15.9) (see Wood (2000) or Hastie and Tibshirani (1990), for more details).

## Appendix II: data sources

The data are taken from the Federal Reserve Bank of St. Louis[21]. The data are quarterly, seasonally adjusted and are all available from 1948:1 to 2001:2. Except for the unemployment rates of the factors labor, $U^l$, and capital, $U^c$, the log of the series are used (see Table 15.4). For reasons of simplicity as well as empirical reasons, we measure the inflationary climate surrounding the current working of the wage–price spiral, see Sections 15.2–15.4, by an unweighted 12-month moving average:

$$\pi_t = \frac{1}{12}\sum_{j=1}^{12}\Delta p_{t-j}.$$

This moving average provides a simple approximation of the adaptive expectations mechanism, which defines the inflation climate as an infinite, weighted moving average of past inflation rates with declining weights. The assumption here is that economic agents apply a certain window (three years) to past observations, here of size, without significantly discounting, see Rudebus and Svensson (1999).

*Table 15.4* Variables used

| Variable | Transformation | Mnemonic | Description of the untransformed series |
|---|---|---|---|
| $U^l$ | UNRATE/100 | UNRATE | Unemployment rate |
| $U^c$ | 1-CUMFG/100 | CUMFG | Idle capacity: manufacturing percent of full capacity |
| $w$ | log(COMPNFB) | COMPNFB | Nonfarm business sector: compensation per hour, 1992=100 |
| $p$ | log(GNPDEF) | GNPDEF | Gross national product: implicit price deflator, 1992=100 |
| $y - l^d$ | log(OPHNFB) | OPHNFB | Nonfarm business sector: output per hour of all persons, 1992=100 |
| $u$ | $\log\left(\dfrac{COMPRNFB}{OPHNFB}\right)$ | COMPRNFB | Nonfarm business sector: real compensation per hour, 1992=100 |

# 16 The distributive cycle with a non-linear wage Phillips curve[1]

## 16.1 Introduction

It is standard in applied macro literature to express the labor market and goods market dynamics by a single Phillips curve, in which the cost pressure on the two markets is working on a single inflation rate. A single Phillips curve for the two markets requires the simplifying assumption that prices are a constant markup on wages.

On the other hand, Post-Keynesian macroeconomic models have recently been considering two separate Phillips curves, one for the labor market (the *wage* Phillips curve) and one for the goods market (the *price* Phillips curve), in order to analyze the interacting dynamics of the adjustment processes (Proaño et al. 2006, Flaschel and Krolzig 2006). Such adjustments are usually referred to as *wage–price spiral*, a well-known process in macroeconomics having to do with opposite sides facing off in wage-setting and trying to maintain their respective purchasing power in view of price variations.

The distributional conflict that is at the source of such adjustments is of obvious interest for Post-Keynesian macroeconomists, and the consideration of two separate Phillips curves provides additional insights in the analysis of the interrelation between income distribution, inflation, and growth. A recent example is the model studied by Flaschel and Krolzig (2006), which constitutes the starting point of our analysis.[2] From a structural form involving both a wage and a price Phillips curve, they derive a dynamic equation for the wage–price spiral as the corresponding reduced form, in which the growth rate of the wage share is affected by the employment rate, the rate of capacity utilization, and the growth rate of labor productivity.

In this chapter, we are interested in the reduced form wage–price spiral that arises from the consideration of two separate Phillips curves in order to extend the now pretty standard (for the readership of a journal such as *International Review of Applied Economics*) structuralist macroeconomic model of demand-led growth and income distribution (Bhaduri and Marglin 1990a, b; Taylor 2004; Barbosa-Filho and Taylor 2006 are just a few examples) and study how this extended model constitutes an improvement towards our understanding of the US economy in the post-World War II era. The aim of structuralist models is to provide a description of the macroeconomy that focuses on the interaction between the rate of capacity utilization and one distributive variable, say the wage share.[3] Such an analysis is meant to be alternative to, and more truthful to Keynes' ideas and the Post-Keynesian tradition than the standard AD–AS framework. The demand side of the structuralist model is obtained from the equilibrium between savings and investment, and leads to a reduced form equation in which the rate of capacity utilization depends on income distribution. Such equation has been called alternatively "IS", or "effective demand regime" in the literature, and its slope depends on the structural characteristics of the economy. In the felicitous terminology coined by Bhaduri and Marglin (1990a), the demand regime is *profit-led*, or *exhilarationist* when capacity utilization reacts negatively to the wage share, whereas a positive impact on the wage share on capacity utilization implies that the demand regime is *wage-led*, or *stagnationist*. The supply side of the model has to do with the behavior of firms, and determines how output is distributed among wage and profit earners. In particular, the interest is in how variations in income distribution (i.e. the wage share) over time are affected by the rate of capacity utilization. The resulting long-run relation is usually called "producer's equilibrium" (PE), or "distributive schedule", and again its slope depends on the structural features of the economy. So far, the literature has been considering linear distributive schedules only. An upward sloping distributive schedule means that the economy displays a *profit squeeze* since the profit share is eroded as capacity utilization approaches its maximum level. Conversely, a downward sloping distributive schedule is traditionally referred to as exhibiting *forced saving*, because usually profit earners have higher propensity to save than wage earners, and therefore the closer the economy gets to full utilization the more the economy is pushed toward higher overall savings by the increase in the share of profits.

The elements of novelty we introduce in this chapter concern the distributive schedule, which we modify relative to the existing literature in view of both theoretical and empirical arguments. First, we provide a non-parametric estimation of the wage Phillips curve for post-war United States, resulting in a robust non-linear relation between wage inflation and employment rate. Second, we notice somewhat trivially that one can make use of Okun's Law, which links variations in capacity utilization to changes in the employment rate, to convert the wage–price spiral in reduced form into a dynamic equation that it is closely related to the distributive schedule. This combination of empirically-based and *a priori* restrictions allows us to study the implications of the estimated non-linearity for the shape of the distributive curve of the economy. An important feature of our distributive curve is that it displays profit squeeze at low and high levels of capacity utilization, and forced savings corresponding to an intermediate region.

Putting together the non-linear distributive schedule with the effective demand schedule, we are able to analyze in depth the dynamic properties of the economy, both in profit-led and wage-led effective demand regimes. Despite the very elementary modeling, the type of non-linearity we introduce gives rise to multiple equilibria in the distributive-demand framework, and these equilibria have different stability properties corresponding to different demand regimes. The possibility of multiple equilibria due to the shape of the distributive curve in a Post-Keynesian demand–distribution model is rather novel in the literature, at least to the best of our knowledge.

The key finding of our model is that a profit-led demand regime, which we show to be the empirically relevant case for the US economy, leads to three equilibria corresponding to different values of the wage share and of the rate of capacity utilization. The two "extreme" equilibria ($E_1$ and $E_3$ in Figure 16.3) are locally asymptotically stable, and display counterclockwise transitional dynamics. These features are qualitatively consistent with the available evidence on post-war United States (Barbosa-Filho and Taylor 2006). In view of such stability properties, we call "stable recession" the equilibrium featuring low capacity utilization (and "high" wage share), and "stable boom" the long-run position involving a high capacity utilization rate. The key force determining the stability properties of both these equilibria, given the profit-led demand, is an upward-sloping distributive curve in their respective regions of the phase space, that is a profit-squeeze effect. The stabilizing (destabilizing) effects of profit-squeeze (forced savings) are already known in the Post-Keynesian literature. The novelty in this contribution is that, differently from the existing investigations on the subject (Taylor 2004) in which a linear distributive curve can either be downward or upward sloping, the non-linearity in our distributive curve allows for both profit-squeeze and forced saving, corresponding to different ranges of capacity utilization.

The fact that a profit-led economy such as the US can have stable recessions and stable booms separated by an intermediate, mostly unstable region, has important implications for demand policies aimed at stimulating or contracting the macroeconomy. In fact, fighting a stable recession through expansionary demand policies requires strong, other than well-targeted measures, whereas cooling down an economy that is deemed to be overheated may result into forcing the system into a slump that will be hard to contrast. An intermediate equilibrium that is only saddle-path stable means indeed that there is only one stable dynamical path (and therefore only one initial condition) leading to it, from which the need of a very well-targeted measure aimed at reaching such equilibrium. The implication is that a weak measure will not be able to push the economy out of the basin of attraction of the stable recession. Conversely, too strong of a restriction to cool down an overheated system may push the dynamics toward the low-capacity equilibrium, which is dynamically stable and therefore hard to turn around.

The chapter is organized as follows. We first present some empirical evidence of demand–distribution cycles in the United States (1956–2004). Then, we review the baseline model by Flaschel and Krolzig (2006), and we introduce a non-linearity consistent with our estimation results into the wage Phillips curve to derive a non-linear distributive curve for the economy. Combining this long-run relation as the only departure from the existing literature with a standard demand regime borrowed from Barbosa-Filho and Taylor (2006), we present our full model of wage share-capacity utilization dynamics in Section 16.6, discussing both profit-led and wage-led scenarios. All these conclusions are drawn assuming an exogenous growth rate of labor productivity. As an extension, we study the implication of endogenizing labor productivity growth in the model, and show that the main conclusions are mostly robust to this generalization in Section 16.7 We then discuss the empirical relevance of profit-led versus wage-led demand regimes for the US economy according to the available evidence in Section 16.8. Section 16.9 concludes. The appendices to this chapter provide derivations of the relevant equations, and an explanation of the methodology used for estimation.

A notational convention, used to facilitate the exposition, is that functional relations are denoted by square brackets. For instance, the expression $\gamma[u - \bar{u}]$ denotes $\gamma[\cdot]$ being a *function* of the difference between $u$ and $\bar{u}$. Conversely, round parentheses are used for multiplication purposes: an expression like $\delta(e - \bar{e})$ denotes that $\delta$ is any variable multiplying the difference $e - \bar{e}$. Also, following the Post-Keynesian literature, we will use the terms *capital utilization* and *capacity utilization* alternatively.

## 16.2 Demand–distribution cycles in post-World War II United States

Demand–distribution cycles in post-war United States have been the subject of several important studies in the Post-Keynesian tradition (Barbosa-Filho and Taylor (2006), Bhaduri and Marglin (1990a, b), Hein and Vogel (2007), Stockhammer and Onaran (2004)). The available evidence points toward Goodwin-style cycles in the employment rate and the labor share. In the empirical plots shown in Figure 16.1 we depict estimated short phase and long phase cycles as against the six business cycles that were observed in the US economy from 1956:1 to 2004:4. The quarterly evolution of employment rate and wage share over time (dots), as well as their estimated non-linear trends, are plotted in the top two panels. On the other hand, the bottom left panel illustrates the observed pairs (dots), and the estimated short phase cycles (the solid line, with circles denoting confidence intervals) occurring in employment rate and labor share, whereas the corresponding estimated long phase cycle is shown in the bottom right panel.[4] As shown in Kauermann et al. (2008), all business cycles have by and large the same counterclockwise orientation, and so does the long-phase cycle. Such paths in macroeconomic fluctuations point toward an explanation that emphasizes the distributional conflict between capital and labor, and the role of unemployment as a discipline mechanism on wage demands by workers. High employment generates wage inflation which, as long as real wages increase more than labor productivity, increases the wage share in output. The resulting decrease in the profit share, in Kaleckian fashion, will however reduce future investment and output. Lower output will in turn reduce labor demand and employment and consequently lead to lower wage inflation or even deflation and thus reduce the labor share. But a higher profit share will produce a surge in investment. This will lead to greater employment and thus improve the bargaining power of workers and consequently wages in Phillips curve fashion. At this point, the wage share in output has increased, and the cycle can repeat itself.

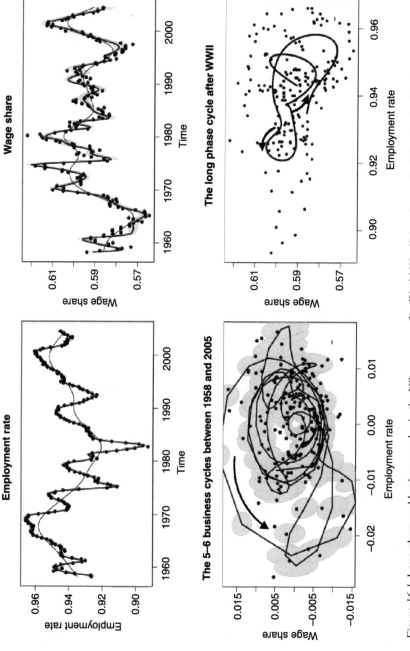

*Figure 16.1* Long phase and business cycles in the US economy after World War II (see Appendix II for the details of the applied econometric technique).

The bottom right panel in Figure 16.1 suggests that the depressed cycles are at most two in number. Nevertheless, the presence of business cycles around low and high equilibrium levels of capacity utilization is hard to justify in models, such as the ones already in the literature, that are capable to produce a single dynamic equilibrium. In what follows, we will see that the inclusion of empirically-based non-linearities in the model can account for persistent periods of booms as well as recessions, and for transition dynamics that cycle for considerable time around either of these equilibria.

## 16.3 Crossover wage–price dynamics

The starting point for our analysis is a simplified version of the model of the wage–price spiral estimated by Flaschel and Krolzig (2006), which we modify to allow for labor productivity growth. The structural form is given by:[5]

$$\hat{w} = \beta_w\left(\bar{U}^l - U^l\right) + \kappa_w\left(\hat{p} + n_x\right) + (1-\kappa_w)(\pi^c + n_x), \quad \hat{w} \text{ wage inflation,}$$
$$\hat{p} = \beta_p\left(\bar{U}^c - U^c\right) + \kappa_p\left(\hat{w} - n_x\right) + (1-\kappa_p)\pi^c, \quad \hat{p} \text{ price inflation,} \tag{16.1}$$

where $w$ denotes the nominal wage, $p$ the aggregate price level, $U^l$ is the rate of unemployment of labor, $U^c$ denotes the complement to one of the rate of capital utilization, the bars indicate inflationary barriers for the two variables, $n_x$ stands for the exogenous rate of Harrod-neutral technical change, and $\pi^c$ is a term that captures expectations about inflation, which we will refer to as *inflationary climate* in what follows. The wage share $v$ is the ratio of the real wage $w/p$ over labor productivity $x$. Define furthermore the labor employment rate as $e \equiv 1 - U^l$, $\bar{e} = 1 - \bar{U}$, and similarly the rate of capital utilization as $u \equiv 1 - U^c$, $\bar{u} \equiv 1 - \bar{U}^c$. In Appendix I, we show that the following reduced-form equation for the evolution of the wage share can be derived from (16.1):

$$\hat{v} = \kappa\left((1-\kappa_p)\beta_w(e-\bar{e}) - (1-\kappa_w)\beta_p(u-\bar{u})\right) \tag{16.2}$$

where $\kappa \equiv (1-\kappa_p\kappa_w)^{-1}$. Equation (16.4) shows that the growth rate of the wage share responds to both utilization rates in labor and capital inputs, other than of course to labor productivity growth.[6] Assuming linear coefficients and Okun's Law $e - \bar{e} = \sigma(u - \bar{u})$[7] it is easy to find that, since $\kappa > 0$ the labor share adjustment responds positively (negatively) to the rate of capacity utilization if and only if

$$\alpha \equiv (1-\kappa_p)\sigma\beta_w - (1-\kappa_w)\beta_p > 0 \quad \text{(respectively} < 0). \tag{16.3}$$

Proaño et al. (2007) denoted the case of a positive response of $\hat{v}$ on economic activity ($\alpha > 0$) as *labor market-led* wage-adjustment process, and defined the wage-adjustment to be *goods market led* when $\alpha < 0$ holds. The intuition is that, when $\alpha > 0$, it is the labor market that drives the adjustment process since the effect of higher employment on wage share growth dominates the effect of higher capacity utilization. Conversely, when $\alpha < 0$ it is the latter effect that dominates in determining the growth rate of the labor share.

In Post-Keynesian macroeconomic modeling, it is common to consider not only a relation like (16.2) in which changes in the wage share respond to the rate of capital utilization, but also the way in which changes in wage share affect the capital utilization rate. Such relation determines the so-called *effective demand regime* of the economy. If capital utilization reacts positively to the wage share, the demand for goods is said to be *wage-led*, while if variations in the wage share cause changes in capital utilization rate of opposite sign the demand regime is said to be *profit-led*.

The sign of the parameter $\alpha$, combined with the characteristics of the demand regime of the economy, determines whether real wage adjustments have stabilizing or destabilizing effects. Wage adjustments will have stabilizing effects if the negative response of investment to changes in real wages outweighs the positive response of consumption, and if wages are more flexible to labor demand pressures than prices to goods market pressures (or both v.v.). Conversely, if investment reacts less than consumption to a change in real wages and wages remain more flexible than prices (in terms each of their own demand pressures), or both v.v., then real wage adjustments will show destabilizing effects. The four possible scenarios are presented in Table 13.2, taken from Proaño et al. (2007), Where however a deeper discussion of such is not within the scopes of this chapter.

## 16.4 Non-linear workforce demand pressure: the distributive curve

Consider now the term $\beta_w(e - \bar{e})$ in (16.2), describing how the wage share reacts to the employment rate level. As opposed to Flaschel and Krolzig (2006), who estimated a VAR for the US economy assuming a constant parameter $\beta_w$, in what follows we will consider instead a p-spline estimation of the US money-wage Phillips curve, where 'p' stands for 'penalized'. The estimation technique is described in Appendix II, and amounts, as it is standard in non-parametric estimation, to assume the functional relation among the dependent and the predetermined variables to be an unknown but smooth function. The outcome of estimation will be a *plot*, as opposed to a vector of parameters which is the outcome of parametric estimation. In particular, we find the non-linear relationship between wage inflation and demand pressure on the labor market shown in the top panel in Figure 16.2: the curve is increasing up to an employment rate of slightly more than 92 percent, then has an almost flat or at most slightly decreasing region, and eventually becomes again increasing for values of the unemployment rate smaller than 6 percent.[8]

A typical element of interest in spline estimates is also the plot of the first derivative of the function. The first derivative of our wage–employment relation is displayed in the bottom graph appearing in Figure 16.2. By looking at the two portions of the figure, we see that the curve is increasing but concave, until an

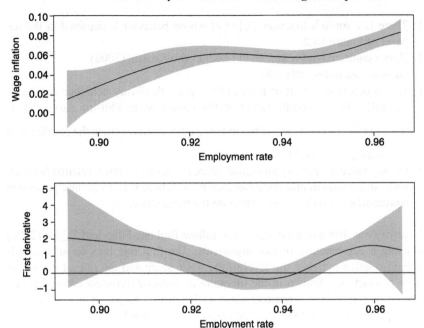

*Figure 16.2* P-spline estimation of the wage-inflation/employment-rate schedule and its first derivative (with confidence intervals shown as grey areas).

inflexion point around a 6.5 percent unemployment rate, after which the curve becomes convex, first decreasing then increasing. Eventually, there is another inflexion point around an employment rate of 95.5 percent or so, and the final portion of the curve is increasing, but concave again. From the bottom graph, we can locate the unconditional mean of the first derivative of $\beta_w$ around 0.6.

A standard Keynesian economic intuition behind the behavior of the curve will focus on the bargaining power of labor supply. For high levels of unemployment, the workers' bargaining power is small: they (or the labor union representing them) will accept only small increases, or even resign themselves to small decreases in the nominal wage in order to increase the employment rate. Corresponding to the center of the curve, there is a flat region where labor is resisting wage inflation decreases at the given expected price inflation. Finally, as soon as the unemployment rate is below its inflationary barrier, workers will exercise their increased bargaining power in requiring significantly more than proportional increases in wage inflation (as compared to price inflation). In view of such arguments, let us reconsider equation (16.2). Given the above non-linearity, it makes sense to consider the term $\beta_w[\cdot]$ as a general, non-linear function of the employment gap, and not a constant parameter.

In order to obtain a distributive curve in reduced form, we make the following assumptions:

1. There is a smooth function $\beta_w[e-\bar{e}]$ whose behavior is depicted in the top panel of Figure 16.2.
2. $\beta_p$ is a constant coefficient, as in Flaschel and Krolzig (2006).
3. Okun's Law holds: $\sigma(u-\bar{u}) = e - \bar{e}$.
4. Very much in the spirit of Rose (1967), price flexibility is higher than wage flexibility in the middle range of the money-wage Phillips curve that is
   $(1-\kappa_p)\sigma\dfrac{\partial\beta_w}{\partial u} - (1-\kappa_w)\beta_p < 0$ within the relevant range (note the parallel with
   $\alpha < 0$ in equation 16.3).
5. For any value of capacity utilization, there is a negative, linear relation between wage share growth and the difference $v - \bar{v}$, where $\bar{v}$ is a constant parameter representing an inflationary barrier on the wage share.

To justify our fifth assumption, we can follow Barbosa-Filho and Taylor (2006) in using a combination of two arguments. The first one lays on an upward-sloping relation between the level of the wage share and the rate of growth of labor productivity, known in the literature as *induced technical change* effect. Generally, this effect is positive since higher wages to pay will induce firms in adopting more labor-saving techniques. The second argument is that the bargaining power of the labor force increases with the wage share. Thus, the rate of growth of the real wage $\hat{\omega}$ should depend positively on the wage share. Assuming both relations to be linear, if the induced technical change effect is higher than the bargaining power effect on the real wage, then the rate of growth of the wage share should be negatively affected by its own level. A different story, which however shares the same ending, is told in Flaschel and Krolzig (2006). They assume that an increasing wage share will dampen the evolution of wage inflation, building on Blanchard and Katz (1999) to "microfound" this negative relation with a bargaining argument. What matters for the purposes of our analysis here is that a negative relation between $\hat{v}$ and $v$ is confirmed by the empirical evidence presented in both papers, and these findings provide further support for our assumption.

We claim that the features of our framework, combining elements coming from empirical findings with *a priori* restrictions on the relations between the variables of interest are interesting enough to be exploited in imposing the following dynamic equation for the evolution of the wage share over time:

$$\hat{v} = \kappa\left((1-\kappa_p)\beta_w[\sigma(u-\bar{u})] - (1-\kappa_w)\beta_p(u-\bar{u})\right) - \beta_{vv}(v-\bar{v}) \tag{16.4}$$

where $-\beta_{vv} < 0$ constant, and $\bar{v}$ denotes inflationary barriers on the labor share.[9] Equation (16.4) implies that the growth rate of the wage share is increasing in capacity utilization when $\dfrac{\partial\beta_w}{\partial u} > \dfrac{1-\kappa_w}{\sigma(1-\kappa_p)}\beta_p$, a case which corresponds to the

labor-market led wage adjustment described above, and that $\dfrac{\partial\hat{v}[\cdot]}{\partial u} < 0$ otherwise.[10]

Therefore, the stationary points of this composite function will lay where
$$\frac{\partial \beta_w}{\partial u} = \frac{1 - \kappa_w}{\sigma(1 - \kappa_p)} \beta_p.$$

We are now ready to characterize the isocline relating wage share to capacity utilization, that is the *distributive curve* of our economy. To do so, it is sufficient to solve (16.4) for $v$ by setting the time-derivative of the wage share equal to zero:

$$v[u, \overline{u}, \overline{v}, n_x] = \overline{v} + \frac{\kappa}{\beta_{vv}} \big( (1 - \kappa_p)\beta_w [\sigma(u - \overline{u})] - (1 - \kappa_w)\beta_p(u - \overline{u}) \big). \tag{16.5}$$

In Post-Keynesian macroeconomics, it is common to look at the sign of the first partial derivative of the function with respect to $u$ in order to interpret the shape of the distributive curve.[11] We say that the economy is "Marxist" or it exhibits *profit-squeeze* if $\frac{\partial v}{\partial u} > 0$, given that an increase in capacity utilization will determine a falling profit share. Conversely, $\frac{\partial v}{\partial u} < 0$ means that the economy displays *forced saving* along "Kaldorian" lines (Taylor 2004), given that the increase in the profit share associated with a higher utilization rate translates *à la* Kaldor into higher savings. Our assumptions ensure that the non-linear distributive curve features profit-squeeze at low and high capacity utilization rates, and forced savings corresponding to an intermediate region of $u$, as shown in Figure 16.3. In particular, since $\beta_{vv} > 0$, the isocline (16.5) will display profit-squeeze for rates of capacity utilization such that $\frac{\partial \beta_w}{\partial u} > \frac{1 - \kappa_w}{\sigma(1 - \kappa_p)} \beta_p$, and forced saving otherwise.

The behavior of the isocline is depicted in Figures 16.3 and 16.4.

## 16.5 The demand regime

The characterization of the demand regime is completely standard in our model. Consider first how the adjustment process of capital utilization rate is affected by variations in the wage share, or equivalently the effective demand regime adjustment process. Departing only slightly from textbook Post-Keynesian macroeconomics (Taylor 2004), assume that there is a linear relation, captured by a constant parameter $\beta_{uv}$, between the growth rate of capacity utilization and the difference $v - \overline{v}$, where $\overline{v}$ is a constant inflationary barrier on the wage share. A profit-led economy corresponds to the case in which $\beta_{uv} < 0$, whereas if $\beta_{uv} > 0$ we say that the economy is wage-led.

Then, consider the impact of capacity utilization on its growth rate, recalling that capacity utilization is defined as the ratio between output (say $X$) and installed capacity, so that the growth rate of $u$ equals the difference between output growth and the growth rate of installed capacity. Two arguments support a negative relation between $\hat{u}$ and $u$. The first one is the rates of output and installed capacity respectively. Barbosa-Filho and Taylor (2006) provide linear equations for the output general consensus on the basic Keynesian stability condition, according to which $\partial \dot{X} / X < 0$.[12] One has, however, to consider also the effect of an increase in the capital utilization rate on the productive capacity of the economy. Generally, capital formation responds positively to the level of economic activity (which can be interpreted as an acceleration principle). It follows immediately that the rate of growth of capacity is negatively affected by the level of capacity utilization.

In view of such arguments, we have the following dynamic equation for the evolution of capacity utilization:

$$\hat{u} = \beta_{uv}(v - \bar{v}) - \beta_{uu}(u - \bar{u}), \quad \beta_{uu} > 0, \quad \beta_{uv} \begin{cases} > 0 & \text{if wage-led} \\ < 0 & \text{if profit-led} \end{cases} \tag{16.6}$$

The isocline $\dot{u}[\cdot] = 0$ will be of the form:

$$u[v, \bar{v}, \bar{u}] = \bar{u} + \frac{\beta_{uv}}{\beta_{uu}}(v - \bar{v}). \tag{16.7}$$

Under the above assumptions, the demand regime of our simple economy has a positive (negative) intercept and negative (positive) slope if the economy is profit-led (wage-led).[13]

## 16.6 The dynamical system

We are now able to study qualitatively the dynamics of the economy described by the system of equations formed by (16.4) and (16.6). Such dynamics take place in the phase space $(u, v)$, where the isoclines describing long-run relations between the two variables of interest are represented by (16.5) and (16.7).

First of all, due to the non-linear shape of the distributive curve, there are likely multiple equilibria in this model, corresponding to different points at which the isoclines intersect. Furthermore, the stability properties of such steady states depend on the features of the demand regime of the economy.

In order to get started in our stability analysis, let us evaluate the Jacobian matrix of the dynamical system at the steady states $(u_0, v_0)$:

$$J[u_0, v_0] = \begin{pmatrix} -\beta_{uu}u_o & \beta_{uv}u_o \\ \kappa(\sigma(1-\kappa_p)\frac{\partial \beta_w}{\partial u}[u_o - \bar{u}] & -(1-\kappa_w)\beta_p]v_o - \beta_{vv}v_o \end{pmatrix}$$

so that we can analyze the profit-led case and the wage-led case by looking at the sign of the parameter $\beta_{uv}$.

### Profit-led demand regime

In the profit-led case, $\beta_{uv} < 0$. Thus, when the distributive curve has a positive slope, the determinant of our Jacobian matrix is positive. Given the negative trace, both eigen-values are negative, and an equilibrium corresponding to this situation is locally asymptotically stable. For such reasons, we will refer to an equilibrium like $E_1$ in Figure 16.3 as a *stable depression* and to an equilibrium like $E_3$ as a *stable boom*, because of the low and high value of capacity utilization respectively. Conversely, when the slope of the locus $\dot{v} = 0$ is negative, the corresponding equilibrium will be a saddlepoint. Figure 16.3 displays the phase diagram corresponding to a profit-led economy when the slope of the locus $\dot{u} = 0$ is such that the two curves intersect three times. As shown in the figure, the dynamics around the steady states $E_1$ and $E_3$ feature the same counterclockwise behavior, although the negative trace of the Jacobian matrix ensures the convergence of these oscillations towards the steady states. As in Barbosa-Filho and Taylor (2006), this is due to the positive slope of the distributive curve in those regions, meaning that there is a stabilizing profit-squeeze effect. On the other hand, since at the intermediate equilibrium $E_2$ the distributive curve has a negative slope and intersects the demand regime "from above", this steady state has the features of a saddlepoint.

Thus, Figure 16.3 can be seen as somewhat combining the two cases discussed in Barbosa-Filho and Taylor (2006) with regard to the US economy (1948–2001): they generally find a stabilizing profit squeeze effect, but in the period 1955–70 the forced saving switch in the distributive curve determines an unstable equilibrium. It must be noted that in their paper Barbosa-Filho and Taylor (2006) have explicit time series thresholds for the change in slope. The explanation we provide is instead in terms of quantitative values of the two variables of interest. Also, while in their paper they found a demand regime steeper than the distributive curve, here the opposite is true. Thus, our intermediate equilibrium

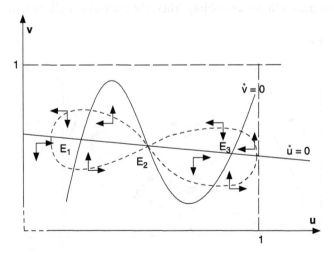

*Figure 16.3* Phase diagram for the profit-led demand regime.

$E_2$ is saddle-path stable. Of course, the slope of the demand regime matters, in what determines how many equilibria we will find in our system.[14]

Given the negative slope of the demand regime in this case, we find a trade-off between short-run growth and redistribution toward wages, which is a traditional feature of a profit-led economy (Bhaduri and Marglin 1990b, Naastepad 2006): in order to stimulate the economy toward a higher capital utilization rate over the business cycle, a reduction in the wage share is needed.[15]

### Remark

If the economy is fluctuating around the extreme equilibria and comes closer to the intermediate one, a small shock may suffice to move it into one of the basins of attraction of the steady states $E_1$ or $E_2$ so that the business cycle will then change its course and converge either do to depressed of a boom situation. Convergence into the depressed basin may for example be the situation experienced in Germany, while the US economy seems to fluctuate outside the basins of attraction of the investigated dynamics, as Figure 16.1 shows.

### *Wage-led demand regime*

A wage-led demand regime leads to some complications in the phase plots. Since the locus $\dot{u} = 0$ has a negative intercept on the $v$-axis, an equilibrium with a very low rate of both capital utilization and wage share could disappear, as it is shown in Figure 16.4. According to the slope of the demand regime curve, there is even the possibility that the only surviving steady state is an intermediate one.

As far as the stability properties of the equilibria in the wage-led case, again we look at the Jacobian matrix of the system. Given the positive value of $\beta_u$, when the slope of the distributive curve is negative, the determinant will be positive, and the negative trace will ensure stability. Then, the clockwise oscillations around an

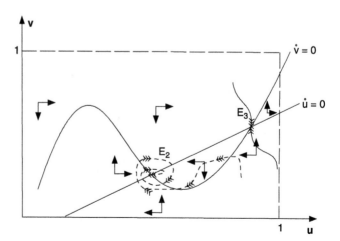

*Figure 16.4* Phase diagram for the wage-led demand regime.

intermediate equilibrium like $E_2'$ will converge eventually to that steady state. Conversely, when the slope of the distributive curve is positive, the corresponding equilibrium will be a saddle. It is worth to observe that the wage-led case appears counterfactual to the empirical situation found to characterize the US economy after World War II: not only the estimated long-phase cycle, but also all business cycles have a counterclockwise orientation.

*Policy implications*

Note also the difference between the two different demand scenarios in terms of policy implications. In a profit-led economy, starting from an equilibrium like $E_1$ in Figure 16.3, fiscal or monetary policy aimed at stimulating the economy needs to be very strong to be effective. If this is the case, it will lead to a situation of the type $E_3$, but will pay a price in terms of distributive conflict. Conversely, suppose that policy makers worry about the distributional implications of an economy fluctuating around an equilibrium like $E_3$ in Figure 16.3, and that they would prefer a situation like $E_2$. Since there is only one stable saddle path leading to the desired equilibrium among the infinite possible ones, a restriction will need to be tailored very closely in order to achieve the desired goal. In fact, if the restriction is too weak, it will fail in moving the dynamics away from the basin of attraction of $E_3$; if the restriction is too strong, it will produce the undesired effect of leading the economy into a stable (i.e. hard to fight) recession.

On the other hand, in a wage-led scenario, if the economy is in (or around) equilibrium, a further stimulus to the economic activity can have a very hard time in achieving the desired effects, because of the uniqueness of the stable saddle path ensuring convergence to an equilibrium like $E_3$. Conversely, if policy makers acting in a wage-led economy deem it overheated at an equilibrium like $E_3$ they will find easy to sort the desire effects adopting restrictive policy measures, but they will pay the price of a lower wage share.

The analysis of these two different kinds of asymmetry in the effectiveness of demand policy deserves further attention, and is left for future research here, together with deeper considerations about the mechanisms behind the agents' expectations.

## 16.7 A simple extension: endogenous productivity growth

We now relax the assumption of exogenous Harrod-neutral technical change we made so far, in order to account for the dynamic effects that arise when labor productivity growth is allowed to respond to variations in capacity utilization and the wage share. The purpose of this section is to show that the behavior of the distributive curve does not change qualitatively when labor productivity varies endogenously with capacity and the distributive shares, so that dynamics of the model studied so far carry over to this more general scenario. First, it is quite standard to assume that the growth rate of labor productivity responds positively to the rate of capacity utilization. The justification for such assumption, known in the literature as the Kaldor–Verdoorn relation, can be found in the presence of increasing returns that make labor more productive as the utilization of installed capacity increases. On the other hand, the traditional (and very well known to economists working in Marxian or Post-Keynesian frameworks) induced technical change mechanism according to which capitalist firms innovate in order to reduce production (in particular labor) costs points toward imposing a positive relationship between the wage share and labor productivity growth (Kennedy (1964), Drandakis and Phelps (1966) are cornerstone papers on induced technical change. Recent developments can be found in Tavani 2009, 2010). To keep things as simple as possible, we impose the following linear relationship:

$$n_x = \bar{n} + n_{xu}(u - \bar{u}) + n_{xv}(v - \bar{v}) \tag{16.8}$$

with $n_{xu} > 0, \beta_{vv} > n_{xv} > 0$. In Appendix III, we show that this new specification for labor productivity growth implies exactly the same dynamics for the distributive curve.[16] Thus, the dynamic analysis presented above survives the endogenous productivity growth scenario.

## 16.8 An empirical comparison

Consider Figure 16.1 again. Inspecting the measured long phase cycle for the US economy in more detail shows that the wage share can increase again during phases of significant unemployment of both labor and capital (top right panel). This further loop is in fact of the Goodwin (1967) type, and is not possible in the many conventional studies of Goodwin's growth cycle model. However, it is perfectly in line with what we have derived in Figure 16.3, and shows that the area around the stable depression is indeed relevant for one episode in the evolution of the distributional conflict in the US economy.

We argue on the basis of this analysis that our simple model is already rich enough to allow for persistent periods of booms, and for considerably long depressions that may need economic policy interventions aimed at avoiding economic breakdowns along some of the trajectories of the dynamics.

We also control for the dramatic increase in wage inequality, in particular the increase in wage earnings at the top of wage distribution which is deemed to be largely responsible for the stability of the wage share and profit share (Piketty and Saez 2003, 2006).[17] Figure 16.5 plots annual data for employment rate and several measures of the labor share, obtained subtracting the share of top 10 percent, top 5 percent, and top 1 percent wage earners respectively from the standard measure of the wage share. The data on the labor share are constructed using the Hodrick–Prescott (HP) filter on the relevant series in the database by Piketty and Saez (2003), while the data on the employment rate is constructed HP-filtering the complement to one of the annual average of monthly unemployment rate from the Bureau of Labor Statistics.[18] As apparent from the plots, the counterclockwise cycles are by and large robust to different specifications of the labor share in national income, at least as far as this sample period is considered.

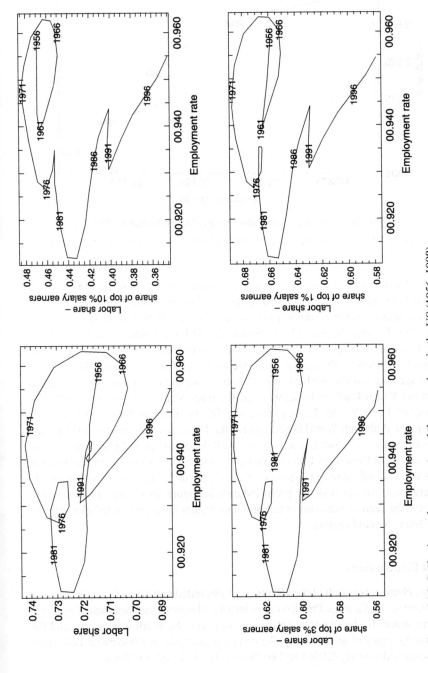

*Figure 16.5* Cycles in employment rate and the wage share in the US (1956–1998).

*Sources:* Piketty and Saez (2003) (Labor Share), annual average of BLS monthly data (employment rate).

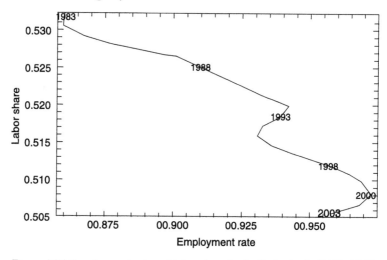

*Figure 16.6* Employment rate and labor share in the Netherlands (1983–2003).

*Sources:* WDI (employment rate), Extended Penn World Table 3.0 (wage share).

Finally, for the sake of cross-country comparisons, it is interesting to look at the behavior of the employment rate against the wage share in a wage-led economy. Several influential studies in the Post-Keynesian tradition (Naastepad 2006, Naastepad and Storm 2008) have found evidence that the effective demand regime in the Netherlands is wage-led. Figure 16.6 displays the (annual) HP-trend of the employment rate plotted against the (annual) HP-trend of the wage share in the Netherlands. The series for the employment rate is taken from the World Bank website, whereas the wage share series is taken from the Extended Penn World Table (3.0) compiled by Duncan Foley and Adalmir Marquetti. Although World Bank data for the Netherlands do not go further back than 1983, and therefore it is hard to see at all the occurrence of cycles in the plot, the movement from top left to bottom right is clear. Such movement is compatible with the kind of wage-led dynamics around the stable equilibrium illustrated in Figure 16.4, but not with the profit-led case in Figure 16.3. Thus, this empirical plot can be seen as confirming the previous results on the wage-led character of the Dutch demand regime.

## 16.9 Conclusions

In this chapter, we studied the effects of an estimated non-linearity in the demand pressure term of a wage Phillips curve into an otherwise standard Post-Keynesian macro model of the dynamic interaction between the distributive curve and the demand regime of an economy. To carry our analysis, we borrowed both from Flaschel and Krolzig (2006) and Barbosa-Filho and Taylor (2006).

We showed that, because of the non-linearity in the distributive curve, multiple equilibria are a likely outcome of this model. In a profit-led economy, which the empirical analysis substantiates to be the relevant case for post-war United States, there are three equilibria corresponding to different values of the wage share and of the rate of capacity utilization: (i) an economic boom with relatively high capacity utilization and relatively low wage share, (ii) a recession with relatively low capacity utilization and relatively high wage share, and (iii) an intermediate equilibrium. Booms and recessions are locally stable in the profit-led scenario of our model, and generate counterclockwise dynamics in capital utilization rate and the wage share. These features are all qualitatively consistent with the available evidence on the so-called distributive-demand cycles in post-war United States (Barbosa-Filho and Taylor 2006). Given the slope of the demand regime, the stability of booms and recessions in our model depends on the stabilizing profit squeeze effect in the distributive curve, consistently to previous findings in the related literature. We also showed that the counterclockwise cycles do not seem to be affected, at least for the sample period considered in Figure 16.5, by the sharp increase in wage inequality occurred in the past two decades and documented in recent literature (Picketty and Saez, 2003, 2006).

The intermediate equilibrium we find is instead saddle-path stable, due to a downward-sloping distributive curve which crosses the profit-led demand regime from above in the relevant region of the phase space. We argued that the instability associated with a saddle-path intermediate equilibrium poses challenges to policy makers both willing to fight recessions and to cool down an overheated economy. In the first case, any stimulus to aggregate demand with the purpose of bringing back the economy to its virtuous circle needs to be very strong to be effective. If the policy makers think instead that the economy looping around its boom phase is overheated, they may end up either finding a small contraction ineffective in what it may not be enough to get away from the basin of attraction of the boom they want to fight, or stuck in a stable recession if the contraction is too strong. These implications are only sketched in the model, because we didn't include any explicit policy variables in it. However, they seem to be interesting enough to be explored in a framework with monetary and fiscal instruments available to policy makers.

## Appendix I: derivation of equation 16.2

Using the newly defined variables $e, u$, the two equations in (1) are then modified as follows:

$$\hat{w} - n_x = \beta_w \left( (1 - \bar{e}) - (1 - e) \right) + (1 - \kappa_w)\pi^c + \kappa_w \hat{p}$$
$$= \beta_w (e - \bar{e}) + (1 - \kappa_w)\pi^c + \kappa_w \hat{p},$$

$$\hat{p} = \beta_p\big((1-\bar{u})-(1-u)\big)+\kappa_p(\hat{w}-n_x)+(1-\kappa_p)\pi^c$$
$$= \beta_p(u-\bar{u})+(1-\kappa_p)\pi^c+\kappa_p(\hat{w}-n_x).$$

These equations capture the dynamics of (nominal) wage share growth and of the inflation rate. Subtracting $\pi^c$ on both sides in both of the last equations, we obtain a two equation system in the variables $\hat{w}-n_x-\pi^c,\ \hat{p}-\pi^c$ which, given that the term $\pi^c$ captures the agents' expectations about the evolution of prices in the economy, captures the expected evolution of the (real) wage share and the forecasting error in the inflation rate. This system can be rewritten in matrix form as:

$$\begin{pmatrix} 1 & -\kappa_w \\ -\kappa_p & 1 \end{pmatrix}\begin{pmatrix} \hat{w}-n_x-\pi^c \\ \hat{p}-\pi^c \end{pmatrix}=\begin{pmatrix} \beta_w(e-\bar{e}) \\ \beta_p(u-\bar{u}) \end{pmatrix}. \tag{16.9}$$

Defining $\kappa \equiv (1-\kappa_p\kappa_w)^{-1}$, the solution of (2) yields:

$$\hat{w}-n_x-\pi^c = \kappa\big(\beta_w(e-\bar{e})+\kappa_w\beta_p(u-\bar{u})\big),$$
$$\hat{p}-\pi^c = \kappa\big(\kappa_p\beta_w(e-\bar{e})+\beta_p(u-\bar{u})\big).$$

Using the fact that $\hat{v} \equiv \hat{w}-\hat{p}-n_x$ in subtracting the second equation from the first one, we immediately have (16.2).

## Appendix II: penalized spline estimates

For the estimation of the wage Phillips curve a penalized spline approach has been used (see for instance Ruppert et al. 2003), such that the (penalized) log likelihood for normal errors can be written as

$$l[\theta] = -\big(y-C\theta\big)^2/\sigma^2 - \lambda_1\theta^T D_1\theta-\ldots-\lambda_m\theta^T D_m\theta \tag{16.10}$$

with the combined design matrix $C = (X\,Z)$ containing the fixed effect design matrix $X = \big(1\,x_{1i}\ldots x_{1i}^{q_1}\,x_{2i}\ldots x_{2i}^{q_2}\ldots x_{mi}\ldots x_{mi}^{q_m}\big)_{i=1,\ldots,n}$ and the truncated spline basis $Z = (Z_1\ldots Z_m)$ with the $j$-th truncated spline basis defined by $Z_j = \big((x_{ji}-\tau_{1,j})_+^{q_j}+\ldots\ldots+(x_{ji}-\tau_{K,j})_+^{q_j}\big)_{i=1,\ldots,n}$ which are constructed with the truncation function $(x)_+^q := \max\{0,x\}^q$ and the $K$ knots $\tau_{1,j},\ldots,\tau_{K,j}$ for the $j$-th dependent variable $x_{j1},\ldots,x_{jn}$. We have chosen different orders of the truncated polynomial, i.e. $q_1,\ldots,q_n$, just to ensure that the structure for the unknown functions for some dependant variables have not been chosen to be too complex and for some variables we need to choose a higher order to visualize the first derivative of the estimated function in a smooth way. In the same way we could have choose different numbers of knots for each variable but to keep things simple we have used the same number of knots for all variables. The main diagonal of the penalty matrix $D_l$ contain a one if the index belong to the truncated spline basis $Z_l$ and otherwise the element contain a zero, i.e. $D_l = \left(d_{ij}\right)_{i=1,\dots,mK+q+1}^{j=1,\dots,mK+q+1}$ with $q = \sum_{i=1}^{m} qi$ and $d_{ij} = 1_{\{i=j\}} 1_{\{i\{q+2+(l-1)K,\dots,q+1+lK\}\}}$. The smoothing parameters $\lambda_1,\dots,\lambda_m$ control the complexity of the structure for the unknown functions and should be chosen carefully. No penalization $\lambda_j = 0$ result in a too complex function with $q_j + K$ degrees of freedom and a highly penalized function ($\lambda_j \to \infty$) result in a function of order $q_j$. We are following the suggestion of Krivobokova and Kauermann (2007) to use the REML estimator for smoothing parameters to avoid misleading parameters because of misspecified autocorrelated errors.

For the wage Phillips curve we are describing the wage inflation (y) by the variables price inflation ($x_1$), the log of the wage share ($x_2$),[19] the employment rate ($x_3$) and the price inflation climate ($x_4$). In a first step we have set the order of the truncated splines to one, i.e. $q_1 = \dots = q_4 = 1$, to avoid misleading estimations because of too complex functional relationships. The resulting estimating show, that the price inflation and the wage share are linear related with the wage inflation. The employment rate and the price climate are in a non-linear way related with the wage inflation, and even more the functional form for employment rate uses more than three degrees of freedom, such that a higher polynomial order could be used. In our second step, setting $q_3 = 2$, the resulting estimation is nearly similar to our first one such that the same smoothing parameters $\lambda_1$ and $\lambda_2$ and the same shape of functions for the employment rate and the price climate are estimated.

Similarly, for the price Phillips curve we are describing the price inflation (y) by the variables wage inflation ($x_1$), the log of the wage share ($x_2$), the utilization rate ($x_3$) and the price inflation climate ($x_4$). But in contrast to the wage Phillips curve the functional shape of the price Phillips curve with respect to the utilization rate is not distinctively different from a linear curve (as was the functional shape of the WPC with respect to the employment rate), which gives the reason why we have omitted the visualization of the PPC estimation.

For the joint estimation of the employment rate ($y_1$) and the log of the wage share ($y_2$) we are distinguishing between long-term and short-term trends which is usually done when estimating business cycles. But instead of treating the deviations from the long-term trend as errors we assume that the business cycles can be described by a functional form. Following Kauermann et al. (2008) we are assuming that the observations $y_t := (y_{1t}, y_{2t})^T$ can be described by a long-term trend $c[t] := (c_1[t], c_2[t])^T$ and a short-term trend $g[t] := (g_1[t], g_2[t])^T$, i.e. $y_t = c[t] + g[t] + \epsilon_t$ with normal residuals $\epsilon_t = (\epsilon_{1t}, \epsilon_{2t})^T \sim N(0, \sigma)$. The structure of the short-term trend is even more specified by setting $g[t] := (\rho[t] \cos \phi[t], \rho[t] \sin \phi[t])^T$ with $\rho[t]$ representing the radius and $\phi[t]$

the angle around the center $c[t]$. For the estimation of the short-term trend $g[t]$ polar coordinates are preferred because we assume that the speed and the direction of the trajectory for the detrended time series $y_t - c[t]$ are smooth functions over the time. The unknown functional forms of the radius $\rho[t]$, the angle $\phi[t]$ and the long-term trends $c_1[t]$ and $c_2[t]$ are captured by a penalized spline approach such that the structure and the degree of complexity has to be estimated with the data at hand. But instead of estimating the short- and long-term functions simultaneously a hybrid version has been used because of numerical reasons. At the first stage, the long-term trend is fitted by a given pair of long-term penalty parameters. At the second stage, the resulting detrended observations $y_t - \hat{c}[t]$ are used to get the estimations for the short-term functions using the REML estimation for choosing the optimal amount of smoothing for the radius and the angle. The optimal pair of long-term smoothing parameters has been chosen by the Akaike Information Criterion, see for justification Kauermann et al. (2008).

## Appendix III: the distributive curve with endogenous productivity growth

Making use of equation (16.8) into (16.4) yields, after some algebra, the following equation in the growth rate of the real wage:

$$\hat{w} - \hat{p} = \bar{n} + \kappa((1 - \kappa_p)\beta_w[\sigma(u - \bar{u})]$$

$$-(1 - \kappa_w - \kappa_n)\beta_p(u - \bar{u})) - (\beta_{vv} - n_{xv})(v - \bar{v}) \tag{16.11}$$

where $\kappa_n \equiv n_{xu}/\kappa$. This equation constitutes the distributive curve in the model with endogenous productivity growth letting $\hat{v} \equiv \hat{w} - \hat{p} - \bar{n}$.[20]

Under $\beta_{vv} > n_{xv}$, that is under the assumption that the effect of the wage share on its own growth rate (which as discussed in Assumption 5 in Section 16.4 already incorporates induced technical change considerations) dominates the (pure) induced technical change effect, it is easy to see that the presence of endogenous labor productivity growth makes very little difference as far as the behavior of the distributive curve is concerned. Indeed, it is actually pretty easy to check that the presence of $\kappa_n$ on the linear term appearing in (16.11) actually makes the inequalities that must be fulfilled for the distributive curve to have the shape under investigation less stringent.

## Appendix IV: data sources

The data for the plots used in Figure 16.1 are taken from the Federal Reserve Bank of St. Louis (see http://www.stls.frb.org/fred). The data are quarterly, seasonally

*Table 16.1* Data used for the plots in Figure 16.1

| Variable | Transformation | Mnemonic | Description of the untransformed series |
|----------|----------------|----------|------------------------------------------|
| $U$ | UNRATE/100 | UNRATE | Unemployment rate |
| $w$ | log(COMPNFB) | COMPNFB | Non-farm business sector: compensation per hour, 1992 = 100 |
| $p$ | log(GDPDEF) | GDPDEF | Gross national product: implicit price deflator, 1992 = 100 |
| $y{-}l$ | log(OPHNFB) | OPHNFB | Non-farm business sector: output per hour of all persons, 1992 = 100 |

adjusted and are all from 1956:1 to 2004:4. Except for the unemployment rate $U$ the log of the series are used.

The employment data for the Netherlands are taken from the WDI website: http://data.worldbank.org/data-catalog. Data for the wage share in the Netherlands are taken from EPWT 3.0, available at http://homepage.newschool.edu/ foleyd/ epwt/.

# Part V

# The road ahead

Neoclassical syntheses
and beyond

# 17 Keynesian business cycle analysis
## Past, present, future

### 17.1 Introduction: Keynesian AD–AS dynamics

During the last decade the New Keynesian approach to macroeconometric modeling has become standard for the study of monetary issues in the mainstream literature, despite its many shortcomings especially on the empirical level. Its advocates, however, stress its solid microfoundations as well as the "rational" forward-looking behavior of all agents as the great advantage of this school of thought.

Interestingly, however, is that the loglinear representation of the baseline New Keynesian model with both staggered wages and prices as formulated by Erceg et al. (2000) features remarkable formal similarities with the modeling of wage and price dynamics which the current authors have developed independently of the New Keynesian approach over the last two decades, see for example Chiarella and Flaschel (1996, 2000), Chiarella et al. (2009) and Chiarella, Flaschel and Franke (2005).

However the similarities between these two theoretical approaches to macroeconomic modeling are really superficial. Indeed, even though the resulting dynamic equations which describe the evolution of the macroeconomy look quite similar (in a striking way) in their state variable and sign structure, the modeling philosophy of each approach (with the New Keynesian focusing on general equilibrium and ours stressing the properties of disequilibria in an economy) are in direct opposition to each other, due to in particular the respective modeling of (inflationary) expectations.

The contrast is due to the non use of the rational expectations solution methodology in the matured dynamic AD–AS approach we are pursuing (where stability is rather achieved through assumptions on economic behavior) and the strict dependence of the New Keynesian dynamics on the rational expectations solution algorithms. These are convergent by definition and construction and at least initially work in a world where only the steady state position is stable in the deterministic core if determinacy is given.

The difference between the two modeling approaches, which cannot be reconciled or compromised, is therefore the way expectations are formed. In our dynamic AD–AS approach we have crossover short-run model consistent expectation coupled with medium-run inflation inertia in the real markets of the economy, made viable by the adjustment behavior in the markets for goods and for labor, whereas the purely forward looking New Keynesian baseline approach with both staggered wages and prices is restricted to the situation where unstable roots are equal in number to the self-referencing forward-looking variables (where then instability is overcome by the choice of an appropriate mathematical solution algorithm that guarantees convergence to the steady state of the dynamics in a stochastic environment). It seems to us that one of these scientific endeavors must sooner or later exhibit serious empirical shortcomings in the explanation of the working of capitalist market economies.

In this chapter we contrast these two competing theories of the business cycle, focusing on the role of the modeling of expectations for the stability (and determinacy) of the system. We start the discussion in Section 17.2 with a brief consideration of the achievements and problems of the traditional Neoclassical Synthesis, the compromise in macroeconomics before the monetarist alternative view became the dominant approach. The remainder of the chapter is structured as follows.

In Section 17.3 we discuss the deterministic skeleton of the New Keynesian AD–AS model and its dynamic implications, as well as its shortcomings. We do this from a continuous time perspective that allows the proof of assertions that are currently inaccessible in a discrete time framework. In Section 17.4 we present our alternative AD–AS model with sluggish price–quantity adjustment processes and show how it can be reduced to a 4-D dynamical system of intensive form variables. In Section 17.5 we analyze the dynamics of the model which reduce to a study of a 3-D dynamical system since one of the intensive form dynamical variables (the expectations of the inflationary climate) does not yet feed back into the rest of the system, due to the interest rate policy employed in this section. In Section 17.6 we outline our estimation procedure and the results of the estimates for the UK economy. Finally, in Section 17.7 we present some conclusions and provide suggestions for future extensions of the model.

## 17.2 Old Neoclassical Synthesis: classical theorems in a Keynesian setup?

In this section we briefly discuss the traditional AS–AD growth dynamics with prices set equal to marginal wage costs, and nominal wage inflation driven by an expectations augmented Phillips curve. Introducing myopic perfect foresight (i.e., the assumption of no errors with respect to the short-run rate of price inflation) into such a Phillips curve alters the dynamics implied by the model in a radical way, in fact towards globally stable (neo-)classical real growth dynamics with real wage rigidity and thus fluctuating rates of under- or over-employment. Furthermore, price level dynamics no longer feed back into these real dynamics and are now globally unstable. The accepted approach in the literature is then to go on from myopic perfect foresight to "rational expectations" and to construct a purely forward looking solution (which incorporates the whole future of the economy) by way of the so-called jump-variable technique of Sargent and Wallace (1973). However in our view this does not represent a consistent solution to the dynamic results obtained in this model type under myopic perfect foresight, as we shall argue in this chapter.

The case of myopic perfect foresight in a dynamic AD–AS model of business fluctuations and growth has been considered in very detailed form in Sargent (1987, Ch.5). The model of Sargent's so-called Keynesian dynamics is given by a standard combination of AD based on IS–LM, and AS based on the condition that prices always equal marginal wage costs, plus finally an expectations augmented money-wage Phillips curve or WPC. The specific features that characterize this textbook treatment of AS–AD–WPC are that investment includes profitability considerations besides the real rate of interest, that a reduced form PC is not immediately employed in this dynamic analysis, and most importantly that expectations are rational (i.e., of the myopic perfect foresight variety in the deterministic context). Consumption is based on current disposable income in the traditional way, the LM curve is of standard type and there is neoclassical smooth factor substitution along with the assumption that prices are set according to the marginal productivity principle – and thus optimal from the viewpoint of the firm. These more or less standard ingredients give rise to the following set of equations that determine the statically endogenous variables: consumption ($C$), investment ($I$), government expenditure ($G$), output ($Y$), interest ($r$), prices ($p$), taxes ($T$), the profit rate ($\rho$), employment ($L^d$) and the rate of employment ($e$, with $\bar{e}$ the rate of employment that reflects the NAIRU rate). These statically endogenous variables feed into the dynamically endogenous variables: the capital stock ($K$), labor supply ($L$) and the nominal wage level ($w$), for which growth laws of motion are also provided in the equations shown below. The equations are

$$C = c(Y + rB/p - \delta K - T), \tag{17.1}$$

$$I/K = i(\rho - (r - \pi)) + n, \quad \rho = \frac{Y - \delta K - \omega L^d}{K}, \tag{17.2}$$

$$G = gK, \quad g = \text{const.}, \tag{17.3}$$

$$Y \overset{IS}{=} C + I + \delta K + G, \tag{17.4}$$

$$M \overset{LM}{=} p(h_1 Y + h_2 (r_0 - r)W), \tag{17.5}$$

$$Y = F(K, L^d), \tag{17.6}$$

$$p \overset{AS}{=} w/F_L(K, L^d), \tag{17.7}$$

$$\hat{w} \overset{PC}{=} \beta_w(e-\bar{e})+\pi, \quad e = L^d/L, \tag{17.8}$$

$$\pi \overset{MPF}{=} \hat{p}, \tag{17.9}$$

$$\hat{K} = I/K, \tag{17.10}$$

$$\hat{L} = n \quad (=\hat{M} \quad \text{for analytical simplicity}). \tag{17.11}$$

We make the simplifying assumptions that all behavior is based on linear relationships in order to concentrate on the intrinsic nonlinearities of this type of AS–AD–WPC growth model. Furthermore, following Sargent (1987, Ch.5), we assume that $t = (T - rB/p)/K$ is a given magnitude and thus, like real government expenditure per unit of capital, $g$, a parameter of the model. This excludes feedbacks from government bond accumulation and thus from the government budget equation onto real economic activity. We thus concentrate on the working of the private sector with minimal interference from the side of fiscal policy, which is not an issue in this chapter. The model is fully backed-up by budget equations as in Sargent (1987): pure equity financing of firms, money and bond financing of the government budget deficit and money, bond and equity accumulation in the sector of private households. There is flow consistency, since the new inflow of money and bonds is always accepted by private households. Finally, Walras' Law of Stocks and the perfect substitute assumption for government bonds and equities ensure that equity price dynamics remain implicit. The LM-curve is thus the main representation of the financial part of the model, which is therefore still of a very simple type at this stage of its development.

The treatment of the resulting dynamics turns out to be not very difficult. In fact, equations (17.8) and (17.9) imply the real wage dynamics

$$\hat{\omega} = \beta_w(l^d/l - \bar{e}), \quad l^d = L^d/K, l = L/K.$$

From $\dot{K} = I = S = Y - \delta K - C - G$ and $\dot{L} = nL$ we furthermore get $\hat{l} = n - (y - \delta - c(y - \delta - t) - g) = n - (1-c)y - (1-c)\delta + ct - g$, with $y = Y/K = F(1, l^d) = f(l^d)$.
Finally, by equation (17.7) we obtain

$$\omega = f'(l^d), \text{ so that }, \quad l^d = (f')^{-1}(\omega) = h(\omega), \quad h' < 0.$$

Hence, the real dynamics of the model can be represented by the autonomous 2-D dynamical system

$$\hat{\omega} = \beta_w(h(\omega)/l - \bar{e}),$$
$$\hat{l} = n - (1-c)\delta - g + ct - (1-c)f(h(\omega)) = \hat{l}(\omega).$$

It is easy to show, see for instance Flaschel (1993), that this system is well-defined in the positive orthant of the phase space, has a unique interior steady state, which moreover is globally asymptotically stable in the considered domain. In fact, this is just the Solow (1956) growth dynamics with a real wage Phillips curve (real wage rigidity) and thus classical under- or over-employment dynamics if $\bar{e} < 1$). There may be a full-employment ceiling in this model type, but this is an issue of secondary importance here.

The unique interior steady state is given by

$$y_o = \frac{1}{1-c}[(1-c)\delta + n + g - ct] = \frac{1}{1-c}[n+g-t]+\delta+t,$$

$$l_o^d = f^{-1}(y_o), \quad \omega_o = f'(l_o^d), \quad l_o = l_o^d/\bar{e},$$

$$m_o = h_1 y_o, \quad \hat{p}_o = 0, \quad r_o = \rho_o = f(l_o^d) - \delta - \omega_o l_o^d.$$

Keynes' (1936) approach is almost entirely absent in this type of analysis, which seems to be Keynesian in nature (AS–AD), but which – due to the neglect of short-run errors in inflation forecasting – has become in fact of very (neo-)classical type. The marginal propensity to consume, the stabilizing element in Keynesian theory, is still present, but neither investment nor money demand plays a role in the real dynamics we have obtained from equations (17.1)–(17.11). Volatile investment decisions and financial markets are thus simply irrelevant for the real dynamics of this AS–AD growth model when *myopic* perfect foresight on the current rate of price inflation is assumed. What, then, remains for the role of traditional Keynesian "troublemakers", the marginal efficiency of investment and liquidity preference schedule? The answer again is, in technical terms, a very simple one:

We have for given $\omega = \omega(t)$ as implied by the real dynamics (due to the $I = S$ assumption)

$$(1-c)f(h(\omega)) - (1-c)\delta + ct - g = i(f(h(\omega)) - \delta - \omega h(\omega) - r + \hat{p}) + n,$$

from which we have

$$\hat{p} = \frac{1}{i}[(1-c)f(h(\omega)) - (1-c)\delta + ct - g - n]$$
$$- (f(h(\omega)) - \delta - \omega h(\omega)) + r = g(\omega) + r,$$

with an added reduced-form LM-equation of the type

$$r = \frac{h_1 f(h(\omega)) - m}{h_2} + r_0, \quad m = \frac{M}{pK}.$$

The foregoing equations imply

$$\hat{m} = \hat{M} - \hat{p} - \hat{K} = -g(\omega) - r_o + \frac{m - h_1 f(h(\omega))}{h_2} + \hat{l}(\omega),$$

as the non-autonomous[1] differential equation for the evolution of real money balances, as the reduced form representation of the nominal dynamics.[2] Due to this feedback chain, $\hat{m}$ depends positively on the level of $m$ and it seems that the jump-variable technique needs to be implemented in order to tame such explosive nominal processes. This means that we have to *assume* that the price level always instantaneously adjusts to a position – after each unanticipated policy shock for example – from where it can converge to the steady state again, that is in the present case, it must jump immediately into its new steady state position, see Flaschel (1993), Turnovsky (2000) and Flaschel et al. (1997) for details on this technique. Advocates of the jump-variable technique, consequently, are led to conclude that investment efficiency and liquidity preference only play a role in appended purely nominal processes (concerning jumps in the price level) and this solely in a stabilizing way, though with initially accelerating phases in the case of anticipated monetary and other shocks (that put the economy onto a stable arm of the new dynamics at the point in time where the considered shock actually occurs). A truly neoclassical synthesis.

By contrast, we believe that Keynesian IS–LM growth dynamics proper (demand driven growth and business fluctuations) must remain intact if (generally minor) errors in inflationary expectations are excluded from consideration in order to reduce the dimension of the model and to simplify the analysis of the dynamical system. A correctly formulated Keynesian approach to economic dynamics and fluctuating growth should not give rise to such a strange dichotomized system with classical real and purely nominal IS–LM inflation dynamics, here in fact of the most basic jump variable type, namely

$$\hat{m} = \frac{m - h_1 y_o}{h_2} \left[ \hat{p} = -\frac{(M/K)_o \frac{1}{p} - h_1 y_o}{h_2} \right],$$

if it is assumed for simplicity that the real part is already at its steady state. This dynamic equation is of the same kind as the one for the Cagan monetary model and can be treated with respect to its forward-looking solution in the same way, as it is discussed in detail for example in Turnovsky 2000, 3.3–3.4). The nominal dynamics assumed to hold under the jump-variable hypothesis in AS–AD–WPC is then of a well-known type.

However, the basic fact that the AS–AD–WPC model under myopic perfect foresight is not a consistently formulated one and also not consistently solved arises from its *ad hoc* assumption that nominal wages must jump with the price level $p$ ($w = \omega p$), since the real wage $\omega$ is now moving continuously in time according to the real wage dynamics. The level of money wages is thus now capable of adjusting instantaneously, which is in contradiction to the assumption of only sluggishly adjusting nominal wages according to the assumed money-wage PC.[3] Furthermore, a properly formulated Keynesian growth dynamics should – besides allowing for under- or over-employed labor – also allow for under- or over-employment of the capital stock, at least in certain episodes. Thus the price level, like the wage level, should alternatively be assumed to adjust somewhat sluggishly; see also Barro (1994) in this regard. We will come back to this observation after the next section which is devoted to new developments in the area of Keynesian dynamics, the so-called New Keynesian approach of the macrodynamic literature.

The conclusion of this section is that the Neoclassical Synthesis, Stage I, must be considered a failure on logical grounds and not a valid attempt "to formalize for students the relationships among the various hypotheses advanced in Milton Friedman's AEA presidential address (1968)", Sargent (1987, p.117).

## 17.3 New Keynesian macrodynamics: the New Neoclassical Synthesis

In this section we provide some succinct propositions[4] on equilibrium determinacy of the four dimensional New Keynesian model with both staggered prices and wages, but also review the relevance of this type of approach from a critical perspective. We here start directly from Galí (2008, Ch.6) textbook analysis of the reduced form representation of the New Keynesian model with both staggered wages and prices.

### *The deterministic 'skeleton' of the New Keynesian AD–AS model*

In the literature on New Keynesian baseline models one often encounters the treatment of the case of a price Phillips curve (PPC), a dynamic IS curve and a Taylor rule (TR) as the point of departure for the New Keynesian and DSGE (dynamic stochastic general equilibrium) modeling approach. A modern model of the Keynesian variety, but also older ones, should in our view accept the proposition that both wage levels and price levels are only gradually adjusting at each moment in time, since they are macro-variables and do not perform noticeable jumps on a daily time scale, which we consider as the relevant time unit for the macro-data *generating* process. This assertion rests on the idea that individual wage and price movements may be occurring in a staggered fashion, but that these staggered movements are not clustered in time as it is generally assumed, also in the empirically oriented New Keynesian approaches. The data collection process in contrast may be a staggered as well as a clustered one, but this does not imply that models that have been estimated on a quarterly data basis should then also be iterated and analyzed with such a crude period length, as far as the rhythm of the data generating process (which is much finer) is concerned. Bunching staggered actions, as period models do, may lead in fact to illegitimate results as in particular the 1-dimensional chaotic macro-models make clear, since they generate trajectories that are totally impossible in continuous time (or for small period lengths).

The foregoing statements in our view suggest that macro-models should be formulated, analyzed and simulated as continuous processes (or quasi-continuous ones, with step size 1/365 with respect to their annualized data framework). This is indeed the perspective that we pursue in this section (and the entire chapter), which allows us to use continuous time methods to analyze models which are normally formulated strictly as period models in the New Keynesian tradition, which we will briefly reconsider from the continuous time perspective in this section.

In our own model, treated in subsequent sections, we go immediately to continuous time as the modeling strategy, since that allows for stability proofs even in high order dynamical systems (which nevertheless can be simulated adequately with a step length of 1/365). In these models, also built on the assumptions of gradually adjusting wages and prices, we can of course consider limit cases where wages, prices or expectations adjust with infinite speed, but these are more a matter of theoretical curiosity than of fundamental importance. Consequently, the natural starting point of the Keynesian version of the New Neoclassical Synthesis and our matured approach to "traditional" Keynesian model building should be staggered wage and price setting as the baseline situation rather than one of its two limit cases.

A theoretical baseline model of New Keynesian type from the theoretical perspective concerning feedback channels and related stability issues (such as our Keynesian reformulation and extension of the traditional Neoclassical Synthesis later on) has not been investigated thoroughly in the literature so far. This is despite the fact that such model types are now heavily used in empirical applications, see Smets and Wouters (2003) for a prominent example.

The loglinear New Keynesian model laid out in Galí (2008, Ch.6) reads

$$\overset{\text{WPC}}{\pi_t^w} = \beta(h)\pi_{t+h}^w + h\kappa_w \tilde{y}_t - h\lambda_w \tilde{\omega}_t, \quad \pi_t^w = (w_t - w_{t-h})/h, \tag{17.12}$$

$$\overset{\text{PPC}}{\pi_t^p} = \beta(h)\pi_{t+h}^p + h\kappa_p \tilde{y}_t + h\lambda_p \tilde{\omega}_t, \quad \pi_t^p = (p_t - p_{t-h})/h, \tag{17.13}$$

$$\overset{\text{IS}}{\tilde{y}_t} = \tilde{y}_{t+h} - h\sigma^{-1}(i_t - \pi_{t+h}^p - r^n), \tag{17.14}$$

$$\overset{\text{TR}}{i_t} = r^n + \phi_p \pi_t^p + \phi_w \pi_t^w + \phi_y \tilde{y}_t, \tag{17.15}$$

with

$$\tilde{\omega}_t \equiv \tilde{\omega}_{t-h} + h(\pi_t^w - \pi_t^p) - \Delta\omega_{t+h}^n$$

as the identity relating the changes in the real wage gap $\tilde{\omega}_t = \omega_t - \omega_t^n$ ($\omega_t^n$ being the natural real wage) to wage inflation, price inflation, and the change in the natural real wage $\Delta\omega_t^n$. Note here also that $\beta(h) := \dfrac{1}{1+h\rho}$ is the discount factor that applies to the period length $h$, and that there holds on this basis $\dfrac{1-\beta(h)}{\beta(h)} = h\rho$, or;

$1/\beta(h) = 1 + h\rho$, when solved for the discount rate $\rho$ of the New Keynesian model, which will be of importance below.

Equation (17.12) describes a New Keynesian wage Phillips curve (WPC), and equation (17.13), analogously, describes a New Keynesian price Phillips curve (PPC), all parameters being positive, see Galí (2008) for their derivation. We assume as in Galí (2008, p.128) that the conditions stated there for the existence of a zero steady state solution are fulfilled, namely that (a) $\Delta\omega_t^n = 0$ for all $t$ and that (b) the intercept in the nominal interest rate rule adjusts always in a one-to-one fashion to variations in the natural rate of interest. The dynamic IS equation (derived by combining the goods markets clearing condition $y_t = c_t$ with the Euler equation of the households) is given by equation (17.14), with $\tilde{y}_t \equiv y_t - y_t^n$ as the output gap ($y_t^n$ being the equilibrium level of output attainable in the absence of both wage and price rigidities) and $r^n$ as the natural rate of interest. Finally, equation (17.15) describes a generalized type of contemporaneous Taylor interest rate policy rule (TR), where the nominal interest rate is assumed to be a function of the natural rate of interest, of the wage inflation, the price inflation as well as of the output gap, see Galí (2008, 6.2) for details.

Note that we have in this formulation of the model three forward looking variables and one equation that is updating the historically given real wage. We thus need for the determinacy of the model the existence of three unstable eigenvalues (three variables that can jump to the 1-D stable submanifold) and one eigen-value that is negative (corresponding to the stable submanifold). In contrast to Galí (2008, footnote 6) we use annualized rates, obtained by dividing the corresponding period differences through the period length $h$ (usually $1/4$ year in the literature). We show herewith which parameters change with the data frequency or just the iteration step-size $h$ when the model is simulated. We thus use the conventional scaling for the rates under consideration, but allow for changes in the data collection frequency or iteration frequency.[5] We consequently consider the equations (17.12)–(17.15) from an applied perspective, so that we take them as starting point for an empirically motivated study of the influence of the data frequency (quarterly, monthly or weekly) on the size of the parameter values to be estimated.

The New Keynesian model completed in this way represents an implicitly formulated system of difference equations, where all variables with index $t + h$ are expected variables. Making use again of the TR and the PPC and using the above representation of $\tilde{\omega}_t$, it can be made an explicit system of difference equations that can be written (with $\eta = \sigma^{-1}$)

$$\pi_{t+h}^w = \frac{\pi_t^w - h\kappa_w\tilde{y}_t + h\lambda_w\tilde{\omega}_t}{\beta(h)}$$

$$= \pi_t^w + h\rho\pi_t^w - h\frac{\kappa_w\tilde{y}_t - \lambda_w\tilde{\omega}_{t-h} - h\lambda_w(\pi_t^w - \pi_t^p)}{\beta(h)}, \tag{17.16}$$

$$\pi_{t+h}^p = \frac{\pi_t^p - h\kappa_p \tilde{y}_t - h\lambda_p \tilde{\omega}_t}{\beta(h)}$$

$$= \pi_t^p + h\rho\pi_t^p - h\frac{\kappa_p \tilde{y}_t + \lambda_p \tilde{\omega}_{t-h} + h\lambda_p(\pi_t^w - \pi_t^p)}{\beta(h)}, \tag{17.17}$$

$$\tilde{y}_{t+h} = \tilde{y}_t + h\eta\left[\phi_w \pi_t^w + (\phi_p - \frac{1}{\beta(h)})\pi_t^p + \phi_y \tilde{y}_t \right.$$

$$\left. + h\frac{\kappa_p \tilde{y}_t + \lambda_p \tilde{\omega}_{t-h} + h\lambda_p(\pi_t^w - \pi_t^p)}{\beta(h)} \right], \tag{17.18}$$

$$\tilde{\omega}_t = \tilde{\omega}_{t-h} + h(\pi_t^w - \pi_t^p), \tag{17.19}$$

which we can represent succinctly through the matrix equation

$$x_{t+h} = x_t + h(J_o + hJ_1(h))x_t = x_t + hA(h)x_t = (I + hA(h))x_t$$

where $J_o$ collects the terms that are linear in $h$ and which therefore will characterize the continuous time limit case.

As already briefly discussed, the model should not depend in its fundamental qualitative properties on the length of the period $h$, in particular when frequencies of empirical relevance are considered. We therefore expect that it reflects the properties of its continuous time analogue, abbreviated by $\dot{x} = J_o x$. The New Keynesian baseline model with both staggered wage and price setting, the Keynesian version of the New Neoclassical Synthesis, reads in its loglinearly approximated form (see Erceg et al. (2000), Woodford (2003, pp.225ff.) and Galí (2008 Ch.6)) and note that there holds $1/\beta(h) = 1 + h\rho = 1$ in the limit:

$$\dot{\pi}^w = \rho\pi^w - \kappa_w \tilde{y} + \lambda_w \tilde{\omega}, \tag{17.20}$$

$$\dot{\pi}^p = \rho\pi^p - \kappa_p \tilde{y} - \lambda_p \tilde{\omega}, \tag{17.21}$$

$$\dot{\tilde{y}} = \eta\phi_w \pi^w + \eta(\phi_p - 1)\pi^p + \eta\phi_y \tilde{y}, \tag{17.22}$$

$$\dot{\tilde{\omega}} = \pi^w - \pi^p. \tag{17.23}$$

### Determinacy analysis

The above representation of the model implies for the system matrix of the considered dynamics the structure

$$J_o = \begin{pmatrix} 0 & 0 & -\kappa_w & \lambda_w \\ 0 & 0 & -\kappa_p & -\lambda_p \\ \phi_w\eta & (\phi_p-1)\eta & \phi_y\eta & 0 \\ 1 & -1 & 0 & 0 \end{pmatrix}.$$

With respect to this model type, it is asserted in Galí (2008, p.128) – and illustrated numerically in his Figure 6.1 – that the New Keynesian model is determinate in the case $\phi_y = 0$ considered below (that is, it exhibits three unstable and one stable root) for all policy parameters $\phi_p$, $\phi_w$ when the following form of the Taylor principle holds: $\phi_w + \phi_p > 1$. We show in this section that this condition is in fact necessary and sufficient for determinacy in the 4-D New Keynesian model for all positive values of the parameter $\phi_y$ in front of the output gap provided that $\rho = 0$ holds. To investigate this assertion one has to consider the eigen-values of the system matrix $J_o$ of our system of differential equations (for $\rho = 0$). Doing so one can derive the following two propositions:[6]

### *Proposition 1*

*Assume that $\rho = 0$ and that $\phi_y > 0$. Then: The characteristic equation $|\lambda I - J_o| = 0$ has 3 roots with positive real parts and 1 negative root if and only if the generalized Taylor principle $\phi_p + \phi_w > 1$ holds true.*

### *Proposition 2*

*Consider $\rho > 0$ and assume that*

$$\phi_y > \rho \frac{-(\lambda_w + \lambda_p) + \eta(\kappa_w \phi_w + \kappa_p(\phi_p - 1))]}{\eta[\lambda_w + \lambda_p - \rho^2]}$$

*holds true. Then: The characteristic equation $|\lambda I - J_o| = 0$ has 3 roots with positive real parts and 1 negative root if and only if*

$$\phi_w + \phi_p > 1 - \frac{\rho(\lambda_w + \lambda_p)}{\kappa_w \lambda_p + \lambda_w \kappa_p} \phi_y.$$

These propositions therefore state conditions – in particular for monetary policy – such that equilibrium determinacy is given, in which case the resulting dynamics need not be excluded from consideration.

The proofs of these two propositions show how a thorough analytical analysis of the determinacy properties of the New Keynesian model with staggered wages and prices is to be conducted by using a continuous time representation of this model. This strategy allows us to circumvent the calculation of the far more complicated conditions which hold for the corresponding discrete time case, see for example the mathematical appendices in Woodford (2003) for the difficulties that exist just in the 3-D case.

However, these considerations concern a mathematical approximation of the true nonlinear model where rational expectations must be of a global nature which need not be mirrored through the rational expectations' paths generated by the loglinear approximation. It may therefore well be that the paths that are generated through computer algorithms in the linearized version have not much in common with the corresponding ones of the true model.

Our approach to determinacy analysis makes use of the (though not unchallenged) view that the intrinsic dynamics and determinacy properties of a dynamic model should not depend on whether such a model is formulated in continuous or discrete time. In other words, the dynamical properties of a model are (or should be) invariant to the assumed frequency of the decision making of the economic agents in the discrete time version of the model.[7] On this basis the approach pursued here makes determinacy analysis of New Keynesian models, studied for example in Woodford (2003), much easier and represents a valid, though indirect strategy for the analytical determinacy analysis of high-dimensional rational expectations models.

### *A critical evaluation of New Keynesian macrodynamics*

A first set of questions concerning the validity of the New Keynesian approach to macrodynamics is its use of the word Keynesian as a label. There is in fact no IS-curve, representing Keynesian demand rationing on the market for goods, as the model is formulated, but simply a Walrasian type of notional goods demand and on this basis the assumption of goods market equilibrium. The theory of rational expectations has also very little to do with Keynes' (1936) views on the difficulties of expectations formation, in particular for the evaluation of long-term investment projects. By contrast, RE expectations formation represents an approach that can be handed over to a computer routine (often simply used as black box) which by construction will deliver at most, if at all, only damped oscillations. Finally, Keynes' liquidity preference theory is no longer a subject to which attention is paid, due to the disappearance (irrelevance) of the LM schedule, which is at best present in the background of a simpler to handle Taylor interest rate policy rule. However it is of interest to note that liquidity preference is now back on the agenda as the recent crises in financial markets show.

Therefore, when compared with Keynes' (1936, Ch.22) "Notes on the Trade Cycle" and its important constituent parts, the marginal propensity to consume out of rationed income, the marginal efficiency of investment (and the expected cash flow that is underlying it) and the parameters that shape liquidity preference, not much of the role of these parameters is left in the New Keynesian approach to macrodynamics, in particular concerning the systematic forces within the business cycle and its turning points as they are discussed in Keynes' (1936, Ch.22).

Moreover, also further important feedback channels, for example the real wage channel, as they have been discussed in Chiarella and Flaschel (2000) and later work, cannot carry out their roles here in the shaping of the cyclical adjustment process and its inflationary consequences, but would only be shifted around by the search for a Taylor rule until they imply the three/one combination of unstable/ stable roots for the Jacobian matrix of the dynamics for a reasonable range of policy parameters.

The constructions and the implications of this New Keynesian approach to macrodynamics are therefore primarily dependent on the stochastic processes that are generally added to this model type. The New Keynesian models are consequently very much governed by the Frisch-Slutzky stochastic shock absorber paradigm. Its rational expectations solutions are nothing but, in a sense, specifically iterated types of suitably chosen stochastic processes, with the iteration being based on the inverse matrix of the Jacobian of the system we considered above.

We conclude from this discussion,[8] that the New Keynesian approach to macrodynamics creates more theoretical problems than it helps to solve. Reasons for this may be found in its following indispensable ingredients:

*Microfoundations*, as stressed by the Rational Expectations school, are *per se* an important desideratum to be reflected also by behaviorally oriented macrodynamics, but agents are heterogeneous, form heterogeneous expectations along other lines than those suggested by the rational expectations school and have short-term as well as long-term views about the economy. The straightjacket postulated by the supporters of the representative agent approach is just too narrow to allow a treatment of what is known as interesting behavior of economic agents and it is also not detailed enough to discuss the various feedback channels of the macroeconomics literature.

*Market clearing*, the next ingredient of the New Keynesian approach, may however be a questionable device to study the macroeconomy in particular on its real side. The data generating process is too fast in order to allow for period models with a *uniform* period length of a quarter or more. So period models of this type, that deviate from their continuous time analogues, should be replaced by the latter modeling approach. In continuous time however it is much too heroic to assume market clearing at all moments in time, but real markets are then only adjusting towards moving equilibria in such an framework (as for example in the modeling approach that we outline later).

Yet, neither microfoundations *per se* nor market clearing assumptions are the true dividing line between the approaches we are advocating and the ones considered in this section. The root of the discontent that our chapter tries to make explicit is the *ad hoc*, that is to say not behaviorally microfounded, assumption of *rational expectations* that by the chosen analytical method makes the world in general loglinear (by construction) and the generated dynamics convergent (by assumption) to its unique steady state.

The basic argument here is that the chosen starting point of the New Keynesian approach – purely forward looking rational expectations – is axiomatically seen to be a wrong one so that complicated additional constructions (epicycles) become necessary in order to reconcile this approach with the facts. In the words of Fuhrer:[9]

Are we adding "epicycles" to a dead model?

By epicycles Fuhrer means habits, indexing, adding lags, and high-order adjustment costs, which are the examples he mentions on the slides from which the above quotation has been taken.

Compared to the disequilibrium AD–AS model that we will formulate in Section 17.4, we find – despite this criticism – many common elements in the structure of the two AS–AD approaches, in particular as far as the formal structure of the WPC and the PPC are concerned. In addition, our model of Section 17.4 also has a dynamic IS-curve and a specific type of Taylor rule. However, we will employ four gaps in the place of only two (concerning various activity measures and real wages) and use Okun's Law to link the labor market gaps to the one on the goods market. In addition, by its origin, our model type will always use hybrid expectations formation right from the start, see Chiarella and Flaschel (1996), based on short-run crossover and model consistent expectations and the concept of an inflationary climate within which the short run is embedded, with the expectation being updated adaptively. We use simultaneous dating and crossover wage and price expectations in the formulated wage–price spiral, in place of the forward-looking self-reference that characterizes the New Keynesian approach on both the labor and the goods market, and – as stated – in addition hybrid ones that give some inertia to our formulation of wage–price dynamics.

We will be able to show stability of the steady state under quite meaningful assumptions on the parameters of our model and can expand our baseline scenario easily in many directions. By contrast, the New Keynesian baseline model faces difficulties when one tries to generalize it (for example to the case where there is steady state inflation). It is moreover not easily extended beyond a non-rationed Walrasian approach concerning the theory of aggregate demand it employs.

Smets and Wouters (2003) have however extended the above baseline New Keynesian model from the empirical perspective towards a more balanced structure where there is not only consumption but also investment and capital stock growth. The loglinear version of their model consists of nine structural equations, for consumption (with habit formation) and investment (with capital adjustment costs and a term representing some form of Tobin's $q$) and goods market equilibrium. Moreover, they then employ a price level Phillips curve (with indexation) and a reduced-form real wage PC (also with indexation). They have finally a labor demand schedule and a Taylor interest rate policy rule. In principle this is a needed extension of the New Keynesian baseline case we have considered above.

Yet, there are drawbacks of such an extension of the baseline case towards an empirically oriented DSGE model. In order to give the model sufficient inertia with respect to a meaningful empirical application there are several *ad hoc* modifications of the purely forward looking New Keynesian baseline story. A discussion of which variables are predetermined and which one are not (and the problem of indeterminacy) is completely bypassed. Instead various techniques for determining a unique solution are available in the form of algorithms which solve this problem automatically in the background of the model and not by a theoretical inspection on the part of the model builder; on this issue we refer the reader to, for instance, Blanchard and Kahn (1980) and Sims (2002), as well as the documentation of the Dynare system on the Dynare site (http://www.dynare.org/).

In such a black box environment it is no longer possible to design monetary policy with a view to relevant feedback channels, as we will do it in the following sections. Finally, the distinction between unanticipated and anticipated shocks is no longer handled in the appealingly transparent form it had in the theoretical saddlepoint investigations of Blanchard (1981) and subsequent contributions. Solving certain optimization problems and reducing the solution to loglinear approximations (when the model becomes too complex, though perhaps more realistic) which then are handled only mathematically and estimated is nowadays a routine task. However though from an academic point of view this is surely a complex task, it is not convincing with respect to a true understanding of how the economy is in fact working during the business cycles and even long-phase cycles (in employment, inflation and income distribution).

We conclude that the New Keynesian approach does not (yet) represent a theoretically and empirically convincing strategy for the study of the fluctuating growth that we observe in capitalist economies. It gives the features of the deterministic core of the considered dynamics (if determinate) by and large a trivial outlook. It reduces the nonlinear growth dynamics of capitalist market economies to loglinear approximations (within which routinized expectations are formed that are convergent by construction) and suggests that such systems when driven by certain stochastic processes are all that one needs to have for a good model of the real–financial market interaction. Altogether, the New Keynesian approach to macrodynamics is too narrowly oriented concerning methodological restrictions and too inflexible concerning substantial generalizations so that a huge effort is needed for only limited generalizations or improvements of the model's structure.

There is thus a need for alternative baseline scenarios which can be communicated across scientific approaches, can be investigated in detail with respect to their theoretical properties in their original nonlinear format, and which – when applied to actual economies – remain controllable from the theoretical point of view as far as the basic feedback chains they contain are concerned. The happy incidence here is that such an alternative indeed exists that does not deny the validity of the traditional Neoclassical Synthesis. This synthesis now appears as a special case of this larger framework, a special case that is however problematic when one attempts to apply it to the study of actual economies. Nevertheless, there is thus continuity in the development of Keynesian macrodynamic models from this perspective, and thus not the total denial of the usefulness of past evolutions in Keynesian macrotheory that the New Keynesian approach is implicitly suggesting.

We formulate in this respect in the next section a dynamic AD–AS model based on gradually adjusting wages and prices, myopic perfect foresight of current inflation rates and adaptive expectations concerning the inflation climate in which the economy operates. The model consists of a wage and a price Phillips curve, a dynamic IS curve as well as a dynamic employment adjustment equation (Okun's

Law) and a Taylor interest rate rule. The model can be reduced to a 3-D dynamical system by a suitable choice of the Taylor rule and implies strong stability results, in particular for an appropriately chosen interest rate policy rule. Through instrumental variables GMM system estimation with aggregate time series data for the UK economy, we obtain parameter estimates which support the specification of our theoretical model and its stability implications.

## 17.4 Disequilibrium dynamics with gradual price–quantity adjustment processes

In this section we provide the alternative to the New Keynesian scenario we have investigated in the preceding section. Quoting again from Fuhrer:[10]

> In a way, this takes us back to the very old models
> — With decent long-run, theory-grounded properties
> — But dynamics from a-theoretic sources

we approach this task by way of an extension of the AD–AS model of the traditional Neoclassical Synthesis (ONS) that primarily improves the AS side, the nominal side, of this early integrated Keynesian AS–AD approach (and which allows for the impact of wage–price dynamics on the AD side of the model in addition).

We call this model type DAD–DAS where the additional "D" stands for "Disequilibrium". We attempt to show that this matured ONS approach can compete with the New Neoclassical Synthesis (NNS) with respect to an understanding of the basic feedback mechanisms that characterize the working of the macroeconomy, their stability properties and their empirical validity. With respect to the latter we consider the UK economy as an example, and refer the reader to related work (see Flaschel (2009, Ch.8)) on the US economy and the Eurozone. Regarding microfoundations we have to face the difficulties that Fuhrer states with respect to dynamics, but will point here to some contributions according to which at least the nominal dynamics can be derived from the behavior of economic agents.

In this section we therefore reconsider a Keynesian D(isequilibrium) AS–D (isequilibrium) AD model as it was first introduced in Chen et al. (2006), and also estimated there and in a later paper by Proaño et al. (2006) We reformulate this model in such a way that it can be reduced to a 3-D core dynamical system which can be easily investigated analytically and which allows for strong stability conclusions, in particular with respect to the role of monetary policy.

The core of our approach with non-clearing labor and goods markets and therefore under- or over-utilized labor and capital is the modeling of wage–price dynamics, which are specified through two separate Phillips curves, each one led by its own measure of demand pressure (or capacity bottleneck), instead of a single one as it is usually the case in theoretical investigations of New Keynesian models, for instance in Galí and Gertler (1999) and Galí et al. (2001). The approach of estimating separate wage and price Phillips curves is not altogether new however: Barro (1994) for example observes that Keynesian macroeconomics is (or should be) based on imperfectly flexible wages as well as prices and thus on the consideration of wage as well as price Phillips curves; Fair (2000) criticizes the low accuracy of reduced form price equations, and in the same study estimates two separate wage and price equations for the United States, using however a single demand pressure term, the NAIRU gap on the labor market.

On the contrary, by modeling wage and price dynamics separately from each other, each one determined by their own measures of demand pressures in the market for labor and for goods, we are able to circumvent the identification problem pointed out by Sims (1987) for the estimation of separate wage and price equations with the same explanatory variables. By these means, we can analyze the dynamics of the real wages in the economy and identify oppositely acting effects as they might result from different labor and goods markets developments. Indeed, we believe a Keynesian model of aggregate demand fluctuations should (independently of whether justification can be found for this in Keynes' General Theory) allow for under- (or over-)utilized labor *as well as* capital and gradual wage and also price adjustments in order to be general enough from the descriptive point of view.

### The model

The structural form of the wage–price dynamics of our framework is given by:[11]

$$\hat{w} = \beta_{we}(e - \bar{e}) + \beta_{wu}(u^w - \bar{u}^w) - \beta_{wv}(\ln v - \ln v_o)$$
$$+ \kappa_w \hat{p} + (1 - \kappa_w)\pi^c, \tag{17.24}$$

$$\hat{p} = \beta_{pu}(u^c - \bar{u}^c) + \beta_{pv}(\ln v_o - \ln v_o) + \kappa_p \hat{w} + (1 - \kappa_p)\pi^c. \tag{17.25}$$

We denote by $e - \bar{e}$ the employment gap on the external labor market and by $u^w - \bar{u}^w$ the excess utilization of the workforce employed by firms. In a similar way, we use $u^c - \bar{u}^c$ to indicate the excess utilization of the capital stock. Demand pressure on the labor market is therefore measured with respect to outsiders and insiders, while there is only one measure as far as the utilization of the capital stock is concerned. The demand pressure terms in both the wage and price Phillips curves are augmented by two additional terms: first, by the log of the wage share $v$ or real unit labor costs, the error correction term discussed in Blanchard and Katz (1999, p.71). The second additional term is a weighted average of corresponding expected cost-pressure terms, assumed to be model-consistent with respect to forward looking, crossover wage and price inflation rates $\bar{w}^2$ and $\hat{p}$, respectively, and a backward looking measure of the prevailing inflationary climate of the economy, symbolized by $\pi^c$.[12] Indeed, while the agents in our model have myopic perfect foresight with respect to future inflation rates, there is no reason to assume that they also act myopically with respect to the past, "forgetting" whole sequences of fully observable, and highly informational, values of past inflation. These two

Phillips curves have been estimated and investigated in detail in Chen and Flaschel (2006).

The microfoundations of our wage Phillips curve are thus of the same type as in Blanchard and Katz (1999) (see also Flaschel and Krolzig 2006) which can be reformulated as expressed in (17.24) and (17.25) with the employment gaps $e - \bar{e}, u^w - \bar{u}^w$ in place of the single measure, the output gap, which is usually employed. We use two measures of demand pressure on the labor market, the external employment rate gap and the utilization gap within firms. Using a physical analogy they can be regarded as forming some sort of capillary system where these two pressure terms are to be related by some sort of Okun's Law.

Concerning the price Phillips curve, a similar micro-procedure can be applied, based on desired markups of firms. Along these lines one in particular gets an economic motivation for the inclusion of (indeed the logarithm of) the real wage (or wage share) with negative sign in the wage PC and with positive sign in the price PC, without any need for loglinear approximations. We use a capacity utilization gap in the price PC as measure of demand pressure on the market for goods (and could add a second measure here too in the form of an inventory gap). Our wage–price module is thus consistent with standard models of unemployment based on efficiency wages, matching and competitive wage determination, as well as markup pricing and can be considered as an interesting alternative to the – theoretically rarely discussed and empirically questionable – purely forward-looking New Keynesian form of staggered wage and price dynamics that we have discussed in Section 17.3.

Note that we have assumed model-consistent expectations with respect to short-run wage and price inflation, incorporated into our Phillips curves in a crossover manner, with perfectly foreseen price inflation in the wage Phillips curve and wage inflation in the price Phillips curve.

The across-markets or *reduced-form PCs* of the WPC and the PPC curves (17.1) and (17.2) are given by (with $\kappa = 1/(1 - \kappa_w \kappa_p))$[13]

$$\hat{w} = \kappa[\beta_{we}(e - \bar{e}) + \beta_{wu}(u^w - \bar{u}^w)$$
$$- \beta_{wv} \ln(\frac{v}{v_o}) + \kappa_w(\beta_{pu}(u^c - \bar{u}^c) + \beta_{pv} \ln(\frac{v}{v_o}))] + \pi^c, \qquad (17.26)$$

$$\hat{p} = \kappa[\beta_{pu}(u^c - \bar{u}^c) + \beta_{pv} \ln(\frac{v}{v_o})$$
$$+ \kappa_p(\beta_{we}(e - \bar{e}) + \beta_{wu}(u^w - \bar{u}^w) - \beta_{wv} \ln(\frac{v}{v_o}))] + \pi^c, \qquad (17.27)$$

with inflation pass-through terms as represented by the parameters $\kappa_w, \kappa_p$. These reduced form PCs represent a considerable generalization of the conventional view of a single-market price PC with only one measure of demand pressure, namely the one in the labor market.

Note that for this version of the wage–price spiral, the inflationary climate variable does not matter for the evolution of the real wage $\omega = w/p$, – or the wage share $v = \omega/z$ if labor productivity is taken into account. The law of motion for $v$ is given by

$$\hat{v} = \kappa\left[(1-\kappa_p)(\beta_{we}(e-\bar{e})+\beta_{wu}(u^w-\bar{u}^w))-\beta_{wv}\ln(\frac{v}{v_o}))\right.$$

$$\left.-(1-\kappa_w)(\beta_{pu}(u^c-\bar{u}^c)+\beta_{pv}\ln(\frac{v}{v_o}))\right]. \tag{17.28}$$

Equation (17.28) shows the ambiguity of the stabilizing role of the real wage channel, already discussed by Rose (1967) which arises – in spite of the incorporation of specific measures of demand and cost pressure on both the labor and the goods markets – if the dynamics of the employment rate and the workforce utilization are linked to the fluctuations of the firms' capacity utilization rate via Okun's Law. Indeed, as sketched in Figure 17.1, a real wage increase can act, taken by itself, in a stabilizing or destabilizing manner, depending among other things on whether the dynamics of the capacity utilization rate depend positively or negatively on the real wage (i.e. on whether consumption reacts more strongly to real wage changes than investment or viceversa) *and* whether price flexibility is greater than nominal wage flexibility with respect to their own demand pressure measures. All parameters shown in the first part of (17.28) (before the minus sign) thus contribute to stability if aggregate demand is profit-led, that is decreases when the real wage is increasing, while the ones after the minus sign contribute to instability in this case (the opposite applies when aggregate demand is wage-led).

These four different scenarios can be jointly summarized as in Table 17.1. As it can be observed, there exist two cases where the Rose (1967) real wage channel operates in a stabilizing manner. In the first case, aggregate goods demand

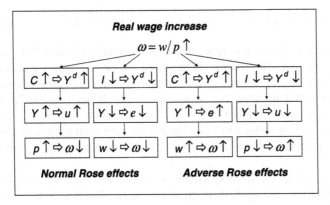

*Figure 17.1* Normal (convergent) and adverse (divergent) Rose effects: the real wage channel of Keynesian macrodynamics.

*Table 17.1* Four baseline real wage adjustment scenarios

|  | Wage-led goods demand | Profit-led goods demand |
|---|---|---|
| Labor market-led real wage adjustment | Adverse (divergent) | Normal (convergent) |
| Goods market led real wage adjustment | Normal (convergent) | Adverse (divergent) |

(proxied in our analysis by the capacity utilization rate) depends negatively on the real wage, which we denote as the profit-led case, and the dynamics of the real wage are led primarily (in column 2 of Table 17.1 by the nominal wage dynamics and therefore by the developments in the labor market. In the second case, given by column 1 on the left hand side of Table 17.1, aggregate demand depends positively on the real wage, representing a consumption-driven wage-led case, where we in addition have that the resulting increase in capacity utilization drives up the price level. In this case, the goods market primarily determines the behavior of the real wages.[14]

Concerning the inflationary expectations over the medium-run, $\pi^c$, that is the inflationary climate in which current wage and price inflation are operating, they may be formed adaptively following the actual rate of inflation (by use of some linear or exponential weighting scheme), may be based on a rolling sample (with hump-shaped weighting schemes), or on other possibilities for updating expectations. For simplicity of exposition we shall make use here of the conventional adaptive expectations mechanism in the theoretical part of this chapter, namely

$$\dot{\pi}^c = \beta_{\pi^c}(\hat{p} - \pi^c). \tag{17.29}$$

The above model of an advanced wage–price spiral is considered in this chapter against the background of a fixed proportions technology, characterized by[15]

$$y^p = Y^p/K = const., \ z = Y/L^d = const., \ u^c = Y/Y^p, u^w = L^d/L^w, \ e = L^w/L.$$

Potential output $Y^p$ is here compared with actual output $Y$, which in this model is demand determined. The ratio $u^c$ is therefore the rate of capacity utilization of firms. Firms employ a workforce of $L^w$ workers who are employed according to actual output and thus have to supply $L^d = Y/z$ hours of work. Their rate of utilization is therefore given by $u^w$. The rate of employment on the external labor market is finally defined by $e$ and has already been contrasted in its implications for wage inflation with the rate $u^w$ in the WPC that we have introduced above.

With respect to the goods markets dynamics, we model them by means of a law of motion of the type of a dynamic IS-equation (see also Rudebusch and Svensson (1999) in this regard) here represented by the growth rate of the capacity utilization rate of firms:[16]

$$\hat{u}^c = -\beta_{uu}(u^c - \bar{u}^c) - \beta_{ui}((i - \hat{p}) - (i - \hat{p})_o) \pm \beta_{uv}(v - v_o). \qquad (17.30)$$

The reduced form (17.30) has three important characteristics; (i) it reflects the dependence of output changes on aggregate income and thus on the rate of capacity utilization by assuming a negative, that is stable dynamic multiplier relationship; (ii) it shows the joint dependence of consumption and investment on the real wage/wage share (which in the aggregate may in principle allow for positive or negative signs before the parameter $\beta_{uv}$, depending on whether consumption or investment is more responsive to real wage changes/wage share changes); and (iii) it shows finally the negative influence of the real rate of interest on the evolution of economic activity.

Concerning the labor market dynamics and its link to the goods market dynamics, we assume a more detailed form of the simple empirical relationship introduced by Okun (1970) as a link between the rate of capacity utilization and the employment rate that we write as

$$\hat{e} = \beta_{eu}(u^w - \bar{u}^w), \qquad (17.31)$$

with

$$u^w = \frac{L^d}{L^w} = \frac{Y^p}{K} \frac{L^d}{Y} \frac{K}{L} \frac{Y}{Y^p} \frac{L}{L^w} = \frac{y^p}{z l_o} \frac{u^c}{e}. \qquad (17.32)$$

This law of motion states that the growth rate of the employment rate is reacting positively to the deviation of the utilization rate $u^w$, the ratio of $L^d$ (employment in hours) to the workforce $L^w$ of firms from its normal level $\bar{u}^w$. The utilization rate $u^w$ depends – as shown in (17.32)– on the rate of capacity utilization $u^c$ and the employment rate $e$ by definition, if a fixed proportions technology is assumed: $y^p = Y^p/K = const, z = Y/L^d = const, L^d$ the employment of the workforce of firms (in hours), and on the ratio of labor supply to the capital stock $L/K$ which is considered as given by $l_o$ here (thereby ignoring the growth aspects behind the model).[17] The essential parameter here is of course the parameter $\beta_{eu}$ in equation (17.31), which characterizes the speed of the hiring and firing process of the economy.

The above two laws of motion therefore reformulate in a dynamic form the static IS-curve (and the rate of employment that this curve implies) that was used in Asada et al. (2006).

Finally, here we no longer employ a law of motion for real balances (an LM curve) as it was still the case in Asada et al. (2006). Instead we endogenize the nominal interest rate by using a new type of Taylor rule compared to the one that is customary in the literature, see for example Svensson (1998). The target rate of the monetary authorities is here determined according to

$$i = (i - \hat{p})_o + \hat{p} + \alpha_{iw}(\hat{w} - \pi^c) + \alpha_{iu}(u^c - \bar{u}^c) + \alpha_{iv}(v - v_o). \qquad (17.33)$$

The target rate of the central bank $i$ is thus here made dependent on the steady state real rate of interest $(i - \hat{p})_o$ augmented by actual inflation back to a nominal rate, and is as usual dependent on the inflation gap and the capacity utilization gap (as a measure of the output gap) and augmented by a further gap impact, the current wage share gap.[18] For the time being we assume that there is no interest rate smoothing with respect to the interest target of the central bank, which therefore immediately sets its target rate at each moment in time. With respect to the inflation gap we use a wage inflation measure, since wages appear to be more flexible than prices with respect to demand pressure (in the US and the Eurozone, see Proaño et al. (2006) and Section 17.6 of this chapter), and use for the time being the inflation climate as a point of reference for this gap (which simplifies considerably the dynamics to be investigated). Measuring the inflation gap in terms of wages gives the labor market more weight in the reaction of the interest rate to inflation, see the reduced form PCs (17.26) and (17.27) we have derived above. The model's behavior will however not be changed qualitatively if the price inflation rate is used in place of the wage inflation rate (if this rate is the one on which the Central Bank is focused) since the feedback structures remain the same.

We note that the steady state of the dynamics, due to its specific formulation, can be supplied exogenously:[19] $u_o^c = \bar{u}^c, e_o = \bar{e}, u_o^w = \bar{u}^w, v_o = \bar{v}, \pi_o^c = \hat{p}_o = \hat{w}_o = 0$, $i_o = (i - \hat{p})_o$. This shows that the model has been constructed around a specific steady state position, the stability of which will be the focus of our analysis in the next section.

Taken together the model of this section consists of the following four laws of motion; capacity utilization $u^c$; the goods market dynamics, for the employment rate $e$; Okun's Law, for the wage share $v$, describing the real wage channel; and for the inflationary climate expression $\pi^c$ (to be supplemented by the derived reduced form WPC and PPC expressions as far as the wage–price spiral is concerned and with reduced form expressions by assumption concerning the goods and the labor market dynamics).[20] We note that the inflation climate here does not feed back into the rest of the dynamics due to the specific formulation of the Taylor rule of the model (where $\hat{w} - \pi^c$ is used as the expression for the inflation). The intensive form dynamics thus read

$$\hat{u}^c = -\beta_{uu}(u^c - \bar{u}^c) - \beta_{ui}((i - \hat{p}) - (i - \hat{p})_o) \pm \beta_{uv}(v - v_o), \tag{17.34}$$

$$\dot{e} = \beta_{eu} \frac{y^p}{zl_o}\left(u^c - \bar{u}^c \frac{e}{e_o}\right) \quad (y^p, z, l_o \quad \text{given}), \tag{17.35}$$

$$\hat{v} = \hat{w} - \hat{p} = \kappa\left[(1-\kappa_p)(\beta_{we}(e - \bar{e}) + \beta_{wu}(\frac{y^p}{zl_o}\frac{u^c}{e} - \bar{u}^w) - \beta_{wv}\ln(\frac{v}{v_o}))\right.$$
$$\left. - (1-\kappa_w)(\beta_{pu}(u^c - \bar{u}^c) + \beta_{pv}\ln(\frac{v}{v_o}))\right], \tag{17.36}$$

$$\dot{\pi}^c = \beta_{\pi^c}(\hat{p} - \pi^c),$$

(17.37)

with the supplementary equations

$$i - \hat{p} = (i - \hat{p})_o + \alpha_{iw}(\hat{w} - \pi^c) + \alpha_{iu}(u^c - \bar{u}^c) + \alpha_{iv}(v - v_o),$$

(17.38)

$$\hat{w} - \pi^c = \kappa[\beta_{we}(e - \bar{e}) + \beta_{wu}(\frac{y^p}{zl_o}\frac{u^c}{e} - \bar{u}^w) - \beta_{wv}\ln(\frac{v}{v_o})$$

$$+ \kappa_w(\beta_{pu}(u^c - \bar{u}^c) + \beta_{pv}\ln(\frac{v}{v_o}))],$$

(17.39)

$$\hat{p} - \pi^c = \kappa[\beta_{pu}(u^c - \bar{u}^c) + \beta_{pv}\ln(\frac{v}{v_o})$$

$$+ \kappa_p(\beta_{we}(e - \bar{e}) + \beta_{wu}(u^w - \bar{u}^w) - \beta_{wv}\ln(\frac{v}{v_o}))],$$

(17.40)

to be inserted into the laws of motion (17.34)–(17.37). Note here that the reduced form of the PPC (17.40) must be used in the law of motion for the inflationary climate of the economy, but that this law does not feed back into the first three laws of motion for the state variables $u^c, e, v$ which therefore can be studied independently of this climate expression and the PPC (as we have already stated this is due to the type of inflation gap that is considered in the interest rate policy rule).

Note finally that we have tailored the Taylor rule in view of the central feedback channels that characterize this economic structure, in particular for the case where the economy is wage- as well as labor-market-led and thus unstable from the perspective of this partial real wage feedback chain. This exemplifies that an understanding of the important feedback channels of the private sector is essential for a proper formulation of interest rate policy rules. It is difficult to see how a New Keynesian framework could fulfill such a requirement, since it tends to imply trivial deterministic core dynamics in general and therefore nothing systematic in the working of the economy.

The stability features of the model of this section are totally different from those of the New Keynesian model with a staggered wage and price setting, as will be shown in the following section, though its structural equations from a formal perspective are in close correspondence to the ones of its New Keynesian counterpart. This implies that it is not possible that both types of approaches can be considered as explanations of the economic world in which we are living.

## 17.5 Stability features

In this section, we formulate some simple assumptions regarding the model of the preceding section and shall derive the local asymptotic stability of the steady state of the implied reduced form dynamics. In addition we shall include some observations on feedback channels and their theoretical implications. We stress that the core dynamics are in 3-D, since the state variable $\pi^c$ does not feed back into them due to our choice of the Taylor rule.

## *Assumptions*

1. *Assume that $\hat{v}_e > 0$ holds, i.e., the parameter $\beta_{we}$ is chosen sufficiently large such that it dominates the effect of changes in e on the utilization rate of the workforce of firms (an outsider-oriented labor market led economy).*
2. *Assume that $\hat{v}_{u^c} > 0$ holds, i.e., the parameter $\beta_{pu}$ is chosen sufficiently small (relative to $\beta_{wu}$ in this case, an insider-oriented labor market led economy).*
3. *Assume that $\hat{u}_v^c < 0$ holds, i.e., the parameter $\alpha_{iv}$ is chosen sufficiently large.*[21]

On the basis of these three assumptions stability propositions[22] 3, 4 and 6 hold true, see Flaschel (2009) for the proofs.

## *Proposition 3*

1. *The assumptions made imply that of the Jacobian of the 3-D system (17.34)–(17.36) at the steady state has the sign structure:*

$$
J = \begin{pmatrix} - & - & - \\ + & - & 0 \\ + & + & - \end{pmatrix}.
$$

2. *This sign structure implies for the Routh–Hurwitz stability conditions (for the parameters of the characteristic polynomial): $a_1, a_2, a_3 > 0$. The remaining Routh–Hurwitz stability condition $b = a_1 a_2 - a_3 > 0$ is fulfilled if the term $J_{13} J_{21} J_{32}$ in the determinant of the matrix $J$ is dominated by the remaining items in $a_1 a_2$. Under this additional assumption the steady state is locally asymptotically stable.*
3. *An increase in the parameter $\alpha_{iu}$ supports the assumed partial dynamic multiplier stability, i.e., the negative term $J_{11}$ in the trace of the matrix J, and an increase in the parameter $\alpha_{iv}$ does the same for the entry $J_{33}$ in the trace of the Jacobian matrix J.*
4. *Setting the parameter $\alpha_{iw} = 0$ implies $J_{12} = 0$. This parameter, representing the inflation gap control of the interest rate, is thus not essential for the control of the private sector of the economy.*

We have indeed designed the Taylor rule such that the Mundell or real rate of interest channel in the dynamics of the goods market is turned from instability towards stability (even without inflation targeting). This holds, since – when our Taylor rule is inserted into the law of motion for capacity utilization – the real rate of interest is totally replaced by the gaps included into the working of the Taylor rule and since all these gaps have a negative impact on the growth rate of $u^c$. The only remaining feedback channel in this model type is therefore the real wage channel discussed in Section 17.3, which presents no problem in the case where the economy is profit-led, since we have assumed above that the real wage dynamics are labor market led. In the case of wage-led goods market dynamics there is a positive influence of $v$ on the growth rate of capacity utilization and thus we need as a sufficient (though not a necessary) condition that the parameter $\alpha_{uv}$ must be chosen sufficiently large in order to turn the effect of $v$ on $\hat{u}^c$ into a negative one. Here the gap term $\hat{w} - \pi^c$ can be of additional help, due in particular to that fact that it includes the Blanchard and Ketz (1999) error correction terms.

The outcome of this stability analysis is that monetary policy should take into account the feedback channels that characterize the economy to which it is applied, namely in the present case the real rate of interest channel and the real wage or wage share channel. These feedback chains should guide the choice of the primary gaps (and the degree of interest rate smoothing) that are to act on the setting of the interest rate which in fact are here not so much the output gap and the inflation gap (the central gaps in the conventional formulations of the Taylor rule and the Taylor principle that is implied by them). The understanding of the central feedback channels of Keynesian macrodynamics, as they are discussed in Chiarella and Flaschel (2000) and the later work they have developed with various co-authors on this behavioral disequilibrium approach to Keynesian monetary growth, may therefore be crucial for the proper conduct of monetary policy (and also fiscal policy).

We note finally that the hiring and firing parameter $\beta_{eu}$ is not really of importance for the qualitative features of the considered dynamics (the same holds for the parameter $\beta_{\pi^c}$ which however may become of importance if the inflation climate does not enter the formulation of the Taylor rule as we have done it in the preceding section). Under the conditions of Proposition 3 we have what we would call a consent economy, see Flaschel, Franke and Semmler (2007), where there is no real conflict between a flexible hiring and firing economy and the existence of a satisfactory stable balanced growth path, since also wage flexibility (with respect to its demand pressure items) is stabilizing. The most important threat to stability in this case is demand pressure driven price flexibility (relative to the adjustment speed of wages) and here in particular the danger of a deflationary spiral and the economic breakdown that may result from it.

### Proposition 4

*Assume that $\alpha_{iw} = 0$ holds in the Taylor rule (17.38). Then: a sufficient increase in the parameter $\beta_{pu}$ gives rise to a Hopf-bifurcation leading to*

local asymptotic instability by way of the birth of a stable limit cycle or
the death of a stability corridor.

The proof of this proposition is straightforward, since we get in this case $J_{31} < 0$ and since this entry of the Jacobian of the dynamics at the steady state is the only one that depends on the parameter $\beta_{pu}$. If one wishes to use monetary policy to avoid the resulting deflationary spirals (in the case of a global loss of stability) it would be necessary to increase its reaction to the utilization gap, $\alpha_{iu}$, to a sufficient degree.

### Proposition 5

Consider now the case of a wage-led economy where monetary policy is sufficiently inconclusive with respect to the wage gap, i.e., where the entry $J_{13}$ is positive. Then: a sufficient increase in the parameter $\beta_{uv}$ (representing the degree to which the economy is wage-led) will destabilize the steady state of the dynamics.

### Proof of Proposition 5

The proof of this proposition is also straightforward, since the product $J_{13} J_{31}$ will enforce a negative Routh–Hurwitz term if $\beta_{u,v}$ becomes too large, see Flaschel (2009) for details.

We remark that the same result can be achieved through an increase in the parameter $\beta_{wu}$, characterizing the behavior of labor market insiders in the case of a weak reaction of the central bank to the wage inflation gap, by way of the Routh–Hurwitz parameter $a_2$, in other words by way of an unstable feedback chain reaction between capacity utilization $u^c$ and the wage share $v$. Similarly, instability can also be generated through an increase in the parameter $\beta_{we}$ characterizing the role of the external labor market (in the case of a weak reaction of the central bank to the wage inflation gap), here by way of the Routh–Hurwitz parameter $a_3 (= \det J)$, that is by way of an unstable three stage feedback chain reaction between capacity utilization $u^c$, the employment rate $e$ and the wage share $v$. The case of a wage-led goods demand can thus become a problem if this effect is too strong or if wages are too flexible with respect to their demand pressure terms. It thus appears that the profit-led situation is the more robust one in the case where the markups of firms on their cost pressure items are not very responsive to demand pressure on the market for goods. This result casts some doubt on the wage-led scenarios often found or favored in Post-Keynesian economics.

Wage-led scenarios with an indeterminate monetary policy may have characterized the evolution in the late 1960s and early 1970s where accelerating wage and price inflation were observed in many countries. However on average we would expect a profit led situation to have prevailed for the major industrialized countries after World War II, and we will investigate this situation briefly in the following section.

Before closing this section we briefly consider the 4-D extension of the model when the interest rate policy rule is of a more conventional type, so that (17.38) is replaced by

$$i - \hat{p} = (i - \hat{p})_o + \alpha_{ip}(\hat{p} - \bar{\pi}) + \alpha_{iu}(u^c - \bar{u}^c) + \alpha_{iv}(v - v_o). \tag{17.41}$$

The Central Bank here has a given inflation target $\bar{\pi}$ and uses the conventional inflation gap. We need not assume that it chooses the parameter $\alpha_{iu}$ such that $\hat{u}_v^c < 0$ holds again as in the case of a wage-led economy. However, we simplify Okun's Law to the form $\hat{e} = \beta_{eu}(u^c - \bar{u}^c)$, so that the recruitment policy of the firms depends only on the rate of utilization of their capital stock. We can then establish the following proposition:

### Proposition 6

1. *The dynamics (17.34)–(17.37) (with (17.38) replaced by (17.41)) are now 4-D, since $\pi^c$ appears in the law of motion of the goods market.*
2. *The determinant of the Jacobian matrix of the system at the interior steady state (which in this case is easily shown to be uniquely determined) is positive.*
3. *The stable 3-D core dynamics (where the influence of $\pi^c$ is neglected) remain stable in their 4-D form if the parameter $\beta_{\pi^c}$ is sufficiently small.*
4. *The dynamics may not necessarily lose stability (by way of a Hopf-bifurcation) if the parameter $\beta_{\pi^c}$ becomes sufficiently large, so that the Mundell-effect is neutralized by way of the chosen interest rate policy rule.*

## 17.6 Keynesian DAD–DAS theory: some empirical evidence

For the econometric estimation of the model for the UK we use the aggregate time series available from the International Financial Statistics database and the National Statistics database (http://www.statistics.gov.uk). The data, described in Table 17.2, is quarterly, seasonally adjusted and concerns the period from 1980:1 to 2003:4.

*Table 17.2* UK data set

| Variable | Description of the original series |
| --- | --- |
| $e$: | Employment rate |
| $u^c$: | Industrial production Hodrick–Prescott cyclical term (calculated with a smoothing factor of $\lambda = 1600$) |
| $w$: | Average earnings in industrial production, sa (year 2000 = 100) |
| $p$: | Gross domestic product: implicit price deflator, year 2000 = 100 |
| $p_c$: | CPI Index, all items, year 2000 = 100 |
| $z$: | Labor productivity, year 1996 = 100 |
| $v$: | Real unit wage costs (deflated by GDP deflator), year 2003 = 100 |
| $i$: | Treasury bill rate |

The logarithms of wages and prices are denoted $\ln(w_t)$ and $\ln(p_t)$, respectively. Their first differences are dated backwards, so that the current rate of wage and price inflation are denoted $\hat{w}_t$ and $\hat{p}_t$. The inflationary climate $\pi^c$ of the theoretical part of this chapter is approximated here in a very simple way by a linearly declining moving average of CPI price inflation rates (measured by $p_c$ in Table 17.2) with linearly decreasing weights over the past twelve quarters, denoted $\pi_t^{12}$.

In order to be able to identify in a structural manner the dynamics of the system and especially of the wage and price inflation (since as discussed in Section 17.3, the law of motion for the real wage rate, given by (17.28) represents a reduced form expression of the two structural equations for $\hat{w}_t$ and $\hat{p}_t$), we estimate the following discrete time reformulation of our continuous time theoretical model (described in Section 17.3):

$$\hat{w}_t = \beta_{we}(e_{t-1} - e_o) + \beta_{wu}\chi\left(\frac{u_{t-1}^c}{e_{t-1}} - \frac{u_o^c}{e_o}\right) - \beta_{wv}\ln(v_{t-1}/v_o)$$

$$+\kappa_{wp}\hat{p}_t + (1 - \kappa_{wp})\pi_t^{12} + \kappa_{wz}\hat{z}_t + \epsilon_{wt}, \tag{17.42}$$

$$\hat{p}_t = \beta_{pu}(u_{t-1}^c - u_o^c) + \beta_{pv}\ln(v_{t-1}/v_o)$$

$$+\kappa_{pw}(\hat{w}_t - \hat{z}_t) + (1 - \kappa_{pw})\pi_t^{12} + \epsilon_{pt}, \tag{17.43}$$

$$\ln u_t^c = \ln u_{t-1}^c - \beta_{uu}(u_t^c - u_o^c) - \beta_{ui}(i_{t-1} - \hat{p}_t) \pm \beta_{uv}(v_{t-1} - v_o) + \epsilon_{ut}, \tag{17.44}$$

$$e_t = e_{t-1} + \beta_{eu}\chi\left(u_{t-1} - \frac{u_o^c}{e_o}e_{t-1}\right) + \epsilon_{et}, \tag{17.45}$$

$$i_t = i_{t-1} - \alpha_{ii}i_{t-1} + \alpha_{iw}\hat{w}_t + \alpha_{iu}(u_{t-1}^c - u_o^c) + c_i + \epsilon_{it}, \tag{17.46}$$

with $\chi = \dfrac{y^p}{zl_o}$ for notational simplicity and all variables with a subscript o denoting sample averages (which can be interpreted as the analogue to the steady state values in the theoretical model). The statistical error terms in each equation are represented by the respective $\epsilon$ term.

It should be noted that rather than using the intensive form dynamics for the wage share $v$ (equation (17.36)) we use the structural forms for $\hat{w}$ and $\hat{p}$ given by (17.24) and (17.25), of which (17.42) and (17.43) are discretized versions. Equations (17.44) and (17.45) are discretized versions of (17.34) and (17.35). Finally we now use as Taylor rule the one shown in (17.46), i.e., for reasons of simplicity one without the term $\alpha_{iv}(v - v_0)$, and also using a lagged adjustment, see our original formulation in (17.33). Whilst this increases the dynamic dimensions of the system to be estimated it has the advantage of setting up interest rate lags that improve the empirical estimations.

In order to account for regressor endogeneity, we estimate the discrete time version of the structural model formulated above by means of instrumental variables system GMM (Generalized Method of Moments) which has the advantage of not relying on a specific assumption with respect to the distribution of the error terms. The weighting matrix in the GMM objective function was chosen in order to allow the resulting GMM estimates to be robust against possible heteroskedasticity and serial correlation of an unknown form in the error terms. Concerning the instrumental variables used in our estimations, since at time $t$ only past values are contained in the information sets of the economic agents, for all five equations we use, besides the strictly exogenous variables, the last four lagged values of the employment rate, the labor share (detrended by the Hodrick–Prescott Filter) and the growth rate of labor productivity. In order to test for the validity of the overidentifying restrictions, the $J$-statistics[23] for both system estimations were calculated.

Since the formulation of the monetary policy rule in Section 17.4 was primarily *ad hoc* – with wage instead of price inflation as the target variable of the monetary authorities – in order to keep the dimension of the model low, we also estimate our model with the current price inflation as the target variable (note that the corresponding coefficient becomes $\alpha_{ip}$ in plane of $\alpha_{iw}$) as is usually done in the literature. We present the structural parameter estimates under these two specifications for the UK economy ($t$-statistics in brackets), as well as the $J$-statistics in Tables 17.3 and 17.4.

At a general level the GMM parameter estimates shown in Tables 17.3 and 17.4 deliver empirical support for the specification of our theoretical Keynesian disequilibrium model and confirm for the UK to a large extent the empirical findings of Flaschel and Krolzig (2006) and Flaschel, Kauermann and Semmler (2007) for the US economy, as well as Proaña et al. (2006) for the Euro area. In particular we find empirical support for the specification of crossover expectational terms, with the wage inflation entering in the price Phillips curve and the price inflation entering in the wage Phillips curve, as well as for the inclusion of the inflationary climate term in both equations. These results stand in stark contrast to the parameter estimates based on New Keynesian wage and price Phillips curves, where no crossover expectation schemes are assumed and were not the present, but rather the one-period ahead expected wage and price inflation rate determine the present wage and price inflation.

Also in line with the previously mentioned studies, we find a statistically significant influence of the Blanchard–Katz error correction terms (the log deviation of the wage share from its steady state value) in both the wage and price inflation equations. Concerning the IS equation, the coefficient of the wage share is negative and statistically significant in both countries, leading to the presumption that the UK like the US and the Eurozone economies (see Proaña et al. 2006) are profit led economies. Our differentiation between "outside" and "inside" employment also finds support in our estimation not only in the wage inflation equation but also in the employment equation. A remarkable result concerning this term is the nearly identical estimated values for $u_o^c/e_o$ as predicted by our

*Table 17.3* GMM parameter estimates (with $\hat{w}$ in the monetary policy rule)

| | *Estimation sample: 1980:1−2003:4* | | | | | | |
|---|---|---|---|---|---|---|---|
| | *Kernel: Bartlett, Bandwidth: variable Newey–West (6)* | | | | | | |
| | $\beta_{we}$ | $\beta_{wv}$ | $\kappa_{wp}$ | $\beta_{wu}\chi$ | $u_o^c/e_o$ | $\bar{R}^2$ | *DW* |
| $\hat{w}_t$ | 1.283 | −0.227 | 0.297 | 1.005 | 1.082 | 0.494 | 1.592 |
| | [17.706] | [8.623] | [7.575] | [15.657] | [1078.1] | | |
| | $\beta_{pu}$ | $\beta_{pv}$ | $\kappa_{pw}$ | | | $\bar{R}^2$ | *DW* |
| $\hat{p}_t$ | 0.358 | 0.227 | 0.386 | | | 0.353 | 2.334 |
| | [3.336] | [4.408] | [9.884] | | | | |
| | $\beta_{uu}$ | $\beta_{ul}$ | $\beta_{uv}$ | | | $\bar{R}^2$ | *DW* |
| $\hat{u}_t$ | −0.367 | −0.014 | −0.097 | | | 0.426 | 1.986 |
| | [15.854] | [2.166] | [7.036] | | | | |
| | $\beta_{eu}\chi$ | $u_o^c/e_o$ | | | | $\bar{R}^2$ | *DW* |
| $\dot{e}$ | 0.030 | 1.068 | | | | 0.979 | 1.197 |
| | [7.744] | [182.71] | | | | | |
| | $\alpha_{ii}$ | $\alpha_{iw}$ | $\alpha_{iu}$ | $c_i$ | | $\bar{R}^2$ | *DW* |
| $i$ | 0.113 | 0.084 | 0.049 | 0.002 | | 0.939 | 1.849 |
| | [84.002] | [7.119] | [3.868] | [6.138] | | | |
| Determinant residual covariance | | | | | 1.80E-19 | | |
| *J*-statistic | | | | | 0.156 | | |

formulation of Okun's Law. It is also remarkable that the parameter estimates in all equations are quite robust to the alternative specification of the monetary policy rule, and that both specifications deliver quite plausible results, with the wage inflation coefficient ($\alpha_{iw}$ in Table 17.4) being actually higher than the price inflation coefficient (denoted by $\alpha_{ip}$ in Table 17.4).

By inserting the estimated parameters of Table 17.3 into the continuous time intensive form dynamic equations given by equations (17.34)–(17.36), we find support for the characterizations of the sign structure of the Jacobian matrix of our Keynesian disequilibrium AD–AS model, namely

$$J = \begin{pmatrix} - & - & - \\ + & - & 0 \\ + & + & - \end{pmatrix}$$

and more importantly, for the validity of the Routh--Hurwitz conditions for local asymptotic stability $a_1 > 0$, $a_2 > 0$, $a_3 > 0$ (see Flaschel (2009, Ch.8) for a thorough

*Table 17.4* GMM parameter estimates (with $\hat{p}$ in the monetary policy rule)

| | Estimation sample: 1980:1–2003:4 | | | | | | |
|---|---|---|---|---|---|---|---|
| | *Kernel: Bartlett, Bandwidth: variable Newey–West (6)* | | | | | | |
| | $\beta_{we}$ | $\beta_{wv}$ | $\kappa_{wp}$ | $\beta_{wu}\chi$ | $u_o^c/e_o$ | $\bar{R}^2$ | DW |
| $\hat{w}_t$ | 1.287 | −0.227 | 0.296 | 1.010 | 1.082 | 0.494 | 1.592 |
| | [17.835] | [9.181] | [7.781] | [15.374] | [1117.4] | | |
| | $\beta_{pu}$ | $\beta_{pv}$ | $\kappa_{pw}$ | | | $\bar{R}^2$ | DW |
| $\hat{p}_t$ | 0.350 | 0.224 | 0.388 | | | 0.353 | 2.338 |
| | [2.992] | [4.318] | [9.323] | | | | |
| $\hat{u}_t$ | $\beta_{uu}$ | $\beta_{ui}$ | $\beta_{uv}$ | | | $\bar{R}^2$ | DW |
| | −0.365 | −0.013 | −0.096 | | | 0.426 | 1.989 |
| | [15.099] | [2.176] | [6.857] | | | | |
| | $\beta_{eu}\chi$ | $u_o^c/e_o$ | | | | $\bar{R}^2$ | DW |
| $\dot{e}$ | 0.030 | 1.068 | | | | 0.979 | 1.197 |
| | [7.488] | [178.53] | | | | | |
| | $\alpha_{ii}$ | $\alpha_{ip}$ | $\alpha_{iu}$ | $c_i$ | | $\bar{R}^2$ | DW |
| $i$ | 0.058 | 0.024 | 0.051 | 0.002 | | 0.933 | 1.816 |
| | [109.90] | [2.745] | [4.251] | [4.904] | | | |
| Determinant residual covariance | | | | | 1.87E-19 | | |
| J-statistic | | | | | 0.156 | | |

analytical calculation of these conditions), as well as

$$b = a_1 \cdot a_2 - a_3 = 0.3162 > 0.$$

In order to confirm this result and also in order to show the qualitative responses of the model with the estimated parameter values we show in Figure 17.2 its dynamic adjustments to a one percent monetary policy shock under a wage and a price inflation targeting scheme (the latter is using the estimated coefficients of the monetary policy rule of Table 17.4).

As Figure 17.2 shows, our calibrated model delivers dynamic adjustment paths which are quite plausible from the qualitative perspective under both specifications, showing that a theoretical framework based on disequilibrium adjustment processes which concern both the goods and the labor markets can indeed be used to analyze the effects of monetary policy in modern economies. This concludes the investigation of integrated Keynesian macroeconomics which will be pursued further in Volume II.

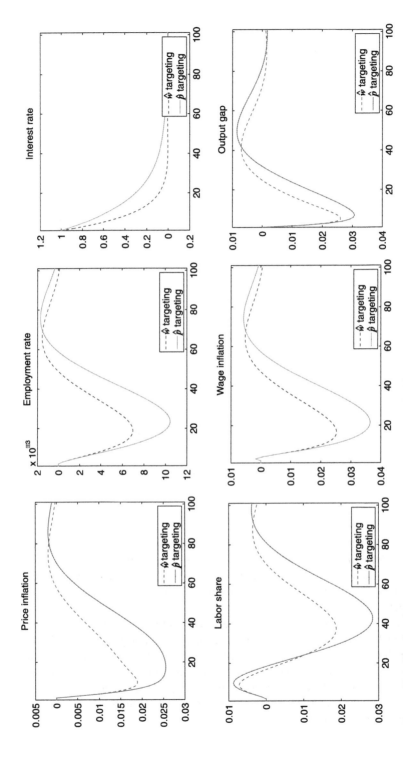

*Figure 17.2* Simulated quarter responses to a one percent monetary policy shock (annualized values)

## 17.7 The next steps: integrated studies of fluctuating growth

In this chapter we have considered two competing approaches to Keynesian macrodynamics which are similar in their formal structure, but radically different in their implications for the working of the economy on the macrolevel.

The established New Keynesian approach is rigorously microfounded and stochastic in nature, but is generally built on loglinear approximations and uses rational expectations algorithms to determine the reaction of the economy to macroeconomic shocks of various types. Its deterministic core is in the baseline cases of a purely forward looking economy with both staggered wages and prices (if determinacy applies) fairly trivial and thus completely devoid of interesting economic statements. Adding elements of inertia like habit formation, indexing and the like may make this approach more applicable, but is often coupled with a loss of rigor as far as microfoundations are concerned. The New Keynesian approach, the Keynesian version of the New Neoclassical Synthesis, represents a complete renunciation from anything that characterizes Keynes' (1936, Ch.22) analysis of the trade cycle and rather represents a new type of, by and large, stochastic approach to macrodynamics based on imperfect competition and staggered adjustment processes.

Our alternative traditional, but matured approach to Keynesian AD–AS dynamics builds on the traditional Neoclassical Synthesis, the microfoundations of which were of a quite different type as compared to the New Neoclassical Synthesis, by adding theory-based wage–price dynamics[24] in the spirit of Blanchard and Katz (1999), see also Flaschel and Krlozig (2006) in this regard. We obtain thereby a wage–price module that is formally similar to the one employed in the New Keynesian approach, but now based on model-consistent short-run expectations (of crossover type using neoclassical dating procedures) and medium-run inflation inertia instead of the non-crossover purely forward looking expectations of the New Keynesian framework. We moreover employ a dynamic IS-curve and a Taylor rule as in the New Keynesian approach and thus have a macrostructure that is easily compared with its New Keynesian alternative. Yet, rational expectation solution procedures are completely absent in this alternative approach, since all variables (inflation rates, output and interest rates) are now predetermined variables and allow us to analyze the model in the way ordinary differential equations are usually analyzed in the mathematical literature. We get interesting deterministic implications of this matured approach to Keynesian macrodynamics (also when it is estimated). However its extension by exogenous stochastic disturbances is still uninvestigated and left for future research.

Taking all this together, our conclusion is that the framework proposed here not only overcomes anomalies of the traditional Neoclassical Synthesis, see Asada et al. (2006), but also provides a coherent alternative to its new formulation, the New Keynesian theory of the business cycle, as for example sketched in Galí (2000). Our alternative to this approach to macrodynamics is based on disequilibrium in the market for goods and labor, as is reasonable in a continuous time framework, and thus on sluggish adjustment of prices as well as wages (in the context of model-consistent inflationary expectations that are interacting with sluggishly changing inflation climate expressions). The dynamic outcomes of our model provide great potential for further generalizations, such as an advanced Metzlerian approach to goods market dynamics and a Tobinian portfolio approach to financial markets (with the short-term interest rate being determined by the central bank), also in the framework of an open economy. Some of these generalizations have already been considered in Chiarella et al. (2000b, 2005), and Asada et al. (2003). These routes to more advanced models of the interaction of real and financial markets, with gradual adjustment at least on the real markets, are in principle much easier to establish than their equivalents in the New Keynesian representative agent approach to macrodynamics.

We will pursue the analysis of integrated Keynesian macrodynamics further in Volume II, with the present chapter just indicating the type of research we will present there. We will do this both in the form of semi-structural integrated approaches like the one of the present chapter as well as completely integrated Keynesian macrodynamics where all behavioral relationships are explicitly shown and all budget restrictions specified, providing – when appropriately arranged – the (flow) social accounting matrix of the economy besides its (stock) balance sheet accounts. In Volume II we therefore study in great detail the matured Keynesian approach as we have obtained it here from the traditional Neoclassical Synthesis (which is an extreme limit case of it). The level of comparison will be the New Keynesian baseline model with both staggered wages and prices and later on also the more general DSGE approaches of the applied New Keynesian literature.

We do not, however, merely mean by a cyclical movement that upward and downward tendencies, once started, do not persist for ever in the same direction but are ultimately reversed. We mean also that there is some recognizable degree of regularity in the time-sequence and duration of the upward and downward movements. There is, however, another characteristic of what we call the trade cycle which our explanation must cover if it is to be adequate; namely, the phenomenon of the crisis – the fact that the substitution of a downward for an upward tendency often takes place suddenly and violently, whereas there is, as a rule, no such sharp turning-point when an upward is substituted for a downward tendency.

Keynes (1936, pp.313–314)

# Notes

## Introduction: Keynesian macroeconomics

1  These three marginal conditions are: the Euler equation defining intertemporal consumption decisions, the marginal rate of substitution equal to the real wage, and the marginal product of labor equal to the real wage.
2  For details on regime dependent multiplier effects, see Mittnik and Semmler (2010b).
3  See Keynes (1936, pp.135–136) for his original proposal of such a definition.
4  The other two parameters merely play the role of amplifiers.
5  Unconstrained is here being used in the sense of no temporary income constraints.
6  The way intertemporal budget equations are made binding is however usually not so obvious in the mainstream approaches and empirically and practically it does not give much guidance as to how the agents should behave in a particular moment of time.
7  Functional income distribution refers not to personal income distribution, but distribution related to economic functions, such as capital, labor etc.
8  The reader is referred to vol. 38 in (2006) of the journal *History of Political Economy* for a variety of articles that discuss the implications of their theorems.
9  See Galí, López-Salido and Valles (2007). For a similar type of model with constrained consumer choice, constrained by employment opportunities, see Semmler and Gong (2011).
10  See Flaschel, Groh, Proaño and Semmler (2008, Ch.1) for a detailed study of the status and the relevance of period models using arguments of this type.
11  See Chiarella et al. (2009) and Part II of this book for further considerations of this type. See also Colander (2006) for a collection of essays that attempt to go beyond Post-Walrasian DSGE macroeconomics.
12  The known Italian philosopher Vico said once that "history is man made history". But his means that also future generations will make their decisions – and will make history – and how do we know what they will decide? If we endow them with rational choices how can we form rational expectations today?
13  For regime dependent responses of fiscal and monetary policy shocks, see Mittnik and Semmler (2010a, b).
14  See also Flaschel, Groh, Proaño and Semmler (2008) and Asada et al. (2010) for more details on the validity of these statements.
15  See Chapter 10 for this type of approach.

## 1 Applicable macro is continuous time macro

1  Note in this respect again, that we focus in this chapter on standard period models and therefore do not yet consider, as in Invernizzi and Medio (1991) and Medio (1991) the role of significant delays in and exponential lags of economic activity.

2   This discrepancy between the frequency of the data generating and the data collecting processes is ignored in the majority of empirical mainstream macroeconomic models, which generally simply assume for the time intervals of the theoretical framework the same periodicity as the data collecting process.

3   An analysis of the accuracy of solutions of non-linear models with respect-to higher order approximations can be found in Becker et al. (2007).

4   We have to thank T. Pampel of making us aware of the fact that this indeed holds for all positive period lengths $h$.

5   See Chen (1988) for a delayed feedback model of economic growth.

6   See Flaschel and Proaño (2009) for another example of "strange" macrodynamics ("strange" attractors) and its detailed discussion.

7   See Fuhrer and Moore (1995) for a variety of models of New Keynesian type that are expressed and analyzed in continuous time.

## 2 Walras' Law and the role of dimensional analysis in economics

1   For this, see for example Buiter (1980, p.4): "an economic agent plans, at time $t - \Delta t_3$, to demand at time $t$ ..., for delivery at time $t + \Delta t_1$, when the length of the interval between markets is $\Delta t_2$."

2   Such approaches typically make use of various sorts of simultaneously conducted limit processes and by only applying them to a small section of the whole structure of the macro-model.

3   It is one of the mysteries of this type of continuous time analysis how the simultaneous occurrence of equations (2.6) and (2.7) can be justified economically, and their implications for the bond stock demand function, in particular in view of their discrete time analogues, cf. Section 2.3.

4   Note here, that (2.8) only concerns private savings and that Sargent's government budget constraint $\bar{G} - \bar{T} \equiv \dot{M}/\tilde{p} + \dot{B}/\tilde{p} \equiv -S_g$ has to be added in order to get $I = S$ as well-known accounting identity.

5   A standard textbook for engineering science with some economic examples is Szirtes (2007).

6   The book of De Jong nevertheless differs in its results significantly from our following dimensional specifications of basic macro-equations and has, in our view, to be read with great care.

7   Note, that $N$ stands for the total number of laborers employed, a "tally" in the language of dimensional analysis. This "tally" has to be included into the formulation of the Phillips curve in the dynamic extension of this model.

8   The first thing to take note of here is the simple fact that in a continuous time setup all "flow" magnitudes such as $Y$ must have the dimension $[G]/[T] = [GT^{-1}]$.

9   This again shows that $N[L]$ – just as $K[G]$ – should be treated as a stock variable which is of the type of a "primary" or non-composed dimension ["men employed"].

10   Note here, that the above analysis implies that dimensional analysis imposes restrictions on the proper choice of possible production functions. Furthermore, its theoretically representation in the form $Y = F(c_k K, c_n N)$ implies that *it must be* homogeneous of degree 1.

11   This reflects the economically plausible circumstance that an isolated variation of the length of the market period should in principle not influence the momentary portfolio decision.

12   In fact, one may even be inclined to discuss a third possibility where N is given the secondary dimension $[LT^1]$ of a flow variable and where the dimensions of $w, p, k$ are adjusted appropriately.

13   This explains the special symbol we have chosen here to denote the goods price in continuous time. Once the meaning of $\tilde{p}$ is understood one can however return to

denote the goods price just by $p$ though it is not of the same dimension as its discrete time analogue.

14  Note, that $\tilde{p}$ is well-defined by the continuous time model. Note furthermore, that the time-dimension of $\tilde{p} = ph$ has been moved here to the right-hand side of equation (2.2″), taking account of the fact that the marginal product of labor depends on the length of the time-period $h$ during which the employed stock of labor $N$ will be at work. Note finally, that labor is assumed to be paid ex post in such a model.

15  Or on the particular economy under consideration.

16  Cf. however the concluding remark of this chapter.

17  Cf. e.g. Sargent (1987, p.73) in this regard.

18  Goods market equilibrium now *implies* $(B^d - \bar{B}) + (M^d - \bar{M}) = 0$ in the continuous case, i.e., an identity of type (2.7) – which thus no longer exists independently of this equilibrium condition.

19  Whether this mathematical rewriting of the $h$-model is indeed successful in the sense that the qualitative study of the derived differential equations will in fact reveal the typical dynamic behavior of the full set of equations of the $h$-economy is, of course, a matter of mathematical investigation or numerical simulation.

## 3 Lucas (1975): too *ad hoc*?

1  Cf. De Jong (1967, Ch.1.4) on the distinction between such entities and pure numbers, such as "men employed"[L], a "tally" in the language of dimensional analysis.

2  Cf. De Jong (1967) for details.

3  Note, that these presentations and our following comments on them differ significantly from the lengthy and mixed discussion in De Jong (1967, pp.34ff.).

4  *Ad hoc* in the sense that the specification is not built on microfoundations but rather on the assumption of certain cross-substitutability between capital and money.

5  What is calculated is $(\ln o\ f\ o \exp)'(\ln x_0) = (\ln o\ f)'(x_0)$.

## 4 Price flexibility and instability: Tobin (1975) reconsidered

1  See also Flaschel and Franke (2000), who provide a shorter and somewhat simplified version of this chapter.

2  There has been a debate in the literature on the issue whether increased price flexibility is stabilizing or destabilizing (two central contributions are De Long and Summers (1986), and Gray and Kandil (1991)). It has, however, to be noted that this discussion is concerned with a different problem. What is studied, in connection with staggered wage contracts and an accompanying rational expectations hypothesis, is the relationship between the variance of the cyclical component of real output and some parameter(s) characterizing the flexibility of prices and wages. The fluctuations themselves are generated by exogenous stochastic shocks. Asymptotic stability if exogenous stochastic shocks are absent is not called into question.

3  Price determination by way of the marginal productivity principle for labor may provide another channel through which falling output translates into falling prices. The price level is then inversely related to the marginal product of labor, which rises when employment falls.

4  In essence, this mechanism was already pointed out by Keynes in Chapter 19 of his *General Theory*, which is devoted to a discussion of "changes in Money Wages". As is well-known, Keynes was very skeptical in this chapter about the beneficial effects of flexible wages. The mechanism of the later so-called "Keynes effect" is indeed the only one he recognized as being of any significance to the classical stance of flexible wages (Keynes 1936, p.266).

5  Tobin calls this effect the Fisher or the real interest effect (Tobin 1989, p.17).

6  The destabilizing effect of high values of $\beta_\pi$ was already pointed out by Cagan (1956). Inequality (4.1) is equivalent to one of the Routh–Hurwitz conditions. Thus, it is only necessary, not sufficient for asymptotic stability. Two of the four Routh–Hurwitz conditions are always satisfied, whilst the fourth may be violated even if (4.1) applies. In this sense also the other parameters of the model may have their bearing on stability.

7  Fluctuations in labor productivity are here neglected.

8  Equation (4.3) is a reduced-form specification of price determination. So price reactions appear sluggish only in a certain formal way.

9  Following Fischer (1972) or Duguay and Rabeau (1988), expected inflation might also be added on the RHS of equation (4.4) (or a similar term; cf. Flaschel 1993, Ch.6 for several proposals in this regard). Such a specification of the price setting behavior of firms would take account of the inflationary climate in which it takes place, and which at the same time it helps to sustain. Equation (4.4), on the other hand, implies zero inflation in the steady state. Similar to Boggess (1983) we assume that a possible self-reference of inflation on price level changes is based on this steady state experience (which may be considered a legitimate assumption in a local stability investigation of steady states). Mathematically, however, the issue is of secondary importance. Including, or not, $\pi$ in (4.4) does not essentially affect the stability propositions in the adaptive framework.

10  It is not so much growth and the endogenous determination of the capital stock that greatly complicates the analysis but the various repercussion effects when $\hat{p}$ in equation (4.3) has to be expressed in terms of the other dynamic variables. Sargent has stopped his formal analysis just at this point.

11  Since we shall continue to disregard capacity effects and long-run growth, our model will no doubt in this respect be less general than Sargent's. The framework of the stationary economy is, however, sufficient to make our main points on the impact of low and high price flexibility on stability. If they are considered sufficiently interesting and relevant, the analysis may later return to Sargent's setup. Based on the findings in Frank (1992a) and some other computational experiences, we are sure that the main conclusions will survive.

12  This is consistent with Sargent's specification of investment as a function of $(F_K - \delta) - (r - \pi)(\delta$ being the rate of capital depreciation). Since he assumes the marginal productivity principle for labor, the first bracket is equal to the profit rate.

13  Note that in the stationary state the marginal propensity to spend is simply given by $C'$ since with $dI/dY = 1/F_N$, one has $dI/dY = I'(1 - w/(pF_N))=0$.

14  Groth (1988) investigates the stability properties of a related model where the expectations mechanism is of a combined adaptive-forward-looking type (on the basis of a positive growth rate of the money supply). Apart from this extension and a somewhat peculiar treatment of taxes (tax levying is a residual in the government budget restraint), his model still suppresses money wages and works with the price Phillips curve (4.2). Groth's results provide further details on the importance of the Tobin condition (4.1) and its relationship to the Cagan (1956) instability condition for models of monetary growth. This analysis is continued in Groth (1993) where also questions of global stability, corridor effects, and the existence of non-local limit cycles are addressed.

15  Since the dynamics is in 3-D, the convenient analytical device of the Poincaré–Bendixson Theorem is no longer applicable. In the end one would, therefore, have to resort to numerical simulations. We may claim that this is not a completely hopeless task (see, e.g., Frank (1992a) for a somewhat related model with dynamic adjustments of a markup factor).

16  For notational simplicity we use the same symbol as in Section 4.3. Note, however, the difference in the arguments of $\phi$.

17 In this case there is no need to resort to the jump-variable technique that is adopted by Sargent in Chapter V.2 of his textbook in order to cope with the immanent instability in the presence of $\beta_\pi = \infty$ as well as $\beta_p = \infty$ (which, likewise, is of saddlepoint type).

18 The case of adaptive expectations could also be easily extended in this way. Though the resulting system is four-dimensional, a local stability analysis may not be hopeless since the Jacobian exhibits a number of zero entries and we know what to look for. Such a complementary investigation is nevertheless beyond the scope of this chapter. In the light of Proposition 4 we do not expect to find anything essentially new, either.

19 A more recent treatment of this issue is provided in Franke and Lux (1993) and Franke (1996).

20 $\beta_p = \infty$ in the first column of Table 4.1 must be interpreted as representing a constant markup over average (not marginal) wage costs. The parameter $\beta_p$ in equation (4.2) (which parallels Tobin's notation) originates with a wage Phillips curve. In accordance with our later notational practice, it may now be better substituted by $\beta_w$ (see the discussion of (4.2)).

## 5 Stock market driven multiplier dynamics: a reconsideration

1 See Chiarella et al. (2009, Ch. 2) for a detailed treatment of this stock and bond market approach to IS–LM dynamics.

2 This analysis is, in fact, a lot simpler than the one in Blanchard (1981), since one does not have multiple equilibria and good and bad news cases in this interaction of output, investment and the long-term rate of interest.

3 Blanchard (1981) also considers the term structure of interest rates. However, the long-term rate of interest does not influence the real–financial interaction he investigates. The role of the term structure of interest rates for the real dynamics is investigated in Blanchard and Fischer (1989, 10.4).

4 Chiarella et al. (2009) does not yet treat labor productivity growth explicitly. Yet, extending this approach by labor productivity growth of the Harrod neutral type is a straightforward exercise and does not alter the presentation of the intensive form of the model.

5 Note that the third law of motion is in particular using the budget equation of firms which reads $p_e \dot{E} = p\dot{K}$.

6 Or a constant that may be larger than one as far as empirical measurement of the long-run ratio are concerned.

7 A (given) risk premium $\xi$ should of course be introduced into this differential equation if empirical applications of the model are intended, see Chiarella et al. (2002).

8 Note here that the Jacobian at the steady state of the dynamics (5.8)–(5.10) exhibits, for $\beta_y (c - 1) + r_0 - n < 0$, a negative trace and a positive determinant, i.e., the unstable manifold of these dynamics is always of dimension 1. The jump-variable technique is therefore in principle applicable, at least from the local perspective.

9 $m = m_0 = ky_o$ and $r_o = (1 - v) y_o - \delta + \epsilon_o - \xi$ by assumption, see the following proposition.

10 See Gantmacher (1959).

11 See Strogatz (1994) for a presentation of the Hopf-bifurcation theorem.

12 Note that we have assumed for reasons of simplicity $k_{p_e} = 0$ in the second law of motion.

13 See Chiarella et al. (2009) for details of such limit cycle generating 3-D dynamics.

14 See Chiarella et al. (2002) for an extrinsically non-linear approach to the estimation of the Blanchard output–stock price dynamics which does not make use of the ratios we employ in this chapter.

15 Note that the $q$ term in goods demand may now also, from the empirical perspective, refer to consumption demand, which may respond positively to increases in Tobin's $q$ too. This further aspect of the features that characterize aggregate demand clearly increases the relevance the model from the empirical point of view.
16 See Chiarella et al. (2000b) for the opposite type of approach.
17 $r = a_m y - b_m m + c_m$, $\epsilon = \hat{p}_e^e$ and $\rho = a_\pi y - c_\pi$.

## 6 Inflation and perfect foresight: implications of non-linearity

1 This chapter is based on Flaschel, P. and Sethi, R. (1998): "Stability in models of money and perfect foresight. Implications of non-linearity". *Economic Modelling*, 16, 221–233.
2 The technique was not always uncritically accepted, particularly in earlier work. Burmeister (1980) argued for the use of sluggish (rather than instantaneous) price adjustment, while maintaining the rational expectations assumption. Oxley and George (1994) pointed to the structural instability of convergence in linear saddlepoint models as a whole. Blanchard (1981, p.135), while accepting the methodology, describes it as a "standard if not entirely convincing practice". For a more recent discussion, see Oxley and George (1994).
3 Chiarella (1986, 1990) derives the perfect foresight case as the limit of adaptive expectations as the speed of expectation revision goes to infinity.
4 This assumption is required also in the Sargent and Wallace model; see Calvo (1977) for the relevant details.
5 For a similar analysis of monetary and fiscal policy changes within a non-linear exchange rate model, see Chiarella (1992).

## 7 Determinacy in the New-Keynesian sticky wage/price model

1 This chapter is based on an unpublished paper by Reiner Franke and Peter Flaschel. We thank Reiner Franke for allowing us to publish this paper in this book.
2 It is thus established that, letting the period tend to zero, the final continuous time Jacobian matrices of the present and the *ad hoc* formulation have indeed identical sign patterns. On the other hand, the (discrete time) high-frequency formulation in Flaschel, Groh, Proaño and Semmler (2008), which rests on a purely formal analogy, can now be seen to be an inadequate representation of the structural relationships of the New-Keynesian model.
3 Which, in particular, implies that there is no scope for endogenous cyclical behavior, or an overshooting wage-price spiral.
4 This $\phi$ may not be confused with the policy coefficients $\phi_w$, $\ln(\phi_p)$, $\phi_y$ in the Taylor rule.
5 Note that solving $\beta = 1/(1+\rho)$ for $\rho$ gives $\rho = 1/(1-\beta)/\beta \approx \ln[1+(1-\beta)/\beta] = \ln(1/\beta) = -\ln \beta$.
6 It is quite a common feature in New-Keynesian models that, in the presence of a positive weight on output fluctuations, determinacy of the steady state is also guaranteed if the central bank raises interest rates a bit less than one-to-one in response to an increase in inflation. A detailed discussion of this issue can be found in Woodford (2003, p.254). Another condition for this to hold may, however, not be neglected, namely, the absence of nominal taxes; cf. Edge and Rudd (2007).
7 Where it is understood that $\phi_w$ and $\phi_p$ vary in fixed proportions. Effectively, in all our numerical experiments $\phi_{wp}^*(h)$ proved to be practically independent of this proportion.
8 Since we could not find an explicit value for $\varepsilon_w$ (until Section 8.3), we assigned the value of $\varepsilon = \varepsilon_p$ from p.52 to it.

9  The eigen-values can here be denoted by the usual letter "$\lambda$" since there will be no more risk of confusing them with the parameters $\lambda_w$, $\lambda_p$ in (7.11) and (7.13).

10  To show them, use the fact that the characteristic polynomial equals $(\lambda - \lambda_1)(\lambda - \lambda_2)(\lambda - \lambda_3)(\lambda - \lambda_4)$ and expand out.

## 8 Disequilibrium growth theory with insider–outsider effects

1  This chapter is based on Flaschel, P. (2000): "Disequilibrium growth theory with insider–outsider effects". *Structural Change and Economic Dynamics*, 11, 337–354.

2  See Chiarella et al. (2000b, Ch.4) for detailed demonstrations of such an assertion.

3  See Flaschel et al. (1997) for presentations (and for extensions) of this prototype model of cyclical growth.

4  The two natural rates $n$, $\bar{e}$ are made dynamically endogenous variables in Chiarella and Flaschel (1998).

5  Note that this means that firms have to consider $e \leq 1$ and $n = \hat{L}^s$ as two separate characteristics of the labor market.

6  Assuming $\beta_l \to 0$ as $e \to 1$ says that it becomes more and more difficult for firms to recruit further workers from the existing labor market when the external rate of employment approaches 1. They then choose instead to operate more and more directly on labor supply decisions $\hat{L}^s$.

7  The parameter values for this simulation of the model are: $\beta_{w_1} = 0.5$, $\beta_{w_2} = 0.05$, $n = 0.05$, $\bar{e} = 0.99$, $s_c = 0.9$, $\beta_l = 0.1$, $\eta = 50$, $a = 0.5$.

8  See Flaschel et al. (2000) for the consideration of smooth factor substitution in an IS–LM–PC model of endogenous technical change.

9  Due to Proposition 1.

10  See Chiarella et al. (2000b) for further investigations on endogenous growth.

## 9 The dominance of Keynesian regimes in non-Walrasian growth

1  This chapter is based on Flaschel, P. (1999): "On the dominance of the Keynesian regime in disequilibrium growth theory: A note". *Journal of Economics*, 59, 79–89. We thank Springer Verlag for permission to re-use this paper.

2  Such asymmetries are not yet incorporated into the present framework, since it is based on purely local considerations.

3  The role of $\bar{u}$ is explained below.

4  The first aspect of this law of motion for the price level can be microfounded in a similar way as the behavior of money wages, leading to a second type of NAIRU, the Non-Accelerating-Inflation Rate of Utilization of the capital stock, while the second influence is due to firms' observation of the labor market and thus to be based on cost-push arguments, see Chiarella and Flaschel (1998, Chs.4,7) for further discussions on the role of $\bar{u}$.

5  This assertion is similar to one in Picard (1983, p.279), but does not allow for alternative regimes in the present framework.

6  See the proof for the expressions that define $a_1 a_2$.

## 10 Steindlian models of growth and stagnation

1  This chapter is based on Flaschel, P. and P. Skott (2006): "Steindl models of growth and stagnation". *Metroeconomica*, 57, 303–338; see also Flaschel et al. (2006) for an alternative analysis of such a framework.

2 We have reservations with respect to some of his claims. The existence of an increasing trend in monopolization, for instance, is debatable (e.g. Semmler (1984), Auerbach (1988) and Auerbach and Skott (1988)).

3 Since it simplifies the analysis, the assumption of a (near-)perfect correlation between the rates of employment and capital utilization is common in the literature. The assumption may be legitimate in the short run but the ratio of the capital stock to the labor force is neither constant nor exogenously given, and the assumption can be highly misleading in the long run.

4 A uniform saving rate out of distributed incomes is in line with Steindl's specification (Steindl (1952, p.214), equation (40 vii)). In the presence of retained earnings, the aggregate saving rate depends positively on the profit share. Thus, the introduction of differential saving rates $s_p$ and $s_w$ for household saving out of wage income and distributed profits would leave the structure of the model substantively unchanged.

5 Although logically possible and used in some models, the condition for Robinsonian instability seems implausible: empirical evidence suggests that the *impact* effect of changes in real wages falls mainly on consumption, rather than investment.

6 Steindl (1952, p.213) uses $Z$ rather than the standard notation $K$ to denote the capital stock.

7 Steindl (incorrectly) suggests that it is the root which is largest in absolute value that will dominate. No harm is done, however, since the large root $\rho_3$ happens to be the largest in absolute value. The analysis (p.220) is slightly flawed also by a failure to realize that the capital stock will be declining from some point onwards (and reach zero in finite time) if the coefficient $c_3$ associated with the dominant root is negative. Meaningful non-negative solutions for the long-run capital stock require that the initial conditions are such that $c_3 > 0$ (or, alternatively, such that either $c_2 > c_3 = 0$ or $c_1 > c_2 = c_3 = 0$); implicitly, Steindl's analysis presumes that $c_3 > 0$.

Note finally that although the stability analysis is conditional on very restrictive assumptions concerning the initial conditions, it is not quite correct, as suggested by Dutt (1995, p.17), that Steindl "does not discuss the dynamic properties of his model" but "only the limiting (or equilibrium) state of the economy".

8 Steindl included overhead cost and, assuming that these costs are proportional to the capital stock, the profit function links the profit share to the markup and the rate of utilization.

9 This second mechanism – introduced partly, perhaps, to get around the ambiguity of the direct effect of changes in the profit share – seems doubtful. If anything, one might expect a *decline* in desired utilization following an increase in oligolization: excess capacity may serve as a deterrent to new entry and the higher the markup, the more excess capacity may be required to deter entry. This type of argument is used in a formal model of growth and cycles by Skott (1989a).

10 Dutt (1995) also obtains two steady state equilibria for some parameter values in his formalization of Steindl's theory. Again, the low equilibrium is unstable while the high is stable. Dutt does not comment explicitly on the plausibility of the high equilibrium but notes (p.28, n.7) that "the model will cease to apply" if the economy hits the full capacity constraint.

11 Other factors, including output movements before period $t - 1$ may influence expectations, too. These complications are irrelevant for present purposes.

12 Both Steindl's graphical illustration on p.128 and his formal specification on p.214 show that he expected negative accumulation rates for low values of the utilization rate. This is contrary to the assumption of a positive constant term in the investment function of the standard model. However, a low sensitivity of accumulation to changes in utilization can be consistent with negative investment at low values of utilization if the accumulation function is non-linear (as in Section 10.3). The key issue therefore concerns the long-run sensitivity of accumulation to changes in the rate of utilization within the relevant range of the utilization rate.

13 Steindl's original specification is preferable in this respect. Although he viewed the long-run accumulation rate as being highly sensitive to variations in utilization, this high sensitivity did not apply to the short run. In his formal model, investment at time $t$ is determined by utilization at time $t - \theta$. Thus, investment is predetermined at any moment, and the impact effect of changes in utilization is zero. As a result, his theory could allow investment to be highly sensitive to changes in utilization in the long run without jeopardizing *short-run* Keynesian stability.

14 A large literature has developed on the long-run relation between actual and desired utilization rates. Kurz (1986) and Auerbach and Skott (1988) are among those who have insisted that actual utilization must equal desired utilization on a steady growth path; Lavoie (1995) surveys the debate.

   Following Amadeo (1986), Lavoie also suggests that the equalization of actual and desired utilization can be reconciled with the long-run variability of the utilization rate: simply treat the desired rate of utilization it self as an endogenous variable whose rate of change is proportional to the difference between actual and desired utilization. As a result, the desired utilization becomes an accommodating variable that can take any value in the long run. From a logical perspective this argument is clearly correct but we find the approach unconvincing, Dutt's (1997) attempt to provide a rationale for the adjustment process notwithstanding.

15 The adjustment of price margins to maintain a "normal" or desired rate of utilization can also be found in Joan Robinson's (1962) writings, e.g.: "let us suppose that competition (in the short-period sense) is sufficiently keen to keep prices at the level at which normal capacity output can be sold" (p.46).

16 It should be noted that Steindl regarded the flexibility of the profit function is a long-run property. While unsatisfactory for long-run analysis, "the rigidity of the profit function is probably realistic for the short run model" (1952, p.228) where the short-run model is defined as one designed to explain "the ordinary business cycle".

17 See Flaschel and Krolzig (2006) for a general analysis of the specification and interaction of wage and price Phillips curves.

18 If $f(u, \pi)$ is continuous and $f(u, 1) < 0$, the inequality $\phi(\pi) = (1 - \pi)f(u, \pi) < 0$ must hold for values of $\pi$ above some threshold $\bar{\pi}$ (that is, for $\bar{\pi} < \pi < 1$). From a mathematical perspective this adjustment equation is similar to Lavoie's (1995, p.811) specification of changes in the "target rate of return".

19 The two cases do not exhaust the set of possibilities with respect to these underlying functions.

20 This paradoxical result is in line with Dumenil and Levy's (1996) data on US trends in profitability after the civil war. Steindl, who did not have profit data for this period, argued that "towards the end of the last century . . . the American economy had undergone a transition which gave considerable weight to the oligopolistic pattern in the total economy" (p.191). He suggested that this transition would have raised profit margins. According to Dumenil and Levy's data, however, the profit share declined at an average annual growth rate of 0.4 percent between 1869 and 1910.

21 Induced technical progress along similar lines are discussed by Dutt (2006).

22 Without the restriction $g_\pi \geq 0$ there may (but need not) be multiple solutions. The restriction is satisfied in the special case analyzed by Dutt (1995) – who assumes $g = a$ and $g_\pi = 0$ – as well as by all exhilirationist cases.

23 These results mirror the effects obtained by Skott (1989a, pp.151–153). In Skott's Marshallian setting, changes in output are related to the difference between realized and target profit margins and, by raising the target, increased monopolization therefore depresses output for any given realized profit margin.

24 To see this, observe that $f(u, \pi) = 0$ at the stationary solution. Total differentiation yields $f_u du + f_\pi d\pi = 0$, and the result now follows from $f_u > 0, f_\pi \leq 0$.

25  These financial aspects are left out in Steindl (1979). This more recent analysis instead emphasizes labor market effects and markup dynamics, although neither of these factors are included in the formal equations.

## 11 Investment of firms in capital and productivity growth

1  For a survey on the earlier literature compare Ziesemer (1995), and for later developments the books of Aghion and Howitt (2009) as well as Barro and Sala-i Martin (2003).
2  For a broad spectrum of models of this type compare Flaschel and Groh (1996).
3  Compare for a similar assumption Sargent (1987, Ch. V).
4  Compare Chiarella, Flaschel, Groh and Semmler (2000a) for a similar model, there, however, with a linear limitational production technology.

## 12 A Harrodian knife-edge theorem in the wage–price dynamics

1  This chapter is based on Flaschel, P. (1994): "A Harrodian knife-edge theorem for the wage-price sector?" *Metroeconomica*, 45, 266 – 278, see also Flaschel and Franke (1996) for a related approach.
2  Unless one insists that one can apply the jump variable technique of Sargent and Wallace (1973) also to the evolution of the actual output–capital ratio.
3  See Gray and Kandil (1991) for a brief survey of this literature and note that these approaches in general only discuss this issue in a model type where convergence to equilibrium is not in question.
4  See Hommes (1991) for a detailed analysis of this approach from the viewpoint of complex dynamic systems.

## 13 Estimating interacting wage–price dynamics

1  This chapter is based on Chen, P. and P. Flaschel (2006): "Measuring the interaction of wage and price Phillips curves for the US economy". *Studies in Non-linear Dynamics and Econometrics*, 10, 1–35. We thank Berkley Electronic Press for the permission to re-use this paper.
2  $dw$, $dp$ wage and price inflation and $\pi^c$ our measure of an inflation climate, here simply a weighted average of past price inflation rates, and $\kappa_w, \kappa_p \in (0, 1)$ the weights of current price and wage inflation in the employed cost-pressure terms, see Chiarella and Flaschel (1996) for the original formulation and Flaschel and Krolzig (2006) for a first estimation of this wage–price spiral.
3  $d$ is the backward difference operator.
4  This holds in the continuous time limit case as was shown in Chapter 7.
5  To simplify the presentation we have assumed here again that the steady state value of the real wage has the value 1.
6  See Flaschel and Krolzig (2006) and Chiarella et al. (2005) for an alternative motivation of the MWPC and the MPPC.
7  Similarly from decreases in utilization rate to reductions in the workforce employed by firms.
8  The conventional literature on Phillips curves generally focuses on the above reduced form for price inflation, and this in the special case where only the labor market matters and price inflation is passively following wage inflation. It thus only provides a very partial representation of the wage–price spiral and completely ignores the resulting effects on income distribution and its laws of motion (for real wages).

9  This data set now employs a homogeneous sectoral measure of the wage share in the place of the hybrid one used in Flaschel and Krolzig (2006).
10  Simultaneous structural models can also present nonstationary variables. see Hsiao (1997) for details.
11  See Engle et al. (1983) for details.
12  Because our interest is not to model the marginal process VAR ($u_t$, $dz_t$, $|\Omega^{t-1})$, it is not explicitly discussed here.

## 14 ES calibration of wage and price Phillips curves

1  The chapter is based on a paper we have obtained from Reiner Franke and which we have adjusted verbally to the contents of this part of the book. We have to thank Reiner Franke for allowing us to make use of this paper.
2  It should also be pursued further in future work, see Flaschel, Krolzig and Proaño (2011).
3  The precise data description is provided in Chiarella et al. (2005).
4  Note: All coefficients are significant, except those on $\pi^c_{dv}$, which in the estimations with one activity variable ($e$ or $u$) are always "highly" insignificant (and so should be directly set to zero). The negative coefficient on $\pi^c_{dv}$ in the fourth column has a $t$-value of $-1.70$.
5  The lower AIC and BIC values also show that the better fit more than outweighs the loss in parsimony by including an additional variable.
6  To be precise, the wage equation would then be part, not of a reduced-form VAR, but of a recursive VAR.
7  Including eight lags of $v^{em}$ on the right-hand side of (14.14) improves reduces standard error to 1.490. On the other hand, this modification is severely punished by not only completely different coefficients on, in particular, the $\hat{w}^{em}_{t-k}$, but they also add up to more than one. A consequence is that when $\hat{w}_t$ is endogenously computed in (14.14), where $\hat{w}^{em}_{t-k}$ is replaced with the previously computed endogenous values of $\hat{w}_{t-k}$, the initial rounding errors cause ever increasing departures of the $\hat{w}_t$ from $\hat{w}^{em}_t$; such that after 20 or 25 years these discrepancies would no longer be tolerable.
8  In principle it might be said that the same residuals $\eta_{w,t}$ would be obtained in (14.14) if $\hat{w}^{em}_t$ and $\hat{p}^{em}_t$ were exchanged on the left-hand and right-hand sides of the equation; in this way the residuals would be only rescaled by the (significantly positive) parameter $\mu_{wp,0}$. Thus, the residuals might just as well be used as shocks in a price Phillips curve. Fortunately, things are not that arbitrary. Although (14.14) has been characterized as an atheoretical equation, there is still a grain of theory in it. For if we view the equation as a regression of $\hat{p}^{em}_t$ and thus the residuals as innovations to the rate of price inflation, we would include utilization $u$ rather than the employment rate $e$ in the list of regressors. In fact, that is what we are doing below.
9  We have verified this as one test when implementing the computer program of the aforementioned search algorithm.
10  It would be logical to call these coefficients "calibrates", but (as long as the method is still new) this coinage seems too artificial.
11  Note: The small bars at the bottom indicate (from left to right) the lower 2.5 percent, the mean value, and the upper 2.5 percent of the distribution. The thin solid line depicts the normal distribution with the same mean and standard deviation.
12  The lowest $p$-value is 0.31.
13  They are computed, not from the standard deviation of the normal distribution, bur directly from the frequency distribution.
14  The RMSD values are here less informative since with the random shocks (14.19) the benchmark values of $RMSD_o$ vary, too.
15  It is interesting to report our experience with the present calibration procedure when it sought to determine the reaction coefficients in a different, and conceptually more ambitious, updating process for the inflation climate $\pi^c_t$; see Table 1 in Franke (2007).

Combining the adjustments with a much simpler price Phillips curve, these experiments were only concerned with the data on price inflation and the output gap. Although in this framework the impact of $\hat{w}_{t-k}$, $\hat{z}_{t-k}$ and $v_{t-k}$ on price inflation in the atheoretical VAR-like equation was subsumed within the exogenous forces, the interplay of these "richer" innovations $\eta_{p,t}$ with the inflation and utilization series gave rise to a similar kind of deterioration in the goodness-of-fit, $\phi$. There, too, the fit was "significantly" better under the estimated innovations than under the bootstrap samples.

16 One fruitful hypothesis was advanced in Franke (2007). After its investigation in a rather limited setting, it would now be time to incorporate it into the present framework.

## 15 Testing non-linear wage and price Phillips curves for the USA

1 This chapter is based on Flaschel, P., G. Kauermann and W. Semmler (2007): "Testing wage and price Phillips curves for the United States". *Metroeconomica*, 58, 550–581.
2 See Chiarella et al. (2005, Ch.5), but also Stock and Watson (1999) and Rotemberg and Woodford (2003) on this latter matter.
3 This feedback channel is generally overlooked in the set of all macroeconomic feedback channels discussed in the literature.
4 The established non-linearities are, however, of different type than estimated for European countries in a parametric approach in Hoogenveen and Kuipers (2000). Other papers on non-linearities in the Phillips curve are Schaling (2004) and Semmler and Zhang (2006).
5 See Galí (2000, 2008) for recent surveys on this approach.
6 With respect to the use of a single curve it is stated in Mankiw (2001): "Although the new Keynesian Phillips curves has many virtues, it also has one striking vice: It is completely at odd with the facts." Eller and Gordon (2003) go a step further by declaring it an empirical failure by all measures. There are of course also exceptions, as for example the paper by Cohen and Farhi (2001) from the applied perspective, and from the theoretical perspective in the area of staggered wage and price setting, where however the concept of a wage–price spiral is rarely discussed, see Blanchard (1986) for its use and Huang and Liu (2002) for a recent contribution to this area.
7 Giving rise to 2-D dynamics when embedded into a larger macrodynamic framework.
8 For reasons of simplicity we here neglect the growth rate of labor productivity which – from a straightforward steady state perspective – would have to be added with a coefficient of unity to the wage equation and with the coefficient of $-\kappa_p$ to the price equation. In the empirical estimates in the next section, however, the role of labor productivity growth is much smaller than suggested by such steady state considerations.
9 See also Rudebush and Svensson (1999) for such a measure.
10 For estimations of a time varying NAIRU, see Gordon (1997), Eller and Gordon (2003) and Semmler and Zhang (2006, Ch.3).
11 Note that we use neoclassical dating of forward looking expectations in the place of the New-Keynesian dating of expectations, see Chiarella et al. (2005) for details.
12 We want to note here that some empirical estimates of the two Phillips curve approaches for the US and Germany are, with some success, already undertaken in Flaschel (2001).
13 $a_4$ should be equal to one from a straightforward steady state perspective, but significantly less than one however when the Blanchard and Katz (1999) approach to the wage PC is adopted.
14 We have neglected here such error correction mechanisms right from the start.
15 Often the case in the Post-Keynesian literature, see Barbosa-Filho and Taylor (2006) on this matter.

16  $k_o = 1/\bar{y}$ the capital/full employment output ratio and $1/y^p$ the capital/full capacity output ratio, which are approximately equal to each other. Underlying this situation, we assume for simplicity a technology with fixed proportions (with Harrod neutral technical change her ignored for simplicity) and abstract for the time being from the distinction between employment in terms of heads and employment in terms of hours, see the concluding section of this chapter for a more general approach.

17  Also called Rose effects (RE) referring to Rose (1967) seminal contribution to the theory of the employment cycle.

18  It has to be reversed in sign in the case of profit-led regimes.

19  Note here that utilization gaps can also be approximated by logarithmic terms in the wags and price law of motion.

20  Note that we are considering in this section only the case where the weights in cost pressure terms sum up to unity – by an imposed restriction of this type.

21  See http://www.stls.frb.org/fred.

## 16 The distributive cycle with a non-linear wage Phillips curve

1  This chapter is based on Tavani, D., P. Flaschel and L. Taylor (2011): "Estimated non-linearities and multiple equilibria in a model of distributive-demand cycles". *International Review of Applied Economics*, forthcoming.

2  See also Flaschel et al. (2005).

3  Bhaduri and Marglin (1990a, b), reason in terms of the profit share, but being distributive shares the complement of one another there is no harm in considering the wage share instead, as we do in this chapter.

4  Table 16.1 in Appendix IV provides a brief description of the data used for these plots. See also Kauermann et al. (2008) for the econometric methodology that allows to separate endogenously long phase cycles from cycles occurring at higher frequency and for empirical applications that are closely related to the ones shown in Figure 16.5.

5  In their model, the authors consider, in both equations, error-corrections for the deviation of the wage share from a certain level $\psi_0$. For reasons of expositional simplicity, we do not analyze in this chapter the consequences of this augmentation in both the money wage and the price Phillips curve.

6  Flaschel, Kauermann and Semmler (2007) provide estimates suggesting that $\kappa, \kappa_p, \kappa_w$ are all positive. See also footnote 8. The growth rate of labor productivity is included in the definition of $\hat{v} \equiv \hat{w} - \hat{p} - n_x$.

7  For basic standard treatments of Okun's Law, see for instance Blanchard (2010, Ch.9), or Mankiw (2010, Ch.9). Abel and Bernanke (2005) provide an estimate of $\sigma$ roughly around 2. Flaschel, Franke and Semmler (2007), instead, parameterize $\sigma = 1$, an assumption that is confirmed by the estimation results in Proaño et al. (2007). Also, Foley and Michl (1999, p.179) can be can be read as arguing that $\sigma = 1$.

8  The other estimated p-spline functions are not statistically different from linear ones – including the price Phillips curve – with the exception of the inflation climate which however does not matter for the law of motion of real wages.

9  There are multiple equilibria in the model, and that is why we refer to multiple barriers as opposed to a single one.

10  Flaschel, Kauermann and Semmler (2007), specifying the inflationary climate as 12 quarter moving-average, obtain estimates of $\kappa_w = .4464, \beta_p = .0026$ and $1 - \kappa_p = .6859$ so that, given the traditional $\sigma = 1/3$, the composite parameter $\dfrac{1-\kappa_w}{\sigma(1-\kappa_p)}\beta_p$ is roughly equal to .0063. Clearly, different specifications for the inflationary climate may lead to

different results. It is worth to keep in mind, however, that recent estimations of the Okun's coefficient, such as the one provided in Proaño et al. (2007), point toward the situation of $\sigma$ not being significantly different from 1.

11  Clearly, $\bar{u}, \bar{v}$ are shift parameters in the model.

12  Skott (1989a, Ch.6) is an authoritative dissenting voice on such stability condition, and especially about its plausibility in the long run.

13  We rule out as uninteresting the case of a demand regime laying entirely in the orthant in which capacity utilization takes only negative values, and therefore we impose $\dfrac{\bar{v}}{\bar{u}} > -\dfrac{\beta_{uu}}{\beta_{uv}}$ to be satisfied everywhere.

14  Note however that the case in which the locus $\dot{u} = 0$ is so steep that there is only one intermediate equilibrium requires an intercept of the curve higher than 1, and this is a case we would like to rule out from the analysis. Clearly, a sound empirical analysis will be crucial on this respect, but we proceed here assuming that the $\dot{u} = 0$ isocline is sufficiently flat.

15  Note finally with respect to Figure 16.3 that there is of course a fourth steady state at the origin of the phase space, that however cannot be reached from the positive orthant.

16  Assumption 5 in Section 16.4 already incorporates induced technical change effects into the evolution of the wage share. In view of this argument, imposing $\beta_{vv} > n_{xv} > 0$ does not seem a very stringent requirement. It must be said however that, if such an assumption is violated, the stability properties of the steady states in the model change (Rezai (2010) analyzes theoretically all the possible cases). Nevertheless, the dynamics observed in the empirical plots in Figures 16.1 and 16.6 should be enough to convince the skeptical reader who likes to engage in Jacobian analyzes.

17  We thank an anonymous referee for suggesting we make such comparisons.

18  The careful reader will have observed that the this plot displays data at the annual frequency, differently from Figure 16.1, which plots quarterly data. The reason is that Piketty and Saez (2003) have annual data in their data set, which is the one we used to construct our series for these plots. Obviously, having to work with annual data like in the Netherlands makes it cumbersome to estimate "long-phase cycles" using the methodology we adopted in Figure 16.1. In other words, there is a potential "apples and oranges" problem that arises from different data frequencies for different countries. This is the reason why simple HP filtered data are used in Figure 16.6. The same considerations apply to the plots in Figure 16.5.

19  As in Blanchard and Katz (1999).

20  Of course, imposing $n_{xu} = n_{xv} = 0$ gives back (16.5) as a special case.

## 17 Keynesian business cycle analysis: past, present, future

1  Since the independent $(\omega, l)$ block will feed into the RHS as a time function.

2  Note that we have $g(\omega, l) = \rho_o$ in the steady state.

3  See Flaschel (1993) and Flaschel et al. (1997) for further investigations along these lines.

4  For the proofs of these propositions we refer the reader to Flaschel, Franke and Proaño (2008).

5  For two analyses of the consequences of such a discrepancy for the resulting dynamics of macroeconomic models see Aadland and Huang (2004) as well as Flaschel and Proaño (2009).

6  See Flaschel, Franke and Proaño (2008) for the proofs.

7 For counterfactual examples where the determinacy properties of the rational expectations equilibrium in an economy do depend on the decision frequency assumed, see Hintermaier (2005).

8 See also Asada et al. (2007) on these matters.

9 See comments by J. Fuhrer on "Empirical and policy performance of a forward-looking monetary model" by A. Onatstu and N. Williams; presented at the FRB San Francisco conference on "Interest rates and monetary policy", March 19–20, 2004. http://www.frbsf.org/economics/conferences/0403/jeff_fuhrer.pdf

10 http://www.frbsf.org/economics/conferences/0403/jeff_fuhrer.pdf

11 We have stressed elsewhere, see Asada et al. (2007) the close formal correspondence of this model of the wage–price spiral with the New Keynesian model of staggered wage and price setting. Yet we have to stress here in this regard that we employ three demand pressure gaps in this spiral in place of the single one (the output gap) that is used by New Keynesian authors. Despite this formal similarity the conclusions drawn later on from our macrodynamic model are in direct opposition to the ones of the New Keynesian macrodynamics.

12 This last term is obtained by an adaptive updating inflation climate expression with exponential or any other weighting schemes that incorporate medium-run developments and therefore inertia with respect to the past wage and price developments.

13 See Flaschel and Krolzig (2006) and Asada et al. (2010) for details.

14 Note here that also the cost-pressure parameters play a role and may influence the critical stability condition that characterizes the real wage channel, see Flaschel and Krolzig (2006) for details.

15 For a simple inclusion of smooth factor substitution – which makes $y^p$ dependent on the real wage – see Chiarella and Flaschel (2000, Ch.5) and see Chiarella et al. (2005) for the discussion of the role of alternative production technologies.

16 Note here that the empirically oriented controversy about the role of income distribution does not play a role in the New Keynesian formulation of the goods market dynamics, due to its reliance on a single representative household (who receives all wage as well as profit income and who thus can be indifferent with respect to changing income distribution if total income remains the same).

17 This assumption is justified if it is assumed that actual labor supply always grows in line with capital stock growth.

18 All of the employed gaps are measured relative to the steady state of the model, in order to allow for an interest rate policy that is also consistent with the steady state.

19 We assume for reasons of consistency: $\bar{u}^w = y^p \bar{u}^c / (z l_o \bar{e})$.

20 As the model is formulated we have no real anchor for the steady state rate of interest (via investment behavior and the rate of profit it implies in the steady state) and thus have to assume here that it is the monetary authority that enforces a certain steady state value for the nominal rate of interest.

21 Only needed in the case of a wage-led economy where monetary policy thus must be sufficiently strict in this respect.

22 Note that propositions on parameter changes always assume that all other parameters are kept fixed in the considered situation.

23 In a GMM context, when there are more moment conditions than parameters to be estimated, a chi-square test can be used to test the over-identifying restrictions. The test statistic can be called the J-statistic.

24 This is given in place of a monetarist type of wage Phillips curve and a marginal cost determination of the price level.

# References

Aadland, D. and Huang, K. (2004), "Consistent high-frequency calibration", *Journal of Economic Dynamics and Control* **28**(11), 2277–2295.

Abel, A. B. and Bernanke, B. S. (2005), *Macroeconomics*, 5th edn, London: Pearson Addison-Wesley.

Aghion, P. and Howitt, P. (1998), *Endogenous Growth Theory*, Cambridge, MA: MIT Press.

Aghion, P. and Howitt, P. (2009), *The Economics of Growth*, Cambridge, MA: MIT Press.

Akaike, H. (1973), "Information theory and an extension of the maximum likelihood principle", in: B. N. Petrov and F. Csaki (eds), *2nd International Symposium on Information Theory*, Budapest: Akademiai Kiado, 267–281.

Akerlof, G. (2002), "Behavioural macroeconomics and macroeconomic behaviour", *The American Economic Review* **92**(3), 411–433.

Alexander, J. and York, J. (1978), "Global bifurcation of periodic orbits", *American Journal of Mathematics* **100**, 263–292.

Amadeo, E. (1986), "The role of capacity utilization in long-period analysis", *Political Economy* **2**(2), 147–185.

Aoki, M. and Yoshikawa, H. (2007), *Reconstructing Macroeconomics: A Perspective from Statistical Physics and Combinatorial Stochastic Processes*, Cambridge, UK: Cambridge University Press.

Asada, T., Chiarella, C., Flaschel, P. and Franke, R. (2003), *Open Economy Macrodynamics. An Integrated Disequilibrium Approach*, Berlin: Springer.

Asada, T., Chen, P., Chiarella, C. and Flaschel, P. (2006), "Keynesian dynamics and the wage-price spiral: A baseline disequilibrium model", *Journal of Macroeconomics* **28**, 90–130.

Asada, T., Flaschel, P. and Proaño, C. (2007), Expectations and the real wage channel. Two competing baseline approaches, Technical report, CEM Bielefeld. unpublished manuscript, Bielefeld University.

Asada, T., Chiarella, C., Flaschel, P. and Franke, R. (2010), *Monetary Macrodynamics*, London: Routledge.

Auerbach, P. (1988), *Competition*, Oxford: Blackwell.

Auerbach, P. and Skott, P. (1988), "Concentration, competition and distribution", *International Review of Applied Economics* **2**, 42–61.

Barbosa-Filho, N. and Taylor, L. (2006), "Distributive and demand cycles in the US economy – a structuralist Goodwin model", *Metroeconomica* **57**(3), 389–411.

Barro, R. (1994), "The aggregate supply/aggregate demand model", *Eastern Economic Journal* **20**, 1–6.

Barro, R. J. and Sala-i Martin, X. (1995), *Economic Growth*, New York: McGraw-Hill.

Barro, R. J. and Sala-i Martin, X. (2003), *Economic Growth*, Cambridge, MA: MIT Press.

Becker, S., Grüne, L. and Semmler, W. (2007), "Comparing accuracy of second-order approximation and dynamic programming", *Computational Economics* **30**, 65–91.

Benassy, J.-P. (1993), "Non clearing markets: Microeconomic concepts and macroeconomic applications", *Journal of Economic Literature* **31**, 732–761.

Benhabib, J. and Miyao, T. (1981), "Some new results on the dynamics of the generalized Tobin model", *International Economic Review* **22**, 589–596.

Beverton, R. and Holt, S. (1957), *On the Dynamics of Exploited Fish Populations*, London: HM Stationery Office. Fishery Investigations Series 2, Volume 19.

Bhaduri, A. and Marglin, S. (1990a), "Profit squeeze and Keynesian theory", in: S.A. Marglin and J. B. Schor (eds), *The Golden Age of Capitalism*, Oxford: Clarendon Press.

Bhaduri, A. and Marglin, S. (1990b), "Unemployment and the real wage: The economic basis for contesting political ideologies", *Cambridge Journal of Economics* **14**, 375–393.

Blanchard, O. and Kahn, C. M. (1980), "The solution of linear difference models under rational expectations", *Econometrica* **48**(5), 1305–1312.

Blanchard, O. (1981), "Output, the stock market, and interest rates", *The American Economic Review* **71**, 132–143.

Blanchard, O. (1986), "The wage price spiral", *Quarterly Journal of Economics* **101**, 543–565.

Blanchard, O. and Fisher, S. (1989), *Lectures on Macroeconomics*, Cambridge, MA: MIT Press.

Blanchard, O. and Katz, L. (1999), "Wage dynamics: Reconciling theory and evidence", *The American Economic Review* **89**, 69–74. Papers and Proceedings of the One Hundred and Eleventh Annual Meeting of the American Economic Association (May, 1999).

Blanchard, O. (2010), *Macroeconomics*, 5th edn, Upper Saddle River, NJ: Prentice Hall.

Blanchflower, D. and Oswald, A. (1994), *The Wage Curve*, Cambridge, MA: MIT Press.

Blecker, R. (1989), "International competition, income distribution and economic growth", *Cambridge Journal of Economics* **14**, 375–393.

Boggess, T. (1983), "A generalized Keynes–Wicksell model with variable labor force growth", *Journal of Macroeconomics* **5**, 197–209.

Brianzoni, S., Mammana, C. and Michetti, E. (2007), "Complex dynamics in the neoclassical growth model with differential savings and non-constant labor force growth", *Studies in Nonlinear Dynamics and Econometrics* **11**(3), Article 3.

Brock, W. and Malliaris, A. (1989), *Differential Equations, Stability and Chaos in Dynamic Economics*, Amsterdam: North Holland.

Buiter, W. (1980), "Walras' law and all that: Budget constraints and balance sheet constraints in period models and in continuous time models", *International Economic Review* **21**, 1–16.

Burmeister, E. (1980), "On some conceptual issues in rational expectations modeling", *Journal of Money, Credit and Banking* **12**, 800–816.

Cagan, P. (1956), "The monetary dynamics of hyperinflation", in: M. Friedman (ed.), *Studies in the Quantity Theory of Money*, Chicago, IL: University of Chicago Press, pp.25–117.

Calvo, G. (1977), "The stability of models of money and perfect foresight: A comment", *Econometrica* **45**, 1737–1739.

Chen, P. (1988), "Empirical and theoretical evidence on economic chaos", *System Dynamics Review* **4**, 1–38.

Chen, P. and Flaschel, P. (2005), "Keynesian dynamics and the wage-price spiral: Identifying downward rigidities", *Computational Economics* **25**(1–2), 115–142.

Chen, P. and Flaschel, P. (2006), "Measuring the interaction of wage and price Phillips Curves for the US economy", *Studies in Nonlinear Dynamics and Econometrics* **10**, 1–35.

Chen, P., Chiarella, C., Flaschel, P. and Semmler, W. (2006), "Keynesian macrodynamics and the Phillips Curve. An estimated baseline macromodel for the US economy", in: C. Chiarella, P. Flaschel, R. Franke and W. Semmler (eds), *Quantitative and Empirical Analysis of Nonlinear Dynamic Macromodels*, Contributions to Economic Analysis, Amsterdam: Elsevier, pp.229–284.

Chiarella, C. (1986), "Perfect foresight models and the dynamic instability problem from a higher viewpoint", *Economic Modelling* **5**, 283–292.

Chiarella, C. (1990), *The Elements of a Nonlinear Theory of Economic Dynamics*, Berlin: Springer Verlag.

Chiarella, C. (1992), "Monetary and fiscal policy under nonlinear exchange rate dynamics", in G. Feichtinger (ed.), *Nolinear Methods in Economic Dynamics and Optimal Control*, Berlin: Springer Verlag.

Chiarella, C. and Flaschel, P. (1996), "Real and monetary cycles in models of Keynes–Wicksell type", *Journal of Economic Behavior and Organization* **30**, 327–351.

Chiarella, C. and Flaschel, P. (1998), "The dynamics of 'natural' rates of growth and employment", *Macroeconomic Dynamics* **2**, 345–368.

Chiarella, C. and Flaschel, P. (2000), *The Dynamics of Keynesian Monetary Growth. Macro Foundations*, Cambridge, UK: Cambridge University Press.

Chiarella, C., Flaschel, P., Groh, G. and Semmler, W. (2000a), "AS–AD disequilibrium dynamics and economic growth", in: M. L. E. Dockner, R. Hartl and G. Sorger (eds), *Optimization, Dynamics and Economic Analysis: Essays in Honor of Gustav Feichtinger*, Heidelberg: Physica Verlag, pp.102–118.

Chiarella, C., Flaschel, P., Groh, G. and Semmler, W. (2000b), *Disequilibrium, Growth and Labor Market Dynamics*, Heidelberg: Springer Verlag.

Chiarella, C., Semmler, W., Mittnik, S. and Zhu, P. (2002), "Stock market, interest rate and output: A model and estimation for us time series data", *Studies in Nonlinear Dynamics and Econometrics* **6**(1): Article 2.

Chiarella, C., Flaschel, P. and Franke, R. (2005), *Foundations for a Disequilibrium Theory of the Business Cycle. Qualitative Analysis and Quantitative Assesment*, Cambridge, UK: Cambridge University Press.

Chiarella, C., Flaschel, P., Franke, R. and Semmler, W. (2009), *Financial Markets and the Macroeconomy. A Keynesian Perspective*, London: Routledge.

Cohen, D. and Farhi, E. (2001), *The Phillips Curves Across the Atlantic: It is the price curves that differ*. London: Centre for Economic Policy Research: CEPR discussion paper No. 3100.

Colander, D. (2006), *Beyond Microfoundations: Post Walrasian Economics*, Cambridge, UK: Cambridge University Press.

Davidson, R. and MacKinnon, J. (2004), *Econometric Theory and Methods*, New York: Oxford University Press.

De Jong, F. (1967), *Dimensional Analysis for Economists*, Amsterdam: North Holland.

De Long, B. and Summers, L. (1986), "Is increased price flexibility stabilizing", *American Economic Review* **76**, 1031–1044.

Debreu, G. (1959), *Theory of Value*, New York: Wiley.

Drabicki, J. and Takayama, A. (1979), "The general equilibrium framework of economic analysis: Stocks and flows – with special application to macroeconomic models", in: J. Green and J. A. Scheinkman (eds), *General Equilibrium, Growth, and Trade*, New York: Academic Press.

Drandakis, E. and Phelps, E. (1966), "A model of induced invention, growth and distribution", *Economic Journal* **76**(304), 823–840.

Duguay, P. and Rabeau, Y. (1988), "A simulation model of macroeconomic effects of deficit", *Journal of Macroeconomics* **10**, 538–564.

Dumenil, G. and Levy, D. (1996), "The acceleration and slowdown of technical progress in the US since the civil war", *Revue Internationale de Systémique* **10**(3), 303–321.

Dutt, A. (1984), "Stagnation, income distribution and monopoly power", *Cambridge Journal of Economics* **8**, 25–40.

Dutt, A. (1992), "Conflict inflation, distribution, cyclical accumulation and crises", *European Journal of Political Economy* **8**, 579–597.

Dutt, A. (1995), "Internal finance and monopoly power in capitalist economies: A reformulation of Steindl's growth model", *Metroeconomica* **46**(1), 16–34.

Dutt, A. (1997), "Equilibrium, path dependence and hysteresis in post-Keynesian models", in: P. Arestis, G. Palma and M. Sawyer (eds), *Capital Controversy, Post-Keynesian Economics and the History of Economic Thought: Essays in Honour of Geoff Harcourt*, London: Routledge.

Dutt, A. K. (2006), "Aggregate demand, aggregate supply and economic growth", *International Review of Applied Economics* **20**(3), 319–336.

Edge, R. and Rudd, J. (2007), "Taxation and the Taylor principle", *Journal of Monetary Economics* **54**, 2554–2567.

Eisner, R. (1997), "New view of the NAIRU", in: P. Davidson and J. A. Kregel (eds), *Improving the Global Economy: Keynesianism and the Growth in Output and Employment*, Cheltenham, UK and Lyme, US: Edward Elgar Publishing.

Eller, J. and Gordon, R. (2003), "Nesting the New Keynesian Phillips curve within the mainstream model of US inflation dynamics". Paper presented at the CEPR Conference: The Phillips curve revisited. Berlin.

Engle, R., Hendry, D. and Richard, A. (1983), "Exogeneity", *Econometrica* **51**, 227–304.

Erceg, C. J., Henderson, D. W. and Levin, A. T. (2000), "Optimal monetary policy with staggered wage and price contracts", *Journal of Monetary Economics* **46**, 281–313.

Fair, R. (2000), "Testing the NAIRU model for the United States", *The Review of Economics and Statistics* **82**, 64–71.

Fehr, E. and Tyran, J. (2001), "Does money illusion matter?", *The American Economic Review* **91**(5), 1239–1262.

Fischer, S. (1972), "Keynes–Wicksell and Neoclassical models of money and growth", *American Economic Review* **62**, 880–890.

Flaschel, P. (1993), *Macrodynamics. Income Distribution, Effective Demand and Cyclical Growth*, Bern: Verlag Peter Lang.

Flaschel, P. and Groh, G. (1996), *Keynesianische Makroökonomik*, Heidelberg: Springer-Verlag.

Flaschel, P. (1999), "On the dominance of the Keynesian regime in disequilibrium growth theory: A note", *Journal of Economics* **70**, 79–89.

Flaschel, P. (2000), "Disequilibrium growth theory with insider–outsider effects", *Structural Change and Economic Dynamics* **11**, 337–354.

Flaschel, P. (2009), *The Macrodynamics of Capitalism. Elements for a Synthesis of Marx, Keynes and Schumpeter*, Heidelberg: Springer.

Flaschel, P. and Franke, R. (1996), "Wage flexibility and the stability arguments of the neoclassical synthesis", *Metroeconomica* **47**, 1–18.

Flaschel, P. and Franke, R. (2000), "An old-Keynesian note on destabilizing price flexibility", *Review of Political Economy* **12**, 273–283.

Flaschel, P. and Krolzig, H.-M. (2006), "Wage-price Phillips Curves and macroeconomic stability. Basic structural form, estimation and analysis", in: C. Chiarella, P. Flaschel, R. Franke and W. Semmler (eds), *Quantitative and Empirical Analysis of Nonlinear Dynamic Macromodels,* Contributions to Economic Analysis, Amsterdam: Elsevier, pp.4–48.

Flaschel, P. and Proaño, C. (2009), "The J2 status of 'chaos' in macroeconomic period models", *Studies in Nonlinear Dynamics and Econometrics* **13**(2).

Flaschel, P. and Schlicht, E. (2005), "New Keynesian theory and the new Phillips curves: A competing approach", in: C. Chiarella, P. Flaschel, R. Franke and W. Semmler (eds), *Quantitative and Empirical Analysis of Nonlinear Dynamic Macromodels*, Contributions to Economic Analysis, Amsterdam: Elsevier, pp.113–148.

Flaschel, P., Franke, R. and Semmler, W. (1997), *Dynamic Macroeconomics. Instability, Fluctuations and Growth in Monetary Economies*, Cambridge, MA: MIT Press.

Flaschel, P., Groh, G. and Semmler, W. (2000), Investment of firms in capital and productivity growth. A macrodynamic analysis. University of Bielefeld: Discussion paper.

Flaschel, P., Gong, G. and Semmler, W. (2001), "A Keynesian macroeconometric framework for the analysis of monetary policy rules", *Journal of Economic Behaviour and Organization* **25**, 101–136.

Flaschel, P., Kauermann, G. and Semmler, W. (2005), Phillips curves, Phillips loops and wage curves. A proposal for model selection. Center for Empirical Macroeconomics, Bielefeld University: Working paper.

Flaschel, P., Asada, T. and Skott, P. (2006), "Prosperity and stagnation in capitalist economies", in: C. Chiarella, P. Flaschel, R. Franke and W. Semmler (eds), *Quantitative and Empirical Analysis of Nonlinear Dynamic Macromodels*, Contributions to Economic Analysis, Amsterdam: Elsevier, pp.415–448.

Flaschel, P., Franke, R. and Semmler, W. (2007), "Kaleckian investment and employment cycles in postwar industrialized economies", in: P Flaschel and M. Landesmann (eds), *Mathematical Economics and the Dynamics of Capitalism*, London: Routledge, pp.35–65.

Flaschel, P., Kauermann, G. and Semmler, W. (2007), "Testing wage and price Phillips Curves for the United States", *Metroeconomica* **58**, 550–581.

Flaschel, P., Franke, R. and Proaño, C. (2008), "On equilibrium determinacy in new Keynesian models with staggered wage and price setting", *The B.E. Journal of Macroeconomics* **8**(1), 31.

Flaschel, P., Groh, G., Proaño, C. and Semmler, W. (2008), *Topics in Applied Macrodynamic Theory*, Heidelberg: Springer.

Flaschel, P., Krolzig, H.-M. and Proaño, C. (2011), Keynesian macroeconomics, income distribution and the wage–price spiral, theory and evidence. Book manuscript. New School University, New York.

Foley, D. (1975), "On two specifications of asset equilibrium in macroeconomic models", *Journal of Political Economy* **83**, 303–324.

Foley, D. K. and Michl, T. (1999), *Growth and Distribution*, Cambridge, MA: Harvard University Press.

Franke, R. (1992a), "Inflation and distribution in a Keynes–Wicksell model of the business cycle", *European Journal of Political Economy* **8**(4), 599–624.

Franke, R. (1992b), "Stable, unstable, and cyclical behaviour in a Keynes–Wicksell monetary growth model", *Oxford Economic Papers* **44**, 242–256.

Franke, R. (1996), "A Metzlerian model of inventory growth cycles", *Structural Change and Economic Dynamics* **7**(2), 243–262.

Franke, R. (2007), "A sophisticatedly simple alternative to the New-Keynesian Phillips curve", in: T. Asada and T. Ishikawa (eds), *Time and Space in Economics*, Tokyo: Springer, pp.3–28.

Franke, R. and Lux, T. (1993), "Adaptive expectations and perfect foresight in a nonlinear Metzlerian model of the inventory cycle", *The Scandinavian Journal of Economics* **95**(3), 355–363.

Fuhrer, J. and Moore, G. (1995), "Inflation persistence", *Quarterly Journal of Economics* **110**, 127–159.

Galí, J. (2000), "The return of the Phillips curve and other recent developments in business cycle theory", *Spanish Economic Review* **2**, 1–10.

Galí, J. (2008), *Monetary Policy, Inflation, and the Business Cycle: An Introduction to the New-Keynesian Framework*, Princeton, NJ: Princeton University Press.

Galí, J. and Gertler, M. (1999), "Inflation dynamics: A structural econometric analysis", *Journal of Monetary Economics* **44**, 195–222.

Galí, J., Gertler, M. and López-Salido, J. D. (2001), "European inflation dynamics", *European Economic Review* **45**, 1237–1270.

Galí, J., López-Salido, J. and Valles, J. (2007), "Understanding the effects of government spending on consumption", *Journal of the European Economic Association* **5**(1), 227–270.

Gandolfo, G. (2009), *Economic Dynamics*, 4th edn, Berlin: Springer.

Gantmacher, F. (1959), *Applications of the Theory of Matrices*, New York: Interscience Publishers.

Gantmacher, F. (1971), *Matrizenrechnung, Teil II: Spezielle Fragen und Anwendungen*, Berlin: VEB Deutscher Verlag der Wissenschaften.

George, D. and Oxley, L. (1985), "Structural stability and model design", *Economic Modelling* **2**, 307–316.

Goldman, S. (1972), "Hyperinflation and the rate of growth in the money supply", *Journal of Economic Theory* **5**, 250–257.

Goodwin, R. M. (1967), "A growth cycle", in: C. Feinstein (ed.), *Socialism, Capitalism and Economic Growth*, Cambridge, UK: Cambridge University Press, pp.54–58.

Gordon, R. (1997), "The time-varying NAIRU and its implications for economic policy", *Journal for Economic Perspectives* **11**, 11–32.

Gray, J. and Kandil, M. (1991), "Is price flexibility stabilizing? A broader perspective", *Journal of Money, Credit and Banking* **23**, 1–12.

Gray, M. and Turnovsky, S. (1979), "The stability of exchange rate dynamics under perfect foresight", *International Economic Review* **20**, 643–660.

Groth, C. (1988), "IS–LM dynamics and the hypothesis of combined adaptive-forward looking expectations", in: P. Flaschel and M. Krüger (eds), *Recent Approaches to Economic Dynamics*, Bern: Verlag Peter Lang.

Groth, C. (1993), "Some unfamiliar dynamics in a familiar macromodel", *Journal of Economics* **58**(3), 293–305.

Harcourt, G. (1972), *Some Cambridge Controversies in the Theory of Capital*, Cambridge, UK: Cambridge University Press.

Harrod, R. (1939), "An essay in dynamic theory", *Economic Journal* **49**, 14–33.

Hastie, T. and Tibshirani, R. (1990), *Generalized Additive Models*, London: Chapman & Hall.

Hayakawa, H. (1984), "Balance sheet identity and Walras' law", *Journal of Economic Theory* **34**, 187–202.

Hayek, F. v. (1933), *Monetary Theory and the Trade Cycle*, London: Jonathan Cape.

Hein, E. and Vogel, L. (2007), "Distribution and growth reconsidered: Empirical results for six OECD countries", *Cambridge Journal of Economics* **32**(3), 479–511.

Hénin, P.-Y. and Michel, P. (1982), *Croissance et accumulation en déséquilibre*, Paris: Economica.

Hintermaier, T. (2005), "A sunspot paradox", *Economics Letters* **87**, 285–290.

Hommes, C. (1991), *Chaotic Dynamics in Economic Models. Some Simple Case Studies*, Groningen: Wolters-Nordhoff.

Hoogenveen, V. and Kuipers, S. (2000), "The long-run effects of low inflation rates", *Banca Nazionale del Lavoro Quarterly Review* **53**, 267–286.

Hsiao, C. (1997), "Cointegration and dynamic simultaneous equations model", *Econometrica* **65**, 647–670.

Huang, K. and Liu, Z. (2002), "Staggered price setting, staggered wage setting and business cycle persistence", *Journal of Monetary Economics* **49**, 405–433.

Ihaka, R. and Gentleman, R. (1996), "R: A language for data analysis and graphics", *Journal of Computational and Graphical Statistics* **5**, 299–314.

Invernizzi, S. and Medio, A. (1991), "On lags and chaos in economic dynamic models", *Journal of Mathematical Economics* **29**, 521–551.

Ito, T. (1980), "Disequilibrium growth theory", *Journal of Economic Theory* **23**, 380–409.

Jaeger, K. (1983), "Diskrete und stetige analyse im IS–LM-Modell", *Zeitschrift für die gesamte Staatswissenschaft* **139**, 229–244.

Kaldor, N. (1956), "Alternative theories of distribution", *Review of Economic Studies* **23**, 83–100.

Kaldor, N. (1957), "A model of economic growth", *Economic Journal* **67**, 591–624.

Kaldor, N. (1966), *Causes of the Slow Rate of Economic Growth in the United Kingdom*, Cambridge, UK: Cambridge University Press.

Kalecki, M. (1935), "A macro-dynamic theory of business cycles", *Econometrica* **3**, 327–344.

Kalecki, M. (1943), *Studies in Economic Dynamics*, London: Allen & Unwin Ltd.

Kalecki, M. (1954), *Theory of Economic Dynamics*, London: Allen & Unwin Ltd.

Kalecki, M. (1971), "Political aspects of full employment", reprinted in M. Kalecki, *Selected Essays on the Dynamics of the Capitalist Economy*, Cambridge, UK: Cambridge University Press.

Kauermann, G., Teuber, T. and Flaschel, P. (2008), Estimating loops and cycles using penalized splines. *Computational Economics* (forthcoming).

Kauermann, G., Teuber, T. and Flaschel, P. (2011), Exploring US business cycles with bivariate loops using penalized spline regression, CEMM working paper, Bielefeld University.

Kennedy, C. (1964), "Induced bias in innovation and the theory of distribution", *Economic Journal* **74**, 541–547.

Keynes, J. (1936), *The General Theory of Employment, Interest and Money*, Cambridge, UK: Cambridge University Press.

King, R. and Rebelo, S. (2003), "Resuscitating real business cycles", in: John B. Taylor and M. Woodford (eds) *Handbook of Macroeconomics, Vol 1B*, Amsterdam: North Holland.

Krivobokova, T. and Kauermann, G. (2007), "A note on penalized spline smoothing with correlated errors", *Journal of the American Statistical Association* **102**, 1328–1337.

Kurz, H. (1986), "Normal positions and capital utilization", *Political Economy: Studies in the Surplus Approach* **2**(1), 37–54.

Lavoie, M. (1995), "The Kaleckian model of growth and distribution and its Neo-Ricardian and Neo-Marxian critiques", *Cambridge Journal of Economics* **19**, 789–818.

Laxton, D., Isard, P., Faruquee, H., Prasad, E. and Turtelboom, B. (1998), *MULTIMOD Mark III. The core dynamic and steady state models*, Washington, DC: International Monetary Fund.

Laxton, D., Rose, D. and Tambakis, D. (2000), "The US Phillips-curve: The case for asymmetry", *Journal of Economic Dynamics and Control* **23**, 1459–1485.

Levy, D., Bergen, M., Dutta, S. and Venable, R. (1997), "The magnitude of menu costs: Direct evidence from large US supermarket chains", *Quarterly Journal of Economics* **112**, 791–825.

Lorenz, H.-W. (1989), *Non-linear Dynamical Economics and Chaotic Motion*, Heidelberg: Springer.

Lucas, R. (1988), "On the mechanics of economic development", *Journal of Monetary Economics* **22**, 3–42.

Lucas, R. E. J. (1975), "An equilibrium model of the business cycle", *Journal of Political Economy* **83**, 1113–1144.

Lucas, R. E. J. (1977), "Understanding business cycles", *Carnegie-Rochester Conference Series on Public Policy* **5** (1), 7–29.

Mankiw, N. (2001), "The inexorable and mysterious tradeoff between inflation and unemployment", *Economic Journal* **111**, 5–61.

Mankiw, N. G. (2010), *Macroeconomics*, 7th edn, New York: Worth Publishers.

Mankiw, N.-G. and Reis, R. (2002), "Sticky information versus sticky prices: A proposal to replace the New-Keynesian Phillips curve", *Quarterly Journal of Economics* **117**(4), 1295–1328.

May, J. (1970), "Period analysis and continuous analysis in Patinkin's macro-economic model", *Journal of Economic Theory* **2**, 1–9.

Medio, A. (1991), "Discrete and continuous-time models of chaotic dynamics in economics", *Structural Change and Economic Dynamics* **2**, 99–118.

Mittnik, S. and Semmler, W. (2010a), "The instability of the banking sector and macrodynamics: Theory and empirics". New York: New School for Social Research. www.newschool.edu/nssr/cem (accessed 25 June 2011).

Mittnik, S. and Semmler, W. (2010b), Regime dependence of the fiscal multiplier. Paper prepared for a Conference on the "The Long-Run Effects of Short-Run Fluctuations", SCEPA Working Paper 2010-8, www.newschool.edu/scepa

Murata, Y. (1977), *Mathematics for Stability and Optimization of Economic Systems*, New York: Academic Press.

Naastepad, C. (2006), "Technology, demand and distribution: A cumulative growth model with an application to the Dutch productivity slowdown", *Cambridge Journal of Economics* **30**, 403–434.

Naastepad, C. and Storm, S. (2008), "OECD demand regimes (1960–2000)", *Journal of Post-Keynesian Economics* **29**(2), 211–246.

Okun, A. M. (1970), *The Political Economy of Prosperity*, Washington, DC: The Brookings Institution.

Oxley, L. and George, D. (1994), "Linear saddlepoint dynamics 'on their head': The scientific content of the new orthodoxy in macroeconomics", *European Journal of Political Economy* **10**, 389–400.

Palacios, J. (1964), *Dimensional Analysis*, London: Macmillan.

Pasinetti, L. (1962), "Rate of profit and income distribution in relation to the rate of economic growth", *Review of Economic Studies* **29**, 267–279.

Phillips, A. W. (1954), "Stabilisation policy in a closed economy", *The Economic Journal* **64**, 290–323.

Phillips, A. W. (1958), "The relation between unemployment and the rate of change of money wage rates in the United Kingdom, 1861–1957", *Economica* **25**, 283–299.

Picard, P. (1983), "Inflation and growth in a disequilibrium macroeconomic model", *Journal of Economic Theory* **30**, 266–295.

Piketty, T. and Saez, E. (2003), "Income inequality in the United States", *Quarterly Journal of Economics* **143**(1–39), 1913–1998.

Piketty, T. and Saez, E. (2006), "The evolution of top incomes: A historical and international perspective", *American Economic Review Papers and Proceedings* **96**, 200–205.

Pitelis, C. (1997), "On Kaldor and pensions", *Cambridge Journal of Economics* **21**(4), 469–482.

Press, W. H., Teukolsky, S. A., Vetterling, W. T. and Flannery, B. P. (1986), *Numerical Recipes in Fortran: The Art of Scientific Computing*, New York: Cambridge University Press.

Proaño, C. R., Flaschel, P., Ernst, E. and Semmler, W. (2007), "Gradual wage–price adjustments and Keynesian macrodynamics: Evidence from the US and the Euro area", Schwartz CEPA working paper, New School University, New York.

Rezai, A. (2010), *Distributional Conflict and Goodwin Cycles: A synthetic note.* Mimeo, Vienna University of Economics and Business.

Roberts, J. (1997), "The wage curve and the Phillips curve". *Finance and Economics Discussion Paper Series*, No. **57**, Federal Reserve Board of Governors.

Robinson, J. (1962), *Essays in the Theory of Economic Growth*, London and Basingstoke: Macmillan.

Romer, P. (1986), "Increasing returns and long-run growth", *Journal of Political Economy* **94**, 1002–1037.

Rose, H. (1967), "On the non-linear theory of employment", *Review of Economic Studies* **34**, 153–173.

Rose, H. (1990), *Macroeconomic Dynamics. A Marshallian Synthesis*, Cambridge, MA: Basil Blackwell.

Rotemberg, J. and Woodford, M. (2003), "The cyclical behavior of prices and costs", in: John B. Taylor and M. Woodford (eds), *Handbook of Macroeconomics*, Vol 1B. Amsterdam: North Holland, 1051–1135.

Rowthorn, B. (1981), "Demand, real wages and economic growth", *Thames Papers in Political Economy* **Autumn**, 1–39.

Rudebusch, G. D. and Svensson, L. E. (1999), "Policy rules for inflation targeting", in: J. B. Taylor (ed.), *Monetary Policy Rules*, Chicago, IL: The University of Chicago Press, Chapter 15.

Ruppert, D., Wand, M. and Carroll, R. (2003), *Semiparametric Regression*, Cambridge, UK: Cambridge University Press.

Sargent, T. (1979), *Macroeconomics*, New York: Academic Press.

Sargent, T. (1987), *Macroeconomic Theory*, New York: Academic Press.

Sargent, T. (1988), *Dynamic Macroeconomic Theory*, Cambridge, MA: Harvard University Press.

Sargent, T. and Wallace, N. (1973), "The stability of models of money and growth with perfect foresight", *Econometrica* **41**, 1043–1048.

Sawyer, M. (1985), *The Economics of Michal Kalecki*, London and Basingstoke: Macmillan.

Sawyer, M. (1995), *Unemployment, Imperfect Competition and Macroeconomics*, Aldershot: Edward Elgar.

Schaling, E. (2004), "The non-linear Phillips curve and inflation forecast targeting: Symmetric versus asymmetric monetary policy rules", *Journal of Money, Credit and Banking* **36**(3), 361–386.

Semmler, W. (1984), *Competition, Monopoly and Differential Profit Rates*, New York: Columbia University Press.

Semmler, W. and Gong, G. (2011), "Macroeconomics with non-clearing labor market", paper prepared for a Festschrift for Bertram Schefold (forthcoming).

Semmler, W. and Zhang, W. (2006), "Monetary policy with nonlinear Phillips curve and endogenous NAIRU", in: C. Chiarella, P. Flaschel, R. Franke and W. Semmler (eds), *Quantitative and Empirical Analysis of Nonlinear Dynamic Macromodels, Contributions to Economic Analysis*, Amsterdam: Elsevier.

Sen, A. (1970), "Introduction", in: A. Sen (ed.) *Growth Economics*, Harmondsworth: Penguin Books.

Sims, C. (1987), "Discussion of Olivier J. Blanchard, aggregate and individual price adjustment", *Brookings Papers on Economic Activity* **1**, 117–20.

Sims, C. (1998), "Stickiness", *Carnegie-Rochester Conference Series on Public Policy* **49**, 317–356.

Sims, C. A. (2002), "Solving linear rational expectations models", *Computational Economics* **20**, 1–20.

Skott, P. (1989a), *Conflict and Effective Demand in Economic Growth*, Cambridge, UK: Cambridge University Press.

Skott, P. (1989b), "Effective demand, class struggle and cyclical growth", *International Economic Review* **30**, 231–247.

Skott, P. and Larudee, M. (1998), "Uneven development and the liberalization of trade and capital flows: The case of Mexico", *Cambridge Journal of Economics* **22**, 277–295.

Smets, F. and Wouters, R. (2003), "An estimated dynamic stochastic general equilibrium model for the Euro area", *Journal of the European Economic Association* **1**(5), 1123–1175.

Solow, R. (1956), "A contribution to the theory of economic growth", *Quarterly Journal of Economics* **70**, 65–94.

Solow, R. and Stiglitz, J. (1968), "Output, employment and wages in the short-run", *Quarterly Journal of Economics* **82**, 537–560.

Spanos, A. (1990), "The simultaneous equations model revisited: statistical adequacy and identification", *Journal of Econometrics* **44**, 87–105.

Stein, J. (1982), *Monetarist, Keynesian and New Classical Economics*, London: Basil Blackwell.

Steindl, J. (1952), *Maturity and Stagnation in American Capitalism*, Oxford: Blackwell.

Steindl, J. (1979), "Stagnation theory and stagnation policy", *Cambridge Journal of Economics* **3**, 1–14.

Steindl, J. (1982), "The role of household saving in the modern economy", *Banca Nazionale del Lavoro Quarterly Review* **35**(140), 69–88.

Steindl, J. (1989), "From stagnation in the 30s to slow growth in the 70s", in: M. Berg (ed.), *Political Economy in the Twentieth Century*, Oxford: Philip Allan.

Steindl, J. (1990), *Economic Papers 1941–88*, London and Basingstoke: Macmillan.

Stiglitz, J. (1997), "Reflections on the natural rate hypothesis", *Journal of Economic Perspectives* **11**, 3–10.

Stock, J. H. and Watson, M. W. (1999), "Business cycle fluctuations in US macroeconomic time series", in J. B. Taylor and M. Woodford (eds), *Handbook of Macroeconomics*, Vol. 1, Amsterdam: Elsevier.

Stockhammer, E. and Onaran, O. (2004), "Accumulation, distribution and employment: A structural VAR approach to a Kaleckian macro model", *Structural Change and Economic Dynamics* **15**(4), 421–447.

Strogatz, S. H. (1994), *Non-linear Dynamics and Chaos*, New York: Addison-Wesley.

Svensson, L. E. (1998), "Inflation targeting as a monetary policy rule", Working Paper 6790, National Bureau of Economic Research.

Szirtes, T. (2007), *Applied Dimensional Analysis and Modeling*, Oxford: Butterworth-Heinemann.

Tavani, D. (2009), "Wage bargaining and induced technical change in a linear economy: Model and application to the US (1963–2003)". EERI Research Paper Series No. 15/2009 ISSN: 2031–4892.

Tavani, D. (2010), *Bargaining Over Productivity and Wages when Technical Change is Induced: Implications for growth, distribution, and employment*. Mimeo, Colorado State University.

Taylor, J. B. (1999), "Staggered price and wage setting in macroeconomics", in J. B. Taylor and M. Woodford (eds), *Handbook of Macroeconomics*, Vol. 1, Amsterdam: Elsevier, pp.1009–1050.

Taylor, L. (1985), "A stagnationist model of economic growth", *Cambridge Journal of Economics* **9**, 383–403.

Taylor, L. (2004), *Reconstructing Macroeconomics. Structuralist Proposals and Critique of the Mainstream*, Cambridge, MA: Harvard University Press.

Thieme, H. (2003), *Mathematics in Population Biology*, Princeton, NJ: Princeton University Press.

Tobin, J. (1975), "Keynesian models of recession and depression", *American Economic Review* **65**, 195–202.

Tobin, J. (1980), *Asset Accumulation and Economic Activity*, Oxford: Basil Blackwell.

Tobin, J. (1982), "Money and finance in the macroeconomic process", *Journal of Money, Credit and Banking* **14**, 171–204.

Tobin, J. (1989), *Price Flexibility and Full Employment. The Debate Then and Now*, New Haven, CT: Yale University.

Tobin, J. (1998), "Supply constraints on employment and output: NAIRU versus natural rate", International conference in memory of Fausto Vicarelli, Rome, pp.21–23.

Turnovsky, S. (1977a), "On the formulation of continuous time macroeconomic models with asset accumulation", *International Economic Review* **18**, 1–27.

Turnovsky, S. (1977b), *Macroeconomic Analysis and Stabilization Policy*, Cambridge, UK: Cambridge University Press.

Turnovsky, S. (1995), *Methods of Macroeconomic Dynamics*, Cambridge, MA: MIT Press.

Turnovsky, S. (2000), *Methods of Macroeconomic Dynamics*, 2nd edn, Cambridge, MA: MIT Press.

Uzawa, H. (1965), "Optimum technical change in an aggregative model of economic growth", *International Economic Review* **6**, 18–31.

Venables, W. and Ripley, B. (1999), *Applied Statistics with S-PLUS*, 3rd. edn, New York: Springer.

Walsh, C. E. (2003), "Labor market search and monetary shocks", in: S. Altug, J. Chadha and C. Nolan (eds), *Elements of Dynamic Macroeconomic Analysis*, Cambridge, UK: Cambridge University Press, pp.451–86.

Wiggins, S. (1990), *Introduction to Applied Nonlinear Dynamical Systems and Chaos*, Heidelberg: Springer.

Wood, S. (2000), "Modelling and smoothing parameter estimation with multiple quadratic penalties", *Journal of the Royal Statistical Society, Series B* **62**, 413–428.

Woodford, M. (2003), *Interest and Prices. Foundations of a Theory of Monetary Policy*, Princeton, NJ: Princeton University Press.

Ziesemer, T. (1995), "What's new and what's old in new growth theory? Endogenous technology, microfoundation and growth rate predictions – A critical overview", *Zeitschrift fur Wirtschafts- und Sozialwissenschaften* **115**(3), 1–44.

# Index

For Product Safety Concerns and Information please contact our
EU representative GPSR@taylorandfrancis.com Taylor & Francis
Verlag GmbH, Kaufingerstraße 24, 80331 München, Germany